THE LIVING AND ACTIVE
WORD OF GOD:

STUDIES IN HONOR OF
SAMUEL J. SCHULTZ

THE LIVING AND ACTIVE WORD OF GOD:

STUDIES IN HONOR OF SAMUEL J. SCHULTZ

Edited by

MORRIS INCH
and
RONALD YOUNGBLOOD

WINONA LAKE, INDIANA
EISENBRAUNS

Library of Congress Cataloging in Publication Data

The Living and active word of God.

   Includes bibliographical references and index.
   1. Bible—Criticism, interpretation, etc.—Addresses, essays,
lectures. 2. Schultz, Samuel J.—Addresses, essays, lectures. I.
Schultz, Samuel J. II. Inch, Morris A., 1925-   . III. Youngblood, Ronald F. BS540.L58 1982   220.6   82-9376
ISBN 0-931464-11-0

THE LIVING AND ACTIVE WORD OF GOD*

Preface xi

List of Contributors xiii

Personal Portrait 1
ERWIN P. RUDOLPH

LEAD ARTICLE

Proposals for New Approaches in Teaching Old Testament
Overview 9
SAMUEL SCHULTZ

SECTION I

How God "Spoke Long Ago to the Fathers"

The Bible and the Environment 15
F. F. BRUCE

The Abrahamic Covenant: Conditional or Unconditional? 31
RONALD YOUNGBLOOD

Gathered to His People: A Study of a Dothan Family Tomb . 47
ROBERT COOLEY

Questions From the Prophets 59
MEROLD WESTPHAL

Right Questions About Isaiah 7:14 75
J. BARTON PAYNE (permission to publish posthumously granted
by his wife)

Jesus and Moses: Rabbinic Backgrounds and Exegetical Concerns
in Matthew 5 85
ALAN JOHNSON

The Promise of God and the Outpouring of the Holy Spirit . 109
WALTER KAISER

SECTION II

How God "Has Spoken to Us in His Son"

Hebrew Thought in the Life of the Church 123
MARVIN WILSON

*Cf. Hebrews 4:12

Apostolic Eyewitnesses and Proleptically Historical Revelation . 137
STANLEY OBITTS

Manifestation of the Spirit 149
MORRIS INCH

Authority for a Going and Sending Ministry in the Christian
Mission of World Evangelism 157
ROBERT CULVER

Textual Variants of the "Apostolic Decree" and Their Setting in the
Early Church 171
JULIUS SCOTT

The Theism of the Apocalypse 185
MERRILL TENNEY

SECTION III

How God's Word Abides With Us

Immanence, Transcendence, and the Doctrine of Scripture 193
MILLARD ERICKSON

The Inspiration of Scripture Among the Seventeenth-Century
Reformed Theologians 207
BONG RO

The Concept of Truth in the Contemporary Inerrancy Debate 225
NORMAN GEISLER

The Clarity of Scripture 237
ROBERT SANDIN

Italics in English Bible Translation 255
JACK LEWIS

The Bible the Foundation for a World and Life View 271
HAROLD LINDSELL

Symbolism, Modeling and Theology 283
WILLIAM DYRNESS

The Bible in an Age of Revolution 301
HAROLD KUHN

The Use of the Bible in World Evangelization 309
ARTHUR JOHNSTON

The Bible in an Age of Revolution 301
    HAROLD KUHN

The Use of the Bible in World Evangelization 309
    ARTHUR JOHNSTON

General Index 321

Scripture Index 333

Author Index 350

Preface

THE author of Hebrews describes the Scriptures not as dead utterances of the past but as a living power for all time. It fathoms the depths of our inner life, so to "judge the thoughts and attitudes of the heart" (Heb 4:12). The articles that follow elaborate on this theme.

If there was one concern that characterized the distinguished career of Samuel J. Schultz, it was to develop in his students a love for Scripture. He hoped that they would cultivate a commitment to the study of Holy Writ and apply its message to their lives. He counted no sacrifice too great to further this goal, and the personal tribute and articles included in this *Festschrift* are an extension of his concern and a way of expressing appreciation on behalf of the contributors and others who join with us for one we highly esteem.

Some years ago Professor Schultz devised a creative approach to teaching Old Testament Survey, and this is the subject of the lead article. The remaining essays are divided into expounding how "in the past God spoke to our forefathers," how God "has spoken to us by his Son," and how "all Scripture is God-breathed and is useful for teaching, rebuking, correcting and training in righteousness." The former sections roughly follow a chronological order with reference to redemptive history. Those articles preceding the close of the first section and introducing the second especially relate the Old Testament to the New.

The final section treats two topics: the authority of Scripture and its relevance. These topics are sometimes more distinct and in other instances blended together in such a way that it is difficult to distinguish between them. One might argue, however, that the first five articles relate more to the issue of authority and the remaining four to Biblical relevance.

Professor Schultz tells a story that seems to sum up what this book is all about. He was visiting in Jerusalem at the time and went to view the famous Qumran scroll of Isaiah that was on display. He waited his turn behind two rabbis who, at the sight of the Isaiah text, wept and lingered—oblivious to the fact that they were obstructing others from viewing the exhibition. Sam accepted their belated but profuse apology and later reflected that "they did not know how deeply I identified with their response to Scripture." We have been encouraged to cherish Scripture because of his own devotion to it, and so in honoring him we identify with those who prize the Word as God's gracious provision for our need.

MORRIS INCH
RONALD YOUNGBLOOD

List of Contributors

F. F. Bruce	Emeritus Professor of New Testament	Manchester University
Robert E. Cooley	President	Gordon-Conwell Theological Seminary
Robert D. Culver	Annual Visiting Professor of Theology	Winnepeg Theological Seminary
William A. Dyrness	Professor of Theology	Asian Theological Seminary
Millard J. Erickson	Professor of Theology	Bethel Theological Seminary
Norman L. Geisler	Professor of Systematic Theology	Dallas Theological Seminary
Morris Inch	Professor of Theology	Wheaton College
Alan F. Johnson	Professor of Biblical Studies	Wheaton College
Arthur P. Johnston	Professor of Missions	Trinity Evangelical Divinity School
Walter C. Kaiser, Jr.	Dean and Professor of Old Testament	Trinity Evangelical Divinity School
Harold Kuhn	Professor of Philosophy of Religion	Asbury Theological Seminary
Jack Lewis	Professor of Bible	Harding Graduate School of Religion
Harold Lindsell	Editor Emeritus	*Christianity Today*
Stanley Obitts	Professor of Philosophy	Westmont College
J. Barton Payne	Late Professor of Old Testament	Covenant Theological Seminary
Bong Rin Ro	Executive Secretary	Asian Theological Association
Erwin P. Rudolph	Professor of English	Wheaton College
Robert T. Sandin	Provost	Mercer University
Samuel J. Schultz	Emeritus Professor of Bible and Theology	Wheaton College

J. Julius Scott, Jr.	Professor of Bible and Theology	Wheaton Graduate School
Merrill C. Tenney	Emeritus Professor of Bible and Theology	Wheaton Graduate School
Merold Westphal, Jr.	Professor of Philosophy	Hope College
Marvin R. Wilson	Professor of Biblical Studies	Gordon College
Ronald Youngblood	Professor of Old Testament	Bethel Theological Seminary West

The chapters that follow conform to the "Instructions for Contributors" section printed on pages 57 to 72 in the March 1977 issue of the *Journal of the Evangelical Theological Society*, a publication that was edited for many years by Samuel J. Schultz.

Personal Portrait

I. THE TASK

To draw a full portrait of a human personality in all of its shades, colors, and relationships is virtually impossible for one hand to accomplish—especially in limited space. Such a task deserves a certain length and development and, better still, a diversity of perspectives. My own viewpoint, while personal and intimate, is, I believe, accurate insofar as it goes, but it will be limited necessarily in its scope of vision.

The full measure of a man must, of course, include both his achievements and personality. The first is easier to assess objectively, for the work of one's hands is open to view and comparatively easy to record. Eternity alone, however, will reveal one's true achievements. The second is more difficult to evaluate, for it is much more complex. Those human characteristics that are open to public view, while apparent and seemingly constant, are incomplete at best and capable of misinterpretation, as setting and context vary constantly. Also when one conducts himself in public he is usually on his good behavior, striving to act "normally" or to find acceptance among his peers. To describe human conduct adequately in its many relationships demands that one take a close look at the man himself when all masks are laid aside and the real likes and dislikes are made known—when the thought life may be seen at close range without the alloy of public opinion. In short, we must try to know the man as he is when no human eye is upon him.

Not only was Samuel J. Schultz one of my esteemed colleagues in college teaching, but I am fortunate enough to count him as one of my best personal friends. I am proud to make such a bold claim, for I feel I have benefited more than he from our relationship. I shall risk presumption to say some things about the man as I know him. I shall also take the liberty of using throughout the less formal appellation "Sam" in personal reference.

II. PHYSICAL MAKE-UP AND HABITS

Tall, straight, and with a shock of pure white hair, Sam is always easy to single out in a crowd. Even strangers are impressed by his striking appearance, as was illustrated one day in Switzerland when a photographer, who was looking for unusual photographic subjects, chose to take Sam's picture as he and I were sitting together in a public place. Beneath a broad forehead are two large limpid, blue eyes set in a kindly visage. The clear countenance is re-enforced by a firmly-set jaw. His manner is deliberate but

1

not slow, thoughtful but not hesitant. Those who know him well attest to his definite beliefs and determination, which are accentuated by his pure Germanic stock.

A man of books and the classroom, Sam is not one to neglect his physical prowess, but he chooses to engage regularly in the more vigorous sports of handball and tennis. Although I was seldom his antagonist in these sports, I was always aware of his competitive spirit in whatever he undertook. The winter months found him methodically seeking out the indoor swimming pool for his half-mile of continuous swimming. His connection with sports was never an end in itself, however. His belief that the body must be a fit temple of the Holy Spirit prompted him to keep in the best physical condition possible. His lithe frame gave evidence of ample exercise and moderate diet.

III. Early Friendship

My wife and I came to know Sam and June during our early years in Wheaton when we lived on adjoining streets in the northern part of the city. Two of our children, Linda and "Zeke," attended the same elementary school. This was in the early fifties. During this time the Schultzes moved into the house on Santa Rosa Avenue diagonally across the street from us, and our paths began to cross more often than before. Their son Dave, in his inimitable, friendly way, would wave to us as he took their dog "Bobo" for his daily walk in the park. Not infrequently we would chat casually with the Schultzes, and we came to know them even better on a few social occasions at the College. Our mutual attraction to each other grew gradually.

IV. Honesty and Integrity

Although I always looked upon Sam as a model Christian, I think two of his dominant characteristics that attracted me most were his intellectual honesty and Christian integrity. He was never one to put on "airs" but was straightforward and sincere in whatever he believed or did. Whenever a controversial matter arose in College affairs, he stood resolutely for what he believed was right—even if that position was unpopular. He was quick to detect sham or hypocrisy in others and was impatient with anything that savored of political maneuvering or legislative "railroading" when he thought such action was detrimental to the College. Especially when the authority of the Scriptures was challenged or Wheaton's long-standing tradition was threatened, he stood resolute and strong. That the Scriptures formed the one solid foundation for faith and practice was uppermost in his thoughts. He believed firmly that a study of the Old and New Testaments was essential to an ideal liberal arts education and that any attempt to substitute other courses for the Bible in the curriculum marked a dangerous departure from sound practice.

Resolute orthodoxy for this man did not come about from bias or narrow provincialism. His was a firm conviction resulting from a deeply pious mind exercised over years of study and reflection. Because of his deep commitment to God, it was natural for him to stand for piety and against compromise in any form.

Just as coming events cast their shadows before them, so harbingers of change in a college sometimes appear unmistakably, if subtly, in the least suspecting places. The Bible department itself is particularly vulnerable to outside pressures. Advocates for alteration of Wheaton's historic positions are ever at work. When these times occur, we can be thankful for those in key positions who stand out against the voices for change. Discriminating in his judgments, Sam has been one of those who have helped to steer the department through many shoals of uncertainty and internal weakness.

As a senior member of the department of Bible and for a time its chairman and later division coordinator, he relished seeing younger colleagues coming into the department to join the others as champions of the undiluted Word of God. At the same time he was grieved whenever he saw inroads of modernism from any quarter that would threaten Wheaton's long-standing position. Even where good men strive sincerely to please God and human motives are above reproach, one must distinguish between the good and the best. Here Sam's sense of discrimination was evident. The benefit of his concern, judgment and personal efforts extended to the Graduate School. Especially in his role as divisional coordinator he helped to harmonize and blend the graduate and undergraduate programs.

That his sound judgment was valued was evident in the wide range of committees both on and off campus on which he served. Here again he was sensitive to problems and wise in his judgments of the various issues that arose. He may not have been the most vocal of the members, but at the right time he would come forth with his opinion that helped the group to ferret out the relevant issues and steer toward a final resolution. If he believed firmly in a matter, it made little difference who disagreed with him. His intellectual honesty and persuasion prompted him to act irrespective of repercussions. Especially where ethical and moral matters were involved he stood unflinchingly for the right, even when his stance might be misunderstood or threatening to an erstwhile friendship. His presence yielded to his colleagues a sense of solidity and confidence. Those in his department attest glowingly to his unwavering loyalty and wise counsel.

V. As Scholar

The ideal scholar-teacher may be judged by his intellectual attainments, his classroom performance, his studious habits, and his writings. The path to high intellectual achievement is a rigorous one, for the way is fraught with hard work and persistence. Sam's early desire for excellence in his chosen field led him early to answer God's call to preach and teach by attending one of America's most prestigious schools. Through self-denial and persistent labor he and June endured the rigor of demanding pastorates and hard study toward graduate school preparation. An undergraduate major in history from John Fletcher College, Sam earned the B.D. degree from Faith Theological Seminary and the S.T.M. and Th.D in OT from Harvard Divinity School. His mind was thus honed by some of the leading Biblical scholars of his day. His early ordination opened up avenues of usefulness for his knowledge of the Bible. He served as pastor of several churches in different denominations during the early years.

The scholar's life, however, has no terminus. He who views himself as a good steward of Jesus Christ probes daily into the vast recesses of learning. He continues to reach for the storehouses of knowledge, knowing that "a man's reach must exceed his grasp." Such a life-style of diligence and disciplined study helped this man to achieve not only the degree credentials of scholarship but to exemplify continuously to the world the true trade-marks of scholarly wisdom. His large personal collection of books enhanced his opportunity for daily study, and his easy recourse to the best libraries kept him abreast of his field. In addition he welcomed the counsel of the learned and sought diligently the prevailing views of the best religious minds of his day.

The classroom gave abundant evidence of the fruits of his learning. Steeped in OT backgrounds, Sam distinguished himself in Biblical and critical studies. His classes were large and his contacts wide. He was well-organized and methodical in his class preparations. He lectured with the same clarity and exactitude that characterized his written word. The many students that he taught in his more than thirty years of college teaching attest to his widespread influence. Alumni at home and abroad speak often of this man's part in opening up God's Word to them, as well as inspiring them by his scholarly bearing. Wherever he went he was continually meeting those whom he had taught. If one was traveling with him, it seemed that somebody was always stopping him with the reminder that he was once their teacher.

Sam's scholarly inclinations prompted him to pursue research and to publish. Feeling the need for more keys to OT studies for layman and teacher alike, he wrote *The Old Testament Speaks*, which has been a standard evangelical authority in its field for many years. This work was written at a difficult period in the life of Sam and June, both physically and financially, and involved a great deal of sacrifice and persistence on their part. Sam could say with the eighteenth-century writer Samuel Johnson after the latter had worked arduously and long towards the publication of his famous dictionary, "[It] was written with little assistance of the learned and without any patronage of the great; not in the soft obscurities of retirement, or under the shelter of academic bowers, but amidst inconvenience and distraction, in sickness and sorrow." But the results have been well worth the efforts. *The Old Testament Speaks* has gone through numerous printings and has been translated into Japanese, Spanish and other languages. Recently it has emerged in a revised third edition by Harper and Row.

Other books by this writer also include *The Prophets Speak*; *Deuteronomy, The Gospel of Love* (1971), which stresses the love relationship between God and his specially chosen people; and *The Gospel of Moses* (1974), which asserts that the book of Deuteronomy is the most important book in the OT and the key to understanding the entire Bible.

Interest in scholarly publications is seen further in his editing for years the *Journal of the Evangelical Theological Society*. He has also written numerous theological articles and has participated in several translations of the Bible.

From my many conversations with Sam I learned that his efforts in publishing derived from a keen sense of stewardship. He was convinced that the well-rounded scholar must be fruitful both in teaching and publishing. He saw no validity in the often-repeated excuse that good teaching frequently precludes scholarly publishing. To him the evidence of one's scholarly achievement must include significant publications, for only by them could one be assured that his work would be remembered.

I cannot refrain from commenting on Sam's literary style. Since so much of his energy was consumed in amassing facts and stressing accuracy of detail, it is unusual that his mind would also be concerned about style and manner of writing. Knowing that I was in the field of literary studies, he would ask me on occasion what I thought of a passage he was composing. Even then he was highly self-critical and wanted what he had to say to be clothed in appropriate prose. He tended to revise what he had written again and again to avoid severity or stodginess or lack of economy. If a suggestion for improvement was good, he recognized it instinctively. I was continually amazed that the writing of a man so engrossed in theological studies could bear the marks of commendable prose as his did.

Much of the attractiveness of Schultz's language was in its clarity and precision. The ability to retain pertinent data without cumbersomeness, to give priority to exactness and detail without tediousness or undue attention to minutiae preserved a winsome quality. When he sought to repeat a point for emphasis, he varied the language adequately. His classical economy of means was consonant with the reserve and conservative judgment displayed in the text. Sentence variation kept the prose free from monotony.

VI. As Friend

Whatever one's accomplishments, no greater human worth can be possessed than the capacity for true friendship. How few there are to whom we can unlock our true selves. Part of that is due to our inability to see in another the human qualities that make for intimacy and trust. How fortunate we are when we find in another those worthy qualities that attract and lead us to cultivate closer ties. Even when we find them, we seldom set about deliberately to bring them to fruition. Rather we are drawn gradually into their magnetic fold. As I reflect upon some of these attributes in Sam, I can appreciate them even more in perspective.

First, the unmistakable marks of the gentleman are upon him. The Victorian John Henry Newman defines a gentleman summarily as "one who never inflicts pain. . . . [He] carefully avoids whatever may jar or jolt in the minds of those with whom he is cast. . . . He is tender towards the bashful, gentle towards the distant, and merciful towards the absurd. . . . He guards against the unreasonable allusions or topics which may irritate; he is seldom prominent in conversation, and never wearisome. He makes light of favors while he does them, and seems to be receiving them when he is conferring. . . . [He] is scrupulous in imputing motives to those who interfere with him and interprets everything for the best. He is never mean or little in his disputes. . . . He may be right or wrong in his opinion, but he is too clear-headed to be unjust."

This apt description adds up to sensitivity toward others, to concern for the welfare of those with whom he deals—in the office, the hallway, the classroom, the home and the public forum. His solicitude for the thoughts and feelings of others conveyed the general impression of care for their well-being and worth. Toward members of his own family this thoughtfulness and sense of caring was especially evident. Students sense instinctively the respect a teacher has for their opinions and appreciate the recognition given to their merit, however slight. They are thus made to feel their own importance. This teacher's gracious solicitude was easily and naturally conveyed to them and to all who had dealings with him.

The kindly and solicitous characteristics easily turn to compassion as the occasion demands. Our own family had opportunities to be the recipients of this genuine concern. Especially at the time of the death of our younger son, both Sam and June were bulwarks of strength. We felt that the sympathy and support afforded us at that time were not forced or dutiful but were prompted by a genuine, natural concern for friends in need. Such a relationship might be termed the "fellowship of suffering" and is a tie that binds friends together by "chains of gold about the feet of God."

The trait of warm, personal consideration was exemplified even on a more daily basis. When either my wife or I had a personal problem, or when his wife June (both his wife and mine had the same given names) had undergone a hard day in the real-estate office, or when things in Sam's day had been trying, our evening times of "eating out" together turned into seasons of mutual sharing and consolation. The course of the conversation on those occasions almost always ended with a new perspective on our problems. Again the combination of interest, compassion and wise forbearance on Sam's part relieved our anxieties. Not infrequently we ended our discussion by laughing at ourselves as we felt lifted above the besetting circumstances.

The Schultzes' zest for travel matched that of our family and provided another means for a burgeoning friendship. One of the most unforgettable experiences of our lives occurred when we met Sam and June in Switzerland for a week of travel to the scenic spots of that beautiful country. I recall vividly Sam's reveling in God's grandeur as he and I scaled the heights of Mt. Pilatus and Zermatt. On the second of these climbs he skilfully helped me to photograph a rare view of the Matterhorn as it was reflected in the still waters of a lake below.

During the several days that we traversed Switzerland's beautiful landscapes and later on a trip to scenic Hawaii, I sensed as never before this man's zest for life and love for God's handiwork. I was amazed at his daring and tireless love for adventure, which again helped to cement a bit more tightly the bonds that held us together. In order to take advantage of his knowledge of Biblical landscapes, I still hope to accompany him some day to the Holy Land for what would be a richly informative and spiritually rewarding experience.

Further manifestations of friendship were revealed during the times we have been guests in their home. There Sam and June have shared their hospitality without stint both with us and with the family of our son Jim. This liberality overflowed into the homes of their children, Linda and David. We felt acceptance on numerous occasions as all members of their family went "all out" to make us a part of their inner circle. Not only in Wheaton, but since retirement in Lexington and Cape Cod, Massachusetts, they have introduced us to many New England landmarks and welcomed us anew to the intimacy of family ties.

The heart of the present matter centers in true friendship. When one has a true friend, he can be what he is without airs or pretense. As Ralph Waldo Emerson puts it, "A friend is a person with whom I may be sincere. Before him I may think aloud. I am arrived at last in the presence of a man so real and equal that I may drop even those undergarments of dissimulation, courtesy, and second thought, which men never put off, and may deal with him with the simplicity and wholeness with which one chemical atom meets another. Sincerity is the luxury allowed like diadems and authority only to the highest rank."

How seldom are we sincere with another. How hypocritical we become as we attempt by compliments or gossip to cover up our true thoughts from him. But a friend is one "who exercises not my ingenuity, but me." How refreshing to possess a friend with whom you may be yourself. Such a rare find should be seized upon.

Francis Bacon has said, "Happy is the house that shelters a friend." Another has commented, "The essence of friendship is entireness, a total magnanimity and trust." Most often we are bound to others by blood or admiration or some other means. But where love draws friends together, one is challenged to be a friend in return. And the character that subsists in my friend makes me great as a result. "True love transcends the unworthy object and dwells and broods on the eternal. True love cannot, therefore, be unrequited."

Such a relationship is not easily shaken. A true friend does not have to be appeased continually. He does not take offense with changeable moods, wounded pride, or even wanton neglect. The real friend stands erect amid the blasts of adverse winds. When friendships are real, they are not "glass threads or frostwork, but the solidest thing we know." We do not have to treat them daintily, "but with the roughest courage."

ERWIN PAUL RUDOLPH

Proposals for New Approaches in Teaching Old Testament Overview

SAMUEL J. SCHULTZ

THROUGHOUT years of teaching courses introducing students to the OT I have been concerned with stimulating interest and excitement in Biblical studies. As I developed and restructured my basic course year after year I could not find a suitable textbook for classroom use. This problem I was able to solve when I was funded by an alumni grant and devoted my efforts to writing *The Old Testament Speaks*, which was published in 1960.

This created another problem. With students having available much of the material that I had previously given in lectures I restructured my course again. By this time the educational climate was anything but favorable for teaching the OT to college students, especially so as a general education requirement at Wheaton College. Scientific and philosophical inquiry as well as rationalism dominated the intellectual climate in college and university classrooms.

Confronted with this challenge, I re-examined my objectives as well as the options I had as to methodology. Was it necessary to have the student read the entire OT for a survey course? Should problems of authorship be included? What was the purpose for maintaining the OT course as a basic requirement in general education in a Christian liberal arts curriculum?

As I analyzed my objectives in this context, I came to a basic decision that affected my teaching. Realizing that many students registered for this course simply to meet a requirement, I accepted the challenge of exciting each student's interest in studying the OT with a prayer that he or she would learn to love it as the Word of God. I was convinced that if a student loved the Bible less after taking my course than when he enrolled I had miserably failed. In view of this I did not require the reading of the entire OT but assigned reading of the material I considered necessary for an overview of the OT. At the same time I challenged the student to select the version or paraphrase that he or she would most enjoy reading. I also revised my quizzes and examinations so as to eliminate the motivation many students have for memorization of lists of facts, names and places. Unfortunately such memorization is too often associated with Bible courses in classroom teaching. I have found that reviews of the Biblical content and examinations should be designed to aid the student in integrating the central meaning of and basic developments in the OT.

9

I. Approaches to Teaching the Old Testament

Over the years many approaches have been used in teaching the OT. The book-by-book method has been very common in Bible institutes, Bible colleges and liberal arts colleges as well as among laity under such course titles as Old Testament Synthesis, Old Testament Survey and Introduction to the Old Testament. In a course in OT synthesis I was given a theme, key verse and outline for each book. For memorizing these with the ability to reproduce them in writing at examination time I received an A in the course. Although much can be gained from such a course under an effective teacher, this method leaves the impression that the OT consists of 39 segments. It also fails to provide an integrated overview.

The historical approach has much in its favor. Such a course can delineate the developments throughout OT times from Genesis to Malachi in chronological order. Where some of the older textbooks were limited primarily to the material given in the Biblical text, the more recent textbooks have been immensely enriched by integration with the vast resources in archaeology available in recent times. Such a course may prepare the student to interact effectively with current OT scholarship, especially in universities and graduate schools.

Typology is another approach that has been used to survey the OT. In such courses the OT is surveyed as a series of persons (e.g., Adam: Rom 5:15), institutions (e.g., offerings: 1 Pet 1:19; Heb 9:28), offices (e.g., priestly duties: Heb 4:14; 9:12), events (e.g., wilderness sojourn: 1 Cor 10:1-11) and actions (e.g., Moses lifting up a serpent: John 3:14), which "were prophetic adumbrations of corresponding realities in the Church and Kingdom of Christ."[1] While this is an interesting approach to the Scriptures, it has limitations in serving as an introductory course to OT studies.

The dispensational approach has been a widely used method in Bible teaching in this century. The first five dispensations are allotted to the OT with the NT era representing the dispensation of grace and the seventh beginning with the return of Christ. Since the major portion of OT content is the dispensation of law—Exod 19:1-Acts 1:26—this approach often leaves the student with the impression that the OT is primarily law or legalistic whereas the NT by contrast represents grace. As a result, students and laity—consciously or unconsciously—relegate the OT to an inferior position. This law-grace emphasis has permeated evangelical Christianity in Bible preaching and teaching to such an extent that the majority of students come to college today with a negative attitude toward the OT (cf. *The Scofield Bible*, which delineates the dispensational framework in its notes).

The historical-critical approach, extensively used in colleges, universities and seminaries, combines the literary analysis of the Graf-Wellhausen

---

[1]See M. S. Terry, *Biblical Hermeneutics* (Grand Rapids: Zondervan) 334-336.

theory in a modified form with the cultural, historical and theological aspects of the OT. Among the popular textbooks reflecting this approach are *Understanding the Old Testament* by B. W. Anderson, *Understanding the Old Testament* by J. Williams, *The People of Ancient Israel* by J. K. Kuntz, and others.

Much is to be said in support of the common concern these authors have in their analysis of the OT. We share their interest in history, which is especially important as archaeology continues to illumine the events recorded in the OT. As we learn more about the cultural setting it is possible to understand and interpret the text of Scripture more fully.

Crucially important, however, are the basic presuppositions common to recent authors in this approach to the OT. It is commendable to find authors stating their assumptions and indicating the perspective from which they are interpreting the OT. G. A. Larue (*Old Testament Life and Literature*, 1968) accepts the documentary hypothesis as the basis for his interpretation because it is the most widely accepted of all theories (pp. 31-33). H. K. Beebe (*The Old Testament*, 1970) states that for OT interpretation the documentary hypothesis still functions as an effective tool in discovering the origins of Israel (p. 122). J. K. Kuntz (*The People of Ancient Israel*, 1974) asserts that current studies indicate that source and form criticism are considered valuable, that Wellhausen's chronological arrangement of strata is generally accepted and that oral tradition is considered important. In conclusion he states his position for interpreting the OT as follows:

> The Graf-Wellhausen documentary hypothesis is still with us. On occasion its doom has been proclaimed, just as the end of the world has been foretold. It seems however that in both instances we have a mistaken prophecy on our hands in which some rejoice and others lament.

John Bright acknowledged that although OT studies were in a state of flux and Wellhausen's theory of the evolutionary pattern of Israel's religion had been abandoned, he still accepted the literary analysis of the Pentateuch as held by Wellhausen as an acceptable theory for OT studies.[2] Although modified by form criticism and the traditio-historical approach with its emphasis on oral tradition, the Wellhausen documentary hypothesis still permeates the classroom, textbooks and commentaries as the basis for OT interpretation.

The covenants can also serve as a basic framework for teaching the OT. By stressing the covenants that God made with Adam, Noah and Abraham the instructor can use the God-man relationship as the unifying

---

[2] J. Bright, "Modern Study of Literature," in *The Bible and the Ancient Near East* (ed. G. E. Wright; Garden City, NY: Doubleday, 1959).

theme in progressive revelation. The Horeb agreement between God and Israel was under Moses in Deuteronomy and Joshua in Canaan. Added to this is the covenant of David and the importance the prophets place on the covenant between God and Israel. This approach emphasizing the God-man relationship throughout OT times provides an excellent background for the study of the new covenant established through Jesus Christ.

Another approach, developed by Walter Kaiser, in surveying the OT is the "promise" theme. Beginning with the promise to Adam and Eve (Gen 3:15) the succeeding promises to the patriarchs, Israel and the future as delineated through the prophets are emphasized. In this way the promise of God is unfolded as it focused on an heir, on an inheritance of the land of rest, and on the heritage of a gospel that issued in a means of blessing the whole world.

II. INDUCTIVE THEOLOGICAL-HISTORICAL-CULTURAL APPROACH

Let me share with you an approach I have found most successful in recent years. This approach can be most effectively developed by beginning the study of the OT in the book of Deuteronomy. There are several advantages to this approach. Ever since DeWette in 1805 identified the D document with Josian times, Deuteronomy has been the focal and pivotal point in OT studies. In recent decades Meredith Kline (*The Structure of Biblical Authority*, 1972) and others have emphasized the cultural setting for its written form as best identified with Moses. Consequently the book of Deuteronomy provides a common basis with current scholarship to begin the study of the OT.

Another advantage is that Deuteronomy provides a common historical basis. Whereas R. H. Pfeiffer would allow for only one slogan in the Pentateuch to come from Moses, current scholars agree that much of the material in Deuteronomy may be Mosaic in origin but transmitted as oral tradition until the seventh century.

When the book of Deuteronomy is used as the starting point for OT study, the student is immediately introduced to the heart of the entire OT revelation. Jesus identified this when he asserted that the two great commandments—love God and love your neighbor—express the essence and core of all that is written in the Law and the Prophets (Matt 22:34-40). The religious leaders agreed with this, adding that these were more important than sacrifice (Mark 12:28-32). Jesus promised the inquiring scribe eternal life if he wholeheartedly loved God and his neighbor (Luke 10:25-28). Consequently in an overview course there is much to be gained by acquainting the student in his or her first lesson with the core of the OT revelation that was climaxed in the NT with the coming of Jesus Christ.

Deuteronomy also provides a very appropriate point in OT times to emphasize divine revelation in an historical setting. Moses summarized for the new generation of Israelites the essence of God's revelation at Mount

Sinai. The historical circumstance was unique. God actually spoke to the Israelites. They heard God speak. No other nation ever heard the voice of God.

It is difficult to find any delineation in the textbooks by Anderson, Gottwald, Larue, Kuntz and others that the message of Moses in Deuteronomy actually had its origin in the spoken word of God. If the text of Deuteronomy 4 is taken seriously, then actual revelation from God to Israel occurred in the spoken word.

Closely related to the above is the fact that the use of Deuteronomy as the starting point introduces the student to the crux of the whole problem of interpreting the OT. Did Moses actually say what is recorded in the book of Deuteronomy? Did Moses actually write the Law and give it to the priests (31:9)? Or is the book of Deuteronomy a compilation of oral traditions that were reworked and re-edited in the Josian reformation?[3] For some earlier scholars like Spinoza and Herder, the Bible represented more or less the product of human imagination. Modern scholars like Mendenhall find the Biblical message in a sociological, anthropological and historical analysis of Israel's history in the context of Near Eastern culture.

Is the book of Deuteronomy a purely human work? Or is Deuteronomy a book divinely inspired, representing what Moses spoke on the Moabite plain and what he gave to the Israelite priests to read publicly every seven years? The teacher can hardly evade these questions as he or she begins to interpret the OT. Peter C. Craigie is keenly aware of these options as he discusses his perspective in attempting to maintain a balance between the theological and scientific approaches to the Biblical text when he says:

> It seems wise, therefore, to indicate the basic point of departure that has been taken in writing this commentary: The approach to the text might be described as theological-historical, or theological-scientific. Thus it is assumed at the outset that the Biblical text, and Deuteronomy in particular, is not a purely human work, a product of man's imagination. The assumption (or belief) that the source of the work is God, though its mediation is human, means that the scientific method is employed with certain limitations. These comments do not mean that this work is ahistorical or ascientific, but the role that the historical and scientifc methods are granted is, relatively, a subsidiary one. Insofar as scientific and historical criticism are an aid to understanding, they are valuable, but they are not considered to be the *sine qua non* for interpreting the Old Testament.[4]

The book of Deuteronomy consequently provides a cultural-historical

---

[3]Cf. M. Weinfeld, "Deuteronomy—the Present State of Inquiry," *JBL* 86 (1967) 249, 262.

[4]P. C. Craigie, *The Book of Deuteronomy* (Grand Rapids: Eerdmans, 1975) 77.

setting in which the theological approach that the Bible is the Word of God can be reasonably projected. Revelation and inspiration consequently are seen in an historical-cultural setting in the renewal treaty between God and Israel in the book of Deuteronomy.

The background for the Deuteronomic renewal treaty is the deliverance from Egypt and the revelation at Mount Sinai. These events, which are the greatest miracle and the most extensive revelation in OT times, provide the history in which the Israelites were established as God's holy nation.

To Moses and the Israelites God identified himself as the God of Abraham, Isaac and Jacob. Consequently the communication between God and the patriarchs as recorded in Genesis 12-50 provides the background for a proper understanding and interpretation of the covenant God established with Israel as a nation. The divine revelation to Abraham, Isaac and Jacob can be seen in a much more comprehensive historical and cultural context than was possible in the early part of the twentieth century.

The first eleven chapters of Genesis are crucially important for understanding the patriarchs. Abraham was called when the human race had been alienated from God. These chapters inform us that the God who spoke to Moses and Abraham had also communicated with Adam, Cain and Noah. The God-man relationship began with Adam but was broken by disobedience. Before the curse came the promise of redemption. In these early developments God manifests love, mercy and judgment in his relationship with the human race. Limited as we are to offer the student extensive information about the historical and cultural context of these introductory chapters of Genesis, the God-man relationship is as vital and real as it is in the subsequent developments recorded in the Pentateuch.

Beyond the Pentateuch the OT can be delineated in its historical and cultural setting in the ancient Near East. The relationship between God and Israel is often strained and again is restored primarily as individuals respond to God. Divine revelation continues and supplements the basic revelation given to and through Moses. Prophet after prophet represents God in his love, mercy and judgment and points forward to the fuller revelation in the Messiah.

When the two great commandments, which Jesus pinpointed as the essence of the Law and the Prophets, are used as the integrating core for teaching an overview of the OT, the historical developments take on theological significance. The uniqueness of the OT will become apparent and meaningful as the interaction between the divine and the human is recognized. In this way the OT unfolds the divine revelation that culminated with Christ, as the author of Hebrews affirms in his opening statement:

> In the past God spoke to our forefathers through the prophets at many times and in various ways, but in these last days he has spoken to us by his Son.

SECTION I

How God "Spoke Long Ago to the Fathers"

The Bible and the Environment

F. F. BRUCE

I. THE CULTURAL MANDATE

THE creation narrative of Gen 1:1-2:4a tells how mankind was made in the image of God in order to exercise dominion over the earth and all the animal life upon it and how God gave them what is frequently called the "cultural mandate" to "be fruitful and multiply, and fill the earth and subdue it, and have dominion" (1:28).

Ecologists of our day have sometimes criticized the wording of this "mandate" and held it responsible for the misuse of natural resources that has now become (and rightly so) a matter of worldwide concern. For one thing, the command to "be fruitful and multiply, and fill the earth" has been thought to encourage overpopulation. For another, the command to "subdue" the earth has been thought to encourage ruthless exploitation. But the command to "be fruitful and multiply" had a positive relevance and justification in its own context of sparse population and should be appraised in that context. To quote it as though it constituted a divine ban on birth control in the vastly different circumstances of today is absurd. As for the command to "subdue" the earth the verb *kābaš* is certainly a strong one, but anyone who has tackled the business of turning a builder's yard into a garden would probably agree that it is not too strong. In any case, however strong it is "subdue" does not mean "exploit." It is indeed the *mot juste* for the back-breaking work involved in transforming forest and wilderness into cultivable land.

II. PARADISE LOST

Even in the most fertile parts of the land of Israel in Biblical antiquity a subsistence could be wrested from the earth only by dint of men's toil and sweat. When cultivated the earth yielded not only the grain for which provision had been made by plowing and sowing but also other things, such as thorns and briars, for which no calculated provision had been made but that impeded the growth of the crops and made the task of reaping them more difficult. There was the recurring hazard of drought and famine, wild beasts were liable to ravage the sown land, and human enemies from beyond the frontiers might work greater havoc than wild beasts. Life was hard and life was short.

In the beginning, however, things were different, and hope was cherished that one day in the future they would be different again. The

15

primaeval narrative of Gen 2:4b-3:24 tells how the first man and woman lived in a well-watered garden that the Creator planted "in Eden, in the east," where every kind of fruitful tree grew spontaneously and provided food in abundance (2:8-17). But the serpent that lurks at the heart of every utopia was present in that first paradise and incited the woman to taste the fruit of the one tree—"the tree of the knowledge of good and evil"—which the Creator had expressly forbidden them to eat on pain of death. She shared it with her husband, and the result was their expulsion from the garden. The way to the tree of life, the fruit of which would have enabled them to live forever, was barred to them. More than that, the man had to hear the sentence (3:17-19):

> Cursed is the ground because of you;
> in toil you shall eat of it all the days of your life;
> thorns and thistles it shall bring forth to you;
> and you shall eat the plants of the field.
> In the sweat of your face
> you shall eat bread
> till you return to the ground,
> for out of it you were taken;
> you are dust,
> and to dust you shall return.

This was, indeed, man's familiar lot. As for woman, her sentence was the equally familiar lot of subservience to her husband and the pangs of childbearing.

Paradise was lost, but from time to time the hope of paradise regained—freedom from toil and pain and death—blazed up brightly. Some alleviation of the sentence was foreseen with the birth of Noah: "Out of the ground Yahweh has cursed," said his father, "this one shall bring us relief from our work and from the toil of our hands" (5:29)—for it was Noah who planted the first vineyard (9:20).

III. THE PROMISED LAND

Among Noah's descendants are found not only the tower-builders of Babylon but also the pastoral family of Abraham, ancestor of the Israelites, who receives the divine promise of blessing, renown and the inheritance of the holy land. Abraham is the first man in Biblical history who is specially called and chosen by God—chosen, not that others apart from him might be excluded from the everlasting mercy but that others through him might be admitted to divine blessing. His descendants pursued a nomadic life in Canaan for three generations and then were driven by famine into Egypt where they remained for four generations, latterly enduring forced labor in the royal building-gangs until they were enabled to leave Egypt in circumstances that left them no option but to recognize the timely intervention of the God of their fathers on their behalf. The Egyptian existence to which they had grown accustomed with its supplies of fish, cucumbers, melons, leeks, onions and garlic (Num 11:5) was now replaced for a generation by life in the desert, mainly in and around the oasis of Kadesh Barnea. From there they struck camp and moved as settlers into the land where their ancestors had lived as nomads. In the desert, too, they entered into a solemn covenant with Yahweh, the God of their fathers—a covenant that was henceforth to be the basis of their religious, social and personal life.

The Canaanites' way of life was integrated with the climate and seasonal pattern of their land. When the Israelites arrived they found the climate and seasonal pattern quite different from what they had known recently in the wilderness and before that in Egypt. In Egypt fertility depended on the annual rise of the Nile, while in Canaan it depended on the regular fall of rain. If they asked the Canaanites how the regular rainfall could be ensured, they would be told that the Baal-cult served that very purpose. Baal (Hadad) was the rain-god who fertilized the earth and made the crops grow. But the Baal-cult and similar forms of fertility worship were irreconcilable with the ethical principles implicit in Israel's covenant with Yahweh, alongside whom no other god could have any place. Israel had to learn that Yahweh was Lord of the sown land as much as of the desert, of the valleys as much as of the mountains. The promised land, they were told, was "a land which Yahweh your God cares for; the eyes of Yahweh your God are always upon it, from the beginning of the year to the end of the year." It was by loving and serving Yahweh that they could be sure of the gift of seasonal rain, gather in their grain, wine and oil, and have grass for their cattle (Deut 11: 10 ff.). When harvest came, it was to Yahweh that the firstfruits were to be presented in acknowledgment of his goodness (26:1-11). But this was a difficult lesson to learn. When they indulged in Baal worship on a national scale in the reign of Ahab, Baal was hit where it hurt him most—in his reputation. When Yahweh withheld the rain for three years, Baal (rain-god though he was) could do nothing about it, and when the long period of drought came to an end it was Yahweh, not Baal, who sent rain once more (1 Kings 17-18). Even so, the prophecy of Hosea a century later shows how slow Israel was to understand that it was Yahweh who gave grain, wine and oil "and who lavished upon her silver and gold which they used for Baal" (Hos 2:8). This time it was not merely by drought but by exile that the lesson had to be learned.

More radical even than prophets like Elijah and Hosea were the Rechabites, who were so convinced that an agricultural economy was a menace to true religion that they renounced that economy. They represented a conservative and puritan movement in Israel, like the Wahhabi at a later date in Islam. They were noted for their exceptional zeal as devotees of Yahweh and (like Israel in wilderness days) lived in tents, not houses. They sowed no seed, planted no vineyards and drank no wine, but followed a pastoral way of life until the Babylonian invasion of Judah compelled them to seek refuge within the walls of Jerusalem (Jer 35:1-11; cf. 2 Kgs 10:15-16).

IV. The Legislation

The terms of the covenant with himself into which Yahweh brought Israel in the desert were spelled out in the national legislation, promulgated in the various lawcodes found in the books of Exodus, Leviticus, Numbers and Deuteronomy, especially those commonly called the "book of the covenant" (Exodus 21-23), the "law of holiness" (Leviticus 17-26) and the Deuteronomic code (Deuteronomy 12-26). The codes may be recognized in their several ways as amplifications of the decalogue, the "ten words" to which Israel swore to be obedient at the inaugural covenant ceremony (Exod 24:3-8; cf. 20:1-17; Deut 5:6-21).

The setting apart of every seventh day as a "sabbath" or day of rest was one of the most ancient and most distinctive of Israel's institutions. When Jesus declared that "the sabbath was made for man, not man for the sabbath" (Mark 2:27) he showed his unerring insight into its original intention. In its short formulation in the original decalogue the sabbath law probably ran: "Remember (observe) the sabbath day, to keep it holy." But as expanded in two rather different forms in Exod 20:8-11 and Deut 5:12-15 it enjoins explicitly that the sabbath rest is to be enjoyed by all members of the community, including servants and resident aliens, and by domestic animals also. The historical sanction at the end of the Exodus expansion is Yahweh's ceasing from his work of creation on the seventh day (cf. Gen 2:2-3). At the end of the expansion in Deuteronomy it is his delivering his people from their servitude in Egypt.

To begin with, there was no need to define the work that was not to be done on the sabbath day. Everyone knew what the daily routine of the other six days was. But what of those agricultural activities that recurred season by season rather than day by day? The ruling was explicit: Even "in plowing time and in harvest you shall rest" (Exod 34:21). Rulings regarding other activities, such as lighting fires or gathering fuel for that purpose, are incorporated in the Pentateuchal laws (35:3; Num 15:32 ff.). Other rulings are recorded in the prophetical and historical books (cf. Amos 8:5; Jer 17:21 ff.; Neh 13:13 ff.), and they were greatly elaborated in the rabbinical age.

The three great pilgrimage festivals of the Israelite year also provided seasonal respites from work (Exod 23:14-17). At an early stage the smallholders were encouraged to attend these festivals at the local sanctuaries by the assurance that no one would encroach on their fields in their absence (34:24). But a time was to come when the land-greed of those whose ambition was to "add field to field" (Isa 5:8) could not be restrained by such religious or humanitarian provisions.

The consideration shown to animals in the sabbath law appears in other contexts, especially in the Deuteronomic code—possibly in the ban on yoking an ox and an ass together (Deut 22:10) and certainly in the commandment: "You shall not muzzle an ox when it treads out the grain" (25:4). A neighbor's straying ox or other domestic animal had to be restored to safety. If it had fallen beneath its load it was to be helped up (Exod 23:4-5; Deut 22:1-4). To the Pauline question, "Is it for oxen that God is concerned?" (1 Cor 9:9), the Deuteronomic answer is "Yes!"

Consideration for wildlife also seems to be implied in the ban on taking a mother bird from the nest along with the eggs or the chicks (Deut 22:6-7). And a general concern for health and safety is reflected in the provisions for the disposal of human waste (23:12 ff.) and for the erection of a protective parapet on the flat housetop (22:8).

Some concern for trees is manifested in the regulations for the holy war in 20:19-20. When Israelite forces besiege an enemy city they must not cut down the fruit trees. "Are the trees in the field men, that they should be besieged by you?" If wood is required to make siege engines other trees may be cut down to provide it, but not fruit trees. Some Assyrian kings boast of cutting down the fruit trees and plantations of resistant or rebellious cities, and even in Israel there is the frank account in 2 Kgs 3:18-25 of how the allied armies of the northern and southern kingdoms, with the Edomite vassals of the latter, felled all the good trees of Moab in addition to stopping up all the springs and covering every fertile field with stones—and that not on the plea of military necessity but in obedience to an oracle of the prophet Elisha.

The sabbatical principle was applied to years as well as to days. The covenant law of Exod 21:1-6 prescribes, for example, that an Israelite must emancipate his "Hebrew" slave after he has given him six years' service. A "Hebrew" slave was so called probably because he belonged to a widespread social group that included the Israelites and other peoples also. According to circumstances these "Hebrews" (if they are to be equated with the ʿApirū of cuneiform inscriptions) hired themselves out as household servants or as mercenary soldiers or organized themselves as gangs of freebooters. The "Hebrew" serf of an Israelite master who did not wish to avail himself of the emancipation legally provided when the seventh year came round had then the option of binding himself to his master in lifelong servitude.

A later form of this provision is laid down in the Deuteronomic lawcode (Deut 15:12-18). This envisages an Israelite (male or female), still called a "Hebrew," who—perhaps because of debt—is sold to another Israelite and serves him for six years at half the cost of a hired servant. Such a servant must be released when the seventh year comes round and given ample supplies to set him up in his independence once again. But again provision is made for the servitude to be lifelong if that is the servant's preference.

In Deuteronomy the seventh year is called the year of "release"—not only because bondservants were given their release then but also because there was to be a general remission of debts "at the end of every seven years" (15:1-6). For all the humanitarian intention of this enactment, it could work only in a very charitable society. The Deuteronomic law realizes this and adds the admonition that a creditor must not withhold a loan from his needy fellow Israelite because "the seventh year, the year of release, is near" and the chance of its being repaid is slender. "You shall give to him freely, and your heart shall not be grudging when you give to him; because for this Yahweh your God will bless you in all your work and in all that you undertake" (15:9-10). The reluctance that the legislator foresaw proved only too real, especially in the changed economic situation of the post-exilic age. Accordingly toward the end of the first century B.C. Hillel (founder of the rabbinical school that bore his name) instituted a provision called the *prozbul*. This was to the effect that if a borrower and lender, before the execution of a loan, made a declaration before the court that the law of release of debts should not apply to it, the debt was not subject to cancellation in the seventh year.

The covenant law also prescribed that arable land should lie fallow every seventh year: "For six years you shall sow your land and gather in its yield; but the seventh year you shall let it rest and lie fallow, that the poor of your people may eat; and what they leave the wild beasts may eat. You shall do likewise with your vineyard, and with your olive orchard" (Exod 23:10-11). This provision guarded against the exhaustion of the soil by too-intensive cultivation. It was repeated and elaborated in the "law of holiness" (Lev 25:1-6, 20-22), where the promise is made that the sixth year will supply a surplus of grain and fruit, enough to cover not only the fallow seventh year but the next two years as well. "When you sow in the eighth year, you will be eating old produce; until the ninth year, when its produce comes in, you shall eat the old" (25:22).

Even so, the sabbatical year may not always have been observed with the care that was originally intended. There is a hint in 2 Chr 36:21 that the land of Judah was allowed to remain desolate for the seventy years of the Babylonian exile in order that it might "enjoy the sabbaths" that it had not been allowed to enjoy for a long time—490 years, presumably (i.e., since the inception of the monarchy), if the reckoning is intended to be exact. However that may be, the sabbatical year was observed throughout the period of the Second Commonwealth. As late as the middle of the first century A.D. the famine in Judaea of which we read in Acts 11:28-30 was the more severe because seedtime and harvest had to be suspended during the sabbatical year A.D. 47/48.

In addition to reaffirming the covenant law of the sabbatical year, the "law of holiness" applies the sabbatical principle to heptads of years as well as to years: the law of jubilee, laid down in Lev 25:8-17. This law provides that after seven sabbatical periods (49 years) the land is to lie fallow in the fiftieth year and that each smallholder is to reoccupy his original family property when that year comes round. The *prima facie* meaning of the law is that the year after the seventh sabbatical year was also to be a sabbatical year, to be inaugurated and observed with special solemnity. The question then arises whether the next jubilee period began with that fiftieth year or (as one might suppose) with the year following it. If with the latter, then there was no correlation of the jubilee periods with the sabbatical periods. Perhaps the late pre-Christian Book of Jubilees (which arranges the narrative from the creation to the giving of the law and the entry into Canaan in fifty jubilees) correctly interprets the year of jubilee as the forty-ninth year—in which case the seventh in each series of sabbatical years was celebrated as an extra-special sabbatical year—although, as has been said, that is not the natural way to understand Lev 25:8 ff. But in fact the historical evidence suggests that the jubilee legislation remained an ideal and was never put into practice—although it was later to find an echo in the preaching of Jesus (Luke 4:19).

Even so, the principle that land should not be perpetually alienated from the group that owned it was firmly entrenched in Israelite law. The land was ultimately Yahweh's. Those who possessed it received it from him as a heritage, and it was not for them to dispose of it at random. "The land shall not be sold in perpetuity, for the land is mine; for you are strangers and sojourners with me. In all the country you possess, you shall allow the redemption of land which has been sold" (Lev 25:23-24). If a man (like Zelophehad) had daughters but no sons, the daughters inherited his land on condition that they married within the tribe (Num 36:1-12). So also Naboth's refusal to sell his vineyard to King Ahab was based on Israel's religious law: "Yahweh forbid that I should give you the inheritance of my fathers" (1 Kgs 21:3). And Ahab, who was as much bound by the law as Naboth was, felt himself obliged to accept Naboth's refusal—with however ill a grace—until Jezebel, who had been brought up in a different culture, took matters into her own hands and procured for her husband by foul means what could not be procured by fair means.

But in the next generations the wealthier classes in Israel were able to do by legal process what Ahab found impossible, foreclosing on mortgages at advantageous opportunities, incorporating their poorer neighbors' smallholdings into their own estates and reducing those neighbors to the status of serfs on what had once been their own patrimony, thus anticipating Oliver Goldsmith's words:

Ill fares the land, to hastening ills a prey,
Where wealth accumulates, and men decay.

The day came, as the contemporary prophets warned, when those fertile acres were turned through invasion and exile into desolate tracts from

which, among the briers and thorns, pastoralists scraped a bare subsistence through their cattle that grazed there.

V. THE HOPE OF PARADISE REGAINED

It was in that period of economic oppression and impending invasion
that a new hope of "paradise regained" began to arise. A popular form of
this hope had existed for generations in the expectation of "the day of
Yahweh"—the day when Yahweh would vindicate his cause and right all
wrongs. Because of a facile assumption that Yahweh's cause and his
people's cause were identical and that his "day" would mark their triumph
and the downfall of their enemies, Amos and the prophets who came after
him had to emphasize that when Yahweh bestirred himself to put down
injustice he would put it down in his own people first and that Israel would
therefore find the day of Yahweh to be "darkness, and not light" (Amos
5:18).

As the fortunes of the dynasty of David sank, men looked back to the
age of David and Solomon and envisaged the new age as a restoration of
the vanished glories of that age under a coming ruler of the same dynasty,
"great David's greater son." David's reign in fact had been one of military
expansion, and when Solomon succeeded to his father's empire—extending
from the Egyptian frontier to the Euphrates—he expended his wealth on
the maintenance of an elaborate court for the sake of which his subjects
had to supply forced labor for one month out of every three. Yet in
retrospect his reign appeared as a golden age: "Judah and Israel were as
many as the sand by the sea; they ate and drank and were happy" (1 Kgs
4:20). Such a time of peace would be reinaugurated under the coming ruler
(Ps 72:7-8):

> In his days may righteousness flourish
>   and peace abound, till the moon be no more!
> May he have dominion from sea to sea,
>   and from the River to the ends of the earth!

With the peace were associated fertility and prosperity (72:16):

> May there be abundance of grain in the land;
>   on the tops of the mountains may it wave;
>   may its fruit be like Lebanon;
> and may men blossom forth from the cities
>   like the grass of the field!

Isaiah sees this state of righteousness and peace extending to the wild
beasts (Isa 11:6-9):

> The wolf shall dwell with the lamb,
>   and the leopard shall lie down with the kid . . . .

They shall not hurt or destroy
    in all my holy mountain;
for the earth shall be full of the knowledge of Yahweh
    as the waters cover the sea.

When exile came the prophets encouraged their fellow countrymen with the assurance that it would not last forever. Restoration would come, and in some strands of prophetic encouragement this restoration was linked with the expectation of the son of David, who would "reign as king and deal wisely" and "execute justice and righteousness in the land. In his days Judah will be saved, and Israel will dwell securely; and this is the name by which he will be called: 'Yahweh is our righteousness'" (Jer 23:5-6; cf. 33:14-16).

The joyful anticipation of return from exile is reflected in a revival of natural fertility and human well-being (Isa 35:1, 5-6, 10):

The wilderness and the dry land shall be glad,
    the desert shall rejoice and blossom;
like the crocus it shall blossom abundantly
    and rejoice with joy and singing. . . .
Then the eyes of the blind shall be opened
    and the ears of the deaf unstopped;
then shall the lame man leap like a hart
    and the tongue of the dumb sing for joy.
For waters shall break forth in the wilderness
    and streams in the desert. . . .
And the ransomed of Yahweh shall return
    and come to Zion with singing; . . .
they shall obtain joy and gladness,
    and sorrow and sighing shall flee away.

The theme of the healing of blind, deaf, lame and dumb is taken up later, in no merely figurative sense, in the gospel narratives of Jesus' ministry, which marks the inauguration of the new jubilee, "the acceptable year of the Lord" (Luke 4:19, 21; cf. 7:22), with a message of release from a deadlier exile than the Babylonian—release from estrangement from God and accordingly restoration to one's true home in him.

VI. Program for the New Commonwealth

More prosaically than the prophets just quoted, Ezekiel presents his blueprint for the new commonwealth that is to be established after the return (Ezekiel 40-48). The land of Israel is to be a holy land, the quintessence of its holiness being concentrated in the sanctuary. The land is divided into twelve parallel zones, each stretching from the Mediterranean to the Jordan, for the twelve tribes. Between the seven northern zones and the five southern zones a "holy district" is set apart for Yahweh, about

seven miles long from west to east by about five-and-a-half miles broad
from north to south. Throughout the blueprint this setting apart of special
sections symbolizes the holiness that is to characterize the new commonwealth. Within the "holy district" a central square on a side of five hundred
cubits is set aside for the temple area. A "green belt" fifty cubits wide
around this square separates it from the surrounding territory, which is
allocated to the priests. To the north of the priests' allocation is that of the
Levites. To the south of the "holy district" is the holy city with the open
country assigned to it. The holy city belongs to the whole nation, not to
any one tribe. The superior holiness of the temple is emphasized by its
being completely separate from the city. Two zones on either side of the
"holy district" and the city area—a western zone bordering on the
Mediterranean and an eastern zone bordering on the Jordan—are set aside
as "crown lands." They are the portion of the "prince" of the house of
David. The prince has no share in the priestly privileges. His lay status is
unambiguous. The one vestige of sacral kingship reserved to him is the
right to enter the temple by the east gate "to eat bread before Yahweh"
(Ezek 44:3). But this falls far short of the privilege of his ancestor David,
who went into the tent-shrine that housed the sacred ark in his day and "sat
before Yahweh" (2 Sam 7:18).

A liberal note is struck with regard to resident aliens: They and their
families are permitted to live among the Israelites and enjoy their inheritance in the tribal territory in which they reside. It may be that here the
Hebrew term for "resident aliens" (gērîm) approximates its later sense of
"proselytes": If they choose to share the Israelites' religion and way of life
they are to be welcomed and made to feel at home (Ezek 47:22-23).

From beneath the temple threshold a stream of water emerges and
flows down the Kidron valley in ever-increasing volume until it reaches the
Dead Sea and makes its salt water fresh so that it teems with fish. On either
side of the river fruit trees spring up, producing fresh fruit month by month
(47:1-12).

This picture gives concrete form to a concept that first comes to
expression in pre-exilic times. Jerusalem, unlike most of the great cities of
the Near East, stood on no river, but what their rivers were to other cities
Yahweh was to Jerusalem (Ps 46:4-5):

> There is a river whose streams make glad the city of God,
>   the holy habitation of the Most High:
> God is in the midst of her, she shall not be moved;
>   God will help her right early.

Again, when Yahweh had protected the city against Sennacherib's threats,
his deliverance was acknowledged in similar terms (Isa 33:21-22):

> There Yahweh in majesty will be for us
>   a place of broad rivers and streams,

where no galley with oars can go
    nor stately ship can pass.
For Yahweh is our judge, Yahweh is our ruler,
    Yahweh is our king; he will save us.

If then Yahweh is the source of his people's life and refreshment, this finds pictorial expression in the stream that flows from his sanctuary. Joel 3:18 tells how, on the day of deliverance,

the mountains shall drip sweet wine,
    and the hills shall flow with milk,
    and all the stream-beds of Judah shall flow with water;
and a fountain shall come forth from the house of Yahweh
    and water the valley of Shittim.

And another post-exilic prophet tells how half of the living waters from Jerusalem will flow to the Mediterranean and half to the Gulf of Aqaba (Zech 14:8). If it be asked how the contours of the land will permit this, the answer is that Jerusalem will stand as a city on a hill while the surrounding territory will be "turned into a plain"—the result, no doubt, of the earthquake that is to split the Mount of Olives in two (14:4-5, 10).

In the sequel, the survivors of the surrounding nations go up to Jerusalem annually to worship the God of Israel at the Feast of Tabernacles. The original purpose of this festival is implied in the threat that any nation that defaults in this respect will be deprived of rain. (The Egyptians, whose land was watered by the Nile and not by rain falling on it, would be punished by plague instead of drought.)

This association of the Feast of Tabernacles with rain underlies the ceremony of the water-pouring that was observed in the early morning of the first seven days of the feast. The ceremony of water-pouring provides in turn the background of Jesus' proclamation on the eighth day, "the great day of the feast," six months before his passion: "If any one thirst, let him come to me, and let him drink who believes in me. As the scripture has said, 'Out of his heart shall flow rivers of living water'" (John 7:37-38). The evangelist explains these words as a reference to the Spirit, who would be given to believers after Jesus was "glorified" (7:38).

VII. THE AGE OF THE SECOND TEMPLE

Ezekiel's blueprint for the new commonwealth was to remain an ideal. There was indeed a return of exiles and the temple was rebuilt in Jerusalem, but it was a modest structure as compared with that of Ezekiel's vision. The new Jewish state did not stretch from Syria to the Egyptian frontier or from the Mediterranean to the Jordan. It comprised a few square miles around Jerusalem. It was, as a contemporary prophet said, "the day of small things" (Zech 4:10). There was indeed some optimistic expectation that internal strife would cause the Persian empire to collapse so that the new Israel would regain independence and extend to its ancient limits, but no such collapse took place. When the Persian empire fell at last (331 B.C.), it was merged in the new empire of Alexander the Great and his successors, and the Jewish state continued to be a tributary to a superior power.

Yet for several generations it enjoyed peaceful conditions—conditions that are reflected in some of the wisdom literature. It also enjoyed a high degree of internal autonomy as a "temple-state" under the theocratic administration of the Zadokite high priests. One OT writer comes very near to regarding this state of affairs as the realization of the ideal. This is the "Chronicler" who, writing toward the end of the Persian empire, brings together much ancient material with more recent genealogies and the memoirs of Ezra and Nehemiah and retells the story of his people from the perspective of his own day. The people of Yahweh dwell in safety, as they once did in Solomon's day, "every man under his vine and under his fig tree" (1 Kgs 4:25). They worship Yahweh and live as his people according to the Law of Moses and the liturgy of David. The reforms of Ezra and Nehemiah have cleansed them from ritual defilement. They have kept at bay the compromising blandishments of their Samaritan neighbors. Was not this the golden age? Could the future promise anything better—unless indeed it were the re-establishment of David's royal dynasty?

If this was "paradise regained" it was doomed to be lost again. The post-exilic temple-state was abolished by Antiochus Epiphanes, who during the years 168-164 B.C. did his best to wipe out the distinctive features of Jewish religious identity. Thanks to the valor of Judas Maccabaeus with his brothers of the Hasmonaean family and their followers, his attempt was defeated. Indeed their successful struggle was followed by nearly eighty years of national independence under a Hasmonaean dynasty of priest-kings (142-63 B.C.). At an early stage in this period of independence some Jews were disposed to think that the kingdom of God had been established on earth: John Hyrcanus (135-104 B.C.), one of the earlier Hasmonaean rulers, was believed to combine in his own person the prophetic charisma together with priesthood and monarchy and thus to be almost a messianic figure. Some of his admirers indeed were willing to transfer the ancient hopes reposed in a prince of the house of David to one of the tribe of Levi (to which the Hasmonaeans, a family of priestly descent, belonged).

But very many Jews, and especially the more pious sections of the population, could not see in the establishment of this dynasty the bringing in of everlasting righteousness. The uprooting of the peaceful temple-state by Antiochus Epiphanes led a number of them to conclude that the long-expected age of righteousness and peace could be inaugurated only by the direct intervention of God, through which his obedient worshipers would receive world dominion and their ungodly oppressors would be destroyed. This hope found vividly pictorial expression in the apocalyptic literature that flourished for the next two or three centuries. It was reinforced when the later Hasmonaeans, imitating their Gentile neighbors, proved to be oppressive despots in their own turn. Any tendency to identify their regime with the messianic age was quickly dissipated. Instead they were denounced as usurpers who had misappropriated the Zadokite high-priesthood or "laid waste the throne of David." The former charge was pressed by the community of Qumran, northwest of the Dead Sea, while the latter charge is voiced in the Psalms of Solomon, a collection of hymns proceeding from another group that, about the middle of the first century B.C., was ardently "looking for the redemption of Jerusalem" (Luke 2:38).

Early in the Hasmonaean period the Qumran community was organized as a miniature Israel in the wilderness, not indeed to embody there and then the conditions of utopia but to prepare itself to be God's chosen instrument when the hour struck—as it surely must soon—for him to execute judgment and establish his kingdom. His kingdom, when it came, would involve the maintenance of righteousness and peace (all the unrighteous having been exterminated) under a Zadokite priest and a prince of David's line in a new Jerusalem with a purified sanctuary and acceptable sacrifices. The Psalms of Solomon contain an eager prayer for the advent of the son of David and of the golden age that he will introduce.

The overthrow of the Hasmonaean dynasty by the Romans (63 B.C.) was hailed by both the groups mentioned (and by others) as divine vengeance on a tyrannous house, but no one imagined that the Roman occupation would inaugurate the kingdom of God. On the contrary it intensified the hope of divine intervention. We hear this note of hope struck in the canticles of Luke's nativity narrative in the NT, emanating from the pious circle into which John the Baptist and Jesus were born— especially the *Magnificat*, celebrating the putting down of the mighty from their thrones and the exalting of the humble and meek, and the *Benedictus*, proclaiming that God's raising up "a horn of salvation" for his people in the house of his servant David meant

> that we, being delivered from the hand of our enemies,
>   might serve him without fear,
> in holiness and righteousness before him
>   all the days of our life.

But in Jesus' own ministry no stress is laid on the promises associated with the dynasty of David. The kingdom of God, he announced, was present in measure in his works of mercy and power. It was manifested wherever God's will was done and it was bestowed on the poor in spirit, even when—or perhaps especially when—they endured persecution for righteousness' sake (Matt 5:3, 10). But it would not come "with power" until the Son of Man had suffered and been rejected (Mark 8:31-9:1). There are some promises in Jesus' teaching that might be given a utopian interpretation—e.g. his promise that the twelve, because they had remained with him throughout his trials, would eat and drink at his table when his kingdom was established "and sit on thrones judging the twelve tribes of Israel" (Luke 22:28-30)—but these promises must be taken along with his other statements to the effect that in his kingdom the highest honor consists in the lowliest service, according to the example set by the Son of Man himself (Mark 10:42-45).

In retrospect we may identify the coming of the kingdom of God "with power" with the outpouring of the Spirit of God on the day of Pentecost, which launched the Christian Church on its career (Acts 2:1 ff.). But the Church in the world has shown few indeed of the features conventionally associated with utopia. Among the other secular standards that Jesus turned upside down must be included the traditional conception of the golden age. The Church "militant here on earth," however, is not the final goal of God's eternal purpose. Rather, as the present fellowship of those who have through Christ been reconciled to God and to one another, it is God's pilot scheme and chosen agency for the reconciled universe to be achieved in the fullness of time, when all things in heaven and on earth will be united in Christ (Eph 1:9-10).

VIII. THE GOAL OF CREATION

There are few more penetrating treatments of our theme in the NT than Paul's comments in Rom 8:19-24 on the cosmic aspects of the redemption that Christ has procured for his people. By faith they enjoy this redemption in measure here and now, but they will enjoy it in fullness on the day of resurrection when they enter into that heritage of glory of which the indwelling Spirit is the present seal and earnest. But on that day it is not only they who will experience liberation and fulfillment:

> For the creation waits with eager longing for the revealing of the sons of God; for the creation was subjected to futility, not of its own will but by the will of him who subjected it in hope; because the creation itself will be set free from its bondage to decay and obtain the glorious liberty of the children of God. We know that the whole creation has been groaning in travail together until now; and not only the creation, but we ourselves . . . groan inwardly as we wait for adoption as sons, the redemption of our bodies. For in this hope we were saved.

In saying that the creation was subjected to "futility" or "vanity" Paul might conceivably have had at the back of his mind the refrain of Ecclesiastes: "Vanity of vanities; all is vanity." But this state, he affirms, is but temporary. Just as man falls short of the divine glory for which he was made, so creation as a whole is prevented from attaining the end for which it was brought into being. Like man, creation must be redeemed—because, like man, creation has undergone a fall. Paul may have thought of the cursing of the ground because of man's sin in Gen 3:17-18, but he probably had something more than this in view: the malign influence of rebellious "principalities and powers," now doomed to defeat because of Christ's victory on the cross (cf. 1 Cor 15:24-28).

In any case, something in the nature of a cosmic fall is demanded by any world outlook that attempts to do justice to the Biblical doctrine of creation and to the facts of life as we know them. Man is part of nature, and the "nature" of which he forms part was created "good" and has been involved in the frustration and futility that is manifested outstandingly in human sinfulness—but it will ultimately be redeemed. It is not by accident that the redemption of nature coincides, according to Paul, with the redemption of man's body, that part of his being that belongs to the material order. Man was put in charge of the "lower creation" and involved it with him in his fall. Through the redemptive work of the "second man" the entail of the fall is broken, not only for man himself but for the creation that is dependent on him. Even now man, who by selfish exploitation can turn the good earth into a dust bowl, can by responsible trusteeship make the desert blossom like the rose. What then would be the effect of a completely redeemed humanity on the creation entrusted to its care? The Christian will neither hold that at present "all is for the best in the best of all possible worlds" nor write the world off as belonging to the devil. The world is God's world, and God will be glorified in all his works. And when God is glorified, his creatures are blessed.

If words mean anything, these words of Paul denote not the annihilation of the present material universe and its replacement by a universe entirely new but the transformation of the present universe so that it will fulfill the purpose for which God created it. Here we have the echo of an OT hope—the creation of "new heavens and a new earth in which righteousness dwells," as it is put in an apocalyptic passage in 2 Pet 3:13, where the language of Isa 65:17; 66:22 is quoted. Apocalyptic language in which "the heavens will pass away with a loud noise and the elements will be dissolved with fire" (2 Pet 3:10) is to be understood in the light of more prosaic statements such as Paul's and not *vice versa*.

With the manifestation of Christ, that is to say, the image of God in man will be fully revealed. And man's environment, no longer selfishly exploited but responsibly administered, will reflect the well-being of man himself.

The Abrahamic Covenant:
Conditional or Unconditional?

RONALD YOUNGBLOOD

ONE of John Bright's primary supporting arguments for his major thesis in his most recent book, *Covenant and Promise*,[1] is his strong affirmation of the widely-held view that the Abrahamic covenant is unconditional and that among the other OT covenants it is most closely akin in that and other respects to the Davidic covenant. Without intending or attempting to undermine Bright's main point—namely, that the apparent irreconcilability of "conditional" covenant and "unconditional" promise was dealt with in various creative ways by Israel's prophets from the eighth century onward—I do wish to take issue with him on his insistence that the Abrahamic covenant was unconditional.

In his chapter on Jeremiah, Bright sets up the tension—the "theological collision," as he terms it—as follows:

> On the one hand, there was the memory of God's unconditional promise to the patriarchs of land, posterity and blessing, which had been taken up and projected into the future through God's eternal covenant with David and his choice of Mt. Zion as his everlasting abode, and which now had hardened into the national dogma which the people clutched to their hearts: *this* nation and *this* dynasty will always endure, for so God has promised! On the other hand, there was the covenant made in the wilderness, based in the prevenient grace of God and issuing in binding stipulations to which the nation was obliged to conform, lately reactivated and made the basis of Josiah's reform and now taken up by the greatest prophet of his day: this nation *can* be destroyed, this nation *will* be destroyed, because it has broken covenant with Yahweh.[2]

The sharp distinction that Bright discerns between these two points of view as he outlines them is blunted seriously, it seems to me, by a statement he makes earlier in his book:

> On the one hand, we see a reaching back to the traditions of exodus and conquest and the old covenant league, which conceived of the immediate future in terms of national destruction, the bringing down of the covenant curses and ejection from the land, which would be followed in the farther

[1] J. Bright, *Covenant and Promise* (Philadelphia: Westminster, 1976).
[2] Ibid., p. 165 (italics his).

31

future by a new entrance into the land and the restoration of the covenant
bond on a deeper level. And, on the other hand, we see a reaching back to the
traditions of Jerusalem and David, which viewed the immediate future in
terms of a terrible chastisement, to be followed in the farther future by the
vindication of God's kingly rule on Mt. Zion and the coming of an ideal king
of the line of David who would fulfill the dynastic ideal and make all the
dynastic promises actual.[3]

The differences in principle between the two halves of that statement are, in
my judgment, too subtle and insignificant to warrant the sweeping conclusions that Bright derives from their supposed disjunction.

However that may be, the time would appear to be ripe for a re-
examination of various aspects of the Abrahamic covenant and its relationship to other OT covenants, particularly the Mosaic. Such an exercise will
hopefully clarify the nature and purpose of the Abrahamic covenant itself.

I. The Covenant Scene in Genesis 15

Although the details of God's covenant with Abraham must be
reconstructed from various passages scattered throughout Genesis 12-22,[4]
the initiating ceremony is delineated in Genesis 15. Bright's own description
of the well-known scene includes his judgment that the covenant it solem-
nizes "is depicted simply as a binding promise—or, better, a promissory
oath—on the part of God. No particular conditions are attached to it."[5]
Although Bright then goes on to qualify that statement to some extent, he
still insists on the passivity of Abraham and the actively self-maledictory
oath of God in the entire transaction. Gerhard von Rad, reflecting on the
same chapter, notes that in vv 1-6 Abraham's "faith is understood as a
decision made in complete consciousness," but that in vv 7-18 Abraham's
"consciousness with all sensual apprehension is completely extinguished,
and God's coming as well as his act receive our sole attention." He
concludes that even though "the two parts are completely different as
regards both their origin and their literary nature," "both parts, precisely in
their dialectical contrast regarding the human attitude toward the proffered

---

[3]Ibid., p. 83.
[4]Cleon Rogers has made the interesting observation that such passages perhaps
parallel the Arpad-KTK treaty recorded on three separate stelae, each of which
exhibits "certain differing features" (C. L. Rogers, Jr., "The Covenant with Abraham and Its Historical Setting," *BSac* 127 [July 1970], p. 250 n. 51); cf. also
A. W. Pink, *The Divine Covenants* (Grand Rapids: Baker, 1973) 112-113.
[5]Bright, *Covenant*, 25-26.

salvation, present in an exemplary and vivid fashion the activity and passivity of the person called."[6]

Neither theological waffling nor critical dissection will help us much here, however, as we attempt to understand Abraham's involvement in Genesis 15. Walther Eichrodt comes closer to the truth by reminding us that it is

> from a methodological standpoint a dubious procedure to use [individual OT] passages as exhaustive statements of the content of the *berith*. The relationship which grows out of the nature of the *berith* could very well include the obligation also of the receiver, without its being expressly mentioned, if it were simply presumed as well known. . . . The *berith*, as part of its very nature, assumes the obligation, also, of the receiver, whereby he enters into the realm of divine order and ordinance. . . . The attempt to understand the *berith* as a solemn assurance which obligates only the giver is seen to be an abstraction which ignores the sociological aspect of the phenomenon. . . . The "basic declaration" of the treaty, before all the single obligations, therefore, named explicitly the loyalty of the treaty partner, his honest intention to live up to the new relationship, as the precondition of all which followed. . . . *Covenant and commandment belong essentially together.*[7]

Eichrodt thus reminds us that whereas a covenant may be formally imposed by a suzerain on a vassal, the very nature of covenant involves relationship—"a relationship under sanctions," to use Meredith Kline's definition,[8] "a relationship between two parties in addition to any relationship they may have had in nature or under law," according to J. J. Mitchell.[9] By way of illustration Mitchell adds that "God's covenant with his people is a relationship to them beyond that of the Creator to a creature." In the specifically Biblical sense a covenant between God and his servant is "a relationship of peace, friendship, brotherhood, or even love."[10] The concepts of "love," "loyalty," "friendship" and the like all find their place in Biblical descriptions of covenant as well as in similar contexts elsewhere in the ancient Near East. It is not without covenant point that Abraham is called the "friend" of God (2 Chr 20:7; Isa 41:8; Jas 2:23).

---

[6] G. von Rad, *Genesis: A Commentary* (tr. J. H. Marks; Philadelphia: Westminster, 1961) 184-185.

[7] W. Eichrodt, "Covenant and Law" (tr. L. Gaston), *Int* 20 (1966) 305, 306, 309-310 (italics his); cf. also D. F. Neufeld in *Ministry* 51/7 (July 1978) 6. See further especially T. P. McGonigal, *"Abraham Believed God": Genesis 15:6 and Its Use in the New Testament* (Ann Arbor: University Microfilms 8117951, 1981).

[8] M. Kline, *By Oath Consigned* (Grand Rapids: Eerdmans, 1968) 16.

[9] J. J. Mitchell, "Abram's Understanding of the Lord's Covenant," *WTJ* 32 (November 1969 to May 1970) 46.

[10] Ibid.

The Hebrew word for "covenant," $b^e rît$, stresses this relationship aspect—but almost certainly not in the way usually thought. The dominant opinion concerning the etymology of the word connects it with the Akkadian noun *birītu*, which occurs frequently enough in various senses but probably never with the meaning "bond," "fetter." Wolfram von Soden separates *birītu* from another noun, *bi/ertu*, which does indeed mean "bond" or "fetter" but is almost always found as a kind of *plurale tantum* in the form *bi/erētu*, "bonds," "fetters." If von Soden is correct—and his examples,[11] as well as those in the Chicago *Assyrian Dictionary*,[12] seem to bear him out—then the crucial long-*î* of the supposed Hebrew cognate vanishes into a zero-element in the Akkadian singular or a mandated long-*ē* in the Akkadian plural. While perhaps such phonological considerations in themselves would not suffice to disprove an etymological relationship, the posited semantic shift from "fetter" to "bond" to "covenant" is a bit difficult to swallow also. It is highly unlikely that a covenant was conceived of as a fetter in ancient times by even the most despotic of tyrants. Whatever the actual facts in any individual case, covenant relationship stressed mutual loyalty and love between even the most exalted monarch and the lowliest slave rather than crushing overlordship or craven submission.

A more acceptable etymology for $b^e rît$—if one is demanded—is not far to seek. Recognizing that "covenants are repeatedly spoken of as being made by one party *with* another, or as existing *between* one party and another,"[13] we think immediately of the Akkadian word *birīt*, "between," used from Old Akkadian and Old Babylonian onward. Note the following examples from the literature: ". . . copy of the written agreement which Tešup arranged between Egypt and Hatti"; "there is peace between them"; "there is agreement between them"; "they drew up a document between them"; and, significantly, two Mari examples: "[they] swore a mighty oath between them"; "we will establish friendly relations between me and him."[14]

But the best example from Mari I have saved till last:

> I went to Ašlakka and they brought to me a young dog and a she-goat in order to conclude a covenant (lit. "kill a donkey foal") *between* the Ḫaneans and the land of Idamaraṣ. But, in deference to my lord, I did not permit (the use of) the young dog and the she-goat, but (instead) had a donkey foal, the young of a she-ass, killed, and thus established a reconciliation *between* the Ḫaneans and the land of Idamaraṣ.[15]

[11]W. von Soden, ed., *Akkadisches Handwörterbuch* (Wiesbaden: Harrassowitz, 1959) 129-130.

[12]*CAD* 2. 254-255.

[13]Mitchell, "Understanding," 45 (italics his).

[14]*CAD* 2. 252, 251, 250, 252.

[15]The translation is that of M. Held, "Philological Notes on the Mari Covenant Rituals," *BASOR* 200 (December 1970) 33 (italics mine). For the analysis here

The Akkadian *birīt* occurs here precisely where we find the Hebrew word *bên*, "between," in similar (including, of course, covenant) contexts—often displaying the same syntactic relationship as well by repeating itself before each relevant noun or pronoun. The Akkadian preposition *birīt*, then, stressing the "between-ness" that is the essence of the covenant relationship, would via Mari—if our theory is correct—have been substantivized and adopted into Hebrew by the Israelites as their specific word for "covenant."

Parallels between Genesis 15 and the last-mentioned Mari example have long been noted. To "kill a donkey foal" corresponds to the Jer 34:18 idiom, "cut a calf," which in turn is parallel there to "cut a covenant"—the phrase used in Gen 15:18 and elsewhere. Jeremiah's double use of "cut" speaks volumes to the origin of "cut a covenant" and demonstrates that it almost certainly refers to the sacrificial ritual that solemnized covenants universally in ancient times.[16]

Another probable relationship exists in the reading "she-goat" instead of George Mendenhall's earlier proposal, "lettuce." Mendenhall read the word in question as a form of *ḥassum* and adduced some questionable supportive examples, including the OT relationship between the Passover lamb and hyssop.[17] It would appear to be far better, however, to read the word as a form of *ḥazzum* = ᶜ*azzum* (*ᶜ*anzum*), "she-goat," cognate with ᶜ*ēz* in Gen 15:9.[18] In any event, the combination "young dog and she-goat" seems more appropriate in a sacrificial context than "young dog and lettuce."

The self-maledictory-oath aspect of Genesis 15 is reflected in at least two extra-Biblical texts: the Abbaᵓilum-Yarimlim treaty[19] and the Bargaᵓayah-Matiᵓil treaty.[20] The latter is especially significant for its making explicit what is implicit in Genesis 15: "As this calf is cut to pieces, so may Matiᵓil and his nobles be cut to pieces" (cf. also Jer 34:18-20).

Before leaving Genesis 15 we observe that the Lord "cut a covenant ᵓ*et*—with"—Abraham (cf. also Jer 34:8 for this idiom). That ᵓ*et* cannot be the sign of the definite accusative here is demonstrated by 2 Kgs 17:35, where the same idiom occurs and where the object is pronominal—ᵓ*ittām*, "with them," rather than ᵓ*ôtām*, "(accus.) them." The use of the preposition "with" in Gen 15:18 assumes bilateral agreement rather than unilateral imposition, and this in turn assumes the presence of conditions.

---

being presented see independently M. Noth, *The Laws in the Pentateuch* (Philadelphia: Fortress, 1967) 112-117.

[16]*Contra*, e.g., Mitchell, "Understanding," p. 34 n. 24.

[17]G. E. Mendenhall, "Puppy and Lettuce in Northwest-Semitic Covenant Making," *BASOR* 133 (February 1954) 26-30.

[18]Held, "Notes," 40.

[19]Cf. Mitchell, "Understanding," 28, and the references there cited.

[20]Cf. ibid., p. 39 n. 37; Kline, *Oath*, 17; M. Weinfeld, "*bᵉrîth*," in *TDOT* 2. 277.

II. Scriptural Statements Implying Abrahamic
Covenant Conditionality

Cleon Rogers, who holds to the view that the Abrahamic covenant is unconditional, refers to only three passages that could conceivably be interpreted as containing conditions: Gen 12:1, 17:1, and 17:9-14—in the first of which, he revealingly admits, "it cannot be denied that a certain conditional element is present."[21] Walter Kaiser adds 22:16 and 26:5.[22] In point of fact, however, the number of conditional passages is much larger than three, or even five, as we shall see.[23]

1. Mitchell goes so far as to say that "Genesis 12:1-3 is *the* Lord's covenant with Abram."[24] While that is doubtless an overstatement it serves the useful purpose of reminding us that formalizing a covenant (as in Genesis 15) assumes previous (Genesis 12) as well as present and future relationships.

"Leave your country ... and go" (Gen 12:1) is a clear obligation imposed on Abraham. The implications in the succeeding verses are clear: If Abraham leaves and goes he will receive the divine benison, and if he does not he will not (indeed, how *could* he?). Since covenant blessing is conditioned on obedience, "Abram left, as the LORD had told him" (12:4). Abraham knew what he had to do to participate in the blessings of God.

"Be a blessing" (12:2). Although the form is a *Qal* imperative, modern translations obscure its force by rendering it as a future indicative ("you will be a blessing" or the like).[25] Mitchell's proviso, that "like 'Be thou

---

[21]Rogers, "Covenant," 252.

[22]W. C. Kaiser, Jr., *Toward an Old Testament Theology* (Grand Rapids: Zondervan, 1978) 92-93.

[23]To say, as Rogers does, that the Abrahamic covenant is "completely unconditional" (Rogers, "Covenant," 252) simply does not square with the Biblical data. It is, however, not completely conditional either—nor is that what I am arguing for in this paper. I would prefer to say that whereas the conditional elements in the Abrahamic covenant preponderate over its unconditional elements, the fulfillment of its promises for a believing remnant (Lev 26:40-45) is guaranteed by its quality of everlastingness (Gen 17:7, 13) which, in turn, springs from its divine establishment (15:18; 17:2, 7). As O. Palmer Robertson helpfully suggested to me in a private communication, one can hold to the conditionality of the Abrahamic covenant while still affirming the certainty of its fulfillment.

[24]Mitchell, "Understanding," 38 (italics mine).

[25]Syntactically one might readily concede a future indicative translation since other comparable examples exist (cf. GKC, sec. 110 i). But the imperatives in Gen 12:1; 15:9; 17:1; 22:2 are sufficient to underscore God's requirement of Abraham's obedience.

perfect,' it can be fulfilled by Abram only in Christ, the promised Seed,"[26] is unnecessary in the light of Matt 5:48. On *tāmîm* in Gen 17:1 von Rad says, "The word that one usually translates 'devout' ... actually means 'whole' or 'complete,' not ... in the sense of moral perfection but rather in relationship to God. It signifies complete, unqualified surrender."[27]

2. At Shechem, Abraham "built an altar ... to the LORD" (12:7). In so doing he acknowledged Yahweh as his God and further demonstrated his intention to serve him.

3. "Abram said to the king of Sodom, 'I have raised my hand to the LORD, God Most High, Creator of heaven and earth, and have taken an oath that I will accept nothing belonging to you" (14:22-23). As Mitchell appropriately asks, "What is this but a solemn oath on Abram's part, an oath that recognizes the peculiar relation that exists between the almighty God and himself, an oath that expresses Abram's confidence in the Lord's ability and the Lord's commitment to bless him in all things? It is the oath of a faithful servant in total commitment to his Lord."[28] I would simply add the observation that such an oath presupposes obedience as well as commitment.

4. "The LORD said to him, 'Bring me a heifer, a goat and a ram, each three years old, along with a dove and a young pigeon.' Abram brought all these to him, cut them in two and arranged the halves opposite each other" (15:9-10). John Calvin's observation is sufficient here: By obeying the command of God, Abraham proved the obedience of his faith.[29]

5. "When Abram was ninety-nine years old, the LORD appeared to him and said, 'I am God Almighty; walk before me and be blameless. I will confirm my covenant between me and you and will greatly increase your numbers" (17:1-2). At the very least, Abram's walk of faith is presupposed in the Lord's covenant confirmation—and the sequel later on in this chapter would seem to prove much more. Calvin calls Gen 17:1 an exhortation to a sincere endeavor to cultivate uprightness and observes that God, in offering his grace to Abraham, requires of him a sincere disposition to live justly and holily.[30] John Wesley's comments are also apropos: "The covenant is mutual," and "upright walking with God is the condition of our interest in his all-sufficiency. If we neglect him, we forfeit the benefit

---

[26]Mitchell, "Understanding," p. 35 n. 28.

[27]von Rad, *Genesis*, 193. On Gen 12:1-3 see further D. P. Fuller, *Gospel and Law: Contrast or Continuum?* (Grand Rapids: Eerdmans, 1980), chap. 4, esp. pp. 100-102.

[28]Mitchell, "Understanding," 40-41.

[29]J. Calvin, *Commentaries on Genesis* (Grand Rapids: Eerdmans, 1948) 412.

[30]Ibid., pp. 444-445.

of our relation to him."[31] R. Allan Killen sees faithful obedience as the condition of the Abrahamic covenant.[32] Again,

> Abraham was justified by faith alone, but the faith which justified him was not alone. . . . Abraham was not justified before God by faith and works but by a faith which worked (see Gal. 5:6). . . . While the covenant promise was not given to Abraham because he fulfilled the law or the covenant conditions, the Bible is also clear that the covenant would not operate apart from obedience on the part of Abraham and his descendants. The covenant fellowship imposed upon him the responsibility of being devoted and upright.[33]

6. "Abram fell facedown, and God said to him, 'As for me, this is my covenant with you. . . . As for you, you must keep my covenant" (17:3, 4, 9). Of the relationship between Gen 17:4 and 17:9 as highlighted by the correspondence between "as for me" and "as for you," Westermann comments: "Die Logik dieser Gegenüberstellung kann doch nur meinen: Ich verhalte mich so zu der berit; du sollst (dich so zu ihr verhalten). Oder: Ich bin der Spender dieser berit; du bist der Bewahrer dieser berit."[34]

7. Gen 17:9-14 describes the institution of the rite of circumcision, an obligatory ceremony to be participated in by Abraham and his descendants as an active demonstration of their acceptance of the covenant. That circumcision was in fact a condition of the Abrahamic covenant has been widely held by scholars (Külling,[35] Pink,[36] von Rad,[37] Wesley, John Murray, etc.). On Gen 17:10 Wesley comments: "They who will have God to be to them a God, must consent to be to him a people."[38] Murray states the issue as follows:

> The emphasis which falls upon the unilateral character of the covenant as a dispensation of grace on God's part and the obligation devolving upon men to keep the covenant might appear to be incompatible. Careful consideration, however, shows that these are complementary. . . . The necessity of

[31] J. Wesley, *Explanatory Notes Upon the Old Testament* (Bristol, England: William Pine, 1765), 1. 68.

[32] R. A. Killen, "Covenant," *Wycliffe Bible Encyclopedia* (C. F. Pfeiffer *et al.*, eds.; Chicago: Moody, 1975), 1. 388.

[33] R. D. Brinsmead, "The Names and Features of the Covenants," *Present Truth* 5/7 (November 1976) 20.

[34] C. Westermann, "Genesis 17 und die Bedeutung von berit," *TLZ* 101/3 (March 1976) 166.

[35] S. R. Külling, *Zur Datierung der "Genesis-P-Stücke": Namentlich des Kapitels Genesis XVII* (Kampen: Kok, 1964) 246-247.

[36] Pink, *Covenants*, 108-109.

[37] von Rad, *Genesis*, 195.

[38] Wesley, *Notes*, 1. 70.

keeping the covenant is the expression of the spirituality involved. Keeping is the condition of continuance in this grace and of its consummating fruition; it is the reciprocal response apart from which communion with God is impossible.[39]

D. N. Freedman, while affirming that the covenant is "unconditional in the sense that no demands are imposed upon Abraham," nonetheless is forced to admit that, on the basis of his own criteria, "P interprets circumcision as a condition of membership in the Israelite community; failure to perform the rite means exclusion from the covenant community."[40]

8. Gen 17:23-27, the report of the act of circumcision itself, underscores Abraham's prompt obedience and performs the same function toward 17:9-14 that 12:4-5 does to 12:1-3.

9. According to Gen 18:19, God said of Abraham: "I have chosen him, so that he will direct his children and his household after him to keep the way of the LORD by doing what is right and just, so that the LORD will bring about for Abraham what he has promised him." Of this verse J. Barton Payne states: "The Abrahamic testament was specifically conditional . . . : only as God's children did justice would God bring upon them what He had spoken."[41] Abraham had to "walk obediently, in subjection to God's revealed will, if he was to receive the fulfillment of the divine promises."[42]

10. "Then God said, 'Take your son, your only son Isaac, whom you love, and go to the region of Moriah. Sacrifice him there as a burnt offering on one of the mountains I will tell you about'" (22:2). This series of commands, a divine demand expecting human obedience, finds its response in vv 3-10. The symmetry of 12:1-3/12:4-5, 17:9-14/17:23-27, and 22:2/22:3-10 is unmistakable: Prompt obedience on Abraham's part follows God's commands. That such obedience springs from divinely-implanted faith in no way negates its reality, its force or its significance.

11. "I swear by myself, declares the LORD, that because you have done this and have not withheld your son, your only son, I will surely bless you and make your descendants as numerous as the stars in the sky and as the sand on the seashore. Your descendants will take possession of the cities of their enemies, and through your offspring all nations on earth will be blessed, because you have obeyed me" (22:16-18). The triple promise of

---

[39] J. Murray, "Covenant," *New Bible Dictionary* (J. D. Douglas *et al.*, eds.; Grand Rapids: Eerdmans, 1962) 265-266.

[40] D. N. Freedman, "Divine Commitment and Human Obligation," *Int* 18 (1964) 425.

[41] J. B. Payne, "Covenant (in the Old Testament)," *Zondervan Pictorial Encyclopedia of the Bible* (M. C. Tenney *et al.*, eds; Grand Rapids: Zondervan, 1975), 1. 1008.

[42] Pink, *Covenants*, 109.

land, progeny and worldwide blessing, implicit in 12:1-3, will be realized because of Abraham's obedience. And Heb 11:17-19 reminds us of the lengths to which such faithful obedience is willing to go.

12. Gen 26:4-5 records these words of the Lord to Isaac: "I will make your descendants as numerous as the stars in the sky and will give them all these lands, and through your offspring all nations on earth will be blessed, because Abraham obeyed me and kept my requirements, my commands, my decrees and my laws." Again we observe that the triple promise is to be fulfilled only on the condition of Abraham's obedience. Before we leave the book of Genesis for a moment, we feel obliged to point out the fact that the command-obedience language of 17:9, 22:18 and 26:5—*šāmar ʾet-bᵉrîtî* ("keep my covenant") and *šāmaᶜ bᵉqôlî* ("obey my voice")—is echoed *verbatim* in the undeniably conditional language of Exod 19:5: "If you obey me fully and keep my covenant, then out of all nations you will be my treasured possession."

13. Commenting on the lengthy curses section of Deut 28:15-68, George Shama states: "The promise made to the seed of Abraham . . . was not unconditional, but clearly revokable. . . . The promises made to the patriarch could be and ultimately have been annulled by national apostacy."[43] While Shama's interpretation may be to some extent politically inspired (he is counselor at the Jordan Mission to the United Nations in New York), his understanding of the relationship between the Abrahamic and Sinaitic covenants is surely on the right track.

14. In Jer 4:1-2 the Lord says to Israel:

> If you put your detestable idols out of my sight
> and no longer go astray,
> and if in a truthful, just and righteous way
> you swear, "As surely as the LORD lives,"
> then the nations will be blessed by him
> and in him they will glory.

John Bright claims that the antecedent of "him" in the last bicolon "is Abraham," and that although "as we read it in Genesis, the promise to Abraham carries no expressed conditions," Jeremiah here "introduces one."[44] Pitting Jeremiah against Genesis will not wash, however. In my judgment the promise to Abraham does carry conditions, and Jeremiah here merely recognizes them.[45]

---

[43]G. Shama in *Christianity Today* (October 6, 1978) 29.

[44]Bright, *Covenant*, 160.

[45]We should mention in passing that the antecedent of "him" is probably not Abraham at all but Yahweh; so C. F. Keil, *Biblical Commentaries on the Old Testament: The Prophecies of Jeremiah* (Grand Rapids: Eerdmans, 1956), 1. 101-103, on the basis of the parallelism within the bicolon, the last line of which

15. "By faith Abraham, when called to go to a place he would later receive as his inheritance, obeyed" (Heb 11:8). Obedience language presupposes the withholding of promised blessing in the absence of obedience.

Since the posited unconditionality of the Abrahamic covenant is often compared to that of the Davidic covenant, I shall now comment briefly on the explicitly conditional elements in the latter. In reiterating the terms of the Davidic covenant to Solomon (1 Kgs 9:4-9), eminently clear conditions are laid down by God. The tension between divine commitment to an unalterable promise on the one hand and the inexorable human bent toward sin on the other is explored in Psalm 89 and in 132:11-12. The latter passage in particular causes no small consternation to both Freedman[46] and Bright,[47] but the fact that a covenant that is everlasting from the divine standpoint may in the course of time be broken by sinful human beings need not give us pause (cf. Isa 24:5).

III. Multiple Fulfillments of the Land Promise

The boundaries of the promised land as sketched in Gen 15:18—"from the river of Egypt to the great river, the Euphrates"—are elaborated upon in greater or lesser detail in such passages as Exod 23:31; Deut 1:7; 11:24; Josh 1:4; Ps 72:8; 80:11; Ezek 47:17-20; 48:1, 28; Mic 7:11-12; Zech 9:10. The Deuteronomy passages are especially interesting, since Deut 1:8 calls it "the land that the LORD swore he would give to your fathers, to Abraham, Isaac and Jacob, and to their descendants after them," while 11:22-25 clearly makes the conquest of that land conditional on whether Israel will "carefully observe all these commands I am giving you to follow—to love the LORD your God, to walk in all his ways and to hold fast to him." Outside the land they had served other gods; in it they were to worship the one true God only (Josh 24:14). As Gleason Archer puts it, "while all of this territory was bestowed upon the seed of Abraham and Isaac by covenant promise, the Hebrew nation was to enjoy actual possession of it (in its entirety, at least) only as long as they were faithful and obedient to God."[48]

According to the OT the land promise was fulfilled at least twice (in the days of Joshua [Josh 21:43-45] and during the reign of Solomon [1 Kgs 4:20-21]). The prophets of Israel predicted that, in effect, it would be

---

contains a verb used exclusively of Yahweh in the OT. Keil, however, would agree with Bright that the verses in question refer to the Abrahamic covenant.

[46]Freedman, "Commitment," 426.

[47]Bright, *Covenant*, 64.

[48]G. L. Archer, Jr., in *Decision* (November 1978) 14; cf. also *Decision* (January 1977) 5.

fulfilled in the future as well. In each of the first two instances the land (or at least large portions of it) was wrenched from the people's grasp because of their sin (Judg 3:8 and *passim*; 2 Kgs 17:1-23; Jeremiah *passim*; cf. also Ezek 33:23-26).

When the kingdom of David and Solomon declined, deteriorated and eventually collapsed, the question of the ultimate fulfillment of the patriarchal land promise took on critical status. The answer to that question, provided by the prophets, has been variously interpreted, as is well known. Equally strong cases can be made for literal fulfillment (of which the present state of Israel could be the culmination or—in the view of others—an incipient stage) and for nonliteral fulfillment (which concentrates on a "heavenly homeland" [Heb 11:13-16] and temple [Rev 21:22] instead of earthly real estate).[49] While this paper is not the place to enter into a detailed examination of this extremely complex subject, it will be apparent to my readers that the issue of conditionality/unconditionality is somewhat more relevant to the former than to the latter.

IV. THE RELATIONSHIP OF THE ABRAHAMIC COVENANT TO THE MOSAIC COVENANT

In his excellent review of Bright's book, Kaiser refers to "the connection between the Abrahamic-David-(re)new(ed) covenant and the Mosaic-wisdom theology in the historical development of the OT" as "one of the most important clarifications needed in Biblical theology today."[50] I would heartily concur and would go on to say that those who sense a more or less strong disjunction between the two covenants are on the wrong track Biblically. M. Weinfeld, for example, refers to the Mosaic covenant as obligatory, modeled on the suzerain-vassal type of treaty, and the Abrahamic/Davidic as promissory, modeled on the royal grant.[51] While such comparisons are instructive they can easily lead to an emphasis on the differences between the various OT covenants at the expense of their similarities and to the ultimate detriment of their overall unity.

Calvin's understanding of the OT covenants was that they were essentially one: "God has never made any other covenant than that He made formerly with Abraham and at length confirmed by the hand of Moses."[52] As Mitchell puts it: "The covenant with Abram is THE covenant God has made with fallen men. The covenant with Noah is a prelude, a preparation of the stage so that the basic covenant may be established.

---

[49] For an apologetic for the latter cf. e.g. G. Goldsworthy, "The Kingdom of God and the Old Testament," *Present Truth* 5/1 (February 1976) 16-23.

[50] W. C. Kaiser, Jr., in *JETS* 21/1 (March 1978) 73.

[51] Weinfeld, "bᵉrîth," 270.

[52] Quoted by Mitchell, "Understanding," p. 24 n. 2.

The covenants that follow are all the outgrowths in time of the original covenant with Abraham."[53]

Freedman agrees that the Mosaic covenant follows from the Abrahamic both logically and chronologically, although he insists on stressing their differences, referring to the latter in terms of divine commitment and the former in terms of human obligation.[54] But Freedman—like Bright— gets into trouble again and again because of the ambiguity he sees in the OT treatment of the Davidic covenant (and by extension the Abrahamic). In his search for a solution, however, he asks a series of rhetorical questions that bring a critical issue into sharp focus: "Can covenant bond be broken—and at the same time persist? Can God sever a relationship as a result of covenant violations—and nevertheless maintain it in perpetuity? The Bible seems to answer in the affirmative."[55] To that I say a hearty "Amen." Freedman has tersely described for us one of the most intriguing paradoxes of the divine-human encounter (and I use each of those terms in their most evangelical sense).

Kline sees the unity of the covenants in "the concept of the kingdom of God, of which they are so many manifestations."[56] He nevertheless feels obliged to speak of the "sharp distinction" between what he calls "promise covenant" and "law covenant."[57]

On the other side of the picture, one of the most outspoken proponents of the conditionality of the Abrahamic covenant was Oswald T. Allis:

> Moses' first stay in the Mount was probably brief. He was to remind the people that the God of the Covenant had delivered them from Egypt, and to offer them the status of a unique people—a kingdom of priests and a holy nation—upon condition of obedience [Ex. xix. 3-6]. We note: (i) While the emphasis is naturally on the recent deliverance by virtue of which Jehovah as their divine Deliverer claimed them as His people (xx. 2), this was because of the Abrahamic covenant (ii. 24, iii. 6, vi. 8). The Mosaic covenant rests on the Abrahamic. (ii) The condition, "if ye will obey my voice indeed", is not new. Abraham's faith was constantly tested in the furnace of obedience (Gen xxii. 18, xxvi. 5).
>
> The claim which is often made that the Abrahamic covenant was unconditional while the Mosaic was conditioned on obedience, finds no support in Scripture. God's first word to Abram was a command: "Get thee out of thy country . . . unto a land that I will show thee" (Gen xii. 1). Abram obeyed this command. The performance of the rite of circumcision was made an indispensable condition to covenant blessing (Gen. xvii). Abram performed

---

[53]Ibid., p. 45 n. 43.
[54]Freedman, "Commitment," 427, 429.
[55]Ibid., p. 429.
[56]Kline, *Oath*, 36-37.
[57]Ibid., p. 25.

it at once. The claim that the Abrahamic covenant was "unconditional" has dangerous implications; for it suggests an antithesis between *faith* and *obedience* which is not warranted in Scripture. Paul joins the two together, when he speaks of the "obedience of faith" (Rom. 1. 5, xvi. 26). The condition, "if ye will obey my voice", is merely the echo, we may say, of Genesis ii. 16, "and the Lord God commanded the man". The reply of the people, "All that the Lord hath spoken we will do", was the oath of allegiance of a loyal people to its ruler or king. They did not realize all that it involved, nor how unable they were to keep the law of God. Their words may show self-confidence and self-righteousness. But God's requirement has always been perfect obedience (Gen. iii. 11). And the law which so stresses this requirement also contains and unfolds that system of expiation by sacrifice by means of which the penitent sinner may find forgiveness and acceptance with his God.[58]

To Allis' list of verses from the Pentateuch indicating that God led his people out of Egypt and into Canaan on the basis of the Abrahamic covenant might be added Exod 6:4-5; 32:13; Lev 26:42; Deut 1:8; 7:7-8.

Although the Sinaitic covenant was clearly an outgrowth of the Abrahamic, it is perhaps going a bit too far to insist that they are to be understood as being one and the same. Although Ps 105:8-11 (= 1 Chr 16:15-18) is sometimes pressed into service in this regard,[59] the "Israel" of v 10 is parallel to "Jacob" in that same verse and should probably be interpreted as the man rather than his descendants (despite the appearance of both singular and plural pronominal suffixes in v 11). In any event, caution is advised in the light of the possibility that Jacob himself is intended. Such factors as the symbolic similarity of the covenant-solemnizing ceremonies in Genesis 15 and Exodus 24, both having to do with the sacrificing of animals as the backdrop for self-maledictory oath-taking, serve to stress the unity of the two covenants without demanding their identity.

V. In Conclusion

By re-examining the covenant scene in Genesis 15, collecting the Biblical passages that attribute conditionality to the Abrahamic covenant, discussing the theological significance of the multiple fulfillments of the land promise, and recalling the close relationships that exist between the Abrahamic and Sinaitic covenants, we have attempted to show that the Abrahamic covenant is conditional. To those who are inclined to agree but are by no means totally convinced, a perceptive and helpful distinction has been called to our attention by John Murray:

[58]O. T. Allis, *God Spake by Moses* (Nutley, NJ: Presbyterian and Reformed, 1958) 72 (italics his).

[59]Cf. e.g. R. D. Brinsmead, "Unity and Tension in the Covenants," *Present Truth* 5/7 (November 1976) 38.

If condition is understood in the sense of meritorious cause, then the Covenant
of Grace is not conditioned.... But if understood as instrumental cause,
receptive of the promises of the covenant, then it cannot be denied that the
Covenant of Grace is conditioned.... The promises respecting salvation are
on condition of faith and repentance, and no one can deny that these
promises are conditional.[60]

Such a carefully-wrought distinction has helped believers of every age and
throughout all the ages to tack skillfully and confidently between the Scylla
of antinomianism on the one hand and the Charybdis of legalism on the
other. "Shall we go on sinning so that grace may increase? By no means!
We died to sin; how can we live in it any longer?" (Rom 6:1-2). Again and
again God asked Abraham to demonstrate through obedience that he had a
faith that worked (Jas 2:20-23)—and so it has been (v 24). "Christ's obedience has not rendered ours unnecessary: rather has it rendered ours
acceptable.... The law of God will accept nothing short of perfect and
perpetual obedience; and such obedience the Surety of God's people
rendered, so that He brought in an everlasting righteousness which is
reckoned to their account."[61]

On the other hand, "a man is not justified by observing the law, but by
faith in Jesus Christ. So we, too, have put our faith in Christ Jesus that we
may be justified by faith in Christ and not by observing the law, because by
observing the law no one will be justified" (Gal 2:16). And so it was with
Abraham: "He believed God, and it was credited to him as righteousness"
(3:6, quoting Gen 15:6). "The apostle Paul refers to the Abrahamic
covenant again and again as foreshadowing and illustrating the privileges
bestowed upon Christians, and of the principle on which those privileges
are conferred—a faith which is evidenced by obedience."[62] Abraham re-
joiced at the thought of seeing, in some sense, the day of Jesus Christ; and
when he did see it, he was glad (John 8:56). We too have seen it, because
the gospel to the Gentiles was announced "in advance to Abraham: 'All
nations will be blessed through you'" (Gal 3:8).

John Bright concludes his book with two eminently worthwile sen-
tences that I concur with, though I do not agree with the premises by which
he reaches them and though I would change a word here and there: "Like
Israel of old, we have ever to live in tension. It is the tension between grace
and obligation: the unconditional grace of Christ which is proffered to us,
his unconditional promises in which we are invited to trust, and the
obligation to obey him as the church's sovereign Lord."[63]

[60]Quoted by R. D. Brinsmead, "Christ and the Promissory Covenants," *Present Truth* 5/7 (November 1976) 56.

[61]Pink, *Covenants*, 106.

[62]Ibid., p. 131.

[63]Bright, *Covenant*, 198. See further D. J. McCarthy, *Treaty and Covenant*
(Rome: Biblical Institute Press, 1978) 296-298.

The apostle Peter said much the same thing in a way that none of us could ever hope to match (2 Pet 1:3-11):

> His divine power has given us everything we need for life and godliness through our knowledge of him who called us by his own glory and goodness. Through these he has given us his very great and precious promises, so that through them you may participate in the divine nature and escape the corruption in the world caused by evil desires.
>
> For this very reason, make every effort to add to your faith goodness; and to goodness, knowledge; and to knowledge, self-control; and to self-control, perseverance; and to perseverance, godliness; and to godliness, brotherly kindness; and to brotherly kindness, love. For if you possess these qualities in increasing measure, they will keep you from being ineffective and unproductive in your knowledge of our Lord Jesus Christ. But if anyone does not have them, he is nearsighted and blind, and has forgotten that he has been cleansed from his past sins.
>
> Therefore, my brothers, be all the more eager to make your calling and election sure. For if you do these things, you will never fall, and you will receive a rich welcome into the eternal kingdom of our Lord and Savior Jesus Christ.

Gathered to His People: A Study of a Dothan Family Tomb

ROBERT E. COOLEY

OLD Testament reference to the celebration of death is scant. No extended passage is to be found that discloses the detail of the burial rite and associated mourning practices. Instead the ritual of burial is summarily described as follows: The deceased was "gathered to his people" or he "slept with his fathers." Varying viewpoints have been expressed by Biblical scholars on the meaning and significance of death and burial in OT times.

Archaeological investigations at numerous sites in Near Eastern lands have yielded abundant data concerning burials.[1] Graves and tombs with their associated burial deposits have been discovered at most of the major sites. These burials are a key source for the reconstruction of life and customs. This has been emphasized by the late American archaeologist Robert Heizer: "More details concerning the life of the people can be obtained from burials than from any other type of feature found by the archaeologist, except data incident to such major catastrophes as the destruction of Pompeii. The reason is simple: burials are almost the only

---

[1]For information on Palestinian sites see the following: P. L. O. Guy, *Megiddo Tombs* (Chicago: University Press, 1939); K. M. Kenyon, *Excavations at Jericho* (two volumes; Jerusalem: British School of Archaeology, 1960, 1965); J. Garstang, "Jericho: City and Necropolis," *Annals of Archaeology and Anthropology* 20 (1933) 14 ff.; P. W. Lapp, *The Dhahr Mirzbaneh Tombs* (Jerusalem: American Schools of Oriental Research, 1966); J. B. Pritchard, *The Bronze Age Cemetery at Gibeon* (Philadelphia: University of Pennsylvania Museum, 1963); S. J. Saller, *The Excavations at Dominus Flevit, Part II: The Jebusite Burial Place* (Jerusalem: Franciscan Press, 1964); O. Tufnell, *Lachish IV. The Bronze Age* (London: Oxford University, 1958); Y. Yadin, *Hazor I* (Jerusalem: Magnes, 1958); *Hazor II* (Jerusalem: Magnes, 1960); R. Amiran, "A Late Bronze Age II Pottery Group from a Tomb in Jerusalem," *Eretz Israel* 6 (1960) 25-37 (Hebrew with English summary); R. W. Hamilton, "Excavations at Tell Abu Hawam," *QDAP* 3 (1934) 74 ff.; *QDAP* 4 (1935) 1 ff.; R. W. Dajani, "Jabal Nuzha Tomb at Amman," *ADAJ* 11 (1966) 48 ff.; E. Grant and G. E. Wright, *Ain Shems Excavations* (Volume 3; Baltimore: J. H. Furst, 1939); J. Ory, "A Bronze-Age Cemetery at Dhahrat el-Humraiya," *QDAP* 13 (1948) 75-89; J. Kaplan, "A Cemetery of The Bronze Age Discovered near Tel Aviv Harbor," *Atiqot* 1 (1955) 1 ff.

major class of archaeological features that one can expect to find in the original complete condition, not worn down by use, and exactly as the people left them."[2]

Our understanding of the celebration of death has been expanded through the discovery of pertinent epigraphic evidence. The Ugaritic texts are especially significant for the reconstruction of Canaanite deathways. Their significance lies in the emotional element and mourning rites that they describe as occurring at the time of death. Since the Canaanites and Hebrews belonged to more or less the same cultural environment, the texts from Ugarit are essential to any delineation of deathways recorded in the OT. Literary evidence from Mari and other Mesopotamian sites is valuable for comparative purposes.

All OT references to Canaanite burial rites are implicit and are found in the Hebrew regulations that are reflections of the Canaanite practice in a negative form. For example, Hebrew practice forbids cutting the flesh, a normal part of the Canaanite mourning rite: "Ye shall not make any cuttings in your flesh for the dead, nor print any marks upon you: I am Jehovah" (Lev 19:27-28). Many of the Hebrew death rites are therefore a conscious reaction against the Canaanite practices (Deut 26:14).

I. EPIGRAPHIC EVIDENCE FOR THE CELEBRATION OF DEATH AT UGARIT

There are three *loci classici* in the Ugaritic texts that describe burial practices.[3] The fullest description of mourning rites in ancient Canaan is furnished by the Baal text. The primary description of the burial of the dead is in the legend of Aqhat, and additional insights into Canaanite mourning rites will be found in the epic of Keret. It is obvious that the literary texts do not give a complete picture of Canaanite burial practice. The material remains of the archaeological data reveal traits that were taken for granted by those who wrote.

An investigation of these texts yields salient points for our understanding of Canaanite beliefs and rituals associated with death. On the evidence of the Ugaritic texts death was viewed as the normal end of the temporal life but not the absolute end of life.[4] It disrupted the community and demanded readjustment. To be dead was to be at "sleep" or "at rest"[5] in the netherworld, which is described as a greedy monster with gaping jaws.[6] Such a life is described as an existence in a subterranean region where food is mud and dirt and where there is constant thirst and languor (cf. Gen 37:35; Job 10:21-22; 17:16; Ps 94:17).

[2] R. Heizer, ed., *The Archaeologist at Work* (New York: Harper, 1959) 84.
[3] *ANET*, pp. 129-155.
[4] Ibid., p. 151 (Aqht A [vi]).
[5] Ibid., p. 154 (Aqht C [iii]).
[6] Ibid., p. 138 (Baal, g. I*AB [ii]).

From the Ugaritic texts we know that the burial of the corpse was undertaken in a spirit of grief and sorrow immediately following death. Elaborate mourning rites always attended the burying rite and for a time following disposition. Very little detail concerning the burial rite can be gleaned from the literary material. No effort was exerted to preserve the body, but rather the body was disposed of by placement in the earth or special necropolis, thereby fixing a social place where the deceased could "sleep" in peace.[7] There is no indication that the place of burial was marked by a monument. The corpse would be placed in a supine position, in an attitude of sleep,[8] and covered with a linen shroud. No reference is made to the depositing of food, furniture or personal items with the corpse. It is precisely at this point that the archaeological data helps us the most to comprehend the total range of burial rites.

II. Mortuary Evidence for the Celebration of Death at Dothan

A fuller understanding of burial rites in the Canaanite-Hebrew culture area is achieved when the evidence from tomb excavations is considered. Its significance lies in the ritual element that may be reconstructed from the material remains.

The body would be removed by relatives, serving in the role of undertaker, to a shaft-chamber tomb located in the limestone escarpment to the settlement. The bones of earlier burials would be unceremoniously swept to the rear of the chamber, thereby providing space for a fresh burial. These were family tombs, and it is reasonable to suppose that this is what the Bible implies when it speaks of being "gathered to one's fathers."[9]

Generally the clothed body would be placed on the floor of the chamber either in an extended or contracted position without regard to a fixed orientation. Vessels, furnishings and personal possessions were either placed around the circumference of the tomb or carefully arranged around the body. These deposits represent a full complement of articles of everyday life and were provided for the dead for their material needs in the afterlife. Food and drink were included in the deposits, and clay lamps in great numbers suggest the importance of light. Following interment the doorway to the chamber would be closed with a blocking stone and the shaft filled with debris.

When a second death in the family occurred and the tomb was to be used again, the debris in the shaft and then the blocking stone were

[7]Ibid., p. 139 (Baal, h. I*AB).
[8]Ibid., p. 154 (Aqht C [iii]).
[9]Gen 25:8; 35:29; Deut 32:50; Judg 8:32; 16:31; 2 Sam 21:12-14; 1 Kgs 2:10; 11:43; 15:8.

removed and the corpse and its deposit were placed in the chamber. Previous burials and deposits were brushed to the sides of the chamber, making room for a fresh burial and deposits. This process was repeated every time a death occurred in a family. Such a burial ritual is amply illustrated by the evidence from tomb explorations. Among the most important excavated tombs for burial reconstruction is one at Tell Dothan.[10]

The Biblical city of Dothan (Gen 37:17; 2 Kgs 6:13) was excavated by the late Joseph P. Free, professor of Bible and archaeology at Wheaton College, for nine seasons between the years 1953 and 1964. The mound rises some 175 feet above the surrounding Dothan plain, and its settled area consisted of some 25 acres. Excavations were carried out in six areas.

Dothan Tomb One is located on the west slope of the tell outside the Late Bronze Age settlement. Its history began about 1400 B.C. and it remained in use until about 1200 B.C. Seventeen to twenty-two feet of Early and Middle Bronze Age stratification existed above the tomb, indicating that the tombdiggers had to cut their way through occupational debris before reaching the native bedrock. Also the remains of an Early Bronze Age wall, four meters thick, had to be removed before arriving at bedrock. A circular stone wall surrounding the tomb shaft served to retain the debris and provide access to the shaft proper. Additional tombs are located nearby. The gentle slope of limestone provided an ideal location for the necropolis.

Dothan Tomb One was a well-cut, irregularly shaped chamber tomb with entrance from west to east. The square-cut entrance shaft was 1.51 m. deep and included three of the seven steps leading down into the chamber. Entrance to the chamber was made through a doorway wider at the base than at the top. A blocking slab of hard stone closed the doorway.

The dome-roofed chamber was extremely large—5.00 m. by 8.30 m.— with an irregular plan that approximates an elliptical layout. Six niches for burial were located about 1.00 m. above the chamber floor. The tomb was cut with a metal blade 2 cm. wide. Vertical and oblique stroke marks are preserved on the chamber walls.

An auxiliary opening or circular window was positioned on the front side directly above one of the chamber niches. Outside the chamber and below the opening two large storage jars had been placed. Each jar contained a dipper juglet for the dead to receive the contents. Similar installations were discovered in the great tombs of Ugarit of the fourteenth and thirteenth centuries.[11] Such provisions give sufficient evidence for the concern of the living to provide the dead with refreshing drinks.

[10]For summary reports on the excavations of Tomb One at Dothan see *BASOR* 156 and 160.

[11]C. F. A. Schaeffer, *The Cuneiform Texts of Ras Shamra-Ugarit* (Oxford: University Press, 1939) 50-51.

It is also possible that the Dothan installation was used for libations. The thirst of the dead had to be quenched. Such a concept was held widely in the ancient Near East, and therefore libations were regularly poured out to the dead.[12] At Dothan water would be poured into the chamber through the window opening and then the vessels placed along the stone retaining wall of the shaft. This would account for the large number of vessels found outside the chamber. Few Palestinian sites have yielded such apparatus to supply water for the thirst of the dead.[13] The ritual purpose of these devices is clearly evident.

The position of the Dothan skeletal material is similar to the general picture of human remains recovered in Palestinian tomb excavations. No coffins were used. Instead the body was placed, either on the chamber floor or on the debris of previous interments, in an extended position. No rule of orientation was followed in the placement of the corpse. In some cases, store-jar sherds were used as a shroud.

The practice of multiple successive burials caused a great deal of destruction to the skeletal material. In places the bone material of many skeletons was fused into a solid mass, making it impossible to evaluate individual burials. The few interments that had not suffered destruction indicate that the full-length or extended position was preferred. Tibia and fibula bones were in an excellent state of preservation. These were often stacked like cordwood, a result of the reuse of the chamber space for fresh burials. The major significance of the Dothan material is not to be seen in the placement or condition characteristics but in the large number of individuals buried in this single-chamber tomb. In all, based upon the skull evidence, 288 skeletons were in the tomb. This number of interments is of far greater amount than any other Late Bronze Age tomb yet excavated.

It was a practice to supply the dead with food, drink, clothing, jewelry, household articles, furniture and weapons for use in the life of the netherworld. The Dothan burial deposits are similar to the repertoire uncovered at other Palestinian sites. Pottery vessels comprised the largest number of household articles. Bowls were the most common vessels. Lamps and pyxides were next in quantity. Three lamps each with seven nozzles, and a lamp with molded figurine, are significant finds. The latter object had a male figure extended across the base of the lamp with the head positioned so as to form a part of the nozzle. Imported Mycenaean and Cypriote wares are well represented also. Other deposits of household articles included an alabaster chalice, faience bowl, bronze bowls and lamp, basalt vessels, limestone platters, spindles and whorls, knives, needles, tweezers and grinding stones.

[12]T. Gaster, *Thespis* (Garden City, NY: Doubleday, 1961) 201 ff.
[13]G. Schumacher and C. Steuernagel, *Tell el-Mutesellim I* (Rudolf Haupt, 1908) 21 ff.

Finger rings were the most popular ornaments represented in the Dothan deposits. The majority were made of bronze and were circular in style. Bracelets and necklaces were rare. Toggle pins, ivory pendants, beads and pins round out the assemblage of personal ornaments.

A limited number of weapons was deposited. Daggers were the most common and were made of bronze with a tang to secure the handle. The handles were of wood as evidenced by wood fragments attached to the tang. One bone handle in excellent condition adds to the variety of materials utilized. Projectile points and spearheads were included in the deposits also.

Few remnants of the food offerings remained. The olive pits and sheep remains attest to the usual flora and fauna offerings. Shellfish were represented in the earliest use of the tomb, and a fish vertebra was found.

Finally, objects connected with religion or ritual are rare. No figurines were found. Scarabs were the only amulets and comprise the largest number of objects in the ritual category. Five zoomorphic vessels were found. All represent the bull and are constructed realistically, including the sexual attributes. These may have been associated with the local fertility cult. The Dothan tomb also included a simple kernos ring. It was in excellent condition and provided free communication between the hollow ring and the standing cups. The kernos ring was probably used for libations: The wine would be poured into the cups to circulate throughout the hollow ring, symbolizing the fertility of the earth. No other ritual ware was identified in the burial deposits. The Dothan practice in regard to objects connected with religion gives no evidence of concern for the spiritual needs of the dead in the afterlife. The tomb deposits considered necessary for the dead in their afterlife were those used in everyday life. The objects were purely domestic and utilitarian. It must be presumed that the Dothanites had some recognition of the existence of an afterlife in this provision of furnishings for the dead, but they seem to have had no feeling for the spiritual needs in this state.

III. THEOLOGICAL AND SOCIOLOGICAL INFERENCES OF THE MORTUARY PRACTICE

Theological and sociological inferences may be drawn from the Dothan tomb study that expand our understanding of the treatment of the body, the nature of the tomb, and the providing of burial deposits. The inferences that may be drawn from the material suggest complete agreement to the mortuary behavior practiced throughout the culture area.

The evidence indicates that a contrast in attitudes existed between the time of the burial of the body and the eventual destructive treatment of the skeletal remains of the same body after the flesh had decomposed. This shift in attitude seems to imply a particular belief in a netherworld as a place where the dead go: Once they are there they are no longer interested in the living and are powerless to influence their lives. Such a concept would explain the burial rites. At the time of burial, scrupulous care was exercised in the placement of the corpse and in the arrangement of tomb equipment. This suggests that the body had to be treated with respect on this particular occasion. Once the body was transformed into a pile of bones it was treated with little respect and regard. It was the normal practice to sweep aside the bones and equipment into a heap, destroying both in the process, to make room for subsequent burials. Apparently it was believed that the deceased was conscious of feeling and actually lived in the tomb as long as the flesh was in existence. Therefore it needed food, drink and personal supplies that were possessions in life. Once the flesh had disappeared the deceased had arrived in the netherworld and no longer needed the mortuary equipment. The descendants could with impunity destroy or remove such equipment. There could be no retaliation. The end of the trip had been accomplished as indicated by the complete decay of the flesh.

In view of the above attitude toward the body, the tomb was not considered as the permanent residence of the dead but a temporary place on the way to the netherworld. It is to be conjectured that this concept explains the general practice of despoliation and destruction of the skeletal material and the lack of evidence for tomb equipment being provided for generations. Once the flesh decayed, the deceased had departed from the tomb for the netherworld. Therefore the tomb served its function as a temporary station. Prior deposits were swept away, broken, and in some instances thrown out of the chamber in order to make room for subsequent burials. Also it may be surmised that valuable or useful deposits were carried away by relatives or strangers. Therefore the tomb served only as a temporary residence and could be used time after time for the placement of fresh burials. In this manner the deceased was "gathered to his people."

The burial deposits consisted of the things a man had needed in his everyday secular life. The afterlife was viewed as a mere extension of terrestrial existence. The material needs of the dead were the prime concern. Deposits related to religious belief or ritual practice are rare, suggesting a curiously materialistic but nonritual burial practice. Furthermore, there is no evidence of any deity to whom the dead could relate, either for enjoyment or protection, in the afterlife. Burial deposits were placed in the tomb to be used in the long and pathetic trip to the netherworld. Once the trip was completed the deposits were no longer needed and therefore could be broken, discarded or removed. There is no evidence that burial furnishings were renewed periodically, nor were additional supplies placed in the tombs in the years that followed interment.

This evidence indicates a belief in an afterlife, but cultic practices were not a part of the activity for the dead.[14]

The Dothan tomb is significant also for the understanding of social institutions in terms of death and dying. A review of the three basic features—the body, the tomb, and the burial deposits—suggests certain social customs.

The dead were respected by inhuming the body in a specially prepared burial site—a large hewn chamber tomb. There is no evidence of cremation, of coffins, or of secondary burials. It was the concern of the Dothanites to properly bury the body in an appropriate "house of the dead." Multiple interments were made in the tomb, indicating that it served a family and its descendants for several generations—possibly two hundred years as indicated by the ceramic tradition. This family vault was associated with other tombs, forming a plot within the necropolis on the western slopes of the tell outside of the settlement area.

Social rank of the deceased has been observed in Palestinian tomb excavations as evidenced by certain deposits or installations.[15] It is thought that persons of rank or wealth were afforded special provision, whereas the vast majority of common people lay on the chamber floors of the tombs. The provision of niches and crypts for a few select individuals at Dothan may suggest that these individuals were important and of greater social rank. The vast majority of deceased individuals was placed on the chamber floor.

No obvious pattern can be detected that would reflect a special social attitude toward the position taken in the placement of the body. The overwhelming evidence indicates a lack of concern. Normally the body was placed supine, sometimes with the knees raised, and without consistency in directional orientation.

The tomb served a practical social function to rid the living of a decaying corpse, freeing them from the nauseous smells of corruption and from the horror of seeing the body decompose. The Dothanites located their tombs outside of the area of settlement, but together in a "city of the dead." It is clear that the city of the dead as a collective representation was considered as a symbolic replica of the living community. Apparently family groups remained intact in death, and the everyday goods were deposited with the dead. Therefore the necropolis is a material artifact reflecting the community life of the settlement.[16]

[14]For another interpretation of the evidence see J. W. Ribar, *Death Cult Practices in Ancient Palestine* (dissertation, University of Michigan, 1973).

[15]Kenyon, *Jericho*, 1. 308.

[16]H. C. Brichto, "Kin, Cult, Land and Afterlife—A Biblical Complex," *HUCA* 44 (1973) 1-54.

It is interesting to note that tombs in the region give very little evidence to indicate levels of society. No evidence is available that would suggest a distinction between royalty and the common people. It could be that the surviving evidence is only representative of the upper levels of society and that the lower levels were not accorded such elaborate burial, since no evidence survives for this segment of the population. It is also possible that no royal burial has yet been uncovered in the area, and therefore the tombs discovered represent a general cross section of society and a uniform burial practice for all social levels. Social status would then be reflected in the quality and quantity of burial deposits and not in tomb architecture.

There was no hesitation to reuse the tomb, with multiple interments being the normal burial practice. The social implications of such a trait are many. First, by the use of existing tombs, efforts in tombdigging were conserved. Second, a few tombs constituted a necropolis. Due to the size of the chambers and the multiple interment practice the few tombs were sufficient for the demand. Third, a single tomb and its interments represent a family vault and group. The continuity of the family unit would be maintained by such practice. It follows that the tomb represents a family plot within the cemetery area. And fourth, the tomb use spanned several generations. When a family ceased to use a tomb, it died its own death and became an historical monument.

The practice of providing the dead with all the requirements of domestic life is of particular interest in supplying evidence for certain social attitudes and practices. It can be deduced from the types of deposits what the normal objects in an ordinary house were. Vessels, furniture, implements and personal and toilet accessories constituted the usual household assemblage. There were very few weapons and hardly any objects associated with religion. The objects that served the material needs of the living also were thought to be capable of serving the needs of the dead.

The quantity and quality of deposits perhaps may be attributed to the social status of the deceased. Trade wares, elaborately manufactured ceramic vessels and bronze containers can be properly explained as only that which is appropriate for an aristocrat. However, none of the deposits suggests great riches. Gold objects for jewelry were extremely rare. Either these were stolen or the inhabitants did not own such precious objects or were not rich enough to spare them as offerings for the dead.

The nature of some deposits suggests certain social notions. Faulty deposits may be interpreted as poverty or stinginess. Bottomless juglets in large storage jars would have been useless to the thirsty spirits of the dead and appear to be cases of fraud. Furthermore, patched jars provide evidence that in some cases relatives were poor or were not wasting a brand-new jar by depositing it with the dead. Evidence of inferior deposits is also seen in the sherds that were used as dishes or lamps. However, this may merely reflect a normal practice of everyday life: When a vessel was broken its usefulness was not terminated. The broken sherds could serve as dippers of liquids, carriers of coals, or oil lamps.

The Dothan tomb contained one dagger, intentionally bent or "killed" and placed in a bowl along with a deposit of food. No doubt it was believed that this practice set free the object's soul to accompany the spirit of its dead owner. Such a find indicates that a complex combination of burial rites and socio-theological concepts existed in Late Bronze Age Dothan.

IV. The Celebration of Death Reconstructed

Death was a most significant event and an occasion set off by ritual and ceremony. The reconstruction of the celebration of death is possible only when the literary evidence and the archaeological data from the culture area are combined. Archaeological data tends to focus attention primarily upon the disposal of the dead, while literary data brings attention to the rites practiced by the living. The combined evidence illuminates a mortuary practice that focuses attention upon the religious as well as the social character of existence, each phase being characterized by a clearly defined rite—a rite of passage. The rite can be divided into three vital functions: separation, transition and incorporation.[17]

At the time of death the related community observed specific rites of separation. Importance was attached to the disposal of the body, and this involved certain physical procedures of separation. The body was clad in a grave shroud or in everyday dress and removed immediately to the burial site (1 Sam 28:14). The burial took place as soon as possible after death. The corpse was interred in a special necropolis or "city of the dead," a social place set aside for this purpose and outside the settlement area. The architecture of the tomb included a deep shaft, an entranceway and a variform chamber. These were common tombs, used by the family over a considerable period. In death, as in life, provision was made for continued association with the family. Two very important functions were served by the tombs: First, it was an established place where the decaying corpse could be disposed of; second, it was a place where the family could maintain and express their intimate relations with their dead.

Multiple successive inhumations were the rule. The general position of the bodies was supine, thereby imitating the position of a person asleep. Social status was signified not by tomb design but by providing special installations for the body and high-quality deposits (2 Chr 16:14; Jer 34:5).

[17] A. Van Gennep, *Les Rites de Passage* (Eng. translation; London: Routledge & Paul, 1960 [1908]).

A man's status in the afterlife was determined by his status on earth. His requirements were thought to correspond to his requirements on earth.

An abundant supply of food, drink and equipment was placed around the body. The deposits represent the equipment used by the dead during his everyday life. Four major types of deposits were considered for mortuary use: personal adornments, military equipment, household articles, and amuletic-ritual objects. Such tomb equipment represents a pathetic attempt to preserve the semblance of the estate of the living.

Following interment the final physical procedure of separation for the dead was the concealment of the chamber entranceway and the filling of the shaft with debris. The separation of the dead to such a nondynamic existence avoided any possibility of upsetting the equilibrium between the world of the living and that of the dead.

The rites of separation for the living, gleaned from the Ugaritic texts, are few in number and very simple in contrast to the elaborate ritual for the dead. A new social role was imposed upon the living—the role of a bereaved person—which served to separate the living from others in the society. The new social role was characterized by the bereaved abstaining from social activities and from public diversions.[18] In such social seclusion the bereaved had opportunity to work through and come to terms with their loss. The mourning period was entered through ritual isolation.

The period of grief reaction constituted the second vital function of celebration and served as a transitional phase marked by intense mourning and violent grief behavior of weeping and crying.[19] Typically the mourners were distinguished by a change in their physical appearance and activity. Garments were torn and sackcloth was worn (2 Sam 3:31; Esth 4:1; Isa 15:2-3; Jer 48:37; Ezek 27:31; Amos 8:10). The pitiful state of sorrow and grief was demonstrated physically by either sitting on a low stool or on the ground and by lying on a bed (Lam 2:10; Ezek 26:16). In this state of complete despair, earth was placed on the head (2 Sam 1:2).[20] It was the practice to self-inflict wounds and disfigure the body and to cut the hair and beard.[21] These practices may be regarded as attempts to focus the attention of the mourner upon himself and therefore hasten his emancipation from the deceased.

There was communal lamentation. Professional female mourners were employed because of their greater emotivity and sensitivity to the requirements of expressing grief (2 Chr 35:25; Jer 9:17-19). Allusions to the length of time given to the transitory period of mourning are scarce.

---

[18] *ANET*, pp. 149-150 (Aqht A [i]).

[19] Ibid., p. 139 (Baal, h. I*AB); p. 143 (Krt A. [i]); p. 146 (Krt B [v]).

[20] Ibid., p. 139 (Baal, g. I*AB [vi]).

[21] Ibid.

The transitional phase of the living had its counterpart in a transitional phase for the deceased: the time required for the flesh to decompose and for the spirit to journey to the world of the dead. This may be a clue to the amount of time engaged in mourning by the living (Num 20:28-29; Deut 34:8; 2 Sam 14:2). Once the body was transformed into a pile of bones, the deceased could no longer influence the living and had no need for the furnishings. Deposits could be broken or removed and the bones pushed aside or swept out of the chamber. The transition period terminated with the incorporation of the deceased into the world of the dead.

Reintegration of the bereaved into the life of society was achieved by certain rites that lifted all the regulations and prohibitions of mourning. Personal interest was again directed outward.

The Ugaritic texts suggest that five rites were observed in the lifting of mourning. First, a rite of purification was performed. The dead were considered unclean, and the rite of washing symbolized the mourner's separation from the dead and his entry into normal intercourse with society. Second, the professional mourners were dismissed. Third, an act of worship was performed. Fourth, the mourning rites were brought to conclusion by a ritual dance. Fifth, a funeral feast served as a rite of incorporation. The meal shared after mourning reunited the survivors with each other. Public acknowledgment and commemoration of a death asserted the viability of the group.[22]

The dead were incorporated into the world of the dead once the flesh had decomposed and not at the time of interment in the tomb. The tomb was not considered as the permanent residence of the dead but a temporary station on the way to the netherworld.

Thus each phase of the celebration of death was characterized by clearly defined rites, which collectively served three vital functions: the disposal of the body, the reorientation of the bereaved, and the readjustment of society back to everyday activities.

The Canaanite viewed death as the lot of all men. It was not the absolute end of life but a crisis transition to a world of the dead characterized as a subterranean region where there was inertia, thirst and dirt for food. Therefore it was essential to bury the dead and ensure the spirit of the deceased admission to that world of the dead. The rites performed at death lend color and richness to our understanding of Canaanite culture as manifested in Dothanite society. While death was accepted, it was accepted only passively. The postponement of death was a joyous occasion (Ps 6:1-5; 88:1-14; Isaiah 38).

[22]Ibid., p. 155 (Aqht C [iv]).

Questions From the Prophets

Merold Westphal, Jr.

O N occasions that seemed appropriate to her, my mother used to recite to me the following piece of didactic doggerel:

Here lie the remains of Jonathan Jay,
Killed in maintaining his right of way.
He was right, dead right as he sped along,
But he's just as dead as if he were wrong.

There is good advice here. There are some battles one cannot afford to win. The debate over propositional revelation may be such a battle for both sides. Those who set out to preserve living encounter and self-revelation by creating a stark antithesis between these and propositional truth run the risk of ending up with a God who can act but not speak and whose very actions evaporate into sentiment and projection because their meaning is given over to completely subjective interpretation.

Wishing to avoid this pitfall, the other side all too easily accepts the false dichotomy between personal and propositional revelation (sometimes unwittingly) by coming to view the Bible as a "golden casket, where gems of truth are stored." Underlying such imagery is a Midas-mercantilist view of truth scarcely more Biblical than the error it was intended to correct, if at all. It expresses a possessiveness vis-à-vis the sacred that is probably more akin to the world-view of magic than to that of theism. That is why the defenders of propositional revelation, among whom I count myself, need to be called back from a victory in which they will emerge dead right. For a theology that forgets that God's word is his living address to his people is the theology of a dead Church. Neither a "high" view of Scripture nor impressive Church growth statistics can give life to dry bones. Only the living word of God can do that (Ezekiel 37).

Paralleling the danger of lapsing into a magical world-view while professing theism is that of falling into mythical patterns of thought even while seeking to preserve Biblical history. Albert Camus has perceptively described the world of myth as one where "there are no more questions, only eternal answers and commentaries."[1] In this light a theology whose supply of answers constantly outstrips the demand arising from vitally

---

[1] A. Camus, *The Rebel* (trans. A. Bower; New York, 1956) 20-21.

urgent questions might be said to exhibit the essence of mythical thinking, even if it denounces those whose scientific naturalism first turns Biblical history into myth and then demythologizes in order to find a truth acceptable to modernity. Such a theology serves as a defense against being put into question by the living word of God. In doing so it domesticates God, and a domesticated God is of course an idol created by man in his own image and for his own purposes.

Jacques Ellul is speaking of this danger when he writes, "We learned that the Bible is not a collection of answers God has given to our questions; on the contrary, it is the place where God addresses us, where he asks *us* the question *we* have to answer. To hear the word of God is to hear the question which God asks of me, to which I must give a response out of my life and faith. I am made responsible (compelled to give a response)."[2]

This lesson is hard to learn and easy to forget. It is always hard to be a good listener, but especially when we are being personally challenged. Our defense mechanisms against the pain of being vulnerable spring into action and we flee the danger of person-to-person presence. With help from the Midas-mercantilist mentality we transform questions that threaten us into answers that we treat as valuable property, generously giving them as gifts to those who will accept them and tenaciously defending them against those who would take them from us or belittle their value to others.

Just as we would like to believe ourselves in possession of an unending supply of fossil fuels, we would like to see ourselves as presiding over a boundless source of theological answers. Fossil fuels are useful to man in pursuing his goals, but only when what was once living has long since been dead. Theological answers can all too easily become the fossil fuels of the spiritual life. They can serve our needs for security, for power and for convenience to the point where we become the slaves of what is lifeless.

A fossil-fuel theology stands in starkest contrast to the word of God. "For the word of God is living and active, sharper than any two-edged sword, piercing to the division of soul and spirit, of joints and marrow, and discerning the thoughts and intentions of the heart. And before him no creature is hidden, but all are open and laid bare to the eyes of him with whom we have to do" (Heb 4:12-13).[3]

This text itself puts us in question. It asks whether we are willing to lie "naked and exposed" (*NEB*) before God or whether like Adam and Eve in the Garden we hide ourselves from the presence of God. It asks us how we read the Bible. But we can easily deflect this awkward question by immediately posing our own question of what the Bible says and making the text answer our questions about God and man. What are the attributes

---

[2]Quoted from the December 1978 issue of *Sojourners*, p. 22 (italics his).
[3]Unless otherwise indicated, all Biblical quotations are from the *RSV*.

of God? What is the nature of man? Our text then becomes a proof text for the claims that God is omniscient and man trichotomous.

Let us avoid misunderstanding here by carefully distinguishing two similar-sounding but very different theses. Thesis I: It does not matter what you believe as long as the how is right—e.g., as long as one believes sincerely, passionately, and so on. Thesis II: The value of getting the what of Scripture right can be effectively neutralized if the how is "properly" distorted[4]—e.g., if the question of our openness to God's living word can be obscured in debates about the nature of God and man. It is the second thesis that I am setting forth and the danger to which it points that concerns me in this essay. For while other theologies may be endangered by tendencies toward heresy, the danger to evangelical theology and preaching is that of being dead right.

How shall we defend ourselves against this danger? Surely not by becoming more orthodox or by becoming louder about our orthodoxy. For this time the problem is not that of sorting out the right answers from the wrong ones but rather of seeing to it that we do not use the right answers to protect ourselves from the hard questions. We can defend ourselves against the danger of dead orthodoxy only by deliberately choosing to be vulnerable to God's living, questioning word. Gabriel Marcel has put the point forcefully in saying that genuine encounter with either persons or truths requires a willingness to be exposed to them.[5] Otherwise we are only adjacent to or in the vicinity of but not really available to God or present to his word.

But the question returns as to how to do this. How do we step out from behind the bushes to stand "naked and exposed" before him with whom we have to do? Perhaps it is a matter of attention, of not allowing our attention to be directed away from the whole of God's word to those parts that we find most attractive. We must abandon any à-la-carte notion of God's word that suggests that we can select what we like and leave for someone else the portions not to our taste. We must rediscover the unity of God's word (singular) in the plurality of his words. Most particularly, we must rediscover that his no belongs to his word as much as his yes, his anger as much as his love—or, rather, to correct the last expression, we must learn again that at least for his people, God's anger is as essential to his love as his gracious smile of approval.

When the writer to the Hebrews reminds us that "the Lord disciplines him whom he loves and chastises every son whom he receives" (Heb 12:6)

---

[4]"Properly" is in quotation marks to indicate a certain perspective—e.g., that of Screwtape and Wormwood in C. S. Lewis' *The Screwtape Letters*. Given their purposes, such a distortion would be proper.

[5]G. Marcel, *Creative Fidelity* (trans. R. Rosthal; New York, 1964) 12. Cf. also pp. 87-89.

he not only quotes from the OT but gives expression to the central notion of covenant. God's covenantal love is not intended to produce spoiled children. It is rather grounded in his righteousness, and as such it includes both a yes and a no, both promises of blessing to those who are faithful and promises of punishment to those who disobey. God's people have perhaps never been free from the Marcionite[6] temptation to save God from his anger, though all such efforts are but thinly disguised attempts to save ourselves from having to deal with that side of God's love. They are, in essence, the rejection of God's fatherly, covenantal love.

The unity of yes and no in God's word is found in the theme of creation as well as that of covenant. The most wonderfully reassuring affirmations of nature and history ring out loud and clear in the matter-of-fact narratives of Genesis and the lyrical theology of creation that permeates the latter chapters of Isaiah. But for a fully Biblical view there is a darker side that comes to expression in the three creation hymns of Amos (4:13; 5:5-9; 9:5-6). They celebrate the sovereignty of God over nature as in a psalm of praise. At first glance they seem to appear abruptly and to fit badly into Amos' tirades against social injustice and idolatry in Israel. A closer look, however, reveals how integral they are to his message. Each one is immediately preceded by a direct warning of impending judgment. They are all prefaced in effect by the words that actually introduce the first one: "Prepare to meet your God, O Israel!" And just who is the God whose anger is about to break forth in punishment? He is God the Father, Almighty, Maker of heaven and earth. The angry words that Amos conveys come from him who spoke the whole world into existence. They are awesome words, for the power to create is also the power to destroy. Israel's very existence is endangered. Like the message of the covenant, the truth of creation is not invariably good news. It puts us in question. Are we living in grateful trust in God's creative goodness, or have we through prideful disobedience put ourselves in danger of experiencing that power as wrath?

It may be argued that this kind of talk has been rendered obsolete by the Pauline doctrine of justification by faith, that the gift of grace through Christ frees us from all anxiety about the divine wrath. Once again we must be careful lest the truth itself become the instrument of self-deception. With Luther and Calvin I understand the Pauline message to mean that the individual believer can be confident that in the age to come God's judgment will be gracious because of the sacrifice of Christ for our sins. But that is quite different from the essentially Marcionite heresy that the God of the

---

[6]The passages already quoted from Hebrews 4 and 12, taken together, are but one indication that God's love under the new covenant is a "severe mercy." Another indication is in Jesus' call to "repent and believe" the good news, a juxtaposition of divine judgment and grace developed in detail in the opening chapters of Romans.

new covenant is no longer one who gets angry. As with earthly fathers, ultimate favor is not incompatible with penultimate, disciplinary wrath, and we have already seen the NT reaffirm the latter reality. Nor is there anything in the Pauline message of grace that suggests that God does not continue to judge the nations in history here and now.

Let us summarize. We are trying to preserve genuine encounter with God through his living word by choosing to expose ourselves to him and his truth. We are trying to allow his word to question us rather than simply using it to refute our opponents. To this end we are trying to keep in focus not only the yes, the good news, the gracious favor he speaks to us in his word, but also the no, the bad news, and the righteous wrath. By giving special attention to the dark side of revelation we are trying to let God's word be free and truly itself rather than making it, through selection, a projection of our own personal or corporate preferences. What is involved is not masochism but simple honesty, a willingness to let God be God and ourselves his creaturely children.

Turning to the prophets at this point is doubly appropriate. What I have called the dark side of revelation is by no means to be found only there, as I have already argued. But it is especially prominent there, and in a manner especially pertinent to our own situation.[7] The second appropriateness is more personal. The prophets first came alive for me while reading them in conjunction with a big book with an orange and blue dust jacket. So it is especially fitting for me to share some reflections on the prophets in a *Festschrift* for the author of *The Old Testament Speaks.*

The prophets are particularly sensitive to the dark side of revelation. Knowing that God himself is a "devouring fire" (Deut 4:24), Isaiah finds that "his lips are charged with wrath and his tongue is a devouring fire" (30:27 *NEB*). For Jeremiah, too, God's word is "like fire, says the LORD, and like a hammer that breaks the rock in pieces" (23:29). For Amos the voice of God is like the terrifying roar of a lion (1:2; 3:8). And Hosea, as if fearing that the metaphors will be misconstrued, resorts to blunt prose: "Hear the word of the LORD, O people of Israel; for the LORD has a controversy with the inhabitants of the land" (4:1).

It is therefore not surprising that the prophets find their message unwelcome. Isaiah finds God's people to be "a rebellious people, lying sons, sons who will not hear the instruction of the LORD; who say to the seers, 'See not'; and to the prophets, 'Prophesy not to us what is right; speak to us smooth things, prophesy illusions, leave the way, turn aside from the path, let us hear no more of the Holy One of Israel'" (30:9-11).[8] Amos charges his audience with having commanded the prophets, "You shall not prophesy."

---

[7] The prophets I shall be especially treating are Amos, Hosea, Isaiah and Jeremiah.

[8] Cf. Isa 28:9-10 in the *Good News Bible.*

They conclude that "the land is not able to bear all his words" either, and in the person of Amaziah the priest they invite him most definitely to take his preaching elsewhere (2:12; 7:10-17). Micah likewise finds his message greeted by a response that is anything but subtle: "Do not preach. . . . One should not preach of such things; disgrace will not overtake us" (2:6).

Perhaps the most dramatic case is Jeremiah's. At the outset God warns him that the whole land—kings, princes, priests and people alike—"will fight against you" (1:18-19). Soon Jeremiah is complaining, "To whom shall I speak and give warning, that they may hear? Behold, their ears are closed, they cannot listen; behold, the word of the LORD is to them an object of scorn, they take no pleasure in it" (6:10). We would find it comforting if this complaint were directed to the theological liberals of Jeremiah's day, who were insufficiently serious about the authority of the Torah. But Jeremiah picks out for special attention just that group in ancient Israel most conspicuous for their high view of Scripture, the scribes: "How can you say, 'We are wise, and the law of the LORD is with us'? But, behold, the false pen of the scribes has made it into a lie. The wise men shall be put to shame. . . . Lo, they have rejected the word of the LORD, and what wisdom is in them?" (8:8-9).

On at least two separate occasions Jeremiah's stubborn insistence earned him death threats if he did not quit or change his message (11:21; 26:7-11). As with Amos and Micah his hearers found it necessary to be blunt: "As for the word which you have spoken to us in the name of the LORD, we will not listen to you" (44:16). It is against this background that Jeremiah utters his desperate appeal: "O land, land, land, hear the word of the LORD!" (22:29).

Israel's rejection of God's word was not grounded in an enlightenment rationalism that wished to replace revelation with reason. They were quite prepared to have God reveal himself to them—so long as they could themselves remain in hiding. But the same word that reveals God to us lays bare the thoughts and intentions of our own hearts, and it is impossible that revelation should be a one-way street.[9] God's word is indivisible, and Israel's refusal to be "naked and exposed" before him with whom we have to do was viewed by God and his prophets as a simple rejection of revelation, even on the part of those whose high view of the Torah gave them a special sense of security. This is why it is so important for us today to hear the prophets' message with fear and trembling, asking whether Jeremiah's poignant plea to hear the word of the Lord is addressed to us as well.

That word exposes us. If we will let it, it asks us questions that put us in question. Given the traditional arrangement of our Bibles, the first chapter

---

[9]In the debate whether we should say that in revelation God reveals himself or truths about himself, both sides may lose sight of the fact that revelation reveals us to ourselves and to God.

of Isaiah is our first encounter with the prophetic message. It may well be the record of a single sermon he preached—uninvited, no doubt. In any case it provides us with a penetrating introduction to what Hosea calls the Lord's "controversy with the inhabitants of the land." It builds to its climax with a message about ingratitude, imperviousness, impiety and injustice.

I. THE QUESTION OF INGRATITUDE (ISA 1:2-4)

The prophets already know the Pauline claim in Romans 1 and 2 that sufficient knowledge of God and his law is available apart from special revelation so that mankind is responsible to worship and obey him. They are therefore not hesitant to announce his judgment on the surrounding nations who are not part of the covenant. But the major part of their concern is with God's own people, and that is where Isaiah begins his report of God's message. "Sons have I reared and brought up, but they have rebelled against me. The ox knows its owner and the ass its master's crib; but Israel does not know, my people does not understand" (vv 2-3). The rebellion of those who have known God's covenant love, who have known him as Father and whom he can call "my people," has an element of ingratitude about it that makes it especially serious.

The image of betrayed love is especially vivid when the prophets portray God's people as a faithless, adulterous wife (Hos 1:2 ff.; Jer 2:32 ff.; 2:6 ff.). A somewhat different but equally forceful picture of ingratitude is involved in the reminder that it is those who were delivered from Egypt in the exodus whose behavior now evokes God's wrath (Hos 12:13-14; Amos 2:10 ff.; Jer 2:6 ff.). It is Amos who gives this motif its most familiar form: "Hear this word [again the plea to hear] that the LORD has spoken against you, O people of Israel, against the whole family which I brought up out of the land of Egypt: 'You only have I known of all the families of the earth; therefore I will punish you for all your iniquities'" (3:1-2).

The prophets did not challenge their audiences' belief that they were God's own people. They simply insisted that, far from providing an unconditional security within history, their privilege gave them a special responsibility, made their sin especially grievous, and left them especially vulnerable to God's disciplinary wrath. The hermeneutical journey from what the text originally meant to what it says to us today is often long and treacherous. Theologians do well to mark its pitfalls carefully. But sometimes the theoretical task is all too easy and only the practical task is hard. This seems to me such a situation. The meaning for us of the ingratitude theme in the prophets is not really hard to figure out, though it is hard to take seriously. It can be expressed in the first of our questions from the prophets.

Question 1: Are we American Christians—who by virtue of our evangelical orthodoxy and piety have a strong sense of being God's

people—resting in a false security, unaware of the ways in which we have
failed truly to hear God's word?

II. THE QUESTION OF IMPERVIOUSNESS (ISA 1:5-9)

Immediately after identifying God's own people as the primary audience of his warnings, Isaiah calls their attention to the fact that God's
judgment has already begun. Their sin has not gone wholly unpunished.
With images of a body already ravaged by disease, of a countryside already
in shambles, and of Zion besieged and defenseless like a toolshed in the field,
he suggests that their own immediate past history has been the kind of
warning that should have shaken them out of their complacency. The fact
that they have not yet awakened and changed their ways reflects a kind of
stubborn, thick-headed imperviousness that bodes ill for their future, since it
may force God to more drastic measures to get their attention.[10] He will do
what he has to to get through to them, for he is not the kind of father or
husband who will be unfaithful to his own love or to the responsibilities
grounded in it.

Isaiah himself returns to this theme (9:13), and Amos builds up to his
"Prepare to meet your God, O Israel" and the first creation hymn that this
warning introduces by citing a long list of such preliminary punishments: "I
gave you cleanness of teeth . . . and lack of bread. . . . I also withheld the
rain. . . . I smote you with blight and mildew. . . . I sent among you a
pestilence. . . . I slew your young men. . . . I carried away your horses. . . . I
overthrew some of you, as when God overthrew Sodom and Gomorrah . . .
yet you did not return to me, says the LORD" (4:6-11). Jeremiah, who seems
to have known the eighth-century prophets intimately, plagiarizes them
shamelessly on this point (2:30; 5:3; 7:28; and perhaps 6:8—see *Good News
Bible*).

There is an hermeneutical hurdle here, but it is a low one. Whereas in
ancient Israel judgment of the nation and judgment of God's people are
identical, we cannot make that assumption for ourselves. Neither the
United States nor the larger North Atlantic community of which it is a part
can legitimately claim a unique covenantal relation with God (though we
sometimes forget this). God does not say to the American or North
Atlantic communities, "You only have I known." Still, the prophetic
critique of Israel's imperviousness speaks very directly to today's covenant
children of God. For as individual Christians and as the corporate Church
we belong, all too fully, to the national and transnational communities
whom God judges in history. The "misfortunes" these communities have

---

[10]For an illuminating analysis of imperviousness see Marcel's discussion of
permeability in *Fidelity*, pp. 87 and 172.

suffered in recent years are open to interpretation as warning signals from God that he is not pleased with our use of power and privilege. If the people of God do not have the courage to perceive God at work in the signs of the times, we are hardly in a position to complain about the secularism of our age and its *Weltanschauung*. When push comes to shove, is ours any different?

What, then, might Amos' "prepare-to-meet-your-God" sermon look like if he preached it to American or North Atlantic Christians today? He might begin by talking about Vietnam and Watergate, about the loss of confidence in our government and its growing impotence in the face of economic and diplomatic crises and even in relation to the basic task of crime control. He would surely talk about runaway inflation, which is causing real hardship to the poor and agonies of anxiety to the rich, including the middle class.[11] He would surely talk about the energy crisis and the threat it poses to our economic, military and diplomatic securities. Then he might ask whether we are open enough to God's word to let the categories of Biblical faith shape our response to these issues. He might do so with questions like these:

Question 2: Has it ever occurred to us that God is trying to speak to us through the traumas of our recent history?

Question 3: If so, are we seriously willing to entertain the possibility that he is speaking to us (Christians) about our sins and not about "theirs," where "they" may be almost anyone but ourselves?

Question 4: Or have we precluded these possibilities from the start by uncritically adopting the view universally put forth by the media and the politicians that it is basically a management question, that the important thing is to find the right persons with the right strategies and the right proportion of charismatic leadership at home and toughness abroad?[12]

Question 5: If the answer to question 4 is yes, can we seriously say that in faithfulness to God's word we have challenged the secular thought patterns of our time by insisting that human experience be interpreted with the categories of Biblical faith?

Question 6: Or have we precluded the possibilities suggested by questions 2 and 3 from the start by uncritically adopting the view that there are simply too few of "us" and that what is most needed is more evangelism and Church growth so that there will be more people like ourselves?

[11]See "The Myth of the Middle Class," chap. 4 of *No More Plastic Jesus* by A. D. Finnerty (New York, 1977).

[12]In *Christianity and Classical Culture* (New York, 1957) C. Cochrane finds the supremacy of the categories of fortune and misfortune to be a key mark distinguishing Roman antiquity from early Christianity. The modern management approach to history is probably just the old pagan view, trimmed of its metaphysical packaging.

III. The Question of Impiety (Isa 1:10-15)

Implicit in the last question is the disturbing possibility that the religiousness of the religious may be part of the problem rather than the solution. This brings us back to Isaiah, for it is just this possibility that he takes up next. In the most undiplomatic language he portrays God as thoroughly fed up with the piety of his people. Of their sacrifices, the heart of Hebrew worship, he says, "I have had enough. . . . I do not delight in [them]." Their offerings are "vain" and their incense an "abomination." Their coming to the temple is "this trampling of my courts." Their weekly, monthly and yearly worship services "I cannot endure. . . . My soul hates [them]; they have become a burden to me, I am weary of bearing them." Of their prayers he says, "I will hide my eyes from you. . . . I will not listen" (a direct response to the people's unwillingness to listen to him). It is quite clear that the problem is not that Israel's "elaborate and well-supplied cultus fostered the notion . . . that Yahweh's demands could be met by ritual and sacrifice alone," but rather that he found "the lavish cultus by which she had hoped to satisfy Yahweh's demands to be unacceptable and offensive to him."[13] There is a considerable difference between saying that the worship of God's people is not all he wants from them and saying that their worship has become offensive to him.

It is the latter point that Isaiah seems quite clearly to be making, to which he returns (29:13; 58:1-12; 59:2-15) and which the other prophets repeat with monotonous regularity.[14] The charge is that the piety of God's people is itself an impiety. This motif in prophetic preaching is not to be confused with a related but distinct complaint: that God's people have gone whoring after Baal and other false gods. The prophets regularly denounce overt idolatry. But in the passage before us and in many like it, it is the "proper" worship of Yahweh that is their target. The religious activities Isaiah mentions are not those of pagan fertility cults but precisely those prescribed in the Torah. A close comparison of Isaiah's sermon with Numbers 28 will suggest that he may well have had just this part of the Law in mind, and his complaint is not that the people have forgotten its precepts nor distorted it with heretical names and attributes of God and immoral practices. It is rather that he has "found a religion which was very religious, which adored what was traditional but which had shaken free from divine revelation."[15]

[13]These two formulations are from J. Bright's discussion of Isaiah 1 in *A History of Israel* (Philadelphia, 1959) 261, 274. The first seems to me to miss the point, the second to capture it precisely.

[14]See Amos 2, 4, 5; Hosea 2, 5, 6, 7, 8; Jeremiah 5, 7, 11, 14 for examples.

[15]J. A. Motyer, *The Day of the Lion: The Message of Amos* (Leicester, 1974) 15. Motyer is speaking of the message of Amos, but his description really fits all the passages mentioned in the previous note.

The idea that their sacrifices, offerings, festivals, fasting and prayers were abhorrent to God must have been a shocking message to ancient Israel, but perhaps the most shocking of all was Jeremiah's temple speech. "Has this house, which is called by my name, become a den of robbers in your eyes? Behold, I myself have seen it, says the LORD" (7:11). For me the most dreadful of these passages is one from Amos. After announcing that he hates and despises their feasts and solemn assemblies and will not accept or look upon their offerings, God continues: "Take away from me the noise of your songs; to the melody of your harps I will not listen" (5:23). Given the importance and the quality of the music in the church I attend, this is a passage that again puts questions very directly to the present without hermeneutical hurdles—questions like these:

Question 7: Does the orthodoxy and elaborateness of our worship provide any assurance that it is not offensive to God?

Question 8: What was it that made Israelite worship, even when not overtly idolatrous, a target of God's wrath, and do those characteristics also apply to our own?

IV. THE QUESTION OF INJUSTICE (ISA 1:15-23)

Question 8 by now seems long overdue. It was not as a general exercise in religious humility that the prophets invited their audiences to entertain the possibility that as the very people of God they were especially vulnerable to God's wrath, that the misfortunes of their recent history were warnings and punishments from God, and that their worship was positively displeasing to him. Had that been the case they could properly be charged with morbid masochism. But the questions of ingratitude, imperviousness and impiety belong to a fourth question that gives them their cash value.

Isaiah's sermon proceeds to this issue by the startling conclusion he gives to his diatribe against the people's religious life. "Even though you make many prayers, I will not listen; your hands are full of blood. Wash yourselves; make yourselves clean; remove the evil of your doings from before my eyes; cease to do evil, learn to do good; seek justice, correct oppression; defend the fatherless, plead for the widow." The issue is economic and political. For reasons that are obvious as soon as one thinks about the nature of Israel's society, reference to widows and orphans comes to be an OT cliché for talking about the poor and the powerless. Oppression and injustice are here defined contextually as the failure to protect the poor and the powerless from those who would take advantage of them.

It is just this failure that underlies the disturbing questions with which Isaiah's sermon begins and that leads him immediately to a very familiar text. "Come now, let us reason together, says the LORD: Though your sins are like scarlet, they shall be as white as snow; though they are red like crimson, they shall become like wool." I wish I had a nickel for every time I have heard this verse without any reference to the specific sin Isaiah was talking about, the sin of economic injustice. If the churches I have worshiped in all my life had been reminded of the poor and powerless everytime they heard this verse, they could scarcely have remained the kind of churches they are.

Once again Isaiah's sermon turns out to be typical. Materialism, greed, complacent affluence, and the oppression of the poor are continuously recurring themes in the prophetic indictment of God's people. This is especially prominent in the hard sayings of the prophets about Israel's worship. Just as Isaiah 1 moves directly from the question of impiety to the question of injustice, so Isaiah 58 links God's rejection of the people's fasting to their neglect and oppression of the poor and hungry. Similarly Amos concludes the passage just cited about God's hating and despising their feasts, not with that reference to their music that I find so painful but with an indication of why their worship is so offensive to him. "Take away from me the noise of your songs; to the melody of your harps I will not listen. But let justice roll down like waters and righteousness like an everflowing stream."[16] And why does Jeremiah's God see his own temple as a den of robbers? The temple speech is explicit: "If you do not oppress the alien, the fatherless or the widow, or shed innocent blood in this place, and if you do not go after other gods to your own hurt . . ." (7:6).

Here overt idolatry, the other major theme of the prophetic indictment, is linked to the economic issue. I have not emphasized it, both because it is barely alluded to in Isaiah 1 and because it is all too easy, by focusing on the question of idolatry, to assume that if we worship the right God by the right name (in Jesus' name) and with the right theology the prophets must be talking to some other audience.

But the questions of idolatry and what I have been calling "the economic issue" are not simply parallel but separate issues. Our own NT should make this clear to us. For Jesus teaches that mammon is a rival of God for our worship (Matt 6:24), and Paul teaches that covetousness is idolatry (Eph 5:5; Col 3:5). The prophets too are aware that there is a link between wrong attitudes toward wealth and the worship of the wrong God. This is perhaps nowhere clearer than in Hosea. He uses the image of harlotry to denounce the Baal worship of God's people. Israel is portrayed as an unfaithful wife who has said, "I will go after my lovers, who give me my bread and my water, my wool and my flax, my oil and my drink" (2:5). God bitterly complains, "And she did not know that it was I who gave her the grain, the wine, and the oil, and who lavished upon her silver and gold which they used for Baal" (2:8). An ungrateful belief about the source of

---

[16]Cf. Amos 2:6-8; 4:1-5. It is clear in context that justice is primarily an economic issue for Amos.

their affluence underlay Israel's attraction for Baal.[17] They would rather see it as resting on the quasi-magical fertility rites associated with his worship than as a gift from Yahweh. For through these rites they felt they had a power over their economic destiny that made dependence, trust and gratitude unnecessary and proud self-sufficiency possible. Like the cheating spouse who wants sexual excitement free from the covenantal responsibilities of marriage, Israel wanted the good life unencumbered by covenantal fidelity to the God who gave them a land flowing with milk and honey.

The prophetic treatment of the "economic issue" is massive and complex. It would take at least a full monograph to do justice to it. Beyond the link between economic oppression and the rejection of Israel's worship of Yahweh and the link between a proud materialism and the worship of Baal, there is only one further aspect I want to make mention of in this context. The prophets regularly complain about the people's indifference to and oppression of the poor. As prosecuting attorneys they also regularly point to the homes the former live in as incriminating evidence about their relationship to the latter.[18] It seems that the prophets saw in the luxurious homes of Israel and the affluent life-styles that accompanied them the most vivid expression of their owners' failure to love the Lord their God with all their hearts and their neighbor as themselves. They see these homes and life-styles as made possible by the oppression of the poor. It is frequently in commenting on these that they talk about the unfair wages, prices, taxes and moneylending practices by which the rich take advantage of the poor and about the unjust laws and corrupt courts that deprive the poor of redress and even serve to legitimate unjust practices.[19]

If, as is often said, indifference is as much the opposite of love as hate is, then we might expect the prophets to protest not only the affluence that depends on active injustice for its support but also the simple conjunction of "the good life" with indifference toward the sufferings of the poor. And indeed Amos complains most bitterly about those who are at ease in Zion, who live in luxury "but are not grieved over the ruin of Joseph" (6:1-8). He sees injustice both in the sources of Israel's wealth (3:10-15; 5:10-15) and in the failure to use that wealth, which they no doubt thought a sign of God's favor and the result of their hard work, to assist the poor and needy. In both these ways they failed to love their neighbor as God had taught them to do.

But the homes of Israel also represented a failure to love the Lord their God. Isaiah concludes one of his diatribes against the people's homes

[17]In his discussion of this passage, Martin Buber calls this "the baalisation of YHWH Himself" in *The Prophetic Faith* (New York, 1960) 118-120.

[18]Cf. Isa 3:14-26; 5:8-12; Jer 22:13-19; Hos 8:14; Amos 3:10-15; 5:10-15; 6:1-8.

[19]Ps 94:20 is pertinent here. In the *Good News Bible* it reads: "You have nothing to do with corrupt judges, who make injustice legal."

and life-styles with the observation that "they do not regard the deeds of the LORD, or see the work of his hands" (5:8-12). Hosea makes the point even more succinctly: "For Israel has fogotten his Maker and built palaces" (8:14). This is but another way of seeing materialism as idolatry, an idolatry grounded not so much in defiant disobedience as in forgetful mindlessness. God and "the good life" compete for our ultimate allegiance, and God is a jealous God.

If we are willing to let them, Isaiah's sermon and its echo throughout the prophetic writings put questions like these to us today:

Question 9: If our worship were to be judged by God in the light of our economic behavior, what would the verdict be?

Question 10: Do false beliefs about the source of our prosperity, the desire to preside over our economic life by ourselves, and either the deliberate or forgetful exclusion of God from our economic attitudes and behavior constitute an idolatry that coexists with our intended worship of the true God?

Question 11: Does the affluence exhibited by our homes and life-styles rest on unjust economic practices and institutions, including those that may have been legitimated in the eyes of man by legislative and judicial sanction?

Question 12: When was the last time that reflection on Christ's command (summarizing the old covenant as well) to love God and neighbor led us to a serious examination of our relation to the poor and the powerless of our day, the majority of whom live in the Third World?

Though questions like these are being more and more seriously discussed throughout the Church, many Christians still find them all but incomprehensible. The difference does not seem to be that some are saintly and some stubborn. It seems rather to stem from the fact that some have been made aware of features of the world we live in of which others remain unaware, partly because our society does its best to keep them out of sight. What I am referring to is the essentially neocolonial structure of the world economy. The literature about this is enormous and rapidly growing. Those willing to risk taking a hard look at some disturbing realities might begin with *Rich Christians in an Age of Hunger* by R. Sider or *Bread for the World* by A. Simon. Both are written from a solidly Biblical framework. *Food First* by Lappé and Collins, *Persistent Poverty* by G. Beckford, and *Global Reach* by Barnet and Müller have no explicit theological framework, but they extend the critical analysis of the modern world beyond what Sider and Simon attempt. These are only samples. The point is simply that there is far more information available than even the most willing reader can absorb, and it is access to such information that gives meaning to the last set of questions from the prophets.

V. WRATH AND REDEMPTION (ISA 1:24-31)

Little needs to be said about the conclusion of Isaiah's sermon. It typically threatens judgment if the people do not repent and change their ways. Just as typically it insists that God is not out for vengeance but is guided by a father's love. The ultimate purpose of his anger and, if necessary, his punishment is to redeem his people and restore them to righteousness. Some of the most lyrical accounts of God's salvation to be found anywhere in the Bible are to be found in the very prophets we have been discussing. These, too, belong to God's word. His yes accompanies his no. But now as then they are only addressed to those who are willing first to be put in question by questions from the prophets.

Right Questions About Isaiah 7:14

J. Barton Payne

WHEN the OT portion of the *RSV* was published in 1952, conservative opposition immediately appeared because of its rendering of Isa 7:14. The wording, "Behold, a young woman shall conceive and bear a son," was clearly unacceptable. But what was not so clear, and still is not clear, is what does constitute an acceptable evangelical understanding of this difficult verse. Ross Price has described conservative Christian thought as oscillating "between two poles"—namely, of fulfillment in the birth of Jesus and in Isaiah's own time.[1] The present writer would, however, suggest that clarification may be aided if we can gain perspective, if we can distinguish the relevant concerns from those that are irrelevant or, at least, less relevant. The goal, one might say, is to ask the right questions. And the following study seeks to distinguish three areas: the primary question, some wrong questions, and the significant question. Perhaps the light that they generate may enable Bible-believing interpreters to thread their way more successfully through this confessedly involved passage.

I. The Primary Question

Basic to all the evangelical discussion of Isa 7:14 is the question, "Does the verse predict Jesus Christ?" Liberalism tends to say no: "The words are not messianic in the proper sense of the word."[2] The following subquestions, however, suggest and seemingly require the answer to be yes.

1. Since the NT states that some the prophecies in Isaiah 9-11 are definite predictions of Jesus (cf. Rom 15:12 on Isa 11:1, 10), we should first ask: "Is 7:14 integral with 9:6-7 and 11:1?" The fact that the newborn son who is called Immanuel in 7:14 seems to have the Palestinian area named after him,[3] as "lord of the whole land of Israel"[4] (8:8), does correspond to the proclamation that the child called *ʾēl gibbôr*, "Mighty God," in 9:6 has no end to the increase of his government on the throne of David (9:7). A

---

[1] R. Price in *Beacon Bible Commentary* (Kansas City, MO: Beacon Hill, 1966), 4. 57.

[2] H. Ringgren, *The Messiah in the Old Testament* (SBT 18; London: SCM, 1956) 35.

[3] E. J. Young, *Isaiah* (Grand Rapids: Eerdmans), 1. 307 n.

[4] H. C. Leupold, *Exposition of Isaiah* (Grand Rapids: Baker, 1968), 1. 170.

contemporaneous reference in Micah reinforces this divine Immanuel-ruler concept as it speaks of a woman giving birth in Bethlehem to One whose goings forth are from eternity, who is to be ruler in Israel (5:2-3). Gleason Archer, indeed, entitles Isaiah 7-12 in its entirety as "The Volume of Immanuel."[5]

2. From the NT viewpoint: "Must 7:14 predict a virgin birth if its use in Matt 1:23 is to remain valid?" Even writers who suggest something other than the virgin Mary in 7:14—e.g. Kenneth Taylor in the notes to his popular *Living Bible*—insist on keeping the translation "virgin," because "otherwise the Matthew account loses its significance."[6] Furthermore, the validity of Matthew involves deciding whether the prediction was meant for the prophet's own day for, as a critic such as Dewey Beegle is quick to point out, "to admit the possibility of an immediate application and still to insist on 'virgin' would put one in the awkward position of holding to a virgin birth in the time of Ahaz"[7]—which, of course, no one does. So when evangelicals sometimes find this verse descriptive of an eighth-century B.C. woman, who "was not a virgin at childbirth,"[8] they are necessarily forced to conclude that Matthew's use "differed considerably from the primary message."[9] This then brings us back to the question of the evangelist's validity, the relevance of which is not to be sidestepped.[10] If Isaiah did not mean Mary, and if there is no other known virgin mother, then Matthew

[5]G. L. Archer in *The Biblical Expositor* (C. F. H. Henry, ed.; Philadelphia: Holman, 1960), 2. 123.

[6]*Living Bible* (Wheaton: Tyndale House, 1971) 538. C. D. Isbell has indeed argued that Matthew's citation of Isaiah is "to portray the birth of Jesus as evidence of divine saving presence in the world . . . because of the word *Emmanouēl* . . . not because of *parthenos*," *The Biblical Archaeology Review* 3 (1977) 19. Yet Matthew's "all this" (1:22), which the Isaianic quote is meant to confirm, can hardly exclude the ideas of 1:18, 20 (Mary's lack of sexual relations with Joseph, and the child's mode of conception and birth), particularly when these ideas reappear in 1:23's Isaianic quotation and correspond to *parthenos* as "virgin" (cf. 1:25, "he did not know her").

[7]D. Beegle, "Virgin or Young Woman?", *Asbury Seminarian* 8 (1954) 34. Isbell thus contends that Matthew cannot have cited Isaiah in support of a NT virgin birth because this would mean that the prophet was "describing an eighth century B.C. virgin birth," *The Biblical Archaeology Review* 3 (1977) 19. His real problem is clearly his presupposition that Isaiah's prophecy had to be meant for its own day.

[8]H. Wolf, "A Solution to the Immanuel Prophecy in Isaiah," *JBL* 91 (1972) 455.

[9]Ibid., p. 456. As he adds, it "went beyond the normal interpretation."

[10]To argue that "the virginity of Mary in Matthew does not depend upon Isa 7:14" (but rather on the facts adduced in the preceding context, Matt 1:18, 20), ibid., p. 455, does not obviate the question of the validity of the evangelist's citation of Isaiah.

erred, for it simply is not right to use a verse that is not about a virgin birth
to substantiate a virgin birth.

II. Some Wrong Questions

Today's discussion of Isa 7:14 may "get off on the wrong foot" if
interpreters ask wrong questions—wrong, that is, in the sense of diverting
attention from what can be seen as the more crucial issues (see section III
below), whether they obscure these issues or are simply extraneous to them.
The following have been selected as representative questions of the diver-
sionary sort.

1. While Matthew's total argument does seem to demand an Isaianic
prophecy of the virgin birth (see above), some may go further and ask,
"Does Matt 1:23's formula of citation require Isa 7:14 to foretell Jesus?"
But here the answer appears to be no. For even though the evangelist's
introductory phrase, *hina plērōthē*, is often rendered "that it might be
fulfilled," and though it may, at certain points, signify the intended
fulfillment of an OT prediction (e.g. Matt 21:4 in fulfilling Zech 9:9), at
other points it may not (cf. Matt 2:15 or 2:17, which merely provide new
applications for the thoughts and phraseology of Hos 1:11 and Jer 31:15).
Jas 2:23, for instance, says that by Abraham's willingness to offer up his
son Isaac "the Scripture was fulfilled which says, 'And Abraham believed
God, and it was reckoned to him as righteousness.'" But these words that
the NT quotes from Gen 15:6 were not originally predictive at all. Abraham's
actions in Genesis 22 simply gave them further illustration. Even so, the
formula in Matt 1:22, "that it might be fulfilled," need not in itself imply
anything more than a verbal allusion and does not require Isa 7:14 to have
been directed toward Jesus.[11]

2. "Does Isa 7:14 have a double meaning, one for Isaiah's day and one
for Jesus' day?" The idea of "multiple sense" is a hermeneutical device to
which conservative interpreters have not infrequently appealed,[12] but liberal
critics are not the only ones who have unmasked it as a kind of "trying to
have your cake and eat it too."[13] Long ago J. A. Alexander cautioned:

> It seems to be a feeling common to learned and unlearned readers, that a
> double sense . . . is unreasonable to assume when any other explanation is
> admissible. The improbability in this case is increased by the want of
> similarity between the two events, supposed to be predicted by the very same
> words.[14]

[11] J. B. Payne, *Encyclopedia of Biblical Prophecy* (New York: Harper, 1973)
77-79, 477.
[12] *Living Bible*, 538; Wolf, "Solution," 449-456.
[13] Payne, *Encyclopedia*, 121-126.
[14] J. A. Alexander, *Commentary on the Prophecies of Isaiah* (Grand Rapids:
Zondervan, 1953), 1. 170.

Such a desperation approach should be recognized for what it is—unacceptable.

3. Another wrong question—though many may not have realized it—is this: "Does the word ᶜalmâ in 7:14 mean 'virgin'?" It does, no doubt about that. Note the *RSV* marginal reading, "Or virgin," which demonstrates its legitimacy. The *RSV* committee simply disfavored it as an option. Or note the *RSV* rendering of ᶜalmâ in Prov 30:19 as "maiden." But still the question is a misleading one because, as Robert Dick Wilson long ago pointed out, "the language itself is not the difficulty. . . . So far as is known, ᶜalma never meant 'young married woman'. . . . The great and only difficulty lies in disbelief in predictive prophecy . . . or in the desire to throw discredit on the divine Sonship of Jesus."[15] Now confessedly there is one other major difficulty that Wilson might perhaps have included (see section III below), but his linguistic contention remains sound: It is not the meaning of ᶜalmâ that lies at the heart of the issue.

4. "Does the definite article with ᶜalmâ demand a virgin well known at the time?" Not necessarily.[16] One of the peculiarities of the Hebrew language is its habit of saying "the (something)" while referring to an object that is as yet unknown to the hearers though present in the mind of the speaker.[17] Furthermore, Hebrew more frequently employs the article to designate classes of objects than do most other languages. Isaiah's reference to "the virgin" needs thus be nothing more than generic, to distinguish her from some other kind of woman—e.g. old woman, married woman, and so on.[18]

5. Today's evangelicals more frequently ask: "Is the ᶜalmâ in 7:14 the 'prophetess' of 8:3?"[19] This, however, still appears to be a wrong question, primarily because of the inherent unlikelihood of such an identification. The prophetess of chap. 8 is Isaiah's wife and the mother of his children—apparently both of Shear-Jashub in 7:3 and of Maher-Shalal-Hash-Baz in

[15]R. D. Wilson, "The Meaning of Alma (A.V. 'Virgin') in Isaiah VII.14," *PTR* 24 (1926) 316; cf. J. B. Payne, "Almah," *The Encyclopedia of Christianity* (Wilmington, DE: National Foundation for Christian Education, 1964), 1. 148-149.

[16]True, Ugaritic studies have demonstrated close parallels to Isa 7:14 (e.g., "A virgin [*btlt*] will give birth . . . ; behold, a maiden [*ǵlmt*] will bear a son," C. Gordon, *Ugaritic Literature* [Rome: Pontifical Biblical Institute, 1949] 75) that were current in the Canaanite milieu of ancient Israel. E. Jacob has specifically claimed: "Immanuel and the ᶜalmâ must have been realities known to the prophet's hearers; the people were waiting for the coming of a divine child of more or less wonderful origin; but in the prophet's mouth this myth becomes present in history" (*Theology of the Old Testament* [New York: Harper, 1958] 336).

[17]GKC 407.

[18]GKC 406; Young, *Isaiah*, 1. 287.

[19]E.g., Archer, *Expositor*, 2. 134.

8:3. The text suggests no other possibility. This proposal seems actually to have arisen from attempts on the part of some to connect the events of 8:3-4 with certain wordings that appear in 7:14-16. This leads us then to the following subordinate questions.

(1) Corresponding to the word "virgin" in 7:14, did not some woman (still in her virginity when the prophet spoke 7:14) marry Isaiah before 8:1 and so become "the [new] prophetess" of 8:3? Probably not, for nothing suggests that Isaiah's allegedly "earlier" wife suffered death or displacement.

(2) Corresponding to the clause that commences "For before the boy knows" in 7:16, is not Maher-Shalal-Hash-Baz (cf. his knowing how to make certain distinctions in 8:4) the same boy as Immanuel? But this similarity in phraseology[20] seems to have arisen out of a deliberate design on Isaiah's part to relate two different prophecies to each other—that is, the immediate verifiability of his prophecy about the Assyrian devastations, which was conveyed by the birth and naming of Maher-Shalal-Hash-Baz, "would thus become as it were a pledge or earnest of the prophecy of the virgin's son."[21] Far from being identical with Immanuel, Maher-Shalal-Hash-Baz differs from him not only in his name but also in its significance, in his parentage (see above), in what he is foreseen as knowing (how to cry out "My father") and in his status (cf. 8:8 on Immanuel's possession of the land).

6. There is a final inquiry that is often heard: "Was Isa 7:14 relevant to Ahaz?" But this question too is "wrong" because it is misleading. Of course the verse was relevant to him. But generally those who most vociferously insist that "the prophecy had to have meaning for the king in his situation"[22] are the ones who then go on to dismiss the messianic interpretation as "such an irrational view," and they do this because they uncritically identify relevance in meaning with immediacy of fulfillment. The proper methodology is rather to inquire, from the king's own context, just how 7:14 was relevant.

III. THE SIGNIFICANT QUESTION

The crucial issue that colors the entire current evangelical debate is the question: "Must Isa 7:14 have had an immediate accomplishment?" In the year 734 B.C. when Isaiah was inspired to address these words to Ahaz, Judah was confronted by a crisis: It was under attack by the allied forces of Ephraim and Damascus (Isa 7:1 [cf. vv 5, 6] = 2 Kgs 16:5)—a crisis that demanded the king's immediate action. It appears in fact that Ahaz had

[20]Young, *Isaiah*, 1. 304, the "formal relationship between the two prophecies."
[21]Ibid.
[22]Cf. Beegle, "Virgin," 28; cf. p. 31.

already resolved upon his course of action, which was one of appeal for help and of abject submission to Assyria (2 Kgs 16:7-8; contrast the prophet's demand for faith in God, Isa 7:9). In a year or two, moreover, the Assyrians did cripple Ephraim (in 733, 2 Kgs 15:29) and crush Damascus (in 732, 16:9). These events that delivered Ahaz from his foes do not, however, require a correspondingly immediate fulfillment to the prophecy of Isa 7:14, nor do they satisfy its broader context, nor do they determine its relevance in regard to the faithless king, as the following subordinate questions are designed to bring into focus.

1. Looking first at the party to whom the Immanuel prophecy is addressed we may ask: "What is 'the house of David' in 7:13?" In v 2 this phrase had identified Ahaz himself and even in v 11 he personally is still being addressed: "Ask for thyself" (*l*^e*kā*, singular). But then a shift occurs just after the king's hypocritical refusal in v 12 to accept a sign from God. Isaiah thus declares: "Listen now, O house of David! Is it too light a thing for you (*mikkem*, plural) to try men's patience . . . ?" (v 13). "Therefore Yahweh will give to you (*lākem*, plural) a sign" (v 14). So the right question to ask is "Why?" At the least, this contextual shift from the king himself to a plurality suggests that Scripture is involving the "members of his family and court";[23] at the most, it may indicate a divine dissatisfaction with the whole later Davidic dynasty, leading to its historical replacement in 586 B.C.

2. Another question of long-range dates that appears in the context of chap. 7 is this: "Does Ephraim's ceasing 'from being a people' (v 8) precede Immanuel (v 14)?" The sequence of verses would suggest so. But this then moves us a full 65 years (v 8) beyond 734 B.C., down to 669 (through the reign and the deportations of Esarhaddon, which are noted in Ezra 4:2). It seems clear that Isaiah's horizon is not limited to the next couple of years after the 734 crisis with Ephraim.

3. Turning now from those time intervals that precede Immanuel and looking at the nature of the Immanuel event itself as this bears on the immediacy of its fulfillment, one may next ask: "Are the 'signs' that are offered to Ahaz nonmiraculous, like the children mentioned in 8:18, or miraculous, like the shadow discussed in 38:7, 22 (or like Mary in Matt 1:18)?" The supernatural alternatives with which Isaiah accompanies his proposal to Ahaz—"Make it as deep as hell or as high as heaven" (Isa 7:11)—seem to favor the latter—i.e., a miracle.

A related though subordinate question that should perhaps be noted in passing is this: "Are the children of 8:18 Isaiah's or Messiah's?" The former is often, uncritically, assumed—some might even want to include Immanuel, with Shear-Jashub and Maher-Shalal-Hash-Baz, as such a "sign"-child of

[23] Alexander, *Commentary*, 1. 166.

the prophet himself (see above). Yet the latter—i.e., the messianic interpretation—is the teaching of Heb 2:13, and its validity is confirmed by a variety of evangelical scholars.[24]

4. A further question on the nature of the prophecy, and a crux for its understanding, is this: "Is 7:14 a threat (per 7:13) or a promise (as in 8:10)?" Answer: The closer context, of threat, must be preferred,[25] not only because 7:13's condemnation of Ahaz's faithlessness—which was "so direct a defiance of God"[26]—specifically introduces the Immanuel prophecy, and not only because chap. 7's whole latter portion threatens him by predicting how "Yahweh will bring on you . . . and your father's house such days as have never come since Ephraim separated from Judah—even the king of Assyria" (7:17) but also because of at least five subordinate questions that arise from the immediate context of vv 14-16.

(1) "Is the meaning of 'Immanuel' providential (God's help will be with us) or incarnational (God's Person will be with us)?" Matt 1:20-23 cites the prophecy because it is seen as teaching the latter, that Jesus in his Person was "conceived of the Holy Spirit."[27] Then too, Isaiah's violent condemnation of Ahaz disfavors the former interpretation. The king's disbelief, in other words, comports badly with any promise of alleged immediate providential consolation.

(2) "Are the curds and honey in 7:15 a sign of plenty or poverty?" The prophet's own explanation in vv 22-23 establishes the latter,[28] that Immanuel's birth will occur under impoverished circumstances. As Micah would soon elaborate, God "will give them up until the time when she who is in labor has borne her child" (5:3), even though this child is "to be ruler in Israel."

(3) "Is 7:16 an encouraging parenthesis between the threats of vv 15 and 17?" Many, including Rice, feel that it is, that Isaiah is here assuring Ahaz of a speedy removal of the foes that he so dreads (cf. 8:4). Yet

---

[24]Cf. ibid., pp. 192-193; Young, *Isaiah*, 1. 315-316. It might be objected that if either this sign or Immanuel refers to the Messiah, they would not be contemporaneous "wonders in Israel," as most OT "signs" are (Isa 20:3; 37:30). Yet a "sign" may be future, not simply as being predicted to occur at a distant time (19:20; 55:13) but also as relevant for the immediate audience; cf. Deut 28:46, where the curses that are to come upon Israel (v 45) constitute a sign not only at the time of their later fulfillment but also then: "a sign . . . on you and your descendants."

[25]Rice, "The Interpretation of Isaiah 7:15-17," *JBL* 96 (1977) 363-369; cf. Young, *Isaiah*, 1. 283: Immanuel as "a pledge of doom."

[26]J. Skinner, *The Book of the Prophet Isaiah* (Cambridge University, 1915), 1. 58.

[27]E. W. Hengstenberg, *Christology of the Old Testament* (Grand Rapids: Kregel, 1956), 2. 43: "The Lord will some day be with us in the truest manner."

[28]The "abundance of the milk" (v 22) is properly defined as irony by Rice, "Interpretation," 365.

because of the basic unlikelihood at this point of such a promise on the prophet's part, Rice feels compelled to deny the authenticity of v 16 as a whole. He dismisses it as a gloss by a later redactor who misunderstood Isaiah's intent.[29] But are we reduced to these straits? Not if the "removal" of which v 16 speaks includes a divine threat against the apostate Ahaz (cf. how the threat of 8:7 follows so hard upon even the promise of 8:4). This possibility of a threatened removal is connected then with two other sub-questions on two particular terms that appear in the passage:

(4) "Does the verb *qûṣ* in v 16 mean what it does in v 6—namely, 'to cut off, tear,[30] *Hiphil* [*KJV, RV*] vex'—rather than what its Hebrew hom-onym connotes in the earlier OT books, 'to abhor, feel a sickening dread'[31]?" If one chooses the latter meaning, then the "two kings" of v 16 become the objects of Ahaz's dread (*RV*—i.e., his Ephraimite and Damascene foes, Pekah and Rezin). If one prefers the former, the kings are then the objects of which "the land shall be forsaken" (*KJV*)—i.e., that land that Ahaz vexes (*Qal*, "troubles").[32] The identity, in turn, of the kings depends on one last subquestion:

(5) "What is the land in 7:16 that is to be forsaken?" Many would propose the combined territories of Ephraim and Damascus, but this is an unusual combination for a prophet to identify by a simple noun like "the land." More likely would be the one Palestinian territory, the home of both Ephraim and Judah, whom Isaiah combines in this immediate context (8:14) under the title "both the houses of Israel." Their abandonments occurred, respectively, under Hoshea in the land's north (722 B.C.) and Zedekiah in its south (586). The relevance of the latter as a threat to Ahaz is obvious, whether in actual history it was of immediate fulfillment or not. This brings us to two final questions that specifically point up the relevance of Isa 7:14 to Ahaz. These would appear to be the "right" sort of questions to ask, since both seek honestly to relate the king's crisis to the prophecy's nonimmediate (i.e., messianic) fulfillment, even though the first should probably be answered negatively and the second positively.

5. "Was Messiah's time-span in maturing (7:16) intended as an indica-tor to Ahaz of speedy (contemporary) deliverance?" The idea often pro-posed is that in a short time—i.e., in a period no longer than the maturing Messiah[33] would need before he could tell right from wrong—Ahaz would

[29] Ibid., pp. 368-369.
[30] KB 834: Arabic *qāḍa*.
[31] Ibid., p. 833: Syriac *qyṭ*.
[32] Payne, *Encyclopedia*, 285 n.
[33] Or any youth (*hannaᶜar*, 7:16), a proposal dating back to J. Calvin, *Com-mentary on the Book of the Prophet Isaiah* (Grand Rapids: Eerdmans, 1953), 1. 250.

be rescued. This kind of approach does provide contemporaneous relevance, but it suffers from at least three objections: (a) the unlikelihood of Isaiah's predicting such a king's deliverance (see above); (b) the opening up of evangelicalism to a charge made by liberalism, that if Immanuel's infancy measures the years immediately following 734 B.C. then to postpone his presence for over seven centuries requires "mental gymnastics involved in ignoring the clear sense of immediacy";[34] and (c) the undesirability of reading into the verb *leda͑tô* in v 15 some special syntax that differs from rendering it as other than a simple infinitive of purpose, "[in order] to know."[35] The normal meaning of v 15 would appear to be that the infant Messiah will have to eat the products of an impoverished land, namely "curds and honey," but he will eat them with the purpose (or result) that he may know right from wrong—i.e., that he may, despite it all, persevere into maturity. Yet however chronologically distant this time of his maturing may be, Ahaz is warned that before it happens his land will be devastated (v 16). The land's very impoverishment, in fact, requires such prior devastation. But no other time-span, particularly one immediately after 734, seems to be needed.

6. "Then would Messiah's coming in poverty (caused by devastations [7:17], even his coming centuries later) constitute a relevant motivation to Ahaz in 734 B.C.?" A positive answer makes good sense. The Assyrian devastations were immediately impending, about the threat of which Isaiah left the king in no doubt at all. The Roman domination, under which Immanuel historically became incarnate, lay centuries in the future, but of course neither Ahaz nor Isaiah was aware of the actual time interval involved, and a threat of any date remains valid as a force in motivating conduct so long as its contemporaries continue to look for it. Our Lord's undatable second coming provides similar motivation for us today (1 Thess 5:2-6). Finally, the very anticipation of Israel's Messiah as the heaven-sent climax to the house of David constituted a standing threat to Ahaz's own status: He could be replaced. As Skinner has summed up the Isaianic situation:

> The sign given to Ahaz is, in short, the birth of the Messiah, the ideal King of the future, born to His people in the hour of their adversity, sharing their afflictions in His youth, and waiting the time when "the government shall be upon His shoulder," and the perfect kingdom of God shall be established. In His presence with His people Isaiah sees the pledge at once of judgment on

---

[34] Beegle, "Virgin," 31; cf. Payne, *Theology of the Older Testament* (Grand Rapids: Zondervan, 1962) 268.

[35] *RSV* "when he knows"; *NASB* "at the time He knows"; cf. Young, *Isaiah*, 1. 291 n.

the existing nation and dynasty and of final redemption for the repentant and believing remnant.[36]

Herein lie acceptable answers to the right kinds of questions, both to the primary one: "Does Isa 7:14 predict Jesus Christ?" (yes), and to the one that is most significant for its understanding by today's Bible-believers: "Must it have had an immediate accomplishment?" (no).

---

[36] Skinner, *Isaiah*, 1. 67, though he adds, "It is no objection to this view that the sign did not come to pass. That is true; but neither did the prophecy to which it was attached."

Jesus and Moses: Rabbinic Backgrounds and Exegetical Concerns in Matthew 5 as Crucial to the Theological Foundations of Christian Ethics

ALAN F. JOHNSON

I T is not inappropriate to begin a study of Christian ethics with Matthew 5-7, the famous sermon on the mount (SM). Christian ethics must as a minimum raise and answer the question, "How does Christ affect the moral life?"[1] These sayings of Jesus in the SM play a more significant part in the NT as a whole than is often recognized.[2]

While there exists important disagreement over the meaning of Christ's teachings in these chapters, all concede the radical nature of the standard set forth by Jesus. Whether non-Christian, Roman Catholic or Protestant, it is recognized that the demands go beyond any other standard of morality known to man. It is primarily because of the radicalness of these statements that there arise divergent views of the sermon as a whole. No system of Christian ethics worthy of that title can fail to seriously confront the pivotal issues that emerge when one seeks to relate these teachings of Jesus to the reality of life in our kind of world.

Although a superficial reflection on these claims of Jesus may only suggest a mild tension between a high ideal and the practical struggle to attain it, a closer consideration reveals the deeper issue of what seems to some to be an impossible ideal in the socio-political arena. How do people who call themselves Christians reconcile these commands with their every-day lives? For example, in personal life who can adopt a literal policy of giving "to him who begs from you" and of not refusing him who would "borrow from you" (Matt 5:42)? Or in public life what would happen if a policeman or a nation adopted the policy of not resisting "one who is evil" (5:39)? Our response to this type of problem is crucial in determining one's whole Christian ethical system. The resolution of the issue involves a

---

[1]J. Gustafson, *Christ and the Moral Life* (Harper, 1968) 3; J. Yoder, *The Politics of Jesus* (Eerdmans, 1972) 16.

[2]W. D. Davies, *The Setting of the Sermon on the Mount* (Cambridge University, 1964) 437.

person's hermeneutics, theology, philosophy, sociology, temperament and other factors.

There are no less than a dozen different views of how the overall injunctions of Matthew 5 can be accommodated to the hard "facts of life."[3] Among the many questions these approaches raise are these: What is the real essence of the ethical teaching of Jesus? Is his teaching relevant to all areas of our life, or is it limited to the personal? Are the commands of Christ in the SM to be taken literally? Are they to be reduced to different principles? Is the ethic of Jesus taught in the SM and elsewhere enough for Christians, or do we need to borrow from other sources?

In a day of renewed Christian concern over what it means to live a responsible life in the world, can we do better than to refocus on the teaching of Christ, the interpretation of which lies at the foundation of the divergent Christian ethical traditions? This chapter recognizes these different approaches and yet attempts to press back beyond them to a more precise understanding of the Biblical text itself in the hope of offering at least a partial reconciliation between Anabaptist and Reformed understandings of Christian ethics.

At the heart of several of these traditions lies the pressing question of the relationship of Jesus' teaching to the Law of Moses. Basically the issue involves the question of continuity versus discontinuity with the OT moral teachings. Anabaptists emphasize discontinuity to such an extent that the "new law of Jesus" seems to some to stand at odds with the old law given through Moses. This is seen particularly in the matter of nonresistance to evil. Reformed exegesis accuses the Anabaptist position of teaching by inference that there are two different Gods—one in the OT and one in the NT—with two corresponding and divergent moralities. Thus the God of the OT allows wars, capital punishment and controlled retaliation, whereas the God of the NT forbids all such activities. Consequently the view of the Anabaptists is rejected by other branches of the reformation.

By stressing instead the continuity of the teaching of Jesus with that of Moses, Reformed exponents attempt to harmonize the SM with the older moral teaching. This is accomplished principally by stressing that in the sermon Jesus merely expounds the inner intention of the Law of Moses

[3]H. K. McArthur, *Understanding the Sermon on the Mount* (Harper, 1960), chap. 4. C. F. H. Henry, *Christian Personal Ethics* (Eerdmans, 1957), chap. 12, discusses seven different views but somehow omits even the standard Roman Catholic interpretation. McArthur has the best summary available of the whole problem. His otherwise excellent treatment is marred occasionally by a less than full view of the inspiration of Matthew's gospel in its present form and by some outdated theories of higher criticism. Two more recent treatments of the SM also deserve careful consideration: R. Banks, *Jesus and the Law in the Synoptic Tradition* (Cambridge University, 1975) 182-235; W. S. Kissinger, *The Sermon on the Mount: A History of Interpretation and Bibliography* (Scarecrow, 1975).

over against the Pharisees' distorted understanding. Any new elements in Jesus' teaching are basically deeper meanings of the OT Law.[4]

Thus there are today two basic positions on this crucial issue: those who with Augustine and the Reformers maintain that Jesus re-established the original intent of Moses' Law, and those who affirm that he went beyond it. Some in this latter group assume that he also abrogated parts of the older tradition. Among the proponents of the former position are Augustine, Luther, Calvin, Zwingli, Theodor Zahn, Martin Dibelius, Carl F. H. Henry, John Murray and others. The latter position is held not only by Anabaptist groups but by many modern NT scholars such as A. Schlatter, Hans Windisch, W. D. Davies, Harvey McArthur, J. Jeremias, John Wenger, John Yoder, Robert Banks, Robert A. Guelich, and others. Those who oppose the Reformers' tradition on this point usually point out that such an interpretation rests on two exegetically indefensible presuppositions: (1) God's law cannot be modified, and therefore the Law of Moses cannot be modified; and (2) Jesus was not a new Lawgiver.

It would be presumptuous in a brief treatment of this question to attempt finally to settle this long-standing debate. However, it will be tentatively argued in the following discussion that (1) Jesus' ethic develops legitimately out of the Mosaic tradition and is not in essential disagreement with it—there is continuity with the old, and (2) Jesus' ethic goes beyond the Mosaic ethical tradition and thereby transforms the older tradition— there is discontinuity with Moses, since something "new" has come with Christ.

I. CONTINUITY WITH MOSES

It is not difficult to argue that the SM shows strong affinities with the Mosaic tradition. Not only was Jesus himself a devout Jew, born and raised within the Jewish community and devoted to the Law, but his frequent appeal to the OT in controversy, his use of language freighted with OT significance in the beatitudes,[5] and his explicit statement in Matt 5:17 indicate that he was no left-wing radical with respect to orthodox Judaism. The fact that the Reformers (Luther, Calvin) have been able to convince the majority of the Church that in the SM Jesus merely expounded the deeper or correct sense of the Mosaic Law is further evidence that the direction, aim and intention of Jesus' teaching was not essentially incompatible with the OT. Finally, the fact that many of Jesus' statements can be paralleled in extant rabbinic literature of the early periods shows that he

---

[4]McArthur, *Understanding*, chap. 1, "The Sermon and the Mosaic Tradition" contains excellent historical material on the whole problem. The author argues for the SM as constituting an "advance" over the Law of Moses.

[5]Davies, *Setting*, 60, 251-252, 288-289.

was not totally outside the traditional Jewish understanding.[6] This continuity with Judaism is due to the common authority they both shared in the Mosaic and prophetic OT Scriptures.

Indeed the text of Matthew itself emphatically emphasizes that Jesus did not come to "abolish" (*katalyō*, "dissolve," "abrogate," "set aside") the Law and the Prophets but to "fulfill" (*plēroō*, "fill out," "complete") them (5:17). Matt 5:17, 18 are so strongly affirmative of the validity of the Mosaic Law that many modern scholars have either denied that Jesus would have so spoken or they think the words are irony: "Think not that I have come to abolish the law and the prophets; I have come not to abolish them but to fulfill them. For truly, I say to you, till heaven and earth pass away, not an iota, not a dot, will pass from the law until all is accomplished" (*RSV* here and elsewhere).[7]

The interpreter, however, must carefully consider the phrase "not to abolish them but to fulfill them" (v 17). The content of the negative clause seems clearly to mean "destroy" or "reject as valid." The disputed term "fulfill" (*plēroō*) in its most widespread interpretation has been understood in terms of setting out the inner "intention," the "true meaning," "spirit," or "basic principles" of the Law so as to "complete," "perfect," "express" its full significance. Thus in this view Jesus wants to emphasize that he upholds or maintains the teaching of the Law and Prophets.[8] In the following section of Matthew (5:21-48), this view maintains, Jesus shows how he in fact upholds the Mosaic Law by contrasting the distorted

---

[6]McArthur, *Understanding*, 49-52, quotes numerous parallels in the teaching of Jesus and early rabbinic and late Jewish apocalyptic writings. This in no way detracts from the fact that Jesus' total ethical impact was unique.

[7]A. M. Hunter, *A Pattern for Life: An Exposition of the Sermon on the Mount* (rev. ed.; Harper, 1965) 47, claims, "These verses as they stand can hardly be words of Christ; for (a) the doctrine of the Law's permanence is pure rabbinism; and (b) Jesus himself 'relaxed' the Sabbath law, annulled the law about purity and rejected Moses' command about divorce." Hunter is not only misled at this point by a diluted view of the inspiration of the NT documents but here exhibits careless exegesis (something he is usually not guilty of). D. Daube (*The New Testament and Rabbinic Judaism* [Arno, 1973] 61 ff.), on the contrary, argues that the statements in vv 17-20 are an integral part of the whole argument of 5:17-48 without which the other sections cannot be understood correctly. T. W. Manson argued that Jesus was speaking ironically in vv 18, 19, which were Jesus' response to a hyperlegalistic attitude: He threw his hands up in despair, saying, "It is easier for heaven and earth to pass away, than for one dot of the law to become void" (cited by McArthur, *Understanding*, 129). While all possibilities should be considered, Manson's suggestion can hardly fit Matthew's context of the saying, especially the immediately preceding verse. R. Banks, on the other hand, argues that v 19 refers to the commandments of Jesus rather than the Mosaic Law (*Jesus*, 220-223).

[8]Daube, *Rabbinic*, 60.

teaching of the Pharisees and scribes with his own true interpretation. Zwingli represents this general Reformed position in his *Commentary on Matthew*. He claims that Jesus fulfilled the law in four ways: (1) by fulfilling its required ceremonies, (2) by fulfilling its prophecies, (3) by fulfilling its ethical precepts, and (4) by fulfilling the Law for us to satisfy divine justice.[9] C. F. H. Henry reaffirms the Reformers' viewpoint:

> The sermon makes no departure from the creation ethic, nor from that of the OT. . . . As God is uniform in his nature, his revelation likewise does not change over time nor does it contradict itself. The ethical norms he addresses to man are constant ones. These ethical norms constitute the one law of God, eternal, unchanging, authoritative for all men at all times. . . . Jesus does not in the Sermon impose upon his hearers a morality which is qualitatively different from the OT claim. What he criticizes is not the Law itself, but contemporary formulations of the Law.[10]

While such a view follows the general lines of the Protestant Reformers, it must nevertheless be seriously questioned. It not only relies on an "inner-outer" dichotomy that cannot be upheld for the NT period, but the approach suffers from an excessive imposition on the Biblical text of a philosophical principle of unity. Additionally, the view flounders exegetically as the following discussion will demonstrate.

In the first place, the word "fulfill" (*plēroō*, 5:17) can also mean "complete" in the sense of filling out or complementing something. Paul uses the same root word when he says, "Love is the fulfillment (*plērōma*) of the law" (Rom 13:10). Paul does not mean that love merely "keeps" the Law but rather that love is the realization of the Law. Love is the direction the Law was pointing in the OT but never reached. While not denying the validity of the Law, Paul argues that the primary authority for the Christian community is no longer the OT Law but the new standard of Jesus (cf. John 13:34, 35). The possibility exists, then, that Jesus could be indicating by this statement (Matt 5:17) that he intends by his teaching to "complete" or "complement" the Law, not simply to expound the inner sense of the older tradition. Thus when he teaches that "anger" and "insult" are as culpable as murder (5:22 ff.) or that "lust" is as culpable as physical adultery (5:28-29) he is not claiming to be merely upholding or keeping or even "adding to" the Law but is teaching that his commandments surpass or transcend the old because he fulfills it. What Jesus requires, then, is not exactly the same as the old nor is it in basic opposition to the old. Instead, it transforms every part of the Law and Prophets.[11]

---

[9]Cited by McArthur, *Understanding*, 39.

[10]Henry, *Ethics*, 306, 309.

[11]Cf. J. Jeremias, *New Testament Theology: The Proclamation of Jesus* (Scribners, 1971), 84-85: "According to b. Shab. 116b, *katalysai* corresponds to the

There are no good reasons, however, to view the teaching of Christ as a new law in the sense that his words were opposed to the basic ethical tradition of the Mosaic Law and the Prophets and thus were being offered as an alternative. However, to stop here with a mere denial of the new-law concept, as many do, would be inadequate in the light of the text of

---

Aramaic *miphat* ('take away') and *plērōsai* to the Aramaic *ʾōsopē* ('increase, add, enlarge'). This understanding of *plērōsai* as 'fill up' matches the usual exegesis of Matt. 5:17b in Jewish Christianity, as we learn from the pseudo-Clementine Recognitions and, recently, from a Jewish-Christian source worked over by a Mohammedan author, which renders Matt. 5:17b as follows: 'I did not come to diminish, but, on the contrary, to complete.'

"On linguistic grounds then there is every probability that the Jewish-Christian tradition has retained the original sense of *plērōsai*.

"Jesus then is countering the insinuation (*mē nomisēte*) that he is an antinomian: His task is not the dissolution of the Torah but its fulfillment. The rendering of *ʾōsopē* ("add") by *plērōsai* in Greek aptly expresses the fact that the purpose of the 'fulfilling' is the reaching of the complete measure. We have here the idea of the eschatological measure, which Jesus also uses elsewhere; *plērōsai* is thus an eschatological technical term. In other words, in Matt. 5:17 Jesus is claiming to be the *eschatological messenger of God*, the promised prophet like Moses (Deut. 18: 15, 18), who brings the final revelation and therefore demands absolute obedience. In fact, this claim of Jesus that he brings the concluding revelation is to be found throughout his sayings. It is expressed clearly in the antithetic pattern of Matt. 5:21-48. This pattern belongs to the bedrock of the tradition, since it involves a conflict with the Torah, something unheard of in the atmosphere of the period. Jesus proclaims that the divine will in the *basileia* stands above the divine will as expressed in the time of the Old Testament (Mark 10:1-12)."

Cf. also Banks, *Jesus*, 210: "What I would argue then, and it is this possibility that seems to have been constantly overlooked, is that precisely the same meaning should be given to the term *plēroun* when it is used of the Law as that which it has when it is used of the Prophets. The prophetic teachings point forward (principally) to the actions of Christ and have been realized in them in an incomparably greater way. The Mosaic laws point forward (principally) to the teachings of Christ and have also been realized in them in a more profound manner. The word 'fulfill' in 5:17, then, includes not only an element of discontinuity (that which has now been realized *transcends* the Law) but an element of continuity as well (that which transcends the Law is nevertheless something to which the Law itself *pointed forward*)." "The term *plēroun* in its present setting, then, would seem to refer to the advent of a new 'Law,' which transcends, and even in parts annuls, the Old Law. Jesus affirms the Old Law and at the same time annuls it" (W. D. Davies, *Christian Origins and Judaism* [Westminster, 1962] 36); so also R. A. Guelich, *"Not to Annul the Law, Rather to Fulfill the Law and the Prophets": An Exegetical Study of Jesus and the Law in Matthew with Emphasis on 5:17-48* (Dissertation; Hamburg University, 1967); contra Banks, see D. Wenham, "Jesus and Law: An Exegesis on Matthew 5:17-20," *Themelios* 4/3 (1979) 92-96.

Matthew itself. Such shortsightedness weakens the development of a distinctive Christian ethic at the most foundational level.

It is at this point that further questions concerning the content of the transcendent substance of Jesus' teaching should be raised. Mark well, however, that this transcendent quality of Jesus' teaching can only be understood in the light of his affirmation of strong continuity with the older tradition. He is no radical revolutionist with respect to the OT tradition.

II. Discontinuity with Moses

We have already noted that there is a general agreement among various interpreters that Jesus in some sense goes beyond the Mosaic legislation by intensifying the Law in condemning anger, lust, and so forth, while admittedly his teaching in these instances does not annul the older teaching. In this case the specific concept of Jesus' transforming or fulfilling the Law for which this chapter argues is not as evident. But are there instances were Jesus' fulfillment of the OT clearly reveals that the old is antiquated by the new? We think that there are cases in Christ's teaching in the SM where this sense of fulfillment is clear: on (1) divorce, (2) oaths, and (3) legal retaliation.

Before we look specifically at these three injunctions it is important to examine carefully the generally misunderstood introductory formula for the six antithetical statements found in Matt 5:21-48.

1. *The Introductory Formula*: "You have heard that it was said . . . but I say unto you." This expression or a variation of it is used six times as an introductory formula to Christ's specific pronouncements in the area of killing, adultery, divorce, oaths, retaliation, and love of neighbor (5:21, 27, 31, 33, 38, 43).

The first question concerns to whom or to what teaching Jesus refers when he introduces each quotation by the phrase, "You have heard that it was said." In two of the six instances the words "to the men of old" are added to the basic formula (vv 21, 33). Who are "the men of old" (*tois archaiois*)? Are they the ancient covenant people to whom Moses spoke the words of the Pentateuch? Or does Jesus refer to the men of old by whom certain teachings were given to the people? In this latter case they could either be identified with Moses and the prophets and/or the rabbinical teachers of old. The Greek construction, some interpreters notwithstanding, allows either interpretation, though there is a slight edge for the "to" sense.[12] Jewish teaching held that the divine Law was laid down by both

---

[12]"To" those of old would be the dative of the indirect object or necessary complement, "by" those of old would be the dative of the agent (cf. BDF, 100, 102). The usual construction for the "agent" with this passive verb of saying is with *hypo* or *dia* and the genitive (Matt 2:15; 3:3; 4:14; etc.). The use of the dative of agent is

the written Torah and the oral Torah or Halakah. The real question is
whether in the six antitheses Jesus is addressing the written Torah or the
oral Halakah. Since an appeal to the expression alone cannot settle the
question, we must look more closely at the content of the quoted materials.

In the first place it can be observed in most of the instances that all or
part of the quotation comes directly from the OT Pentateuch: "You shall
not kill"; "you shall not commit adultery"; "whoever divorces his wife"; and
so on.[13] Secondly, in three instances (first, fourth and sixth) further
qualifying words are added to the quotation that do not appear in OT
phraseology as such. Added to "you shall not kill" is the further expression
"and whoever kills shall be liable to judgment" (5:21). Added to "you shall
not swear falsely" is "you shall perform to the Lord what you have sworn"
(5:23). Finally, to "you shall love your neighbor" is added "and hate your
enemy" (5:43). It is easily agreed that the first two instances (first, fourth)
are a natural interpretive conclusion or summary of OT teaching where the
death penalty is imposed for murder or encouragement is given to do one's
vows (based on such passages as Exod 21:12; Num 35:16-33; Lev 19:12;
Deut 23:21). These instances are completely acceptable paraphrases of the
OT written Law.[14]

However, the third addition concerning "hating the enemy" raises a
question. Are these latter words a reasonable conclusion or summary of
OT teaching or does it represent a departure from the written OT, imposed
by a corrupt rabbinic Halakah, which Jesus corrects by saying, "But I say
to you, 'Love your enemies . . .'"? Those who desire to stress the unity of
the moral revelation of the OT with the NT and to reinforce their
conclusion that Jesus teaches nothing new in the SM that was not already
in the OT, at least in intent, claim that this case clearly represents a corrupt
rabbinic interpretation of the OT Law. It is an easy step, then, to generalize
from this one supposed corrupt Halakah to conclude that the other five
antitheses are likewise directed not toward the written Torah and Prophets
but the Pharisaic Halakah.[15]

It may be argued that the "neighbor" in the OT refers predominantly
to a fellow covenant Israelite or "compatriot," being parallel in Lev 19:18

---

usually confined to the perfect passive. Furthermore, in the parallel construction,
egō de legō hymin, the dative is clearly an indirect object. Thus most modern
interpreters prefer the translation "to the men of old."

[13]Cf. Exod 20:13; 20:14; Deut 24:1-4. On oaths cf. Lev 19:12; retaliation, Exod
21:24; love of neighbor, Lev 19:18.

[14]It is also possible that these formulations may have occurred in the Targums
(paraphrases of the OT in Aramaic). This material is only now beginning to be
studied thoroughly in relation to the NT; cf. M. McNamara, *Targums and the New
Testament* (Eerdmans, 1973).

[15]So Henry, *Ethics*, 306, 307.

with "the sons of your own people" and in the preceding verse with "your brother." Even though the Israelite was commanded to love the stranger who sojourned with them in their land (Lev 19:33) there is no direct command in the OT or in rabbinic literature for them to love their enemies, although they were commanded to spare their enemies' cattle (Exod 23:4). The phrase "hate your enemies" is likewise not found in the OT but, as Jeremias points out, it probably was a popular maxim qualifying Lev 19:18.[16] There is a question concerning whether the "enemy" is a personal enemy (i.e., an "adversary") or a national enemy (see n. 16). However, the OT seems to lay no special burden on the Israelite to love either of these. For example, Deut 23:3-6 states concerning the national enemies Moab and Ammon that "you shall not seek their peace or prosperity all your days forever." With reference to the personal enemies Ps 139:21-22 might be cited: "Do I not hate them that hate thee, O LORD? And do I not loathe them that rise up against thee? I hate them with perfect hatred; I count them my enemies."[17] But these OT citations are not really parallel to the statement of Jesus. More direct is the Dead Sea scrolls, where the following exhortation to the community is found:

> To love all the sons of light, each according to his lot in the Council of God, and to hate all the sons of darkness, each according to his guilt in the vengeance of God (IQS 1:9-11).[18]

Again, this statement does not really parallel Jesus' remarks since it refers to the eschatological judgment, not the present. In fact the rabbinic materials can be searched in vain for such a statement.[19]

Therefore it seems perfectly appropriate to see in the phrase "hate your enemies" a legitimate paraphrase of OT attitudes and render it as: "You

---

[16]Jeremias, *Theology*, 252, 253 n. 3: "Three things should be noted about the popular maxim Matt. 5:43, qualifying Lev. 19:18: all are connected with its language. First, the pair of opposites *plēsion/echthros*: *plēsion* (Lev. 19:18 LXX) is a rendering of *rēa*^{c} = 'compatriot'; thus in Matt. 5:43 it is not to be loaded with the meaning 'neighbour', which only Jesus gave it. *Echthros* means a man's personal enemy, his adversary, and not a national enemy (cf. Luke 6:27f.). Secondly, in a contrasting pair in Semitic languages, the negative part is very often no more than a negation of the positive. This is also the case here: so *misein* is accordingly not to be rendered 'hate,' but 'not love.' Finally, the Aramaic imperfect which underlies the two Greek futures *agapēseis-misēseis* only rarely has a future significance; usually this significance is virtual. In *agapēseis* the virtual nuance is jussive ('you shall'), in *misēseis* it is permissive ('you need not'). The translation therefore must be: 'You shall love your compatriot (Lev. 19:18) (but) you need not love your adversary.' "

[17]Hunter, *Pattern*, 61.

[18]Cited by W. S. LaSor, *The Dead Sea Scrolls and the New Testament* (Eerdmans, 1973) 240.

[19]Banks, *Jesus*, 199.

need not love your adversaries" or in the Aramaic equivalent: "You shall hate your enemy" (see n. 16). Only when the NT revelation of Jesus' concept of "neighbor" is read back into the OT do we conclude that the popular paraphrase is a Pharisaic corruption of the OT.

There are further reasons that this sixth antithesis should be understood as another case of Jesus' addressing not rabbinic Halakah but the OT written Torah. In the first place, the previous two additive statements to the OT commands about killing and oaths are wholly compatible with other OT references and do not represent Pharisaic Halakah on the OT. If these earlier two paraphrased additions are legitimate, why not also in the third case? Furthermore, the introductory formula, "It was said," is a common form used in the NT, not to introduce rabbinic interpretations but OT Scripture quotations (Matt 1:22; 22:31; Rom 4:18; 9:12; Heb 4:3). Additionally, in several of these NT passages the phrase specifically introduces a statement specifying that the quote comes from "the law" or "the prophets" (Luke 2:24; Acts 13:40). Hence it is probably correct to paraphrase the expression as follows: "It was said by God." While there certainly were Pharisaic Halakah teachings about the Law that Jesus elsewhere refuted,[20] it is contended that the primary intent of Jesus as set forth in Matthew 5 was not to refute erroneous Halakah interpretations but to show that because of his authority he is now presenting a new order that surpasses or transcends the old ("but I say to you").

2. *The Literary Structure.* The second important observation about each of these six antitheses is their literary structure. Important rabbinic materials can now aid the interpreter in understanding the form of the discourse. As Daube has effectively demonstrated, a common method of rabbinic teaching followed the form of "general principle multiple illustration."[21] The procedure was first to state a broad principle, then to follow the principle with one or more illustrations that more concretely showed how the principle operated in certain specific situations. Eccl 3:1 ff. may be cited as an illustration of this method. The passage begins with a general statement or principle: "To everything there is a season and a time to every

---

[20] Jeremias, *Theology,* 208, shows that Jesus especially opposed the Halakah on the Sabbath and on questions of purity (Mark 3:1-5; 7:1-16).

[21] Daube, *Rabbinic,* 85 ff. We cannot, however, accept Daube's conclusion that the expression "You have heard" is intended originally (*Sitz im Leben*) by Jesus to correspond with the rabbinic formula, "I hear, I might understand (literally), but you must say (the true meaning)." In this case Jesus would be arguing that the commonly understood literal interpretation was erroneous and he was giving the true sense (pp. 56-57). Beside creating a false dichotomy between Jesus' intent and Matthew's, Daube's explanation still leaves the main question dangling—i.e., "What is Jesus' relation to the OT legislation itself?" McArthur rightly questions this type of exegesis of the six phrases (*Understanding,* 42).

purpose." Then follows a series of specific illustrations based on and expounding the central principle: "A time to be born, and a time to die; a time to plant," and so on. Daube cites many examples of this method in rabbinic literature including a chapter in the Mishna that begins: "If a man wounds another, he is liable on five counts, for injury, for pain, for healing, for loss of time, and for the indignity inflicted." The text goes on to deal with each of these five "counts" in detail.[22] The suggestion of Daube fits well the material in Matthew 5 and helps illuminate not only the general structure of the whole passage but also the format within each of the six individual antitheses.

In the words, "I came . . . to fulfill [the law and the prophets]. . . . Unless your righteousness exceeds that of the scribes and Pharisees" (vv 19-20), we find the general statement of the whole passage, which is then followed by six specific examples, "You have heard," and so on, answering the questions, "How have you fulfilled the law?" and "How does the new righteousness exceed the old?"

Furthermore, and quite importantly, each of the six specific examples is in turn prefaced with a general principle and is followed itself by one or more illustrations. For example, "But I say to you, 'Do not resist one who is evil'" (v 39) states the general principle. Then follow four or five specific cases that illustrate the application of this general statement, such as, "If any one strikes you on the right cheek, turn to him the other also" (v 39), and so forth.

The significance of this distinction between general principle and specific cases becomes important when the question is raised concerning the application to Christian ethics of each of the more specific injunctions. It should be noted that while the general statement admits of few or no exceptions, the individual cases are concrete cultural illustrations applying the general principle in quite specific situations. As such the latter type of injunction must be understood as concrete illustrations of the general principle and should not themselves be made into general principles literally binding in every situation. This perhaps explains why even Jesus himself did not turn the other cheek when he was smitten by one of the officers of the high priest. Instead he protested and rebuked the man for his unjust deed (John 18:22-23). While Jesus did not resist the evil inflicted on him (a literal fulfillment of the principle), neither did he in this case literally turn his other cheek.

But care must be exercised at this point that the radicalness of the ethic taught in the illustrations not be softened, nor should there be a prohibition against a literal keeping of the illustrations in certain circumstances as the most appropriate way to obey the general command. The point to be emphasized, however, is that the illustrations are quite culturally

[22] Daube, *Rabbinic*, 63-64.

specific and hence must admit of numerous exceptions depending on the similarity or dissimilarity of the situation depicted in Jesus' cases with our own situations. The specific cases cannot be taken as general commands or a new legislation (as we can with the leading statements) to be applied in all circumstances. Just when and how the specific cases can be applied literally must be settled on solid exegetical ground that considers the original cultural setting and seeks to find the nearest modern equivalents.

Thus it is concluded that in the series of six statements introduced by the expression, "You have heard . . . but I say to you," Jesus is expounding his own general statement in vv 17 and 20 that he came to fulfill the Law and the Prophets and that unless the righteousness of the disciples of Christ exceeds that of the scribes and Pharisees they cannot enter the kingdom that Christ was calling man into through his ministry.[23] Jesus does this by contrasting the old righteousness with the new righteousness that he brings by setting forth six pointed antitheses. To repeat, his teaching is not primarily set over against rabbinic Halakah, corrupt or otherwise, but over against the Torah and Prophets. Jesus indeed brings something that is new, yet not at the expense of repudiating the divine validity of the old. The old was valid for its time but a new time has come. The old must now be seen as it is fulfilled in himself and in the kingdom that he inaugurates. The whole of the Law is thus affirmed, yet only through its transformation by the teaching of Christ, which was new and unique in comparison. What is more important is not the Law but Jesus and his teaching. This conclusion is further reinforced by considering three specific teachings of Jesus in Matthew 5: divorce, oaths, and retaliation (antitheses 3, 4 and 5).

3. *Divorce, Oaths, and Retaliation.* As previously indicated, the specific teaching of Jesus in three areas not only clearly goes beyond the OT legislation but also, and by his new revelation, effectively supersedes the Mosaic in these areas.

a. *Divorce* (Matt 5:31-32). Moses clearly assumed the right of the Israelite man to divorce his wife. In the only OT passage dealing directly with the problem of divorce, Deut 24:1-4, divorce is not prohibited but simply regulated. While the rabbis disputed to what extent the words "some indecency" might be carried, Jesus seems to cut across even the most conservative interpretation of the day and permit divorce only on the grounds of unchastity.[24]

---

[23]G. E. Ladd correctly emphasizes that the force of Matthew's "But I say unto you" is identical to John's "Truly, truly, I say to you" (John 3:11, etc.): *The Presence of the Future* (Eerdmans, 1974) 285.

[24]The school of Hillel was most liberal, allowing divorce for even "poor cooking," while that of Shammai was quite conservative. Recent studies, however, have documented the fact that even Shammai allowed divorce for other reasons

In defense of his more radical teaching, Matthew at another place records that Jesus appealed to the exemplary nature of the original creation of one man and one woman as sufficient grounds for rejecting divorce as God's will (Matt 19:7-9). The Pharisees ask, "Why then did Moses command that a certificate of divorce should be made out and the man put away his wife?" Jesus replies, "For your hardness of heart Moses allowed you to divorce your wives, but from the beginning it was not so" (19:8). Divorce was allowed under the old order to bring some order and justice out of what would have been chaotic and more harmful, especially to women. While it is true that Jesus appeals to the creation narratives to support his view that Moses only allowed divorce because of man's "hard heart," should we therefore conclude that any devout Israelite could have so understood this from Genesis or elsewhere in the Pentateuch? The OT merely indicated a procedure for divorce to limit its abuse. It did not prohibit it altogether. Even God divorced Israel for her adultery (Jer 3:1-8).

Yet Jesus completely sets aside this aspect of the Mosaic legislation by showing that the standards of the kingdom of God that he inaugurates in his ministry go beyond the old and in this instance abrogate the earlier legislation. This does not mean that Moses was wrong or uninspired in his divorce legislation. Rather this should teach us that there is a progress in God's revealed will as it is now fulfilled in Jesus. In some instances the new revelation annuls the old. We must not say that this new order was already revealed in the old and that Jesus is simply "expounding" the sixth commandment or giving the true "intent" of Deut 24:1. This would deny the full sense of what is meant by historical revelation. It will not do to try to harmonize at this point the injunctions of the old with the new by saying that they have the same "intent" or "goal" and are therefore really and essentially the same. Rather there is here a clear surpassing of the old in what Jesus is teaching. This chapter argues that the whole tradition from Augustine through the Reformers, Luther and Calvin, down to the present has unconsciously or deliberately forced the interpretation of this passage to conform it to an extra-Biblical philosophical principle of the unification of all revelation. One example from Calvin will have to suffice. He argues that Moses in reality sought to "condemn" divorce by prescribing a bill of divorce to be written.

> Although what relates to divorce was granted in indulgence to the Jews, yet Christ pronounces that it was never in accordance with the Law, because it is directly repugnant to the first institution of God, from whence a perpetual and inviolable rule is to be sought. . . . And undoubtedly the bill or scroll of

than unchastity, thus indicating the more accentuated and unique position of Jesus; cf. T. V. Fleming, "Christ and Divorce," *TS* 24 (January 1963) 106-120.

divorce, whilst it cleared the woman from all divorce, cast some reproach on the husband. . . . We see, then, that husbands were indirectly condemned by the writing of divorce, since they thus committed an injury against their wives who were chaste, and in other respects what they should be.[25]

Calvin reads into the OT text the NT truth to support his prior assumption of the once-for-all revelation of the eternal moral law of God. Some support for Calvin's position might be seen in Malachi's condemnation of divorce: "For I hate divorce, says the LORD, the God of Israel" (Mal 2:13-16). However, a careful study of the historical context favors the view that the prophet was concerned with a proliferation of divorces as well as the pernicious treatment women were receiving from their husbands.

While the argument of a common "intention" between the old and the new serves to show that the commands were going in the same direction, it cannot be used to prove that the old in fact reached the same end as the new. This distinction enables the NT interpreter to argue for a difference in the ethics of the kingdom of God as preached by Christ and the apostles from that of the Law and the Prophets.

We conclude then that Jesus' teaching on divorce is different from the older revelation through Moses and the Prophets. In fact it nullifies the old at this point, thus illustrating that Jesus' person and teaching "fulfills" the entire old order by surpassing it. Nevertheless the old still stands as a witness against the Pharisees concerning their "hardness of heart." But the standards for those in God's kingdom "exceeds" even the strictest and most accurate understanding of Moses. Something new has now dawned in history through the ministry of Jesus.

b. *Oaths* (Matt 5:33-37). As in the case of divorce, no decalogue command is involved. Jesus first reiterates the OT Torah teaching by a direct quote from Lev 19:12, "You shall not swear falsely." This is followed by an accurate summary of other OT statements bearing on oaths, "but you shall perform to the Lord what you have sworn" (cf. Deut 23:21-23). What is an oath? It is a serious invoking of God as witness to affirm the truth of a statement. Oaths testify to the fact that men are often liars (v 37, "comes from evil"). The presence of oaths presupposes the recognition that among men there are two kinds of affirmations: One type, accompanied by an oath, is binding; another, lacking the oath, is equivocal.

The Jews, and orientals in general, are fond of the habitual use of oaths to underscore the truthfulness of remarks in everyday speech, the only notable exception being the Essene Dead Sea sect, which prohibited all oaths except the initiatory oaths into the community.[26] A casuistical

---

[25] J. Calvin, *The Harmony of the Four Last Books of the Pentateuch*, on Deut 24:1, cited by McArthur, *Understanding*, 47.

[26] Hunter, *Pattern*, 55: "However, the Gentiles also greatly abuse oaths and vows." "The Rabbis generally accepted them but with reluctance" (Davies, *Setting*,

hierarchy of the seriousness of an oath was also practiced (Matt 23:16-22). To the whole practice of oaths, whether initiatory or regular, Jesus makes a sweeping statement: "But I say to you, 'Do not swear at all'" (v 34). This is the general principle followed by four specific methods of swearing common in Jesus' day (by heaven, by earth, by Jerusalem, by one's head). None of these forms was used in court as a legal device.[27] Each of the specifics appears to be a substitute for actually naming God as the witness. The point is that to invoke any authority in creation as a witness is to ultimately invoke God (Matt 23:21-22). Men and women of the kingdom of God are always to speak the truth. A plain "yes" or "no" is enough. When there is truth in the heart it will also be on the lips. Whatever must be said more than this reveals a lack of total honesty in the words we speak (Jas 5:12).

Whatever else may be said about this passage on oaths, one thing is clear. Jesus' teaching on the whole oath-making practice runs counter to the OT teaching. Oaths, like divorce, were permitted but regulated under the old economy. Christ does not merely correct their first-century abuse. In the kingdom of God, which he is now inaugurating, all oaths are to be set aside, and nothing but truth in all our statements is to be the standard. True, the OT oaths were to be truthful and not false, but their tolerance in the total life of the community (not just the civil-legal) was a moral imperfection that the new order in Christ's kingdom does not permit. Again, Christ fulfills the Law by surpassing its prescriptions. Something new has come that again at this point annuls the old.

It is tempting here to point out that even this more general principle against invoking God as a witness is subject to a situational conditioning. Paul in the unusual circumstance of being attacked as a deceiver must impress his audience on more than one occasion that he tells only the truth by invoking an oath with God or something else as his witness (1 Cor 15:31; Rom 9:1; Gal 1:20; 2 Cor 1:23). This does not suggest that the general principle Jesus teaches is not in normal relations fully binding but alerts us to the fact that the general commands are never totally absolute without regard for special circumstances.

At this point it is evident that we must part company with traditional absolutist Anabaptist and Tolstoian understandings of the words of Jesus. In the first place the context indicates from the several illustrations given that Jesus has in mind the habitual everyday use of oaths in common speech and not the use of an oath in court. The more official oath of adjuration in legal proceedings was honored by Jesus when he finally broke his silence and responded to the high priest's order (Matt 26:63-64).

---

241 ff.). Cf. Jeremias, *Theology*, 220. Banks rightly insists that the "oath" should not be confused with the "vow" (*Jesus*, 194 n. 1).

[27] Jeremias, *Theology*, 220.

Finally, Paul apparently did not feel that he violated Jesus' commandment on oaths when he appealed to God as his witness in the unusual circumstances of defending false charges brought against him.

c. *Retaliation* (Matt 5:38-42). There is one further evidence that the teaching of Christ concerning the kingdom ethics surpasses the OT Torah —namely, his statements about retaliation. In this case, as in the instance concerning adultery, Jesus begins his remarks with a direct quotation from the OT written Torah without any further qualifying phrase: "You have heard that it was said, 'An eye for an eye and a tooth for a tooth' " (v 38). This is a direct quotation found in three passages from the Pentateuch (Exod 21:24; Lev 24:20; Deut 19:21). In these OT references the expression relates to civil-legal procedure and involves the notion of justice. In brief it states that the punishment or compensation for an offense committed against another person is to be equivalent to the harm done, no more or no less. This is known as the *lex talionis* (the law of retaliation).

In the time of Jesus an elaborate money system of damages perhaps took the place of the older literal retaliation.[28] Thus a problem arises. Precisely to what practice does Jesus refer? Does he address the OT Torah command or the current interpretation and practices? Part of the answer must be discovered by studying the alternative action Jesus suggests in his contrasting statement: "But I say to you, 'Do not resist one who is evil' " (v 39). The correct translation of this statement must first be determined. The *KJV* has "Resist not evil"; the *NEB* reads, "Do not set yourself up against the man who wrongs you." In the Greek we have simply, "Do not oppose the wicked" (*tō ponērō*). The term "the wicked" might be rendered "the evil one"—that is, the devil (Matt 13:33; John 17:15). This rendering, though grammatically possible, is highly improbable in this context and would counter other NT exhortations to "resist the devil" (Jas 4:7). Again, "the wicked" could mean "the wicked man" and have reference to anyone who opposes the disciple unjustly. This translation would admirably fit the context since the four illustrations that follow (vv 39-42) generally refer to someone's actions whose demands might be resisted. A third possibility translates the expression with the *KJV* as, "Do not resist evil."[29] The four illustrations then would show various ways in which the evil in the world is manifested by human actions and how the disciple is to respond. This latter rendering seems likewise appropriate to the context, to Matthew's usage, and to the rest of the NT (Rom 12:17, 21).[30]

There follow in vv 39b-42 four illustrations of the general principle of not opposing evil (or evil men). Each of these must be examined more

---

[28] If we can assume that in this case the practice of the first century was similar to that of the end of the second or third when the Mishna and Mekilta were formulated, it can be so argued (Daube, *Rabbinic*, 255).

[29] A. H. McNeile, *The Gospel According to Matthew*, 69.

[30] Harder, *"ponēros,"* *TDNT* 6 (1968) 567.

carefully before any final conclusion can be reached about the precise meaning of Christ's general principle. In the first illustration Jesus says, "If any one strikes you on the right cheek, turn to him the other also" (v 39b). This sounds at first glance like a simple case of personal injury, inflicted by a blow to the face whereupon the disciple is to refrain from retaliation and to offer instead the other side of his face. But why the right side of the face, especially since most people are righthanded and the left side of the face would thus be struck in the case of an offensive blow?

In answering this question the following may be noted. It is quite inappropriate to reduce these specific illustrations to general principles, in this case to the broad principle that we should not retaliate for various sorts of personal injuries done to us. Instead we must press for the actual offense referred to in its more concrete historical sense. We find in the Mishna, in Roman law, and in the East today that the blow to the right side of the face, a blow with the back of the hand, is an insulting blow.[31] Jeremias asks further how it would happen that Jesus' disciples would be insulted. He answers, "When they are dishonored as heretics." This follows, Jeremias argues, because whenever Jesus refers to insult, persecution, hatred and anathema coming to the disciples it is because they follow him and are thus spurned by the political or religious establishment.[32]

Thus it seems clear in the first illustration of nonresistance to evil that Jesus is dealing with the question of compensation for insult, which under Jewish law of the time would be linked to the OT Scripture passage, "An eye for an eye and a tooth for a tooth."[33] Jesus' disciples will truly show themselves as his disciples by refusing to expect or require any compensation when they are insulted. The point of the illustration is not to teach a general principle—such as "when wronged do not retaliate"—or to teach that disciples should refrain from hitting back or harming the other in formal retaliation. Rather Jesus calls them not to expect or require legal compensation from the offender. Instead the followers of Christ are to give themselves to the wrongdoer in humility and to allow themselves to be insulted again and again if need be—i.e., to "turn the other cheek."

We may conclude two things from this first case: (1) Jesus is using the OT *lex talionis* reference probably not to refer to the older practice of actual mutilation but to the current practice of the rabbis of allowing legal monetary compensation for insult. However, in the final analysis from the OT point of view we probably should not make a sharp distinction between retaliation and compensation. In the Pentateuch, as Daube points out, the

[31] Daube, *Rabbinic*, 28, 257.

[32] J. Jeremias, *The Sermon on the Mount* (Fortress, 1963) 28-29.

[33] Daube, *Rabbinic*, 259-265, argues effectively that the rabbinic law of the late first century onward in the Mishna was in the process of alteration and there is good reason to believe that Jesus' treatment of the *talion* reflects an authentic earlier stage in the whole development.

references to legal retaliation for wrong done (including mutilation) can be understood as a form of recompense to the injured.[34] (2) This legal practice of compensation for insult fell under the part of jurisprudence known as civil law or private law. Jesus is not at this point considering what a Christian should do when the criminal law has been broken. Perhaps in this regard it is significant that Jesus omits from the OT Torah quotation the actual part of the *talion* that would include the criminal angle—i.e., "life for life." These two aspects of the legal procedure were separate in the minds of the Jewish people of Jesus' day and separate here also in Jesus' mind. He does not abrogate the legal system but instead instructs his disciples how they are to surpass the Law and what their response should be when they are wronged either personally or publicly as his followers.

Turning to the second illustration we are again confronted with an apparent legal situation: "If anyone would sue you and take your coat, let him have your cloak as well" (Matt 5:40). In the first place it is not certain how the translation should read. The verb translated "sue" (*krinō*) means either to enter into a legal judgment—i.e., a trial with someone—or less formally to simply dispute, debate, quarrel with someone.[35] Since Luke reports Jesus as simply saying "from him who takes away your cloak" the interpreter might favor adopting in Matthew also this nonlegal sense of "debate" or "dispute" (Luke 6:29).[36] The point of the passage is not affected by whether this is a personal or a judicial debate.

The two words used for the garments are instructive. First, the opponent takes the less expensive "coat" or "jacket" (*chitōna*, "under-garment"). In response the disciple is to freely give up also his more expensive outer "cloak" or "overcoat" (*himation*). This outer garment or overcoat was for warmth and was so indispensable to a person in the culture of the day that the Law required that when taken as a pledge it had to be returned before nightfall (Exod 22:26-27). As in the first illustration the disciple is not only to refuse to resist the evil affront but he is also to act positively to bring benefit to his opponent.

But why should Jesus use this illustration of the taking away of a shirt in debate or trial to support his general statement that a disciple should "not resist the evil"? Why should anyone want to take away a person's "jacket" in the first place? It is difficult to establish any symbolical or

---

[34]D. Daube, *Biblical Law* (Cambridge, 1947) 114 ff. Banks likewise concludes that the principle of retribution was very much alive in the first century as a basic tenet in rabbinic teaching (*Jesus*, 199).

[35]BAG, *krinō*.

[36]On the other hand the Lukan reversal of "cloak" for "coat" in the order of the sentence suggests the order of a forceful removal of the outer cloak first, in response to which the disciple is to give also the under "coat" (or garment), whereas in Matthew the less expensive coat is taken in law settlement (?) and the disciple gives up freely the more expensive overcoat or toga.

representative meaning for the word "coat" or "jacket" (*chitōna*). It seems to refer literally to a piece of apparel sought by an opponent. Could it be that only the very poor in material goods would have nothing of more value than the clothing on their backs? May it not indirectly suggest the gospel theme of the "poor" who are poor in this world because they have taken a strong stand in identifying themselves with Jesus and his way of life? (Cf. Matt 5:3; 11:5; Phil 3:8; Heb 10:32-34; 1 Cor 4:4-13; 2 Cor 8:9; Rev 2:9.)[37] We may follow here also Jeremias' earlier suggestion that everything in the SM has presupposed the response to the gospel and the commitment to Jesus. Thus this manifestation of evil takes the form of an opponent unjustly extracting clothing from a poor disciple—poor because he is a follower of Christ and a member of his community. If this interpretation is correct, the question of all sorts of civil trials involving petty charges, claims, and so on, which do not arise directly out of the disciple's identification with Christ as a form of persecution, is not under consideration and cannot be settled by appeal to this teaching of Jesus.

Paul, however, does mention certain types of trials that were going on among the Christian members of the Corinthian Church. His advice is to the effect that such trials are altogether a "defeat" for the Christians. He suggests two ways to deal with this less-than-desirable situation. First, let the innocent, who are sued, willingly suffer loss by an out-of-court settlement so as not to drag these petty offenses before the unbelieving world in the civil courts. Second, if Christians cannot do this willingly they should allow the elders of the Church to settle the dispute rather than drag Christians into the public courts (1 Cor 6:1-8). Again as in Jesus' teaching the issues are civil matters and not criminal law. This latter point needs to be emphasized because some have alleged that Jesus' teaching, if followed literally, would undermine the whole judicial system. This would be true only in criminal cases, not in civil matters involving personal losses where the law only demands prosecution when charges are preferred by the wronged party.

In the third case or illustration that Jesus cites we have an incident involving forced transportation: "If any one forces you to go one mile, go with him two miles" (Matt 5:41).[38] A government official or soldier in the

---

[37] Jeremias, *Theology*, 108-171.

[38] The Greek for "forces you" (*angaranō*) comes from a Persian loan word meaning ᵤriginally the action of postal couriers (*angaroi*) who were permitted by Cyrus to make requisition of men, cattle or carriages from station to station for the carrying on of their journey (H. A. W. Meyer, *A Critical and Exegetical Handbook to the Gospel of Matthew*, 137). Here the sense is broadened to include any type of compulsory transportation pressed on the disciple by an official of the government or military. Josephus refers the word to compulsory transportation of military baggage (*Ant.* 13.52). See Matt 27:32 where Simon from Cyrene was compelled by the military soldiers to carry Jesus' cross. Was it already known that he was a

first century could compel (legally) any person to carry baggage or to
transport other items if he so wished. If given such an order the disciple is
not only to comply with the initial request but, as in the former examples,
he is also to respond positively by willingly (not through compulsion)
offering more service than required. As in the previous cases we may
assume that it is because the person is a follower of Christ that this special
case of compelled service comes to him in the form of persecution. When
this is not the case other considerations must impinge.

A final fourth illustration involves requests made to the disciple in the
form of begging or borrowing: "Give to him who begs from you, and do
not refuse him who would borrow from you" (Matt 5:42). In the first place
we must ask why this example is subsumed by Matthew under illustrations
of "not resisting evil." It has been argued that in the other three cases a
disciple because he is a disciple would receive the evil actions of men in the
various forms cited. But how is begging and borrowing an evil directed
toward the followers of Christ? Perhaps Luke gives us a clue. He puts the
matter of lending in the context of love for enemies: "But love your
enemies, and do good, and lend, expecting nothing in return . . . and you
will be sons of the Most High; for he is kind to the ungrateful and the
selfish" (Luke 6:35-36; see also vv 30-34). In other words there underlies
this begging and borrowing a malicious or at least a selfish motivation and
an ungrateful attitude. Could the reason the disciple as a disciple is
approached by these people be because of his loving, generous and kind
reputation? Malicious persons will come to Christians intent on exploiting
their generosity for selfish reasons. Hence they may not even have a
genuine need. The natural response would be to turn them away. But not
the Christian response. Since the Father is kind (giving benefit) to the
ungrateful and selfish, the disciple will also give to these kinds of persons
("enemies"). This is the point. The illustration is not a general principle,
encouraging a generous spirit (however Christian this may be), but the
teaching concerns our response to evil in the form of selfish requests from
people who we know are exploiting us and who will not be grateful for any
amount they receive. We are to overcome their evil by the good that we in
love show them. The illustration does not answer questions about how
often we should do this or whether we will add to a person's dereliction by
giving to him. It is simply a case in point where the disciple instead of
resisting the evil that comes to him through selfish requests responds by
willingly accepting it and positively bringing loving benefit to the one doing
the evil.

To sum up this important section on retaliation (Matt 5:38-42) the
following may be noted. The *KJV* rendering of the general principle in

---

follower of Christ, and was he compelled because of his identification with Christ?
Cf. Rom 16:13 and Mark 15:21.

v 39, "Do not resist evil," comes closest to the intended sense than some
other translations (although "wicked men" is also acceptable). The disciple
is confronted with the manifestation of evil in various forms of persecution.
He is not to resist the evil acts done to him. What it actually means to "not
resist evil" is elucidated by four culturally specific illustrations.

The observation of Jeremias has been adopted to the effect that the
teaching of Jesus in the SM is directed to Christians as disciples of Christ.
Therefore the evil acts done to them in the context are acts directed at them
because they are his disciples. They are not simply general evils visited
upon us because we are men in the midst of unjust men and societies.
Christians are treated unjustly, as was Jesus, because of their Christian
confession. As such the acts take on the form of persecution. Under these
conditions how is the disciple to respond? The four illustrations of the
general principle are taken from various areas of life, involve different
manifestations of this kind of evil and all point to the same answer. The
believer is to confront such evils in a twofold manner: (1) by not pressing
his rights or attempting retribution, and (2) by showing beneficial love by
doing good to the one who manifests such evil.

By not seeking financial or other compensation (retribution) for insults
directed to them because they are Christians and by offering themselves
instead for further insults, disciples will show that they are following
Christ's commands—i.e., that they are truly his willing servants. When a
disciple is unjustly forced to relinquish his suit of clothes he is not to seek
redress for the wrong but instead is to freely give his adversary the more
indispensable outer toga or overcoat. When the disciple, because he is a
disciple of Christ, is persecuted by a government official or soldier who
requires him to transport something for him he is not to refuse the demand,
and furthermore by transporting the person or thing more than the
required distance he is to show beneficial love. By giving and lending to
selfish persons intent on exploiting our Christian generosity because we are
disciples of Christ we will not only be refusing to resist evil but we will
also manifest beneficial love to those who seek to do this evil toward us
because we belong to Christ.

If we should ask why Christ asks us to so respond to evil or whether
such action on our part will really help or compound the problem, we must
turn elsewhere in the NT for answers. It is outside the limits of this
discussion to do more than barely to suggest an answer. Paul in Rom
12:14-21 seems to offer precisely the same exhortations as Jesus: "Bless
those who persecute you. . . . Repay no one evil for evil. . . . Never avenge
yourselves. . . . If your enemy is hungry, feed him. . . . Do not be overcome
by evil, but overcome evil with good." But how will this action affect the
evil perpetrator? Paul actually does not discuss the problem. He is more
interested in the Christian stance of "servanthood" in the world as a witness
to Jesus than the possible pragmatic effects in terms of a deterrent to evil.

Such a servanthood stance creates a witness of love and forgiveness that characterizes Christ himself (cf. John 8:1-11). This way stands over against the way of one "who stands on his rights and honor instead of humiliating himself before his fellow-man."[39]

Only in one bare statement taken from the OT is there a suggestion as to the reason for such Christian response: "If your enemy is hungry, feed him . . . for by so doing you will heap burning coals upon his head" (Rom 12:20 quoting Prov 25:21-22). While it is possible to undersand the burning coals as a reference to the judgment of the evildoer, it is better to understand the figure to refer to the burning conviction of the conscience that may take place in the offender when he confronts love instead of retaliation. Such a person will be confronted with Christ in the action of the believer, and such a confrontation will go further to promote the will of God in society than retaliation for the wrong. Yet Paul recognizes that this form of loving response exists alongside of and not as a replacement for civil government and its retaliation on criminal offenders (Rom 13:1 ff.). Is this not true also for Jesus? (Cf. Matt 21:21; John 19:11.) And Peter as well? (Cf. 1 Pet 2:21-23; 3:9, 16.)

Under the OT Torah teaching the Israelite was permitted to redress wrongs done against him by his personal enemies. But under the new law of the kingdom of God the Christian is not to seek compensation for evil directed to him in any manner that involves visiting a like evil in return. Again the teaching of Jesus surpasses and again in this case effectively nullifies the older legislation.[40]

III. Conclusion

Despite the difficulty of reaching any acceptable conclusion to the problems this chapter addresses, it may be possible to tender several brief summary statements.

1. The ethic of Jesus develops legitimately out of the Mosaic tradition and is not in essential disagreement with it—there is continuity with the old.

2. Jesus' ethic fulfills or surpasses the Mosaic ethical tradition and thereby radically transcends the old—there is discontinuity with Moses and the Prophets. Something new has come with Christ.

3. The two basic assumptions of the Reformers (Luther and Calvin) are exegetically indefensible—i.e., (1) God's Law cannot be modified, and

[39] Daube, *Rabbinic*, 258.

[40] To these three specific abrogations could also be added Jesus' teaching about defilement from unclean foods: "Thus he declared all foods clean" (Mark 7:19), a clear case of abrogation of the old. Also we should note Jesus' statement about the relationship of the kingdom of God he was inaugurating to the old order in Matt 11:13: "For all the Prophets and the Law prophesied until John."

therefore the Law of Moses cannot be modified—there is no progress in moral revelation; and (2) Jesus was not a new Lawgiver.[41]

4. Anabaptist literalism, while rightly stressing discontinuity, yet without regard to a more precise hermeneutic, has produced an unwarranted absolutism that has restricted and at times misdirected Christian ethical action.

5. A proper grasp of both the aspect of continuity with the old and an appreciation for discontinuity with Moses and the Prophets will provide a more adequate foundation for Christian theological ethics.

6. The final authority for Christian ethics is not the Torah or even the Prophets but Jesus and the Holy Spirit.[42] Perhaps the concluding summary of Banks' impressive study may serve also as a fitting conclusion to this chapter's aims:

> In the passages with which we have had to deal, Jesus appears as "the man who fits no formula", whether Jewish or modern. It has been the contention of this study that the same may be said of his teaching. This has no counterpart in the traditions of the Old Testament and the inter-testamentary literature and has no parallel in the teaching of the Jewish parties of the time. As we have seen, it no less calls into question the emphasis that has been placed upon the Natural Law, Decalogue and love-commandment as foundations for ethics in much Christian moral instruction. The teaching of Jesus is at once more radical and more complex than such presentations of it have been willing to allow. In view of this fact, it still has something to contribute to contemporary ethical discussion, including contemporary Christian ethical discussion, for the full potential of his insight into the human situation and the behaviour that should characterise it has yet to come into its own, and the basic relevance of his call to discipleship to even the most modern of modern men has still to be presented in more meaningful terms. Certainly his teaching

[41]Cf. W. D. Davies, *The Sermon on the Mount* (Cambridge, 1966) 149 ff. Davies argues that indeed Matthew has presented Jesus as a second Moses, a new Lawgiver. He also argues that this presentation of Jesus was aided by certain forces at work in the contemporary Jewish communities. We need not follow Davies in separating the mind of Matthew from that of Jesus to appreciate his careful scholarship. One could also refer to Matt 7:28-29 as an indication of the authority of Christ not only as an interpreter of Torah but also as a legislator of a new ethic: "The crowds were astonished at his teaching, for he taught them as one who had authority and not as their scribes." Also Jesus' new commandment highlights this newness of the ethic of Jesus (John 13:34).

Banks rightly argues against the "new Torah" view of Jesus' teaching by stressing that the Law must be seen in its relationship to Jesus and not Jesus in his relationship to the Law. He is the One to whom all attention must be directed (*Jesus*, 226).

[42]C. F. D. Moule, "Important Moral Issues, Prolegomena: The New Testament and Moral Decisions," *ExpTim* (September 1963) 370-373.

questions the legitimacy of that polarity between law and love, order and freedom that is so widely presupposed in much contemporary secular and Christian thought.[43]

The Promise of God and the Outpouring of the Holy Spirit: Joel 2:28-32 and Acts 2:16-21

Walter C. Kaiser, Jr.

E VANGELICAL students of Scripture have experienced such unusual amounts of rapprochement in recent years that many of the older distinctions made between various theological systems now need heavy qualification or major readjustment. As a parade example one could cite recent writings and the revival of interest in the theology of the land of Israel[1] or the present participation of the Church in the new covenant made with a future national Israel.[2] One could only hope that this spirit of earnest Bible study and evangelical collegiality might continue.

Another area where some new work in exegetical and Biblical theology could contribute to this new rapprochement is Peter's use of Joel 2:28-32 in his Pentecost speech. Did he mean to say that Pentecost fulfilled Joel's prophecy or merely illustrated it? Did Joel intend that the scope of his prophecy should include Gentiles as well as Jews? At what time did Joel believe that his prophecy would be accomplished? And what would the results of the outpouring of the Spirit be? Were all the events in Joel 2:28-32 to be literally fulfilled, or were some to be realized figuratively? But before these issues can be considered, a word must be said about the interpretation of prophetic literature.

I. Hermeneutics and Prophecy

1. *The issues.* Several interpretive issues have perennially confronted the Church in her use of the prophetic statements in Scripture. (1) There is the concept of prophetic perspective, which deals with the question of the time relationships between the original predictive word and the future events they signaled. Was the prophet aware of a time lapse between his

---

[1]For example see W. Brueggemann, *The Theology of the Land* (Richmond: John Knox, 1977); H. Berkhof, *Christ the Meaning of History* (Richmond: John Knox, 1966), esp. pp. 134-179.

[2]Notice that many recent dispensational writers affirm that there is one new covenant, not two; e.g. R. L. Saucy, *The Church in God's Program* (Chicago: Moody, 1972) 77-81.

ultimate hope and his present realizations? (2) There is the issue of prophetic cognizance of the material the prophet wrote. Did the human recipients of God's revelation understand less than what they wrote? Or were they aware only of the immediate application of their words? Did they seldom if ever know what was the messianic or eschatological significance of their words about the future? (3) Prophetic fulfillment is likewise another important aspect of this topic. Did the words of the prophets receive partial fulfillment, complete fulfillment, double fulfillment, or continuous fulfillment? Such are some of the key issues demanding good answers if evangelicals are to make progress in their hermeneutical analyses of prophetic statements.

2. *Generic predictions.* A basic factor to deal with in Biblical prophecy is the phenomenon of prophetic foreshortening. The perspective of the prophet in certain predictive passages often simultaneously included two or more events that were separated from the time of their fulfillment, yet there often was no indication of a time lapse between these various fulfillments in the predictive word as they were originally given.

How then shall we handle this perspective? It is best to note that this is what may be termed a "generic prediction."

> A generic prediction is one which regards an event as occurring in a series of parts, separated by intervals, and expresses itself in language that may apply indifferently to the nearest part, or to the remoter parts, or to the whole—in other words, a prediction which, in applying to the whole of a complex event, also applies to some of its parts.[3]

The fundamental idea here is that many prophecies begin with a word that ushers in not just a climactic fulfillment but a series of events, all of which participate in and lead up to that climactic or ultimate event in a protracted series that belong together as a unit because of their corporate solidarity. In this way, the whole set of events makes up one collective totality and constitutes only one idea even though the events may be spread over a large segment of history by the deliberate plan of God. The important point to observe, however, is that all of the parts belong to a single whole. They are generically related to each other by some identifiable wholeness.

3. *The day of the Lord.* One prominent example of this common phenomenon in the OT is the "day of Yahweh." Consistently in all the prophets this day is viewed as one day, yet it is obviously a collective event as seen from this threefold dilemma: (1) The day of Yahweh is "near" and "at hand" (Obad 15; Joel 1:15; 2:1; Isa 13:6; Zeph 1:7, 14; Ezek 30:3), and yet these same prophets who announced the identical message about the

---

[3]W. J. Beecher, *The Prophets and the Promise* (Grand Rapids: Baker, 1975) 130.

imminence of that day also spanned a period of four centuries.[4] (2) These prophets also identified different immediate events as the "day of the Lord." For Obadiah it was the destruction of Edom, for Joel it was a contemporary locust plague, and Zephaniah held that it was the pending destruction of Jerusalem in 586 B.C. Were they all correct? (3) Nevertheless the "day of the Lord" also was for each of those five prophets a future day. It was to be the day when the Lord of hosts "destroys the whole earth" (Isa 13:5), a day when he will reign as "King over all the earth" (Zech 14:1, 8-9), a day when "the elements will be dissolved . . . and the earth and the works that are in it will be laid bare" (2 Pet 3:10) as well as a day of salvation and deliverance for all who would but call on the name of the Lord (Joel 2:32).

The only solution to this three-way puzzle is to view the "day of Yahweh" as a generic or collective event in which are gathered all the antecedent historical episodes of judgment and salvation along with the future grand finale and climactic event in the whole series. Thus God's previous interventions into history were but previews, samples, down payments and guarantees for his final visitation in connection with the second advent of Christ.

4. *The prophets' meaning and understanding*. But did the prophets understand and intend to convey such collectivity? Were they aware that they were contributing to a larger whole when they also realized some of the immediate fulfillments of their prophecies? Indeed they were. This prophetic concept both as applied to the people (e.g. "seed") and to many events such as the "day of the Lord" was fairly common to the Hebrew mind. The frequent interchange between singular and plural pronouns in the Hebrew text when the antecedent was Judah/Ephraim or Jacob/Israel is one obvious witness to the practice. But even more directly the prophets would often announce an event as being both "near" (e.g. Joel 1:15; 2:1) and also quite removed in the future (e.g. 3:14) all in one and the same breath.

Even when the prophets spoke of the Messiah and of those of us in the Christian era who were to believe they were well aware of the particular contribution they were making by the revelation of God even if the total subject matter of the Messiah and the Church remained beyond their abilities. What they wrote they spoke accurately and knowingly, but they did not write and know comprehensively. For this bold claim we have the

---

[4]Generally, conservatives regard Obadiah and Joel as ninth-century B.C. writers, Isaiah as eighth-century, Zephaniah as seventh-century and Ezekiel as sixth-century. For an early dissenting view on Joel see G. B. Gray, "The Parallel Passages in 'Joel' in Their Bearing on the Question of Date," *The Expositor*, fourth series, 8 (1893) 208-225. On the day of the Lord see R. W. Klein, "The Day of the Lord," *CTM* 39 (1968) 517-525, esp. p. 521; J. Bourke, "Le Jour de Yahvé dans Joël," *RB* 66 (1959) 5-31, 191-212.

authoritative declaration of 1 Pet 1:10-12. There Peter asserted that the prophets were aware of five facts. They knew they were writing about (1) Messiah, (2) Messiah's sufferings for us, (3) Messiah's triumphant kingly glory, (4) the sequence of suffering first and then glory, and (5) the fact that we Christians were to share in the things they were writing to Israel.

Thus we would conclude that the truth-intention of the prophet was always singular and never double or multiple in sense. Yet by design that same word often embraced and encompassed an extended period of time by describing protracted events, giving characteristics that belonged to several periods of time, or, in the messianic line, it would link a whole string of persons who in their office, function and person pointed to the last one in the series who shared at least some of the identical features specifically prophesied about them.

We believe this is exactly the perspective Joel had when he announced the connection between the locust-plague-induced revival with its attendant resumption of the much-needed rain for the crops and the imminent appearance of the day of the Lord with its constituent parts of judgment and salvation.

It is our hope that we may offer some help to God's people on these issues. It is an added pleasure to contribute this essay to a volume that honors Samuel Schultz, my first teacher in the study of the OT texts.

II. JOEL 2:28-32 [HEBREW 3:1-5]

1. *The significance of the passage.* Varying estimates have been placed on the meaning of Joel's prophecy of the outpouring of the Holy Spirit and its connection with the event of Pentecost in Acts 2. For a significant number of Biblical interpreters the blessings predicted in these five verses of Joel refer in their entirety only to a future millennial kingdom. Thus Peter's citation of these verses on the day of Pentecost was merely used as an illustration of his point. They were not, according to this recent popular view, cited in any sense as a fulfillment.[5] While the point is usually granted

---

[5]"Clearly Joel's prophecy was not fulfilled at Pentecost. . . . The events prophesied by Joel simply did not come to pass" (C. C. Ryrie, "The Significance of Pentecost," *BSac* 112 [1955] 334). Likewise M. F. Unger opined, "It seems quite obvious that Peter did not quote Joel's prophecy in the sense of its fulfillment in the events of Pentecost, but purely as a prophetic illustration of those events. . . . Peter's phraseology 'this is that' means nothing more than 'this is [an illustration of] that which was spoken by the prophet Joel'" ("The Significance of Pentecost," *BSac* 122 [1965] 176-177). C. L. Feinberg also called it an "illustration" (*Joel, Amos, Obadiah* [New York: American Board of Missions to the Jews, 1948] 29). However, a quiet change is underfoot even in this school of interpretation as can be seen in W. K. Price, *The Prophet Joel and the Day of the Lord* (Chicago: Moody, 1976) 66: "Pentecost fulfills Joel's prediction about the coming of the Spirit. It does not

by this interpretation that there is a "close similarity"[6] between Joel's prophecy and the marvelous outpouring of the Holy Spirit on the day of Pentecost, the usage of the OT Scriptures at this juncture in Peter's message is "primarily homiletical"[7] and not theological argumentation.

However, the hermeneutical problems encountered in this passage are very similar to those faced in the use of the new covenant passage (Jer 31:31-34) in the book of Hebrews. For while the address of Jeremiah's word is distinctively to the "house of Israel and the house of Judah" (Jer 31:31; Heb 8:8), still it is also found to be a fitting prediction of the NT age and the Church.[8] So serious was this problem that many championed the view for a while that there were two new covenants—one for Israel and one for the Church. Fortunately, few hold to this view anymore.

Accordingly, the fact that Joel 2:30-31 predicted that there would be world- and cosmic-shaking events in connection with the day of the Lord need be no more of a detraction from the view that the day of Pentecost was at least a partial fulfillment to this prophecy than the fact that the new covenant also includes the provision for a future restoration of Israel to her land (Romans 11, esp. v 27). Meanwhile it is also affirmed that we already are ministers of the new covenant and that we now participate in some of its benefits.

Neither may it be argued that the introductory formula[9] of Peter is wrong if he had in mind any kind of fulfillment logic. Why is it that "this is that" cannot mean this Pentecostal event is the fulfillment of that word predicted by Joel? The truth of the matter is that there is no single formula[10] used consistently in Acts or elsewhere in the NT for that matter.

Nor can it be successfully argued that Joel's prophecy cannot be fulfilled "until Israel is restored to her land, converted and enjoying the presence of the Lord in her midst (Joel 2:26-28) [sic]."[11] To insist on these criteria would logically demand that the new covenant's current benefits to the Church likewise be rescinded until Israel is restored to her land. There was no way around it: "This" outpouring of the Holy Spirit on the day of

---

exhaust it, however." It must also be noted that J. F. Walvoord wrote the introduction for this book.

[6]Unger, "Significance," 176.

[7]Ryrie, "Significance," 334.

[8]See W. C. Kaiser, Jr., "The Old Promise and the New Covenant," *JETS* 15 (1972) 11-23.

[9]Ryrie, "Significance," 334.

[10]See W. C. Kaiser, Jr., "The Davidic Promise and The Inclusion of the Gentiles (Amos 9:9-15 and Acts 15:13-18): A Test Passage for Theological Systems," *JETS* 20 (1977) 106-107. Also see the references there to additional literature.

[11]Ryrie, "Significance," 334.

Pentecost "is that" eschatological outpouring of the Holy Spirit predicted by Joel centuries before.

However, already that "day of the Lord," which some would deny to Peter, had come as a destruction from the Lord (Joel 1:15; 2:1). The dark clouds of locusts (whose Latin name, incidentally, means "burners of the land") had come as a flame and an invading army (2:2-11). And if that was a preview of the ultimate and final day of the Lord, so also was the repentance of the people a foretaste of the climactic revival and the healing of the land. Why could not Peter's experience of the outpouring of the Holy Spirit on the day of Pentecost likewise be a foretaste of God's ultimate flood of the Holy Spirit?

2. *The organization of the book of Joel.* The message of Joel revolves around the pivot verse of Joel 2:18. Prior to that verse Joel had issued two separate calls for Israel to repent (1:13-14; 2:12-17). Only by turning from her sin in repentance could Israel begin to experience the blessing of God again. Only then would her land be healed.

Thus when Joel 2:18 suddenly announced in the past tense[12] that the Lord "was jealous," "had pity," "answered" and "said," we may be sure that the people did repent. That then is the reason why 2:19-27 gave the immediate and temporal effects of this repentance while 2:28-32 went on to list the distant future and more spiritual results of God's response to the people's repentance.

3. *The shape of Joel 2:28-32 [Hebrew 3:1-5].* This portion of Joel's prophecy is divided into three sections, each section beginning with a Hebrew verb form called a converted perfect tense.[13] Thus the three sections are: 28-29, 30-31, and 32. The first and third sections employ the literary device known as inclusio—i.e., the section is, as it were, bracketed by a repeated clause or phrase coming at the beginning and the end of the section. Verses 28a and 29b both begin and end the section with "I will pour out my Spirit" while v 32, the third section, begins and ends with the almost identical "who call on the name of the LORD" and "whom the LORD calls."

Such an analysis is sufficient to suggest that there are three distinct movements or parts to the passage. Two of these sections also conclude with a reference to the fact that the events described in them will take place

---

[12]Those translations (e.g. *KJV, NIV, NASB*) that fail to translate the *waw*-conversive with the imperfect tense of the verb as a narrative past tense are in error. Whatever else remains ambiguous about the Hebrew verb, this one form is constant and without any variation.

[13]The three verbs are wᵉhāyâ (v 28), wᵉnātattî (v 30) and wᵉhāyâ (v 32). This division is the same as L. C. Allen, *The Books of Joel, Obadiah, Jonah, and Micah* (Grand Rapids: Eerdmans, 1976) 97.

"in those days"[14] (Joel 2:29) or "before[15] the great and terrible day of the LORD comes" (2:31). The exegetical problem would appear to be the temporal relationship between the three parts.

4. *The temporal setting for the text.* But before the internal relationships are established it is necessary to determine how the entire block of vv 28-32 is related to the preceding and following context. The phrase "after this" in v 28 [Hebrew 3:1] does not appear in and of itself to be an eschatological expression even though the passage clearly does include at least two such formulae—namely, "in those days" (v 29 [Hebrew 3:2]) and "before the great and terrible day of the LORD comes" (v 31 [Hebrew 3:4]). Rather Joel intended to show that the promises of vv 28-32 would come after those immediate and material blessings promised in vv 19-27.

The key temporal term in vv 19-27 is found in v 23: "in the first [act of blessing?]" (*bārîʾšôn*). The Lord God would send both the autumn and spring rains in this his first act of blessing. Thus the pastures, the fields, the trees and the vines would thrive once again as God revived the land that had just been decimated by the locust invasion and the accompanying drought.[16]

Then a second, subsequent act would come "afterward" or "after this": a shower of natural rain. But the text does not say how long after that first act. Thus the text clearly sets apart two distinct blessings in a clear order of

---

[14]While the "day of the Lord" is not formally linked with "that day," "those days" or the "latter days," Deut 31:17-18 does connect God's coming judgment with "that day" to come. See W. C. Kaiser, Jr., *Toward an Old Testament Theology* (Grand Rapids: Zondervan, 1978) 186, 188-191. G. E. Ladd, *A Theology of the New Testament* (Grand Rapids: Eerdmans, 1974) 344, has created an unnecessary problem when he has Peter separating the "last days" from the "day of the Lord" and "re-interpreting" them so that they could appear in history rather than the consummation. Ladd misunderstands the OT prophetic perspective we have explained above.

[15]A phrase repeated verbatim in Mal 4:5 [Hebrew 3:23].

[16]It is impossible to enter into the question of the translation of *hammôreh liṣʿdāqâ* of v 23. The suggested translations are almost unlimited: "rain at the proper time" (H. Ringgren, *Israelite Religion*, 83); "rain in abundance" (M. Dahood, *Psalms I*, 146); "the autumn rain in token of covenant harmony" (Allen, *Joel*, 86); "rain according to what is fit" (Calvin); "rain moderately" (*KJV*); "rain in just measure" (*RV*); "rain in due measure" (*NEB*); "rain amply" (Moffatt); "teacher for righteousness" (*NIV*). This last suggestion has much to commend it. See Prov 5:13; 2 Chr 15:3; 2 Kgs 17:28; Job 36:22. Note that the messianic King who brings "righteousness" to his people gives blessings to his country "like rain falling on the mown grass, like showers that drip on the earth" (Ps 72:6). See C. Roth, "The Teacher of Righteousness and the Prophecy of Joel," *VT* 13 (1963) 91-95; J. Weingreen, "The Title *Moreh Ṣedek*," *JSS* 6 (1961) 162-174; G. W. Ahlström, *Joel and the Temple Cult of Jerusalem, VTSup* 21 (1971) 98-110.

appearance, yet it refrained from telling us the time that would intervene
between the two.

One might fairly conclude that the second blessing (vv 28-32) was
more intimately tied to God's distant future work, since vv 29 and 31 used
the formulae of the day of the Lord and the passage was so closely joined
to the eschatological events of the last chapter of Joel where God would
regather Judah and judge all the nations of the earth for scattering Israel
and partitioning her land (3:1-8 [Hebrew 4:1-8]). However, even while
making this strong tie with the events of the second coming we must not
refuse on basic principles to allow any fulfillments of this word in the
Christian era any more than we have for a prophecy like Jeremiah's new
covenant with the house of Israel and the house of Judah.

In fact Peter introduced his famous "this is that" reference to Joel
2:28-32 with a new temporal clause for Joel's "after this": "It shall come to
pass in the last days, says God." For the NT writers the Church already
was in the "last days." Heb 1:2 is one good example of this declaration:
God had spoken to the NT saints "in these last days" in his Son Jesus. Thus
the last days had broken in upon the Church, but they were only a sample,
an "earnest," a foretaste of what the "age to come" would be like in all its
fullness when Christ returned a second time. We conclude then that
nothing in the temporal formulae of this passage prejudices us against the
use of this passage or finding its partial fulfillment[17] in the early Church
and that nothing limits this passage to the total fulfillment at Pentecost
apart from any second advent realizations. For Peter specifically the event
he experienced inaugurated the last days and was itself part and parcel of
the final consummation.

5. *The outpouring of God's Spirit.* Here is the heart of the matter.
Three basic items need to be noted here: (1) the distinctiveness of this
"outpouring" of the Spirit; (2) the identity of the "all flesh" on whom the
Spirit would come; and (3) the results of this outpouring.

Never had an individual in the OT been completely without the aid
and work of the Holy Spirit. Certainly Jesus held that the subjects of the
new birth and the special work of the Holy Spirit in the gift of salvation
were not new or inaccessible doctrines to OT men and women before the
cross. In fact he marveled that Nicodemus could have been a teacher in
Israel and still have been so totally unaware of this fact (John 3:10). Thus if
salvation is not of works so that no man or woman ever could boast and is
a gift of God to all who ever believed so that it might always forever be by

---

[17]See the fine statement by Price, *Prophet*, 65-66: "Therefore, Joel's prediction
has *initial* fulfillment at Pentecost, *continuous* fulfillment during the Church age,
and *ultimate* fulfillment at the second coming of Christ" (italics his).

grace (Eph 2:8), then OT saints were indeed regenerated by the Holy Spirit.[18]

Likewise John 14:17 is especially important, for it affirms that our Lord's disciples already had known the "Spirit of truth" because he was living "with" them and he was already "in" them. The prepositions are *para*, "with," the same word used in John 14:23 of the Father and the Son's abiding in the disciples—a nonfluctuating relationship,[19] and *en*, "in," with a present tense verb *estai*, "is" (rather than "will be" as in *RSV*, *NASB* and *NIV*).

However, there are a number of NT passages that would seem to suggest that the Holy Spirit had not yet been given to believers even during our Lord's earthly ministry. He must come at Pentecost (John 7:37-39; 14:16; 16:7-11; Acts 1:4-8; 11:15-17; 15:8). We have deliberately deleted from this list John 14:25-26; 15:26-27; 16:12-15, for these promises of the Holy Spirit's coming were solely directed to those disciples whose distinctive work it would be to write the NT. The Spirit would "bring to their remembrance all that [Jesus] had said," and they would be witnesses to Christ since they "had been with [him] from the beginning [of his earthly ministry]". The disciples would teach doctrine ("what is mine"), future events and past deeds. Thus only these men were promised the Spirit's leading them into revelational truth.[20]

Even allowing for these exemptions, how shall we explain the apparent tension between these two sets of texts on the Holy Spirit? Had the Holy Spirit been given or had he not? Was Pentecost necessary or was it not?

The answer is similar to one given for the necessity of the death of Christ. Men were truly forgiven and made part of the people of God in the OT on the basis of God's promise to send the Suffering Servant. If Christ had not given his life as a ransom and been raised from the dead, then all the OT saints would have believed in vain. Likewise, had the Holy Spirit not come visibly at Pentecost with all its evidential value, then the previous ministry of the Holy Spirit in the lives of individuals would also have been in vain. Just as Passover is linked to the "Feast of Weeks" (Exod 34:22; Lev

[18]G. W. Grogan argues in "The Experience of Salvation in the Old and New Testaments," *Vox Evangelica* 5 (1967) 13, that "the same Spirit of faith" in 2 Cor 4:13 means that Paul claims that our faith is the product of the same Holy Spirit who was at work in the author of Ps 116:10 whence he derived the quotation in 2 Cor 4:13.

[19]See ibid. We have developed this point in our article, "The Single Intent of Scripture," *Evangelical Roots* (ed. K. Kantzer; Nashville: Nelson, 1978) 133-134.

[20]This should not be viewed as restricting the meaning of "you" too severely as if it would defeat the universal reference of "you" in the great commission of Matt 28:18-20, for 28:20 clearly has the broader idea in mind when it says, "Lo, I am with you always, even to the end of the world."

23:15-21), so the cross is linked to Pentecost. Thus Goodwin correctly commented: "[The Holy Spirit] must have a coming in state, in solemn and visible manner, accompanied with visible effects as well as Christ had."[21] This we believe to be one of the main reasons for emphasizing the necessity of the Holy Spirit's coming at Pentecost: He must come visibly as an exhibition that all who had previously depended on the ministry of the Holy Spirit were totally vindicated just as those who had depended on the future death of Christ.

Moreover, what had now happened at Pentecost was both climactic and effusive. This new, outward, evidential coming of the Holy Spirit would be a downpour—a word conveying abundance in contrast with the previous scarcity. Thus Joel had carefully selected the verb meaning to "pour out."[22] This verb easily links up with the one Jesus would use: the "rivers of living water" that would come on all who believed (John 7:38-39)—indeed the very baptism of the Holy Spirit (Matt 3:11; Mark 1:8; Luke 3:16-17; Acts 1:5; 8:15-17; 11:16). If this connection is correct, as we believe it is, then there was something additional and unique about this ministry of the Holy Spirit that first occurred at Pentecost, Samaria and Caesarea. Now a believer was not only regenerated and indwelt to some degree by the Holy Spirit but, beginning at Pentecost and following, all who believed were simultaneously baptized by the Holy Spirit and made part of the one body (1 Cor 12:13).[23]

If Joel was written in the ninth century, then his word was the basic teaching passage on the coming advent of the outpouring of the Holy Spirit and the forerunner of those in Isaiah and Ezekiel. The eighth-century prophet Isaiah affirmed the same word: "[Jerusalem would be deserted] until the Spirit is poured on us from on high and the wilderness becomes a fertile field" (32:15). "I will pour out my Spirit on your seed and my blessings on your descendants" (44:3).[24] Likewise the sixth-century Ezekiel also took up the same theme of the outpouring and linked it with Israel's restoration to the land of promise as had Isaiah: "I will gather them to their own land . . . for I will pour out my Spirit on the house of Israel" (39:28-29). Yet in three other passages Ezekiel does not use the verb "to pour" but

---

[21]T. Goodwin, *Works* (Edinburgh: 1861), 6. 8, as cited by G. Smeaton, *The Doctrine of the Holy Spirit* (London: 1958) 49, and Grogan, "Experience," 14.

[22]There are five Hebrew verbs for "pouring out": *nātak, nāsak, nābaᶜ, yāṣaq*, and the one used here (*šāpak*). Also note the apocryphal work, Enoch 62:2: "The Spirit of righteousness has been poured out on him [i.e., Messiah]." See also F. F. Bruce, "The Holy Spirit in the Qumran Texts," *ALUOS* (Leiden: Brill, 1969) 53.

[23]Yet even here there were careful anticipations of the fact that Christ is over his house, the one in which Moses was faithful, the same house we are in if we hold on to our courage and our hope (Heb 3:2-6).

[24]The other Isaianic references to the Spirit and the coming Servant of the Lord are slightly different in that he has the Spirit "put on" him (42:1; 59:21; 61:1).

the verb "to put": "I will give them one heart and I will put a new Spirit in them" (11:18-19); "I will give you a new heart and put a new Spirit in you. . . . I will put my Spirit in you . . . and you shall dwell in the land that I gave to your fathers; and you shall be my people and I will be your God" (36:26-28); "I will bring you back to the land of Israel. . . . I will put my Spirit in you and you will live" (37:12-14).

Clearly, then, the ultimate and final downpour will still take place in the land in connection with the future restoration of Israel to the land in that complex of events belonging to the second coming of our Lord—a downpour of the Holy Spirit indeed.

But who will the recipients of this downpour be? Joel had it fall on "all flesh." This expression, *kol bāśār*, appears 32 times in the OT outside of Joel. In 23 of these occurrences the expression refers to Gentiles alone. For example, in four of these 23 instances it is used as a synonym for the "nations" (Deut 5:26; Isa 49:26; 66:16; Zech 2:13). Certainly the preponderance of usage favors the meaning of "all mankind"[25] without distinction of race, sex or age. Thus Isa 40:5-6 declared that "all flesh" will see the glory of the Lord. The extent of this expression had been set as early as Gen 6:13. There God had told Noah that he was going to put an end to "all flesh" because of the violence they had done on the earth.

Seldom if ever may "all flesh" be reserved and restricted to all Israel. The two passages cited for this exclusive meaning both turn out to be larger references than what had at first been assumed. Ps 65:2, "to thee shall all flesh come," refers also to Gentiles since v 5 claims that this offer is the "hope of all the ends of the earth" (see also Isa 66:23; cf. 66:20). Likewise Ps 136:25, "who gives food to all flesh," is also universal in its scope as can be seen from the identical sentiment in Ps 104:27; 145:9.

But what about Joel's use of this expression? He explained what he meant by the term by first listing sons, daughters, old men, young men. Then by way of surprise the prophet abruptly declared "and also" or "and even" (*wᵉgam*) menservants and maidservants would receive the Spirit of God. It is this epexegetical addition that was marked by the "and even" phrase that forces the interpreter to acknowledge that Joel had "all mankind" in mind here. Even the Gentile slaves[26] in the Jewish households would benefit in this outpouring. Thus the Jews were not the only ones fit to receive this visitation of God's Spirit (as Rabbi Ibn Ezra had claimed) but literally "all mankind."

[25]For the most recent word study on this expression see A. R. Hulst, "*Kol baśar*. . . ," *Studies in the Book of Genesis*, OTS 12 (1958) 47-49. Many recent commentators, however, unnecessarily restrict this phrase in Joel to Israel.

[26]The LXX translators apparently could not believe their eyes, so they deliberately changed the servants of men into servants of God by rendering "my servants" and "my handmaids."

The NT therefore was once again on the mark when it also invited the Gentiles to receive the gift of the Holy Spirit (Acts 2:38). The reason was obvious: The promise was for Israel and for "all who are afar off"[27] (*pasin tois eis makran*; Acts 2:39). To describe someone as belonging to "those who were afar off" was merely a circumlocution for saying "Gentiles." This is plain from Paul's usage in Eph 2:13, 17: Christ has abolished the wall of partition between Jew and Gentile and has brought "those who once were afar off" (or "far away") into the commonwealth of Israel and the covenants of promise. And Acts 10:45 is conclusive, showing that God had intended that the gift of the Holy Spirit would also be "poured out even on the Gentiles."

Thus this gift would be given without regard to age (old men, young men), sex (sons, daughters), social rank or race: It would provide for both the Gentile servants and handmaids of the Jewish employers as well as their owners.

Joel must have startled his audience both by his reference to the Gentiles and to women. Yet this is not to say that they were totally unprepared for this truth. Had not Moses prayed, "I wish that all the LORD's people were prophets and that the LORD would put his Spirit on [all of] them" (Num 11:29)? And that was exactly what was to be inaugurated at Pentecost but totally realized in the day of the Lord.

Finally, we may ask, what were the results of this outpouring of the Holy Spirit? Put in the most succinct terms they were these: Everyone would immediately and personally know the Lord. There would no longer be a need for someone to teach each child of God. In this sense Joel explains the means (the outpouring of the Holy Spirit) by which Jeremiah's later revealed fact of the new covenant would be implemented (similarly, Jer 31:34: "they will all know me, from the least to the greatest"). Heretofore it took the mediation of a prophet to have God revealed to the people (Num 12:6) or a priest to have the people represented to God (8:15-19). But now everyone, regardless of age, sex or social status, would be able to prophesy, dream dreams and see visions.

True, there were OT examples of the Holy Spirit coming on almost every one of the categories Joel mentions.[28] There were sons (Bezalel, son of Uri; Exod 31:2-3), daughters (Deborah, Judges 4-5; Huldah, 2 Kgs 22:14), old men (Moses was 120 years old when he wrote Deuteronomy), young men (young Jeremiah, Jer 1:6; young Daniel, Daniel 1), and menservants (perhaps the messengers of Saul, 1 Sam 19:20-23). But nowhere did any of these receive the Holy Spirit in such profusion as was now promised in this outpouring.

[27]For a study of this expression see H. Preisker, "*makran*," *TDNT* 4 (1967) 373-374. He notes how Eph 2:17 sets Isa 57:19 in the context of salvation history with a similar phrase for the Gentiles.

[28]These were pointed out to me by my student Keith Ghormley.

However, some results promised by Joel did not take place at Pentecost, Samaria, Caesarea or anywhere else as yet. Especially troublesome to many interpreters is that second or middle section of Joel's prophecy, vv 30-31. Even though some interpreters[29] have attempted to show that God did fulfill his promise to put "wonders in the heavens and on the earth" ("blood, fire, billows of smoke, the sun turned to darkness, the moon to blood") in his first advent, the argument is not very convincing. Hermeneutical talk about figurative language must be stretched to the breaking point (all without any of the requisite textual clues that we are dealing with such figures), or certain phrases must be seized while others are conveniently dropped from the discussion. So for some the darkness is easily related to the hours Christ spent on the cross. But what shall we say of the "moon being turned into blood" or the "billows of smoke"?

Likewise we also find unsatisfactory the conclusion that "what is recorded in Acts 2:19-20 [=Joel 2:30-31] is simply a connecting link between two key points in his argument"[30]—i.e., between vv 28-29, what "the Spirit was able to do,"[31] and v 32, the invitation to accept the Messiah. But Hengstenberg[32] had already solved this problem. He pointed to Acts 2:40: "With many other words he warned them. . . . Save yourselves from this corrupt generation." Accordingly, Hengstenberg correctly concluded that Peter had deliberately used these words from Joel 2:30-31 in order to bring before his hearers a proper respect for the God who could right then and there deliver them from threatened judgments to come. For that was exactly the connection made by Joel. Thus while there has not yet been any fulfillment of vv 30-31 in that they await our Lord's second advent, nevertheless Peter used this truth in the same way that Joel used it in his day: It was an incentive to call on the name of the Lord.[33]

The coming wonders would certainly remind mankind of the terrible plagues of Egypt. Such descriptions of future cosmic judgment are similar

---

[29]M. W. Holmes, "The Interpretation of Joel in the New Testament" (unpublished M.A. thesis, Trinity Evangelical Divinity School, 1976) 68 n. 61, did point to an article by F. Gardiner, "Descriptions of Spiritual Phenomena Under the Figure of Natural Convulsions," *Old and New Testament Student* 9 (1889) 162. His argument is that since Pentecost fulfills Joel 2:28-32, therefore there is "inspired authority" that these signs were fulfilled at the same time and accordingly must be interpreted figuratively. Many contemporary interpreters also opt for this explanation. The problem with this logic is its assumption that there is a total fulfillment here.

[30]Ryrie, "Significance," 335.

[31]Ibid.

[32]E. W. Hengstenberg, *Christology of the Old Testament* (abridged by T. K. Arnold; Grand Rapids: Kregel, 1970 [1847]) 533.

[33]Note Paul's use of this verse in Rom 10:12-13; note also Kaiser, "Davidic," 103-104.

to numerous other descriptions of the day of the Lord. Yet in the midst of such catastrophes God's offer of salvation shone through clearly.

III. Conclusion

We conclude that the promise of the outpouring of the Holy Spirit in the last days has received a preliminary fulfillment in the series of events at Pentecost, Samaria and Caesarea. But these events and the subsequent baptisms of the Holy Spirit that take place whenever anyone receives Christ as Lord and Savior and is thereby ushered into the family of God are all mere harbingers and samples of that final downpour that will come in that complex of events connected with Christ's second return. However, these events—past, present and future—make up one generic whole concept, for in the prophet's view there is a wholeness and a totality to what he sees.

Furthermore, Joel specifically intended to announce that this blessing was to fall on the Gentiles as well as the Jews. In its final realization it was always connected by Isaiah and Ezekiel with the restoration of the people of Israel to the land just as it was in the Joel prophecy. Thus the spiritual benefits may not be abstracted and isolated from the national and political promises made to the patriarchs and David. The plan of God is a single plan that embraces the entirety of soteriology and the historical process. Anything less than this must be attributed to our western tendencies to dualism, docetism and spiritualizing.

Finally, in no way must this special profusion of the ministry of the Holy Spirit that operates much in accordance with the blessing found in the new covenant be interpreted in such a way as to suggest that the individual OT saints and believers were unaware of any ministry of the Holy Spirit in their lives apart from temporary endowments of the Spirit for special tasks at special times. On the contrary, the Holy Spirit was the author of new life for all who believed in the coming man of promise (=regeneration), and he also indwelt these same OT redeemed men, at least to some degree, even as David testified in Ps 51:11. There David pleaded with God: "Do not cast me away from your presence, and do not take your Holy Spirit from me." His reference did not seem to be to the Spirit's gift of government and administration but rather to his personal fellowship with God. This judgment is strongly supported by Jesus' pre-cross affirmation in John 13:17: "[The Holy Spirit] lives with you and is [now] in you."

What believers knew only in a seminal and preliminary form was now promised for "those [coming] days" as a veritable downpour. The baptism or incorporation act would not only bring all believers together in one body, but it would also so gift each individual that ultimately in that last day everyone would personally and directly know the Lord without being taught. And that would be a most unique outpouring of God's gift.

SECTION II

How God "Has Spoken to Us in His Son"

Hebrew Thought in the Life of the Church

MARVIN R. WILSON

In each new generation, one of the great challenges facing the Church is that of inculcating within its members a healthy and Biblical view of life. The Christian's view of man, the family, the Church and the world must firmly rest upon sound building blocks that are scripturally secure. And what is the nature of this Biblical foundation? It is characterized by a perspective on life and the world that is profoundly Hebraic in nature. Indeed the roots of Christianity run deep into the soil of Judaism. Thus if we want to understand the Bible correctly in its original life setting we must look primarily not to Athens but to Jerusalem for the Biblical view of reality. For the Scriptures are without question Hebraic in their composition and orientation.

Now this is not to say that the Greek or Roman or Canaanite or Egyptian cultural backgrounds are unimportant in understanding certain aspects of the Biblical text. To be sure, the Biblical world did embrace many different cultures. (Witness for example the Egyptian background of the exodus, the Canaanite linguistic insights vital to our understanding many of the Psalms, and the Greek imagery behind such NT terms as *logos*.) Rather it is to say that the writers of Scripture were, almost without exception, Jews. And it is because they were part of the Jewish religious world that they reflect primarily and fundamentally a Hebraic way of looking at life. Their thought forms betray a Hebraic mind-set. They viewed life through Hebrew eyes.

The last nineteen hundred years reveal how relatively easy it has been for the Church to lapse and become uprooted from her Hebraic way of thinking and approach to life. And right here, in my opinion, is a great tragedy—we may even call it an insidious heresy—in the life and history of the Church. For whenever the Church has departed from her Judaic roots and claimed a western or Greek heritage rather than a Middle Eastern and Hebraic heritage, detrimental and ofttimes dire consequences have resulted. It is thus my purpose in this chapter to point out some of these negative consequences. But I also intend to show why education that is authentically Biblical in scope can never afford to take lightly the Hebrew Scriptures and the Hebraic perspective on life derived from them.

It is more than a matter of arbitrary decision why most Christian colleges introduce their students to the Bible not with the NT but with the OT. Why is the OT considered foundational and prerequisite to all other Bible courses? The reason primarily lies in the fact that the theology produced by the writers of the NT is essentially Jewish theology. It is revelation brought to its fullest development by what God had done for hundreds of years through the Hebrew people of old. This revelation was brought to its culmination through Israel's Messiah—namely, Jesus the Jew. In effect Judaism was the parent and Christianity the child. The former gave birth to the latter. As Edith Schaeffer reminds us by the title of one of her recent books, "Christianity is Jewish."

A cursory look at the historical origin of Christianity reveals a Church that was, at the outset, exclusively made up of Jewish people. The Church was viewed as a sect within Judaism. Only gradually did Gentiles begin to infiltrate the ranks. When the number of Gentile believers sufficiently increased, at that point a council was called in Jerusalem. The proceedings of that council are recorded in Acts 15. The middle wall of partition of which Paul writes in Eph 2:14 was beginning to break down. Unfortunately, however, this breakdown meant more than accepting Gentiles into a formerly all-Jewish Church. Indeed the very Jewish moorings foundational to the Church were soon to stand in jeopardy.

To be specific, in the latter half of the first century the Church began to feel the impact of a rapidly growing process, that of de-Judaization. Christianity began to be understood in non-Jewish ways. For instance, the name "Christian" was derived from *Christos*, a Greek rendering of the Hebrew word for Messiah. The lingua franca of Palestine was now Greek, and so the NT was written in a non-Hebraic and non-Semitic tongue. The gap between Jew and Gentile was increased even further as the NT denunciation of Jewish religious leadership (witness, for example, Matthew 23 and 1 Thess 2:14-16) was thought to be a condemnation of all that was Jewish.[1] In addition the fall of Jerusalem in A.D. 70 to Gentile armies was seen as proof that God had rejected the Jewish nation. Toward the end of the first century, Church and synagogue had parted company.[2] By the year A.D. 160 (the time of Justin Martyr) the Church had begun to use for herself the title "Israel." The Church now considered herself to be the new and true Israel of God.[3]

Also in the middle of the second century an anti-Jewish polemic arose within the Church as men like Marcion sought to rid Christianity of every

[1]D. C. Juster, *Jewishness and Jesus* (Downers Grove, IL: InterVarsity, 1977) 11.

[2]E. M. Yamauchi, "Concord, Conflict, and Community: Jewish and Evangelical Views of Scripture," *Evangelicals and Jews in Conversation* (eds. M. H. Tanenbaum, M. R. Wilson and A. J. Rudin; Grand Rapids: Baker, 1978) 162.

[3]P. Richardson, *Israel in the Apostolic Church* (Cambridge: University Press, 1969), 1, 205 ff.

trace of Judaism. Marcion went so far as to teach that the God of the Hebrew Bible, the OT, was a different God from the God revealed in the pages of the NT.

In addition to Marcion, other Church fathers (Justin Martyr, Ignatius, John Chrysostom) spoke with such contempt against Jews and Judaism that any recognition of the Hebraic cradle in which the Church had been born was accordingly shunted aside. With the eventual triumph of Christianity as the state religion in the fourth century, its indebtedness to Judaism had largely been forgotten. Judaism was now treated as obsolete. Because Jewish people had rejected Jesus as Messiah, what need did Gentiles have to associate with or feel indebted to those of a dead, legalistic religion?

The Jewish roots of Christianity had thus virtually been severed. In its place stood a Church that had become largely Grecianized through the influence of Platonic thought. From this point on, "contrast and contradiction rather than acknowledgment of roots, relatedness and indebtedness, became the perspective."[4] And so today we must give serious consideration to the question of whether "we who once were not his people, and who have become his people only through his grace, can learn nothing from those who from of old have been his people."[5] Abraham Heschel put the question clearly in focus when he said, "The vital issue for the church is to decide whether to look for roots in Judaism and consider itself an extension of Judaism or to look for roots in pagan Hellenism and consider itself as an antithesis to Judaism."[6]

How are the Jewish roots of the Christian faith being truncated today? A quick perusal of the curriculum in many seminaries will reveal that all too frequently OT courses, the study of Hebrew, and Jewish cultural backgrounds are given second-class status. The Westminster Confession of Faith (1646), however, to which the majority of conservative seminaries subscribes, affirms that all 66 books of the Bible are fully authoritative. Indeed, though most Protestants give lip service to this belief, in practice the OT and the Jewish backdrop of Christianity have for too long been sadly neglected. Consequently we must emphasize that redemptive history is more than NT fulfillment. It embraces hundreds of years of OT promises.

The OT comprises about 80% of the Bible, the NT about 20%. But in many churches one would be hard pressed to ever hear a series of sermons preached from the OT. Such neglect is really Marcionism revisited, a kind of benign heresy that has been actually present in the Church since the middle of the second century.

[4]A. J. Heschel, "Protestant Renewal: A Jewish View," *The Insecurity of Freedom* (New York: Schocken, 1972) 169.

[5]W. S. LaSor, "The Messiah: An Evangelical Christian View," *Evangelicals and Jews*, 93.

[6]Heschel, "Renewal," 169-170.

One of the positive results of the deepening of evangelical-Jewish relations in this country has been the fact that evangelicals are now beginning to realize that great benefit can come from discussing the Jewish origin of the Christian faith face to face with those whose ancestors gave us the Bible. Many religious Jews of our day are committed to embodying the social, ethical and spiritual concerns and values so central to the Jewish Scriptures. In my experience I have found that it is often these Jewish friends who help most in putting the Scriptures in their proper and original Semitic setting. It is they who can help us better understand the Jewishness of our own faith for, as the NT puts it, "salvation is from the Jews" (John 4:22).

In these opening paragraphs we have sought briefly to make the case that learning to think and respond Hebraically must be basic to Christian teaching and hence the Christian experience. To be sure, as Karl Barth forcefully reminds us, "one has either got to be a Jew or stop reading the Bible. The Bible cannot make sense to anyone who is not 'spiritually a Semite.' "[7]

Now the tragedy of the matter is that we have not consistently followed this advice. We must therefore return to the position of the early Church that challenges today's Christian to

> claim the Old Testament, as the New Testament did, for it belongs to him no less than it did—and does—to Israel. Indeed, the Christian has through Christ in the truest sense been made an Israelite, grafted onto Israel like a wild branch onto a tree (Rom. 11:17-24). He must therefore see the Old Testament history as *his* history, the history of his own heritage of faith, its God as *his* God, its saints and sinners as men who had to do with that God. The Christian who refuses to see it so, flies in the face of the New Testament's witness and does no less than reject his own past.[8]

There are a number of areas where today's Church stands in need of redirection by returning to its Jewish Biblical roots. The following areas that will be surveyed have rather profound implications for the quality of life each Christian intends to live within his own believing community. But these matters are also crucial for the life of service he is called in Scripture to render to the larger outside community as well.

We turn then to a discussion of our first corrective, one taught by the Jewish writers of Scripture: *We must view ourselves and our world not dualistically but in terms of dynamic unity and oneness.* As students of western civilization and the history of ideas we stand in awe when we

[7]Quoted in T. Merton, ed., *Conjectures of a Guilty Bystander* (Garden City, NY: Doubleday, 1968) 14.

[8]J. Bright, *The Authority of the Old Testament* (Nashville: Abingdon, 1967) 199-200 (italics his).

consider Plato and other Greek philosophers for their great impact not only upon the thought of the ancient world but also upon ours today. We owe much to Plato and his later disciples for what they have taught us through their penetrating insights about reason, truth, wisdom, beauty and the good life. Nevertheless, there is a darker side of Plato and other Greek thinkers that has manifested itself through a dualistic kind of thinking that has proven to have largely negative consequences upon the history of the Church. We must therefore succinctly note what this Greek dualism was and how the Hebrew view of man and his world differed from it.

Platonism holds to dualism of two worlds, the visible (material) world and the invisible (spiritual) world. The visible or phenomenal world is in tension with the invisible or conceptual world. Because it is imperfect and a source of evil, the material world is inferior to that of the spiritual. In this view, man's soul originates in the heavenly realm from which it fell into the realm of matter. Though man finds himself related to both these worlds, he longs for release from his physical body that his true self (his soul) might take its flight back to the permanent world of the celestial and divine.

Related to Plato's dualistic view of the cosmos, then, is a dualistic view of man. Plato likens the body to a prison for the soul. The immortal soul, pure spirit, is incarcerated in a defective body of crumbling clay. Salvation comes at death when the soul escapes the body and soars heavenward to the invisible realm of the pure and eternal spirit. Centuries after Plato the Gnostics (a sect against which certain NT writings such as Colossians and 1 John seem to hold some sort of apologetic) viewed matter itself as being evil.

Unlike the ancient Greek, the Hebrew viewed the world as good. Though fallen and unredeemed, it was created by a God who designed it with man's best interests at heart. So instead of fleeing from the world man experienced God's fellowship, love and saving activity in the historical order within the world. According to Hebrew thought there was no cosmological dualism of two worlds, for the world was not evil per se. Neither was man viewed in dualistic terms of soul versus body. To the Hebrew mind, man was a dynamic unity of body-soul. He was called to passionately serve God his Creator with his whole being within the physical world. To be sure, the saints of the OT could never have brought themselves to sing such patently foreign and heterodox words as the following, which may be heard in churches today: "This world is not my home, I'm just a-passin' through." To any Jew of Bible times this kind of language would be a "cop-out." It seeks to abandon the present material world and focus on achieving the joys of the truly spiritual world to come.

What are some of the implications of these two contrasting views for the life of the Church? For purposes of illustration we shall note how this dualistic way of viewing man and his world has impacted upon the area of marriage and the family.[9]

The Bible is clear that marriage is an institution God calls holy and good (1 Tim 4:3-4). But the Church has always had those who have looked with suspicion or negatively at marriage and the family, seeing it as an inferior way of life. For many of these people, dualistic thinking has either consciously or unconsciously had a role to play in bringing them to such a conclusion. Thus, we are forced to ask some serious questions of the Biblical text: Is marriage only for the spiritually weak and those who are too much this-worldly minded? Is celibacy or a life of singleness ipso facto a higher if not more "God-honoring" way of life? Are clergy and monks living under the vow of chastity really closest to God because they have denied the fleshly temptation of marriage and the worldly desires of the flesh? Were some of the early Gnostics right who taught that marriage is a "foul and polluted way of life" and that eternal life cannot be obtained if one remains in this relationship? Was the great Church father of the fifth century, Jerome, being faithful to Scripture when he taught that "he who loves his own wife too ardently is an adulterer"? Did the Church follow clear, Biblical teaching in declaring not only the immaculate conception of Mary but also her perpetual virginity for fear that the womb that gave our Savior birth might be defiled should Jesus have actual brothers and sisters?

The Biblical and Hebraic answer to all these questions is a thunderous no. From the beginning God, through Moses, affirms the dignity and purity of the marriage relationship. Marriage and sex are from God and are therefore good. Gen 1:31 teaches that everything God had made was "very good." But what God made beautiful man at any time has the potential of distorting because of sin. To be sure, "the fall of man did not create passion; it only perverted it."[10] In God's eyes sex is neither sin nor salvation. In the context of marriage, however, the Hebrew Scriptures pronounce it to be a blessed gift because it is tied to the birth of children, an occasion worth rejoicing about (see 1 Sam 2:1-10).

In sum, the Scriptures view both man and his world in terms of dynamic unity, not dualistically. As such the Bible upholds the dignity, rightness and purity of the marriage relationship. Marriage and the family are gifts from God and hence judged by the Jewish Biblical writers as "very good" (Gen 1:31; cf. 1 Tim 4:4).

A second corrective from the Biblical world of Hebraic thought is this: *The fixation upon other-worldliness so much a part of evangelical Christianity must be brought back into Biblical balance by a return to this-*

[9] I will soon publish a parallel and expanded treatment of this section on the influence of Platonism on Christian marriage.

[10] D. A. Hubbard, "Old Testament Light on the Meaning of Marriage," *Theology, News and Notes* (Pasadena: Fuller Theological Seminary, March 1969) 6.

worldly concerns. For too long, Christianity in general and a notable segment within evangelicalism in particular has given expression to a pallid kind of ascetic, other-worldly "spirituality." This stands in stark contrast to the robust, life-affirming, this-worldly spirituality of the early Jewish believers. The Jews of Bible times were not life-denying people. Spirituality did not come by negating the richness of life's experiences or withdrawing from the world. Instead they found a sense of holiness in the here and now. There was no division between the sacred and secular areas of life. It was all God's world, and it was to be enjoyed without a sense of shame or guilt. In Paul's words, "to the pure, all things are pure" (Titus 1:15). As trustee and steward of God's world, man was to live within it and use it in accord with divine directives. Again, in Paul's familiar Hebraic idiom, "so whether you eat or drink or whatever you do, do it all for the glory of God" (1 Cor 10:31). It must be pointed out, however, that the Jew of Bible times did not see the need to bless food, drink or other physical properties. He only focused on blessing God,[11] the Giver. He alone was worthy of receiving the blessing and praise. The post-Biblical notion that man needed to sanctify, cleanse or purify what God had already created and declared to be good would be foreign theology to the apostle Paul. It implies that food and drink are profane until sanctified.

Unfortunately, the pages of Church history reveal that when Christians have become too fixated with seeking to find the God of heaven and of that other world to come they have often missed finding the God of earth and history, the Creator of this world, in the here and now. Unlike the Jews of Bible times who looked up to heaven but kept both feet square on the ground, Christians have not always learned so to balance themselves. It is the age-old problem man experiences of how he can keep the invisible from consuming the visible, the spiritual from negating the material, the theoretical from eliminating the practical, and the creed from making him blind to the deed. It can be shown in the life of the Church that a number of basic Christian doctrines and values have been lopsided or thrown out of balance because of this fact. Let us look at several of these, noting first the doctrine of salvation.

In the Middle Ages the concept of salvation revolved around the idea of being "lifted out of life." Salvation came when one was delivered from the world. At the end of life this was often called the "beatific vision" as one was taken beyond the world to realms sublime. The good life was the life

---

[11]The ancient prayer and benediction used in Judaism as grace before meals reflects this point: "Blessed art thou, O Lord our God, King of the universe, who bringest forth bread from the earth." See J. H. Hertz, ed., *Daily Prayer Book* (rev. ed.; New York: Bloch, 1948) 962-963. See also A. Hertzberg, ed., *Judaism* (New York: Washington Square, 1961) 240-247.

of contemplation by which man could escape the pressures of this mortal life and achieve a quality of peace that was akin to a little taste of heaven.[12]

By contrast, the Hebrews did not primarily view salvation as deliverance from this world. Their commitment was not to escape this life but to know God's power and presence, which could transform their lives and their society. The Hebrews sought to live life to the hilt, entering into the fullness of the human experience. They knew that to seek flight from this life by death was no permanent solution to the ills of this world. (The example of the Greek jailer at Philippi who thought of ending his life the moment Paul and Silas escaped from prison would have been a strange action to the Hebrew mind-set of the former Pharisee Paul.) The Hebrews sought not to kill time but to sanctify time in their daily round of activities. Salvation was not to escape this fleshly veil but to walk faithfully and triumphantly throughout life with God, who redeems the whole man. The Hebrews boldly affirmed their God-given humanity. In Scripture, again and again, we find that their identity was found in society, not in isolation from others. The earth was never seen as an alien place but as a part of creation. It was on earth and on earth alone that man's highest duty and calling could be performed—namely, that of bringing glory to his Maker through the praise of his lips and the work of his hands. So strongly did the rabbis of old feel about the importance of man's enjoyment of this life and God's created order that they wrote: "At judgment day every man will have to give account for every good thing which he might have enjoyed and did not" (*y. Qidd.* 66d).

A second potential area of imbalance, and one in which a thoroughgoing this-worldly orientation is needed, is that of education. To the Hebrew mind the goal of education and learning was far from producing students who were so heavenly minded they were no earthly good. Unlike their Greek counterparts the Hebrews were not primarily interested in an educational model that sought mainly to transfer knowledge in the intellectual or technical areas. In the Greek world, teachers provided intellectual exercises for those whose reasoning skills needed sharpening, athletic training for those in need of specialized development of the physical body, lessons in comportment for those whose manners needed upgrading, and cultural and artistic expertise for those interested in music, art, sculpting or drama. In short, the main function of the teacher (*didaskalos*) in secular Greek literature was to hone the skills and talents of a student in the particularly desired area of instruction. After all, for the Greeks only the wealthy could afford the leisure to be educated.[13]

---

[12]J. Spong, *This Hebrew Lord* (New York: Seabury, 1974) 24.

[13]Note that our English word "school" derives from a Greek root meaning "to have spare time, be at leisure."

By contrast the Hebrews viewed education as anything other than idle time, or simply a rich person's way of avoiding the degrading tasks of manual labor. Rather they viewed education as something embracing more than one specialized area of skill or interest. Theirs was education of the whole man, with his whole person—body and soul as a unit—in mind. They were interested in producing what Jewish psychiatrists and educators today call a *mensch* (a Yiddish word for one who has his total life put together in an exemplary way). Such provides a worthy goal and model of education for Christian liberal arts colleges.

The Hebrew saw his God-given vocation—whether it be that of farmer, herdsman, fisherman, tax collector, teacher or scribe—as a means of bringing glory to God by the very privilege of work itself. (It should not be forgotten that the Hebrew word for "work," ʿăbōdâ, is also translated "worship.") There were no secular occupations and there were no sacred ones. Every domain of life belonged to God. The Jews were pragmatists. They were never interested in making education a game of storing up abstract concepts or theoretical principles. Education had to be useful in meeting the challenges and needs of this world. To know something was to experience it rather than merely to intellectualize it. In short, to "know" was to "do" and learning was life. The whole person was engaged in what John, a NT Jewish writer, calls "doing the truth" (1 John 1:6).

If the educational process of the Church is to remain authentically Biblical it must never lose sight of this practical dimension. Truth must be incarnate in each member of the community. Quality education from a Biblical point of view is concerned with integrating learning with faith and living. This is the Hebrew model, and it is the lifelong task to which each Christian must continually address himself.

Yet another realm in which imbalance between otherworldliness and this-worldliness is often found centers upon our understanding of the concept of faith. What does it mean for today's Christian to have "faith"? For many evangelical Christians—particularly those ignorant of the Jewish background of this word—"faith" is understood to be mainly an activity of the mind. To "believe" or "have faith" is, for these Christians, purely a matter of intellectual assent to some proposition. The Hebrews, however, looked at faith differently. To them it meant to have the capacity to "enter life with courageous expectation."[14] The man of faith did more than believe in his mind. He stepped out into life to act on that belief. His mental assurances and convictions were transformed into action. For the Hebrew, faith was more than a theory. It was wed to a life of service. Indeed he could serve God through his work. The Jew of Bible times knew that God was always met in history, in the context of events, the world of activity and doing. The man of faith was one who was so committed to God that

[14]Spong, *Lord*, 23.

he, like Abraham, ventured into the unknown with the full expectation that God would meet him there. Thus to have "faith" in the Biblical sense was to move out in life and know God would be there waiting. It was "the call to step boldly into tomorrow, to embrace the new—with confidence that every new day would prove to be a meeting place with the holy and eternal God. The opposite of faith was to cling desperately to yesterday, fearing that if one ever left it, one would leave God."[15]

How does this Hebrew concept of faith apply to the vocation and mission of today's Christian? Like the Hebrews, his faith must be this-worldly oriented. For either God has the power to change lives now, in this world, in the market places of life, or the gospel for the life to come is little worth talking about. The world needs to see an evangelical Christian faith with less rhetoric, one that demonstrates its credibility in this world in tangible terms. A faith that is truly Biblical will demonstrate its credibility when it brings healing to relationships in the office, or when it serves with dedication and unselfishness in the classroom, or when it goes beyond the call of duty on the playing field. Likewise it will demonstrate to others that it is a believable faith if it provokes others with a refreshing honesty in the political arena, or if it enables a businessman to serve ethically and cheerfully in the course of his pressure-packed day.

This is the Hebraic and Biblical model of faith. Though conscious of heaven, it is a faith that operates in, and is only at home in, the realm of flesh and blood. Removed from the sphere of the angels, such faith confronts idols and addresses the inhumanities and injustices of a sin-plagued world. This Hebraic and Biblical quality of faith has the possibility of transforming this life so that those thereby changed may be worthy of the life to come.

We may sum up our second main point, then, by saying that whether it be faith, or salvation, or education—these must be more than theoretical values. Each must have a practical and decisively this-worldly orientation.

There is a third and final Hebraic corrective that I would suggest ought to be brought to bear on the Church: *The current display of "rugged individualism" and private Christianity within evangelicalism must give way to a greater emphasis on the corporate life of the community of faith.* Unhappily, one of the characteristics of contemporary fundamentalism and evangelicalism is its emphasis upon what might be called "lone ranger" Christianity. That is, people seem to be losing their Biblical sense of accountability to each other and think they can, for the most part, operate on their own. Today we may observe an assorted array of dominating and independent Church leaders who, through spiritual-sounding language and intimidation, impose their will upon the group. Frequently their conversa-

[15]J. Spong, "The Continuing Christian Need for Judaism," *Christian Century*, September 26, 1979, p. 919.

tion is punctuated with such phrases as "the Lord told me" or "God revealed to me." And we need not limit our examples to Jonestown-type situations.

Somehow the community-centeredness of the body of Christ is now in danger of being replaced by the rugged individualism of a private kind of faith. And perhaps we who are evangelicals have, in part, brought this upon ourselves. Let us think for a moment. Could it be that we have so stressed soul liberty, the individual priesthood of each believer, the importance of personal devotions, the right to privately interpret the Bible for ourselves, the priority of private confession of sin directly to God, and the encouragement of independent churches and separatistically autonomous parachurch agencies—could it be we have so stressed these things that we have come to believe we can function not only in these, but also in other areas, as self-sufficient believers?

This issue was put in clear perspective by the Catholic priest who once was asked by a religious news reporter if he could briefly distinguish the major difference between evangelical Protestantism and Catholicism. "That's easy," the priest replied. "The evangelical Church says to people, 'The Church needs you,' but the Catholic Church says, 'You need the Church.'"

Now it is obvious that such a reply paints an overly simplistic picture of evangelical Protestantism. Nevertheless, what this priest said is in large measure true—namely, that the Church must be more than a group of independent individualists each going his own way. The individual can never survive apart from the group. Man was created to be a social being. And God has so constituted his people to function within a body. Man's true meaning derives from relationships with God and his fellowmen (Matt 22:34-40).

Since Bible times the Jewish community has embodied this concept in an exemplary way. It has been said that the religion of Israel was characterized by an organic link between two principal elements: "faith and folk."[16] This Biblical emphasis upon "folk"—that is, the group—is underscored by the fact that most Jewish prayer employs the plural "we," not "I." It expresses the "cry of the whole community."[17] One of the best known Biblical prayers gives expression to this in its opening words: "Our Father, who art in heaven." In the words of an old Hasidic saying, "A prayer which is not spoken in the name of all Israel is no prayer at all."[18]

Central to the Hebraic concept of community is the idea of "corporate personality."[19] This means that the individual was always thought of in the

[16]R. Gordis, *The Root and the Branch* (Chicago: University Press, 1962) 19.
[17]D. deS. Pool, *Why I Am A Jew* (Boston: Beacon, 1957) 93.
[18]M. Buber, ed., *Ten Rungs: Hasidic Sayings* (New York: Schocken, 1947) 31.
[19]See H. W. Robinson, *Corporate Personality in Ancient Israel* (Philadelphia: Fortress, 1964) 3-9.

collective (family, tribe, nation) and the collective in the individual. This corporate solidarity was further reinforced by the fact that the entire community (past ancestors and future members) was viewed as one personality, "a living whole, a single animated mass of blood, flesh and bones."[20]

The very fact that the Hebrew language is full of what we refer to in English as "collectives" gives additional undergirding to this concept of organic solidarity.[21] For instance, in the Hebrew Bible the word ʾādām may refer to man as an individual or mankind in the collective sense. Thus all Israelites are mutually accountable for one another and mutually participate in the life of one another. A striking example of this is the ancient Biblical practice of blood revenge.[22]

In the modern Jewish community, at Passover each Jew is obligated to regard himself as if he personally had come out of Egypt, not simply his ancestors.[23] In addition each Jew is taught to think of himself as personally standing at Mount Sinai in order to receive the Torah. Thus the Law is given to every Jew, not one Jew.[24] In a similar way, the concept of the sacredness of human life is basic to the idea of corporate personality. In the Talmud we read, "He who destroys a single life is considered as if he had destroyed the whole world, and he who saves a single life is considered as having saved the whole world" (*m. Sanh.* 4:5).

And how does this concept apply to the life of the Church? As a visible body of believers, the Church is the spiritual Israel (Rom 2:29; 4:11, 16; Gal 3:26-29). "There is no mere individualistic experience for Christians, but a corporate one."[25] In Paul's words, "we were all baptized by one Spirit into one body—whether Jews or Greeks, slave or free" (1 Cor 12:13 *NIV*). Thus the Pauline idea of the Church as the body of Christ is firmly rooted in the OT concept of the corporate personality. Accordingly for Paul, as in the Israelite community of old, the individual "incorporates in himself the group which he heads, who illustrates in his person and in his life the ideals by which the group professes, and from whom the group derives its life and its distinct identity."[26]

---

[20]Ibid., p. 4.

[21]T. Boman, *Hebrew Thought Compared with Greek* (New York: W. W. Norton, 1960) 70.

[22]See A. Gelin, *The Key Concepts of the Old Testament* (New York: Paulist, 1963) 64.

[23]I. Breuer, *Concepts of Judaism* (ed. J. S. Levinger; Jerusalem: Israel Universities Press, 1974) 296.

[24]S. Umen, *Jewish Concepts and Reflections* (New York: Philosophical Library, 1962) 39.

[25]J. A. Fitzmyer, *Pauline Theology* (Englewood Cliffs, NY: Prentice-Hall, 1967) 66.

[26]J. McKenzie, "The Significance of the Old Testament for Christian Faith in

In effect the Church is a community of faith, learning and living, just as the synagogue serves as a house of worship, study and assembly. As such, a Christian's actions within that fellowship are not solely a private matter. When one members suffers, the whole body shares the grief. When one rejoices, all share in that joy. The body of Christ is never stronger than the sum of its individual members, for the Church, like Israel, functions as a corporate personality. The lives of its members are intertwined and find their truest meaning in a network of relationships within this body. As an ancient rabbi once observed, "There is no room for God in him who is full of himself."[27] In the Bible, piety is always oriented toward community. God and one's neighbor belong inseparably together. The Church must never become so self-centered and self-sufficient that it fails to grasp this fact. For the concept of the priesthood of the believer means that each Christian functions as a priest not only unto God but also unto his neighbor.

In the ancient synagogues of Israel, whenever the congregation completed the reading of one of the books of Moses it was the practice for the entire congregation to loudly exclaim, "Be strong, be strong, and let us strengthen one another." It is with this same sense of mutual dependence that today's Church must learn to stand in the full strength of its Hebrew heritage.

Roman Catholicism," *The Old Testament and the Christian Faith* (ed. B. W. Anderson; New York: Harper, 1963) 113.

[27]Buber, *Rungs,* 102.

Apostolic Eyewitnesses and Proleptically Historical Revelation

Stanley Obitts

"What is all too frequently lacking in New Testament scholarship practiced by Christians is not scholarship but a certain toughness of mind," declares Van A. Harvey.[1] Among the evidences of a lack of rigorous reasoning that he finds is "too hasty an appeal to the apostolic eyewitnesses." The genuinely critical historian knows that historical "witnesses and sources are themselves a web of inferences" that the historian must evaluate unless "he is willing to settle for the mere transmission of tradition." Anyone familiar with the process of historical reasoning recognizes that "the historian does not accept the authority of his witnesses; rather, he confers authority upon them . . . after subjecting them to a rigorous and skeptical cross-examination."[2]

What Harvey has in mind by this "cross-examination" is succinctly presented in what he calls elsewhere "a much neglected" book. According to T. A. Roberts, the Biblical historian must search for "the significance of the fact that, meaning what they do, the gospel writers wrote what they did write." That is to say, "at every point these gospel statements must be challenged, for the only evidence they furnish is the evidence which answers the historian's own questions."[3]

In criticism of C. H. Dodd, for example, Roberts claims that to say that

> the apostles or the early Church are the best judges of the significance of events which they experienced, is tantamount to denying the role of historical criticism and a negation of the task . . . of asking whether the gospel record is true. Historical criticism alone can answer this question, and historical criticism starts with the awareness of the possibility that the gospel record may be mistaken.[4]

But what criteria is the historian to use in ascertaining the authenticity and reliability, much less the veracity, of the Biblical reports of miracles

---

[1] V. A. Harvey, *The Historian and the Believer* (London, 1967) 111.
[2] Ibid., p. 107.
[3] T. A. Roberts, *History and Christian Apologetics* (London, 1960) 18.
[4] Ibid., p. 113.

and fulfilled prophecies? The insuperable problem facing Roberts and Harvey in meeting this requirement becomes obvious when their appeal to Troeltsch's principle of analogy is noted.[5]

According to Roberts a nonanalogous or unique occurrence, such as a miracle, cannot be authenticated by historical criticism. Indeed faith in a miracle runs contrary to the presuppositions of historical criticism, geared as they are for nonunique events. On what basis, then, is belief in a miracle such as the resurrection justified? Roberts' enigmatic answer is "faith."[6] In his opinion theological language in which the term "resurrection" appears, having "a 'logic' of its own, . . . is not historical language and is not . . . supported by appealing to historical considerations."[7] Harvey's solution, somewhat reminiscent of Wilhelm Herrmann's,[8] is expressed thus: "No event or miracle that others tell us about can acquire the force of something we know for ourselves, and if one has the experience for himself, the appeal to a past fact is important largely because it provides us with an image to which we can return again and again and use in our present relationships with others."[9]

These solutions to the problem—the problem so influentially articulated by Troeltsch concerning the relation of critical history to Christian faith—are of course typical of the general approach taken by many leading theologians in the twentieth century. Rather than attacking Troeltsch's position on the philosophical issues of historical explanation and objectivity, many theologians have sought simply to insulate themselves from the theological implications Troeltsch drew as the systematizer of the *religionsgeschichtliche Schule.*[10] For example, Bultmann argues for a dialectical

---

[5]Harvey, *Historian*, 3-19; Roberts, *History*, 144-174 (implicitly). In his important essay, "Über historische und dogmatische Methode in der Theologie," *Gesammlte Schriften* (Tübingen, 1922), 2. 729-753, E. Troeltsch laid down three principles for the truly critical historical method that he took to be different from those adopted traditionally by Christians. The second principle specifies the criterion for determining the probability of a past event or tradition to be the analogy of the past with the present. If an alleged event is of the kind unknown in the present, then it cannot be conceived as happening in the past.

[6]Roberts, *History*, 167.

[7]Ibid., p. 171.

[8]See e.g. W. Herrmann, *The Communion of the Christian with God* (2nd ed.; trans. J. S. Stanyon; New York, 1906) 72, 84; *Faith and Morals* (trans. D. Matheson and R. W. Stewart; New York, 1904) 32.

[9]Harvey, *Historian*, 283.

[10]Troeltsch states his position succinctly in *Die Bedeutung der Geschichtlichkeit Jesu für den Glauben* (Tübingen, 1911). Two recent authoritative treatments of Troeltsch's position are W. Bodenstein, *Neige des Historismus—Ernst Troeltschs Entwicklungsgang* (Gütersloh, 1959), and E. Lessing, *Die Geschichtsphilosophie Ernst Troeltschs* (Hamburg-Bergstedt, 1965).

relationship between history and revelatory events because he agrees with Troeltsch that "the historical method includes the presupposition that history is a unity in the sense of a closed continuum of effect" in a way that "cannot be rent by the interference of supernatural, transcendent powers."[11]

Wolfhart Pannenberg, however, has self-avowedly abandoned (*verlassen*) the concepts of revelation taken by the "Theology of the Word" and existential theology.[12] Within the world of theology there are two positions against which he must defend his primary doctrine that "history is the most comprehensive horizon of Christian theology," reports Pannenberg. One is the existential theology of Bultmann and Gogarten. The other is the theology of Barth, which separates secular history from salvation history (*Historie abgegrenzte heilsgeschichtliche Theologie*). The extra-theological motif (*aussertheologisches Motiv*) shared by both positions is their starting point in the conviction that "the scientific establishment" through "historico-critical research" of the events that have happened in the history of salvation is impossible. Pannenberg says he takes the opposite starting point.[13]

He has developed his willingness to bring such miraculous events as the resurrection of Jesus out from the hiding place of faith for the scrutiny of historical science so far as to make historical knowledge the very ground of Christian faith: "It is not at all necessary for one first to have faith in order to find the revelation of God in the history of Israel and Jesus Christ. Rather, true faith is first awakened through an unprejudiced observation [*unbefangene Wahrnehmung*] of these events."[14] That Pannenberg has not wavered on this point over the years can be seen from one of his most recent declarations on the same theme: The "affirmation" of "the resurrection of Jesus . . . is not to be based on authority rather than on a critical evaluation of evidence."[15]

But what is an "unprejudiced observation" of the Biblical events? Pannenberg's reply, we hope to show, reveals that he has not moved as far from the threat posed by Troeltsch[16] as one might have surmised from his

---

[11]R. Bultmann, *Existence and Faith* (ed. S. M. Ogden; New York, 1960) 291-292. Cf. E. Troeltsch, "Historiography," *The Encyclopedia of Religion and Ethics* (ed. J. Hastings; Edinburgh, 1913), 6. 716-723.

[12]W. Pannenberg, *Offenbarung als Geschichte* (ed. W. W. Pannenberg; Göttingen, 1970) 132.

[13]W. Pannenberg, "Heilsgeschehen und Geschichte," *Probleme alttestamentlicher Hermeneutik* (ed. C. Westermann; München, 1960) 295-296.

[14]Pannenberg, *Offenbarung*, 100-101. For a concatenation of similar assertions by Pannenberg see P. Althaus, "Offenbarung als Geschichte und Glaube," *TLZ* 87 (May 1962) cols. 322-323.

[15]W. Pannenberg, *Human Nature, Election, and History* (Philadelphia, 1977) 89.

[16]In particular we have reference to the threat posed by Troeltsch's historico-

affirmed openness to the historicity, in Troeltsch's sense, of the resurrection of Christ.[17]

In Pannenberg's opinion God's communication is always indirect, never "having God as the content in any direct manner."[18] First, the content of some act or activity of God is "perceived for its own value," and then when that event is viewed from a different perspective "it is also seen that the event defined in this way has God as its originator." This does not mean that an event reveals, or God reveals himself through it, as its originator, however, for any single event can illuminate God's being only partially, including the Christ event. Nonetheless, as an act of God an event is used by him to say something indirectly about himself.[19]

If no one event in history can convey a full and complete indirect self-revelation of God, and if no human being can gain a comprehensive view of all historical events together, then how can Troeltsch's repudiation of the Christ event as having absolute meaning be avoided? Maybe Troeltsch is correct in seeing Christianity incompatible with the universal historical viewpoint.

Firmly maintaining the indirect nature of God's revelation of himself, Pannenberg admits that without the doctrine of an inspired interpretation of the meaning of history, in the manner of the "supernaturalist theologians," he cannot claim that God's revelation is fully comprehended until the end of history. Nonetheless, he rejects the doctrine of an inspired

---

critical method, but more broadly to Troeltsch's attack upon the absoluteness of Christianity. The current significance of this attack is attested by the recent republication of Troeltsch's *The Absoluteness of Christianity* (Richmond, 1971). Concerning the resurgence of interest in Troeltsch see Harvey, *Historian*, 3-4; C. Pinnock, "Prospects for Systematic Theology," *Towards a Theology for the Future* (ed. D. F. Wells and C. G. Pinnock; Carol Stream, IL, 1971) 99-100. Pinnock says, "As far as contemporary theologians are concerned, however, no name is more important than Ernst Troeltsch (1865-1923). His reflections on the nature of historical thinking, especially his principle of 'analogy,' have done more than almost anything else to precipitate the crises of Twentieth-century theology" (p. 99).

[17]The "historical knowledge" presupposed by Christian faith, as defined by the Reformers and with which he agrees, says Pannenberg, "comprises not only what historical positivism would allow as history, but also Jesus' resurrection from the dead and the incarnation." W. Pannenberg, *Basic Questions in Theology* (trans. G. H. Kehm; London, 1971), 2. 36.

[18]He argues that Barth's restriction of divine revelation to a direct self-revelation stems from an Hegelian concept for which there is no Scriptural support. The Biblical view is that of "an indirect self-revelation of God in the mirror of his dealings in history" (*in Spiegel seines Geschichtshandelns*). *Offenbarung*, 16.

[19]*Revelation as History* (ed. W. Pannenberg; trans. D. Granskow and E. Quinn; London, 1969) 14-16.

interpretation of God's revealing actions in history while at the same time affirming the uniqueness and absoluteness of God's revelation in Jesus Christ. He claims to be able to accomplish this by describing the self-revelation of God in the resurrection of Jesus Christ as being eschatological in nature.

> Only in the sense that the perfection of history has already been inaugurated in Jesus Christ is God finally and fully revealed in the fate[20] of Jesus. With the resurrection of Jesus, the end of history has already occurred, although it does not strike us in this way. It is only the eschatological character of the Christ event that establishes that there will be no further self-manifestation of God beyond this event. Thus, the end of the world will be on a cosmic scale what has already happened in Jesus.

Pannenberg even goes so far as to make the solution for the non-Jew of the philosophical questions of God's existence and nature dependent upon "the eschatological character of the Christ event as the anticipation of the end of all things."[21]

The advantage of making the absoluteness of God's self-revelation in the resurrection of Jesus dependent upon the eschatological nature of that event is, of course, that it permits the time-bound human historian paradoxically to stand also at the end of history from which stance alone the full meaning of any event can be comprehended in the light of the totality of God's historical actions. But having eliminated the possibility of an inspired interpretation of the Christ event, how does Pannenberg justify his claim to know with certainty[22] the ultimacy of the Christ event? His answer is that while we cannot know all the ramifications of the resurrection, "what we appropriate" from that event, "namely, our life's reality in the light of the final decision, does place us in a position to speak about the self-revelation of God" in it.[23]

This appropriation of "the transforming power" of the divinely-revealed events, particularly the Christ event, derives from the nature of the event itself, not from an attitude of faith brought to the event, however. "The knowledge of revelation is not supernatural." The divinely-revealed events,

---

[20]"Geschick," *Offenbarung*, 104. According to E. F. Tupper, author of a comprehensive study of Pannenberg's theology, this term "should be translated as 'destiny' instead of 'fate,' for it positively connotes resurrection as Jesus' end beyond the disaster of the cross. 'Destiny,' therefore, coheres with 'prolepsis,' the anticipation of the '*eschaton*' in the Christ event" (*The Theology of Wolfhart Pannenberg* [Philadelphia: Westminster, 1973] 50 n.).

[21]*Revelation*, 142. See also "The Revelation of God in Jesus of Nazareth," *Theology as History* (ed. J. M. Robinson and J. B. Cobb, Jr.; New York, 1967) 104-109.

[22]Pannenberg, *Revelation*, 138.

[23]Ibid., p. 143.

if "taken seriously for what they are, and in . . . the traditio-historical context . . . to which they belong, speak their own language, the language of facts." Anyone should be able to grasp these facts for what they are by using his native reasoning ability. "It is through an open appropriation of these events that true faith is sparked" rather than faith being "the basis for finding the revelation of God" in these historical occurrences. Faith concerns the future. It is a trust in the future based upon God's revelation in "the fate of Jesus." Only the future can justify or falsify the Christian's faith.[24]

It is important to notice that "the language of facts" that the divinely-revealed events speak is not the language of the "pure facts of positivistic historiography," since the latter are merely abstraction from the original historian's interests and the context in which the facts appeared.[25] Rather, it is "the *inherent* meaning of the reported event" as the content of the historical knowledge presupposed by the historical faith of the Christian.[26] He is not willing to distinguish in God's revelation between the events and their meaning, as if the meaning was relative to an individual's preference and thus needed inspiration to assure its truth quality. The "original meaning" is "recognizable" when the events are understood in the context provided by "the history of the transmission of tradition." In his opinion, "events always bring their original meaning along with them from the context to which they have been assigned by their having happened." As far, then, as the resurrection of Christ is concerned, says Pannenberg, "it is a matter of the God of Israel having revealed his deity in this event—a conviction that, I admit, can be justified only in view of the universal connection of all events, and therefore always stands to come under new discussion."[27]

This admission by Pannenberg may indicate that he is aware of his tendency to go in two directions at once in the matter of faith and history. This tendency becomes more apparent when what has been seen above about his stress upon the grounding of faith upon historical events whose inherent meaning is recognizable for even the "non-Jewish" person—i.e., the person not viewing God's revelatory events in their Jewish context—is compared with his discussion of the proleptic character of faith. By his radical rejection of *Heilsgeschichte* and his equally radical identification of revelation with the history apprehended in Troeltsch's manner—i.e., through the historico-critical method—Pannenberg realizes that the final meaning

[24]Ibid., pp. 137-138. See also "Eschatologie und Sinnerfahrung," *KD*, January-March 1973, pp. 39-52, esp. pp. 51-52.

[25]Pannenberg, *Basic*, 2. 39.

[26]Ibid., 2. 35 (italics his). See also "Nazareth," 125 ff.

[27]Pannenberg, *Basic*, 2. 39-50. See also "Kerygma und Geschichte," *Studien zur Theologie der Alttestamentlichen Überlieferungen* (ed. R. Rendtorff and K. Koch; Neukirchen, 1961) 129-140; *Human Nature*, 86-89.

of any and all of God's revealing acts can be conceived as being known only at the end of history.[28] Yet he wants to remain within the ranks of those who have maintained against Troeltsch, as spokesman for the *religionsgeschichtliche Schule*, the absoluteness of Christianity.

The real position Pannenberg takes on the relation of history to faith, however, comes out in his discussion of the proleptic character of faith, for he there tips his hand by unmistakably espousing in addition a proleptic view of revelation. A few quotations will suffice:

> God's revelation in Jesus Christ is indeed only an anticipation of the final event. And yet . . . the final event will not bring anything decisively new. . . . To this extent, Jesus is already the revelation of God.
> The matter must remain thus: revelation as history, anticipatorily summed up in Jesus Christ—but *for* faith, which lives between the prolepsis of the end in the Christ event and the universal onset of this end. The proleptic structure of faith (in the future reference of trust) corresponds to the structure of the Christ event, and it is just for this reason that only in faith is this event received. . . . To this extent, event talk about the revelation of God in Jesus Christ is proleptic.[29]

Now it would seem to us that if God reveals himself only proleptically, then history as the sole medium of that revelation is only proleptically such a medium. That is, God has not actually revealed himself through history. Rather the future state of affairs when the revelation will have been given historically is just conceived in a quasi-hypothetical manner as presently existing. Even as an analogical predication of God must have a point of univocity in order to avoid equivocating, so also a proleptic manifestation of God or a proleptic state of affairs mediating that manifestation must possess a point of nonprolepsis to serve as its ground or basis. As long as Pannenberg identifies revelation with history he is logically on the side of Troeltsch, unable to establish the uniqueness and absoluteness of God's revelation in Jesus Christ. As Pannenberg himself puts the alternative he imagines himself to have avoided: "When the totality of reality in its temporal development is thought of as history and as the self-communication of God, then we find ourselves on the road which German idealism has taken since the time of Lessing and Herder."[30]

---

[28] W. Pannenberg, *Jesus—God and Man* (trans. L. Wilkins and D. Priebe; London, 1968) 69; see also his *Theology and the Philosophy of Science* (Philadelphia, 1976) 64-70 (notice especially his version of the distinction between *Historie* and *Geschichte*, pp. 69-70).

[29] *Basic*, 2. 44 (italics his). See Pannenberg, *Jesus—God and Man*, 107-108. "When we speak today of God's revelation in Jesus . . . our statements always contain a proleptic element" (p. 108). See also his treatment of "the proleptic element in Jesus' claim to authority," pp. 53-66.

[30] *Revelation*, 16.

So far we have seen him attempting epistemologically to establish a nonproleptic element in history as revelation by appealing to a faith-apprehension of the resurrection of Jesus as a proleptically existing full disclosure of God. But we must now press Pannenberg for the metaphysical justification for this faith-apprehension. Could the resurrection of Jesus actually exist as the full disclosure of God? In a system that describes history in its entirety as the exclusive means of revelation it is inconceivable that a single event within history could exist having this function. We have seen that Pannenberg is aware of this, but he has also been seen trying to sidestep its implications by reverting to the epistemological possibility of proleptically viewing the Christ event as that full revelation through faith. He simply leaves the metaphysical problem hanging in abeyance, thereby joining by default the idealists in their view of historical revelation.

If this be the case, then the contingency of any historical event upon a transcendent God is beyond Pannenberg's epistemological range. He can talk of the continuity of history but not the unique contingency of a particular event within history. A fortiori he cannot use that event as the basis for his assertion of its contingency. That is, he cannot consistently ground his assertion that the central event of Biblical history and thus of all history is the Christ event upon the claim that history must be viewed apocalyptically and then turn around to justify an apocalyptic view of history upon the eschatological interpretation of the Christ event.[31]

It will next be contended that, given the truth of the above analysis, Pannenberg's attempt to break free of Troeltsch's use of the principle of analogy in the historico-critical method is left without support.

Of the three principles Troeltsch laid down for what he regarded as the truly critical method of historical investigation[32] he gave the primacy of importance to the principle of analogy.[33] It will be recalled that the use of this principle eliminated for him the traditional Christian belief in God's

[31]The following excerpt from "Nazareth," 125, succinctly expresses the fallacious logical move we are accusing Pannenberg of making: "Jesus' resurrection . . . has its eschatological significance only because it is a proleptic occurrence of the general eschatological salvation expected by the Jews of that time, and *hence* only in the context of the totality of human history, whose ultimate future it unveiled.

"Is this significance of Jesus' history recognizable from within itself? And is such a recognition already a knowledge of the revelation of God in him? Or is some supplementary explanation necessary, an explanation emerging out of faith in Jesus and not derivable from the bare facts of his story?" (Italics mine.) Pannenberg answers the first two questions in the affirmative and the last question in the negative.

[32]See n. 5.

[33]"Denn das Mittel, wodurch Kritik überhaupt erst möglich wird, ist die Anwendung der Analogie. Die Analogie des vor unseren Augen Geschehenden und in uns sich Begebenden ist der Schlüssel zur Kritik." *Gesammelte Schriften*, 2. 732.

incursion into history to do the new and unique—i.e., the miraculous. Hence in order to view history as essentially apocalyptic and to make good his claim that, contrary to Barth and Bultmann, theology had nothing to fear and literally everything to gain from the historico-critical scrutiny of Biblical history Pannenberg had either to repudiate Troeltsch's principle of analogy or to show that the same principle could be used to yield conclusions opposite to Troeltsch's. Choosing the latter alternative Pannenberg argues that Troeltsch did not understand the limitations which should be placed upon the use of analogies. Otherwise he would not have made them serve as a criterion of what can be declared real in an historical tradition. A reported event for which there is no analogy may quite well have happened. The principle of analogy is to be applied to decide the validity of historical reports when the reports themselves, not the events reported, are analogous to myths, legends or visions. The principle of analogy should never block theology's access to the transcendent God's "individual, special contingent" acts in history, declares Pannenberg.

The historicity of an event like the resurrection of Jesus can be judged upon a careful examination of the reports to ascertain whether they are analogous to nonfactual kinds of historical accounts. The prejudgment that all historical events must be essentially the same simply rules out the historicity of the resurrection before the historian can begin his investigation, explains Pannenberg. For example, he does not agree with those who think that in his influential essay *Der Ablauf der Osterereignisse und das leere Grab* Hans von Campenhausen confused the historical and the kerygmatic by claiming as an historian to be able to account for the empty tomb by the possibility of the resurrection of Jesus.[34]

But to hold open the possibility of the resurrection of Jesus as an historical explanation of the empty tomb is one thing. To decide that this possibility has been actualized is quite something else. In order to substantiate his welcome assertion that Troeltsch's use of the principle of analogy can be set aside without debilitating the principle itself, Pannenberg must adduce a methodological criterion for the proper employment of the principle. But his placement of both history and revelation in the category of prolepsis leaves the epistemological support for the needed criterion begging. In his system, as we have seen, it is only from the perspective afforded by the end of history that one will be able to devise a criterion by which he can affirm that, as a matter of fact, the reports of the resurrection are not mythical or, at least, are probably true in the factual sense,

---

[34] "Heilsgeschehen und Geschichte," *KD* 5 (1959) 266-267, esp. n. 22. The views expressed by von Campenhausen in this essay, published in Heidelberg in 1952, lie "in the background" of "the Pannenberg group" who studied in Heidelberg at this time, reports J. M. Robinson, "Revelation as Word and as History," *Theology as History* (ed. J. M. Robinson; New York, 1967) 25.

whatever be their genre. But until he can devise that criterion he has no basis for claiming to use the Biblical reports to affirm as an historian that the possibility of the resurrection of Jesus accounting for the empty tomb was actualized. How crucial it is for him to be able to use the Biblical records in this way can be seen by recalling his contention that God's activity in history cannot be adequately comprehended at any time until his unique disclosure of his deity in the resurrection is grasped.

We must conclude, therefore, that Pannenberg has not successfully challenged Troeltsch's use of the principle of analogy in the historico-critical method.

Is our reaction to Troeltsch, then, a reversion to some kind of *Heilsgeschichte*, or the radical fideism of Roberts, or the Ritschlian-like attempt by Harvey to verify Christianity through inner experience? Must these thinkers be allowed to determine the methodological significance of an appeal to the apostolic eyewitnesses? Not so, if a way could be found for establishing on other than Pannenberg's faulty grounds his reformulation of Troeltsch's principle of analogy.

Pannenberg has correctly repudiated the positivistic view of historical facts that holds them to be discrete entities discovered by the historian who, upon closer examination, will observe their causal connections. Fortunately, he has no use for Taine's maxim: "Apres la collection des faits, la recherche des causes."[35] But although he basically stands with the nonpositivists on the issue of historical explanation and objectivity[36]—for instance, he says, "In spite of our statement that the meaning of an event is inherent to its original context and is not something injected into it by the interpreter, nevertheless that meaning can be determined only in relation to the vantage point of the particular inquirer"[37]—as described above, he has allowed his theory of the proleptic viewing of historical events to intensify the notion of an inherent meaning of an event in its original context to such an extent that he is left in a quasi-positivistic fashion with an objective, unbreakable union of event and meaning. We would deem it wiser to keep any such union from forming in order that no logical difficulties arise to hinder our acceptance of another of Troeltsch's three principles of the historico-critical method—namely, that "judgments about historical events can attain only varying degrees of probability."[38]

---

[35] Quoted in P. Gardiner, *The Nature of Historical Explanation* (Oxford, 1961) 70.

[36] For a lucid summary and comparison of the positivistic and nonpositivistic positions on these issues see P. Gardiner, "The Concept of Man as Presupposed by the Historical Studies," *The Proper Study*, Royal Institute of Philosophy Lectures (Macmillan, 1971), 4. 14-31.

[37] "Nazareth," 127; see *Jesus—God and Man*, 89.

[38] *Gesammelte Schriften*, 2. 731.

Harvey, who roundly criticizes orthodoxy for being incapable of following Troeltsch's historico-critical method, declared that "the difficulty with all orthodox attempts to ground the credibility of revelation in something objective like miracles or the fulfillment of prophecy is that they fail to see that there is no intrinsic connection between such external events and faith, *unless faith is already presupposed*" (which he thinks it should be).[39] It seems to us that so far from being the "difficulty" this is the beauty of the orthodox view. By denying any intrinsic connection between miraculous events and faith orthodoxy can maintain a genuinely critical stance as it "attempts to ground the credibility of revelation" in miracles.

Purported eyewitness accounts of the resurrection of a man, Jesus, need not be rejected out of hand because the event reported is not analogous to present-day experience. Pannenberg is right and Troeltsch is wrong here. But that this man, Jesus, was God's Christ, as the eyewitnesses interpret him to be—who but God or his inspired confidants would be in a position to know? The only viable question for the historian to seek to answer is: "What probability is there that the meaning they give this event constitutes a revelation of God and is, thereby, true?" Even if he tries to look at the resurrection proleptically in faith he is still faced with the necessity of establishing the fruitfulness of this method. Pannenberg is wrong and Troeltsch is right here. Pannenberg wisely recognizes that "even the supernatural interpretation does not necessitate it." But he unwisely fails to recognize the role that authority must play when he goes on to assert that the occurrence of a miracle, which he calls "an extraordinary event," is "a question of historical experience and judgment and not necessarily of authority."[40]

Assuming, then, the logical separability of the events three days after Jesus' entombment from their meaning for any historian, whether he claim the status of an eyewitness or not, on what basis could the present-day historian judge the credibility of the apostolic eyewitnesses' accounts of those events and their meaning? As already indicated the credibility of these accounts does not hinge on their recounting events analogous to what can be expected to be witnessed today. Rather the task of the Biblical scholar would be to determine the literary form to which the accounts themselves were analogous, or in other ways to ascertain the type of epistemological pretensions which, analogous to similar kinds of historical accounts, they have. If these pretensions are found to be of the high level traditionally held, then the question of their credibility becomes one of their veracity. Keeping in mind that there could neither be known to be nor reasonably be believed to be an intrinsic connection between the events reported and their interpretation in faith by the eyewitnesses as miraculous

[39] Harvey, *Historian*, 282 (italics his).
[40] *Human Nature*, 89.

revelations of God, we must confess that our belief that the eyewitness accounts are true derives logically, although perhaps not psychologically, from the truth of our belief that they are apostolic. Contrary to Harvey or Roberts, the historical theologian could never be capable of "conferring" the authority of those witnesses upon them, not even when viewing the eyewitnesses proleptically, as proposed by Pannenberg.

Manifestation of the Spirit

Morris Inch

ONE often picks up the comment that the Holy Spirit is manifest in the life of some individual or congregation. When pressed for evidence, the person who made the comment seems to have in mind some extraordinary incidents (miracles), enthusiasm, individual piety, or a combination of two or more of these factors. This perception influences the way he thinks of others and his own self-image as a seeker after the fullness of God.

The thesis I mean to set forth is a simple one, and I do not intend to make it appear any more difficult than is in fact the case. I suggest that the book of Acts represents the community of faith as the prime manifestation of the Holy Spirit. I am further convinced, although I shall not attempt to labor the point at this time, that the gospel of Luke is consistent with this conclusion. However, there are complicating factors in Luke, growing out of its synoptic character and the theological transition of the Spirit in the life and ministry of Christ to the messianic community that followed.

I. The Common Alternatives

I identified for the purposes of my study 48 episodes in which the Holy Spirit was manifest. Was the miraculous constantly evident? No. In less than twenty instances, assuming a more generous interpretation of what qualifies as miracle, were extraordinary events reported. Likewise of interest, all but four of these instances were related to the apostles and might best be understood as attesting to their particular office rather than the general manifestation of the Holy Spirit in the life of the Church.

I am reminded of C. S. Lewis' comment on the occurrence of miracles: "They come on great occasions: they are found at the great ganglions of history—not of political or social history, but of the spiritual history which cannot be fully known by men. If your own life does not happen to be near one of those great ganglions, how should you expect to see one?"[1] How indeed? Unless we have a distorted idea of how the Holy Spirit manifests himself, unless we fail to recognize that miracles fall out in great ganglions, such as in the deliverance of Israel from Egypt, the struggle of the prophets with Baalism, the life and ministry of Christ, the acts of the apostles.

[1]C. S. Lewis, *Miracles* (New York: Macmillan, 1947) 201.

That is not to argue that miracles never appear at less likely times but that they should not be taken as the necessary or primary manifestation of the Holy Spirit. Miracles are not the necessary manifestation, for the Spirit does not always or generally reveal himself in that fashion. They are not the primary manifestation, for (as we shall see) there is a predictable way in which we may expect him to be revealed.

The matter of enthusiasm is largely a moot question. Was the company of believers less inhibited, bubbling over with joy and borne along by ecstasy? The further one reads in Acts the less this common perception seems likely. The isolated proof text for being intoxicated with the Spirit (Acts 2:15) wears thin when stretched to accommodate the subsequent experiences with the Holy Spirit.

There is probably more reason to suppose that life in the Spirit was and is characterized by the full range of emotions than a constant high. The sage observed that there is "a time to weep, and a time to laugh; a time to mourn, and a time to dance" (Eccl 3:4). I suspect that the experience of the earliest Christians should be understood in this light.

If there was a contrast between the Christian and his contemporary in terms of disposition, I think that lay in the area identified by Oscar Cullmann, who recalls the contempt in which the Stoic emperor Marcus Aurelius held the Christians: "The alacrity with which the Christians met their death displeased him. The Stoic departed this life dispassionately; the Christian martyr on the other hand died with spirited passion for the cause of Christ, because he knew that by doing so he stood within a powerful redemptive process."[2] The Christian took life as the arena of God's redemptive program, where he might play some meaningful role. Thus he drank deeply of life, its bitterness as well as its sweetness, and so he followed in the footsteps of the Master.

But, I repeat, it is a moot question as relates to enthusiasm in the sense of some overriding emotional high. One must build from the bits and pieces of the Biblical record a mosaic of the Christian's experience. And the end result, no matter how persuasive it may appear, can hardly be the distinguishing mark of the Holy Spirit.

The alternative of individual piety has more to say for it. Acts takes great care to promote the guilelessness of the earliest Christians and to exonerate them from the charges leveled by their protagonists. Acts is something of an apologetic for the Christian faith, which rests in part on the piety of its adherents.

Nevertheless, this emphasis on personal piety seems meant less to distinguish the Christians from other men of good will than to include them along with others. And even when some distinctive may be implied,

[2]K. Stendahl, ed., *Immortality and Resurrection* (New York: Macmillan, 1965) 46.

the ambiguity of the reference suggests that this was not intended as a unique manifestation of the Holy Spirit.

There may be more at issue in this connection than we first suppose. Dietrich Bonhoeffer suggests that "two things are called penultimate in relation to the justification of the sinner by grace, namely being man and being good."[3] He means that it is possible to speak of manhood and goodness before and apart from the experience with Christ. This implies to me that no ethic can in and of itself be the primary manifestation of the Holy Spirit. Christians ought to live good lives in keeping with their profession, but this is neither synonymous with grace nor does it qualify as the distinctive manifestation of the Holy Spirit.

These common alternatives (miracles, enthusiasm, individual piety) hold out at best some partial truth and at worst are thoroughly misleading and even a snare to those seeking the fullness of God. They can lead us into fruitless exploration of some religious fad or another and away from the goal we mean to pursue.

II. The Thesis

What theme does the book of Acts set forth as the distinctive manifestation of the Spirit? I discovered that in 40 of the 48 episodes studied there was a reference to the community of faith, the messianic people of God. This fact, so obscured by popular opinions as to the manifestation of the Spirit, seems clearly evident.

Reflect on the emphasis in one of the texts: *Those who* received Peter's word were baptized, and *they* continued devoting *themselves* to the apostles' teaching and *fellowship. Everyone* experienced a sense of awe with the wonders and signs taking place through the apostles, and *all those* who had believed were *together*, holding *their* possessions in *common*, and selling *their* property in order to *share with all*, as *anyone* might have need. So *they* continued with *one mind* in the temple and taking *their* meals *together* with gladness and sincerity, praising God and having favor with all the people (Acts 2:41-47). Thus was the Lord adding to their number daily those regenerated by the Holy Spirit. Christian community appears as the critical indicator of the Spirit at work.

A veteran missionary helped firm up my conviction at this point. He told me how that one night, as he was returning from a meeting with Christians at the other end of an African village, he suddenly came upon a frenzied pagan ritual with the participants gyrating to the beat of drums. He stopped short in his tracks, overcome by a terribly stifling feeling of oppression that seemed to fill the air around him. The missionary cried out in anguish for God to rebuke the evil and demonstrate his power. It seemed

---

[3]D. Bonhoeffer, *Ethics* (New York: Macmillan, 1955) 133-134.

as if a hushed voice were speaking to him and inquiring as to where he had come from. "Why, from the other end of the village," he responded. "And what were you doing there?" the voice pressed further. Then it dawned upon him that the community of believers, squatted around the hut in prayer and Bible study, had only recently been participants in the pagan rite. Had the Holy Spirit been at work? Yes. What was the manifestation of the Spirit? That messianic community, which had been called out to serve the living God and minister in his name.

We naturally want to inquire into the nature of this community as manifesting the Holy Spirit. This fellowship exists, when it exists at all, in response to the call of Christ and by his grace. It does not come into being because it proposes to do so and is not sustained by its own endeavor. It is Christ's community.

The road this community takes is a difficult one, as the book of Acts testifies. There is oppression from without, discord within, and circumstances sufficient to discourage the most resolute among us. Yet the way is in a sense easy, so long as we follow the Master closely. We dare not lose sight of him or fail to take his gentle reprimand.

Dietrich Bonhoeffer concludes that "the separation of Church and world is now complete," but "the separation is never permanently assured; it must constantly be renewed."[4] The separation is complete, for these have decided to follow Jesus. Out of all the alternative possibilities they have decided to follow Jesus. In spite of obstacles raised to dissuade them they have decided to follow Jesus. This may seem a small thing to some but it makes a profound difference. It creates a great chasm between the Church and the world that appears greater still in eternity.

But the separation must also be renewed each step of the way. There can be no turning back, and when one stumbles he must reach up to grasp the extended hand of Christ and press on. There are those who seem so little to resemble the disciples of Jesus as to raise doubt as to their genuineness. That is not for us to determine. God is not through working with them. The fruit of the Spirit is sometimes late in blossoming.

There are others that seem so exemplary that this misleads us into thinking that they are choice servants of God. They may even deceive themselves. So while we may not know, God knows whose are his.

We can be certain of one thing: that our separation must be renewed. It was so in the past and so it must be on our dying bed, when we sense the time at hand to give an account for what we have done with our God-given opportunities.

We may conclude that the Spirit manifests himself in relationship to Christ. Jesus promised, "He will bear witness to me" (John 15:26)—and so he does. The Spirit directs our attention to Christ, the Savior of men. He

[4]D. Bonhoeffer, *The Cost of Discipleship* (New York: Macmillan, 1963) 212.

preempts our other interests, of whatever nature, and including an undue emphasis upon himself. He fixes "our eyes on Jesus the author and perfecter of faith" (Heb 12:2), not the author alone but the perfecter as well.

Thus when the Corinthian Church began to emphasize the gifts of the Spirit, and the less profitable ones at that, Paul reminded them of their place in the body of Christ. Their gifts were to be used to edify others rather than promote self. Christ should have the preeminence.

There were more subtle nuances in regard to the community of faith that impressed me in the review of Acts. Proclamation was one of these. F. F. Bruce observes, "The early apostolic *kerygma* regularly falls into four parts, which may be summarized thus: (1) the announcement that the age of fulfillment has arrived; (2) a rehearsal of the ministry, death, and triumph of Jesus; (3) citation of OT scriptures whose fulfillment in these events prove Jesus to be the Messiah; (4) a call to repentance."[5] This preaching appears to be a calculated supplement to the prophets, so that while "in the past God spoke to our forefathers through the prophets," "in these last days he has spoken to us by his Son" (Heb 1:1-2).

Once when the apostles were warned against teaching in the name of Jesus they responded, "We must obey God rather than men" (Acts 5:29). With this they proclaimed their message boldly and without regard for the cost it might involve. Luke concludes with the observation that "every day, in the temple and from house to house, they kept on teaching and preaching Jesus as the Christ" (5:42). Later on a great persecution arose against the Jerusalem Church, but when the believers "were all scattered throughout the regions of Judea and Samaria" they "went about preaching the word" (8:1, 4). The Spirit manifested himself not only in their singular attention to Christ but their faithful proclamation concerning him.

This was also a sharing community, for each as he was able to each as he had need. R. B. Rackham comments:

> Their success depended first on the local unity—they were all together; and then on the unselfishness of individuals. Many of the brethren must have come from the ranks of the poor, and the preaching of the gospel prevented the apostles from practising their trades. Hence the charge "go sell all that thou hast and give to the poor" must have been urgent on the wealthier converts. Accordingly many sold their possessions (lands and property) and goods (furniture and valuables). The money realized was given to the apostles and for the relief of want, as every man had need.[6]

As the Church expanded, it could no longer be "all together," and as a matter of historical record the Jerusalem congregation continued to require

[5] F. F. Bruce, *Commentary on the Book of the Acts* (Grand Rapids: Eerdmans, 1954) 69.

[6] R. B. Rackham, *The Acts of the Apostles* (London: Methuen, 1947) 42.

help. But the principle of sharing remained, "and the selling of possessions was succeeded by the sending of alms from one church to another."[7]

The concept of sharing was and is by nature reciprocal. It is both being available to others in their need and allowing them to minister to us as they are able and inclined. And it should not be construed in legalistic terms. Our contribution may not be to the one who has served us, let alone in the same measure. We seek to be generous to one another as the opportunity is afforded and do so in the larger service of Christ.

Francis Schaeffer carries our discussion one step further. He asks, "What is the final apologetic? 'That they may be one; as thou, Father, art in me, and I in thee, that they also may be one in us: that the world may believe that thou hast sent me.' This is the final apologetic."[8] It is the orderly fitting together of lives in cooperative ministry that helps round out our understanding of the Holy Spirit as manifested in community.

We recall that the first association the Hebrew people made with the Spirit was with bringing order out of chaos (Genesis 1). This undercurrent of thinking seems to flow throughout Acts. One dips in at any point and discovers it present. For instance, James' disposition of the Gentile issue (Acts 15) seems to reveal this perspective. He argues that God "was taking from among the Gentiles a people for his name. . . . Therefore it is my judgment that we do not trouble those who are turning to God from among the Gentiles" but urge them to abstain from those things especially repugnant to the Jews, who have "in every city those who preach him [Moses]." The Spirit does not manifest himself in the sowing of discord but in harmony and constructive endeavor.

Sin alienates men from God and from one another. Salvation reconciles us to the Almighty and to one another. The Spirit is manifested in life together, a people in communion with God and community among themselves. This is Schaeffer's "final apologetic," an evidence of the Spirit at work.

The final aspect of the community I wish to call our attention to is the creative diversity that manifests the Spirit's presence. Acts centers primarily on Peter and Paul, but there is an interesting array of lesser performers. These are, more times than not, portrayed as tokens of the Spirit's ministry.

C. S. Lewis introduces a helpful distinction that seems pertinent at this point. He observes that "a cruel man oppresses his neighbour, and so does simple evil. But in doing such evil, he is used by God, without his own knowledge or consent, to produce the complex good—so that the first man

---

[7]Ibid.

[8]F. Schaeffer, *The Mark of the Christian* (Downers Grove: InterVarsity, 1970) 15.

serves God as a son, and the second as a tool."[9] That is to say, some men cooperate with God's purposes as tokens of the Spirit's work, while others for all of their lack of intentional cooperation serve in the furthering of God's sovereign will.

Acts has its own quota of sons and tools. Each contributes through God's sovereign means to the rapid expansion of the Christian faith: from Jerusalem, throughout the region, and to the extent of the Roman empire.

These features we have mentioned (concerning proclamation, sharing, a harmonious cooperation, and a creative diversity) are only variations on the one theme. They suggest some of the more subtle ways in which the Spirit is manifested in community. The critical factor is the focus brought upon Christ and life together in him. Here is where we began to outline our thesis and with this emphasis we will conclude.

Dietrich Bonhoeffer extrapolates, "In the incarnation we learn of the love of God for His creation; in the crucifixion we learn of the judgment of God upon all flesh; and in the resurrection we learn of God's will for a new world."[10] Thus do we perceive life from the vantage point of the Christian community. We learn to appreciate God's creation, to be warned of man's defection, and to anticipate the final deliverance from this present evil world. And this community, living as it does between fulfillment past and future, is in itself the special manifestation of the Holy Spirit.

[9]C. S. Lewis, *The Problem of Pain* (New York: Macmillan, 1962) 111.
[10]Bonhoeffer, *Ethics*, 130-131.

Authority for a Going and Sending Ministry in the Christian Mission of World Evangelism

ROBERT DUNCAN CULVER

PAUL'S situation when he wrote the tenth and fifteenth chapters of his famous epistle to the Romans is important to understanding the argument of those chapters. In them he argues that some Christians must go to regions where Christ has not yet been named and others must send the ones who go.

He had long been engaged as Christ's missionary to the Gentiles. His initial conversion experience, both as Luke reports it directly (Acts 9:6) and as he quotes Paul (Acts 22:10-21), shows that from almost the first moment he was aware of a personal command from Christ to evangelize the heathen. As he paused at Corinth on this third missionary journey from Antioch he could write of how fully (up to then) he had fulfilled the duty laid on him by Christ: "From Jerusalem and round about even unto Illyricum, I have fully preached the gospel of Christ; yea, making it my aim so to preach the gospel, not where Christ was already named, that I might not build upon another man's foundation" (Rom 15:19-20). This means that according to his own standards and his mission as he understood it he had evangelized most of the eastern Roman empire. He had not visited those portions of the empire to which (like Alexandria and Egypt) others had previously taken the gospel, nor did he evangelize regions where the Spirit expressly forbade him. Further, we must understand "fully preached" in the sense of establishing witnessing congregations in urban centers from which by "spontaneous expansion" (to borrow Roland Allen's striking phrase) the churches carried the message to the countryside. Paul's aims were not unlimited. The *oikoumenē* (= Roman empire) was how he understood the geographical limits of his field, and only the policed and civilized portion of that.[1]

He felt he had fulfilled his commission in the eastern empire. It would have been a good time to retire, assigning to others the arduous task of evangelizing the west and visiting the churches in the places mentioned in later letters to Titus and Timothy. Instead he then began making practical,

[1] See R. D. Culver, *Toward a Biblical View of Civil Government*, 208-239.

157

tactical plans to evangelize the west personally in the same manner he had already evangleized the east.

The tactics would not essentially be new. It was only that he wished to have a new base of operation, nearer to the scene of work: Rome, the center of the Latin west and springboard for commerce, communication and government of the Occident in a way it never could be for the older and more sophisticated Orient.

There is no evidence I know of that this mission to the west was ever explained to Paul's home church at Antioch on the Orontes or that he ever sought their authorization for it. It is possible to make far too much of Paul's alleged dependence on the Church of Syrian Antioch for missionary authority. True, the congregation there had set aside Barnabas and Saul (Paul). But it was only in recognition of "the work" to which the Holy Spirit had already called them (Acts 13:1-3). When they went forth it was "being sent forth by the Holy Spirit" (13:4). Acts 13:1-4 is good grist for the mill of congregational polity but not quite a sufficient guide for authority in pioneer missionary evangelism. Paul's authority came more directly from the Lord, for he had known from the first that he was Christ's ambassador, not merely the Church's messenger. He preached as Christ's servant primarily.

He believed, as we shall see, in "comity" arrangements, determining never to build on others' foundations. Yet he needed human helps of many kinds, even financial help when his "own hands" were not quite up to earning a living and preaching too. Perhaps tents were not needed in Spain (cf. Acts 18:3-4). So he is respectful now to the Roman churches, which he had no part in founding, wishing to impose no personal authority on them to gain support of his cherished goals other than his apostolic authority as a teacher (see Rom 15:13-16).

Yet Paul needed and wanted their help in the projected mission to Spain—and who can doubt that he meant to reach all the Roman provinces northwest and west of Rome? How did he appeal to them for this help? What was the basis of the appeal?

The doctrinal declarations and clarifications of chaps. 1-8—"the gospel" with "the whole counsel of God"—constitute an agreed apostolic basis for any Christian mission at all. But there were many weaker brethren at Rome, probably the converted Jews of a predominantly Gentile congregation plus converts from the proselytes to Judaism and the "God-fearers" (those who, approving the Jews' religion, never formally became Jewish by religion). These people would need to be convinced of at least three things before Paul's plan could be effected: (1) the universality of Christianity—i.e., that one need not become a Jew to be a Christian; (2) the need that some Christians become missionaries to all the world—the whole of mankind—to preach the gospel to all men; and (3) that other Christians make it possible for the missionaries to go by sending them. All of Romans

9-11 is related to these matters, but the present study is limited to the most explicit part—to chap. 10 and to 15:8-33, where the argument is brought to conclusion.

One might suppose that Paul would simply have quoted the "great commission" to the Roman believers. What could be more explicit, we seem to think, than Matt 28:19-20 or Mark 16:15? True, there is nothing said about sending people, but who has not taken the leap of pulpit logic that goes about like this: "God commands every Christian to go. If you cannot go, then send someone else"? Of course the gospels may not have been written yet when about A.D. 56 Paul sent off his letter from Corinth to Rome by the hand of Phoebe, deaconess of nearby Cenchrea. The sayings of Jesus, reported in part in Jesus' speeches in the gospels, were in circulation far and wide and had been for a quarter century. Paul frequently cited teachings of Jesus later reported in the gospels. One thinks of 1 Corinthians 7 and the several times therein where Paul appeals to Jesus' teaching. And Paul could cite Jesus directly also, sometimes sayings found nowhere else than in Paul's quotation (e.g. Acts 20:35).

What is more in line with fact is that Paul did not cite Jesus' commands to provide authority for a general Christian mission of going or a duty to send missionaries because there were no such commands to quote, either from the gospels or pre-gospel tradition. There is really a wide gap between popular exposition of Matt 28:19-20 and parallels and the meaning adduced there from the Greek text in the critical commentaries and the great grammatical writers. In the main the preachers have not got together with the Greek text nor with the authors who have.

No one questions that the Church in the world has been committed "by her Lord" to a task of world-wide evangelism. Some time ago I showed by examination of the relevant texts, chiefly Matt 28:19-20, that from Jesus' perspective "the church is already deployed upon the field of activity."[2] Its members need not go anywhere at all to fulfill the great commission. Because the churches failed to take the gospel seriously in the home "parishes" and too frequently failed to take the gospel along wherever they went ("As ye go, make disciples") we now have to mount going and sending missions to refound the churches in the very regions where earlier the Church was strongest (North Africa, the eastern Mediterranean regions, and so on) in the first centuries. This has become true even in western Europe, as the names of several recently founded "foreign" missionary organizations ("Greater Europe Mission," "Slavic Gospel Mission," "Mission to Greeks," and the like) testify. I invite any who are disturbed by these words here to read my earlier article referred to above. The evidence has impressed many and convinced more than a few.

[2]R. D. Culver, *BETS* 10/2 (Spring 1967).

I do insist that if Paul had been able to cite a general command of Jesus for the going and sending of foreign missionaries he would have done so in the case of the mission to Spain. What he actually did was far different.

He employed only such authority as was available to him and, as we shall see, that was considerable. He knew that his own commission to go was from Christ himself. He apparently knew of no such direct demand for all Christians, so he employed Scripture and rational arguments to build a case for the necessity of a going and sending mission in chap. 10 of his letter. When he got around to specific support for his mission to Spain he used a similar method with a different set of Scripture texts in chap. 15. We cannot deal with quite everything in these chapters, not even everything that might feasibly apply to the foreign mission enterprise. Our pursuit must be focused on the topic of authority for a going and sending ministry in the Christian mission of world evangelism. Such authority as Paul could muster for his own project of going and sending, once recognized, becomes ours also.

I. THE ARGUMENT OF ROMANS 10

For brevity's sake I shall proceed mainly with propositions that summarize the teaching of the passage. The apostle's leading statement is that Christ is the end (*telos*) of the law to everyone who believes (v 4). Whether "end" be understood as goal, consummation or termination (and there are respectable advocates of each view) the righteousness (or salvation) offered by God to man is clearly intended for anyone and everyone who believes. Christianity is for all men, truly a universal offer of righteousness by faith. Paul wants to show why believers must see that this good news must reach the ends of the earth (cf. Psalm 19; Rom 10:18 and chap. 15). He supports his leading statement by two arguments drawn from the OT (10:5-9, 10-11). He then draws the conclusion that faith righteousness is freely available to heathen as well as Jews (vv 12-13). Then he shows how this leads logically to the necessity of a going and sending mission to the heathen (vv 14-15). He concludes this section by showing how response to the message, whether in unbelief or faith, is voluntary. Therefore God is not the cause of unbelief (vv 16-21).

1. *The first scriptural argument.* The word of faith, or the righteousness of faith, or the gospel, was already universal in the teaching of the Torah, truly allied to interior human nature.

"For Moses writeth that the man that doeth the righteousness which is of the law shall live thereby. But the righteousness which is of faith saith thus, Say not in thy heart, Who shall ascend into heaven? (that is to bring Christ down:) or, Who shall descend into the abyss? (that is to bring Christ up from the dead.) But what saith it [i.e., the righteousness which is by faith]? The word is nigh thee in thy mouth and in thy heart: that is the word of faith which we preach: because if thou shalt confess with thy mouth Jesus as Lord and shalt believe in thy heart that God raised him from the dead, thou shalt be saved" (Rom 10:5-9).

There is "an antithesis between the idea of righteousness which is of works and the inward essence of righteousness [vv 5-6]. But it is clear from the place of the citations, that this antithesis means no contradiction between the Old and New Testaments. The quotation in v. 5 is taken from Lev. 18:5; v. 6 from Deut. 30:11-14. It is evident, therefore, that the Apostle places two aspects of the law in contrast, one of which is an external Jewish law of works, and the other is an inward law of righteousness which is of faith, or a law designed for the inward life; the one is transient, the other permanent."[3] As is well known, Deuteronomy anticipates many of the teachings of the OT prophets on the prior place of evangelical repentance and faith in salvation, law-keeping being always a fruit of righteousness rather than its cause. Some writers with a special care to find no teaching of grace of any kind in a book of the Torah make Moses' words about the law typical but nevertheless have Moses telling of the gospel of grace, albeit in future tense. Especially helpful is this comment: "Therefore, as the former revelation put aside all effort to obtain a knowlege of His will, so the second revelation puts aside all effort to obtain righteousness . . . . Consequentially the words of Moses apply with still greater force to the gospel: and Paul is justified in calling them a voice of the righteousness of faith, proclaiming the end of the law. For the law implies doing: and according to Moses, the gospel puts an end to doing as a means of righteousness. If we admit, as Paul did, the divine origin of the words of Moses, we cannot doubt that it was mainly with a view to the gospel that the Spirit moved Moses to speak thus."[4] I see nothing in Paul's use of Deuteronomy to decide questions of covenant theology, dispensations, and so on, which are suggested inevitably by this discussion.

2. *The second scriptural argument.* The universality of the offer of the righteousness of faith, set forth by Moses, is known now by experience though previously declared by the OT prophets also.

"For with the heart man believeth unto righteousness; and with the mouth confession is made unto salvation. For the scripture [Isa 28:16] saith, Whosoever believeth on him shall not be put to shame" (Rom 10:10-11). Mention of heart and mouth, the inner being of man and the medium of its expression, takes the reader back to Moses' words just quoted from Deut 30:12, 14 and connects with Paul's last previous argument about universal grace in the Mosaic literature. Paul quoted Isa 28:16 earlier at Rom 9:33, as here, to show that the Gentiles have equal access to God with

---

[3]M. B. Riddle, *Commentary on Romans* (ed. J. P. Lange), ad loc.
[4]J. A. Beet, *Commentary on Romans*, 291.

Jews in the gospel. In each case Paul makes Isaiah's words distinctly Christian by adding "in him"—that is, in Christ. The LXX has, simply, "He that believeth shall never be put to shame."

3. *The conclusion to be drawn.* From Pentateuch, Prophets and experience we learn that all religious distinctions based upon race are foreign to the gospel. First, Paul puts the conclusion in remarkably clear language of his own and then in the words of a prophet (Joel 2:32; cf. Rom 10:12-13): "For there is no distinction between Jew and Greek: for the same Lord is Lord of all, and is rich unto all that call upon him: for whosoever shall call on the name of the Lord shall be saved."

4. *A practical "missionary" result of this conclusion.* Men must hear if they are to be saved. Thus the special going of some to preach and a sending of these by others are necessary if men are to be saved: "How then shall they call on him in whom they have not believed? and how shall they hear without a preacher? and how shall they preach except they be sent? even as it is written [Isa 52:7], How beautiful are the feet of them that bring glad tidings [Greek: of those who evangelize] of good things" (Rom 10:14-15).

The technical commentaries debate several questions herein. Is Paul thinking of a universal apostleship—that is, is he preparing for his own mission to Rome and beyond to Spain? Are those who "call on the name of the Lord"—that is, those who believe, specifically both Jews and Gentiles—in the thinking of Paul here? Is the sending of preachers definite—that is, Paul and his party? Or is it indefinite, referring to all missionaries of the gospel who are now going to be sent? And finally, is the sending done by God or by congregations of Christians? I think some of these questions can be answered and some cannot. The conclusion he makes is sustained however they are answered. Therefore we press on.

In any case the points being made are (1) that God has appointed that the gospel shall be preached everywhere on earth and (2) that God has appointed agents and means whereby the necessary preaching of the gospel in distant places shall be done. Messengers must go and they must be sent. Charles Hodge has written, "It is an argument founded on the principle, that if God wills the end, He wills also the means." M. B. Riddle, having surveyed the Greek text in detail and weighed the various arguments, comments that "the beautiful precision of the Greek requires us to find an intimation of the certainty of the universal gospel proclamation." He further says that "in the last [of Paul's series of questions], we have *ean mē*, which indicates that however men may fail to call and hear, those who will preach will certainly be sent forth."[5]

The last verses of the chapter present the contrasting responses of men to the hearing of the glad tidings. There is another Jew-versus-Gentile

[5]Riddle, *Romans*, 348.

contrast—of glad belief as opposed to sullen unbelief on the part of the hearers.

To conserve the readers' interest for the next part of the paper I shall forego commenting extensively on each of the final verses (16-21), for space does not allow further treatment except for v 17 a bit later. The concluding section as a whole may be summarized as follows:

5. *There is a universal Christian duty*. The gospel must be preached to all men everywhere without distinction for, even though some will reject it as national Israel did, others will receive it as the Gentiles are now doing. Both responses (rejection and faith) are part of God's plan and purpose and hence predicted in the OT (Paul cites Ps 19:4; Deut 32:21; Isa 65:1-2).

Verse 17 is important for focus on the topic of the going and sending mission of the Church. If all "belief" ("faith" *KJV*) comes of hearing and all true "hearing" of the gospel comes by the word of Christ ("of God" *KJV*) it is therefore incumbent upon believing people to organize missions to the unevangelized and to support them. The "hearing" of v 17 must refer to the message heard ("report") as in v 16, where it is equated with the gospel. The passage quoted from Isa 53:1 fitly employs a passive participle meaning "that which is heard by us." This message is the Word of God (or of Christ). It might help the case for a sending authority if the "Word" (v 17) were a direct command to the apostles and others to go. Such does not seem to be the case. The Word as cause and content of faith and as salvific instrument is what Paul means. It is important to know that the divine Word as recognizable content of the message has always been the decisive token of the authority of God's messengers—from Moses onward (see Deuteronomy 13; John 3:34; 17:8).

II. THE ARGUMENT OF ROMANS 15

Chapters 11-14 provide progress to 15:8-31. The topic of treatment of the weaker brethren even provides some transitional thoughts. Romans 15:8 nevertheless seems to appear abruptly, for here Paul begins in earnest to press the Roman believers for participation in his (and others') going to Spain as gospel preachers. He wants them to do nothing less than to approve the mission in brotherly affection, to join him in it, and to support it with material gifts and with prayer.

Paul is not by any means as direct in his approach as my preceding paragraph might suggest. He had nothing directly to do with founding the Church at Rome. They owed him respect and obedience due an apostle of Christ but not the affection due a father, upon which he based appeals in the two letters to Corinth and the Galatian letter. Whatever his rights and authority in a matter of practical action (the mission to Spain), Paul did not employ or appeal to them. Neither, significantly, did he appeal to any command of Christ regarding world evangelism. I think we may confidently

assume that in this as in so many other such "practical" matters he would
have appealed to the "dominical" authority of the personal words of Jesus
if he had known of any to which he might appeal. But he did not. So he
resorted fully to other kinds of argument: history (v 8), the direct teachings
of OT Scripture (vv 9-13), his own apostolic mission (vv 14-21), practical
strategy and current need (vv 22-23).

1. *Argument from the history of Christ's earthly mission (v 8)*: "For I
say that Christ hath been made a minister of the circumcision for the truth
of God, that he might confirm the promises given to the fathers."

There might have been some questions raised by Jews of the Roman
Church as to why Paul would want to take his ministry to heathen nations
when the Lord Jesus himself never devoted any extensive ministry to
Gentiles, even commanding his apostles on their first mission to go not into
any way of the Gentiles. Paul explains that there were special reasons. For
one, "the truth of God" was at stake. The promise of a Messiah was to the
Jewish people. From the first "promise to the fathers," the message of God
to Abraham, to the last promise in the last chapter of Malachi the Jews
had a special place in God's plan. They were the only people of God as yet.
To them belonged the covenants and promises. They were custodians of the
oracles of God. Those covenants, promises and oracles were theirs in the
first place. Even the gospel, Paul says elsewhere, is to the Jew first. Hence
Jesus lived out his days as a minister to the circumcision, authenticating
thereby the promises made to Israel. The nativity accounts all bear this out.
There is nothing in the NT more intensely Hebraic than those early
chapters of Matthew and Luke. When Jesus cried, "It is finished," among
the items consummated was his distinct function as "a minister of the
circumcision." As a nation they simply rejected him and, for all they knew,
simply did away with him. As minister exclusively to the Jews, Jesus is no
example for us. He was unique in this special responsibility to Israel. Yet
Paul says nothing to denigrate Israel, the special chosen people. The
expression "minister of the circumcision" (used nowhere else in Scripture)
is likely used here to check the pride of "the strong" (chap. 14 and 15:1-8),
the Gentile believers at Rome, by elevating the people of the covenant (9:1-
3) to their proper dignity. This also must be said for the sake of "the truth
of God."

It is worthy of note that though Paul does not quote the first form of
the promise "made to the fathers" (Gen 12:3) it did include a provision that
"in thee [Abraham and his posterity] shall all the families of the earth be
blessed."

2. *Argument from the teachings of the Old Testament Scriptures (vv 9-
13)*: "And that the Gentiles might glorify God for his mercy; as it is written
[Ps 18:49], Therefore will I give praise unto thee among the Gentiles, and

sing unto thy name, And again [Deut 32:43], Praise the Lord, all ye Gentiles, And let all the peoples praise him. And again [Isa 11:10], Isaiah saith, There shall be a root of Jesse, And he that ariseth to rule over the Gentiles; on him shall the Gentiles hope. Now the God of hope fill you with all joy and peace in believing, that ye may abound in hope, in the power of the Holy Spirit."

Many things impress the reader here: In the first place, Paul, the former disciple of Rabbi Gamaliel, quotes from all three parts of the OT: the Law (Deuteronomy), the Prophets (Isaiah) and the Writings (Psalms). He is finding whole-Bible authority for a Church sending mission to the Gentiles. He follows Jesus in the then-"new" Christian understanding of what we Christians have come to call "the Old Testament," for "he interpreted to them in all the scriptures the things concerning himself" (Luke 24:27).

In the second place, the praise of God from the majority section (Gentiles) of the human race rather than from a small tribe (Israelites) is an important thrust of the meaning of these select passages. "Praise . . . among the Gentiles. . . . Rejoice ye Gentiles with his people. . . . Praise the Lord, all ye Gentiles. . . . let all the peoples [plural] praise him." No longer shall a remnant from the nations of earth (the Hebrews) alone have a saving covenant and receive salvation's praise-inducing benefits. All "the Gentiles"—i.e., nations (*ethnoi*)—shall "glorify God for his mercy" (v 9).

In the third place, Paul carefully distinguishes covenant promise from mercy. God made covenant with Israel (merciful, to be sure; but, once made, a matter of fidelity on God's part), but he had and has mercy on the Gentiles. He confirms promises to Israel but extends mercy to Gentiles (v 9). The covenant with Abraham and his seed mentions Gentiles, but it is never with the Gentiles in any primary sense. The Gentiles are never an Israel so far as I can see—spiritual or otherwise. Of the Israelites Paul says elsewhere that theirs is the adoption (*huiothesia*, "son-placement") and the glory and the covenants and the giving of the Law and the service (*latreia*, "ritual worship") of God and the promises. What God has done in Christ for Israel (in Romans often referred to obliquely as "us" or "we") is indeed a matter of special arrangement in ancient covenant. For the Gentiles (in Romans often "ye" or "you"), however, God's saving actions are a matter of mercy apart from covenant.

It is reassuring, if likewise disconcerting, to find that Paul seems almost naive to some of our doctrinal distinctions, now favoring what looks like one kind of modern evangelical theology, then another, and sometimes seeming to amalgamate them.

This section again presents a hornet's nest of vexing textual problems—LXX renderings versus Hebrew, Pauline adaptation versus strict quotation, and so on. But these in no case seem to detract from Paul's plain thrust, so we simply summarize and pass on.

3. *Argument from Paul's own apostolic mission (vv 14-21):* "And I
myself am persuaded of you, my brethren, that ye yourselves are full of
goodness, filled with all knowledge, able also to admonish one another. But
I write the more boldly unto you in some measure as putting you again in
remembrance, because of the grace that was given me of God, that I should
be a minister of Christ Jesus unto the Gentiles, ministering the gospel of
God, that the offering up of the Gentiles might be made acceptable, being
sanctified in the Holy Spirit. I have therefore my glorying in Christ Jesus in
things pertaining to God. For I will not dare to speak of any thing save
those which Christ wrought through me, for the obedience of the Gentiles,
by word and deed, in signs and wonders, in the power of the Holy Spirit;
so that from Jerusalem and round about even unto Illyricum, I have fully
preached the gospel of Christ; yea, making it my aim so to preach the
gospel, not where Christ was already named, that I might not build upon
another man's foundation; but as it is written [Isa 52:15], They shall see, to
whom no tidings of him came, and they who have not heard shall
understand."

These are verses (as indeed in all of chap. 15) to try the pulpit
expositor's patience and skill. Not many sermons are preached on them.
The point of the chapter—an effort to solicit agreement, prayer and
support for the mission to Spain—is slow in coming. But let us be patient
with Paul. There were reasons for his circuitous approach. We remind
ourselves again that he was proposing something new—perhaps unheard of
in Rome: Christians should not only take the gospel along wherever they
go. Jesus' command was plain enough about that. They should also mount
campaigns of evangelism. They must dedicate life and treasure to send
gospel messengers abroad to "foreign" parts. (How strange the word
"foreign" sounds in our age of pussyfoot terminology! We now hear only of
"overseas" missions, a misnomer if there ever was one.) And some Christians
must go. They must also, from another perspective, be sent. So let us
quietly submit to the courteous usages of another age when men were not
so ready to "let it all hang out" or so impatient to "get to the point" and
demanding that everyone "tell it like it is." There are personal reflections of
the author to ponder and his personal history: "I myself am persuaded. . . .
I write the more boldly. . . . I should be a minister. . . . I have therefore my
glorying. . . . I will not dare to speak. . . . Christ wrought through me. . . . I
have fully preached . . . making it my aim . . . that I might not build upon
another man's foundation." This sort of rumination takes an intimate
approach that seems odd for one who was a stranger to most of his readers.
This mixing of personal sentiment and emotion with the serious business
being proposed should only heighten our awareness of the great delicacy of
the matter of proposing a great project on a grand scale to people strangers
to Paul's person.

The author seeks to build a bridge of mutual respect between writer and readers in vv 14-15a: "But I myself also am persuaded of you, my brethren, that ye yourselves are full of goodness, filled with all knowledge, able also to admonish one another. But I write the more boldly unto you in some measure."

They are, he says, well-taught, mature believers (v 14). Perhaps these words of praise expressing high esteem are intended to overcome any antagonism produced by his rather sharp negative criticisms of chap. 14. This serves to put those criticisms in the realm of loving reproof within family relationships. He also calls them "my brethren." Furthermore, though "I write the more boldly," he says, it is only "in some measure"—i.e., partly (*apo meros*). The very same expression elsewhere in Romans (11:25) means "in part, partly." This phrase seems best to be taken in the sense of part (only certain portions of his letter) as opposed to the whole. In addition to chap. 14 there are other rather severe statements, but generally the apostle says very little by way of direct reference to the Roman congregation.

Next the apostle carefully explains the special character of his own work and its unique value to God. He explains how that in Christ's own arrangement of affairs for mankind he (Paul) is "minister of Christ Jesus unto the Gentiles." He asserts that it is a special ministry, of a high value and apparently generally recognized by Christians: "as putting you again in remembrance, because of the grace that was given me of God, that I should be a minister [a priestly minister, *leitourgos*] of Christ Jesus unto the Gentiles, ministering [officiating as a sacrificing priest, *hierourgounta*] the gospel of God, that the offering up [presenting a sacrificial victim, *prosphora*] of the Gentiles might be made acceptable, being sanctified by the Holy Spirit" (Rom 15:15b-17).

The figures drawn from the sacrificial ritual rites of the ancient world, both pagan and Jewish, are transparent. They serve only to convey the religious-spiritual values, not to teach anything at all about any genuine Christian ritual sacrifice or ritual priesthood. Both he and they know they have no place in Biblical Christian religion. This device is not strange or unusual in Paul's writings, for even in the next chapter (v 5) "Epaenetus . . . is the firstfruits of Asia unto Christ" (cf. 11:16; 1 Cor 15:10, 23). In this manner Paul puts the projected mission of evangelists going to Spain and of others sending on the very highest possible level of human religious effort. It is difficult for the exegete even to discuss this passage without employing (albeit symbolically) ritual language ordinarily abhorrent to the sons of the Protestant Reformation. Yet nothing could more fully convey the holiness of the project.

Finally, Paul deftly prepares to connect the "novel" missionary project with his own reasons for writing them a letter: "For I will not dare to speak of any things save those which Christ wrought through me, for the obedience of the Gentiles, by word and deed, in the power of signs and wonders, in the power of the Holy Spirit; so that from Jerusalem, and round about even unto Illyricum I have fully preached the gospel of Christ; yea, making it my aim so to preach the gospel, not where Christ was already named, that I might not build upon another man's foundation; but as it is written [Isa 52:15], They shall see, to whom no tidings of him came, And they who have not heard shall understand" (Rom 15:18-21).

Let a few comments serve to make the necessary connection of Paul's argument for support of his western mission with the argument of this essay for authority in all Christian missions of evangelism. The Romans should be informed that his policy, under Christ's special assignment, is to do strictly pioneer work, gospelizing only in regions where others have not previously done so. This mission, amply authenticated by divine signs and power, has now been completed throughout the eastern empire. Paul has evangelized from Jerusalem along the Mediterranean littoral northwest through the regions of what we now call Syria and Asia Minor, Greece and Macedonia to Illyricum, also called Dalmatia, a Roman province lying north of Macedonia. It lay west of Moesia and south of Pannonia and on the east coast of the Adriatic Sea—i.e., in territory approximately the same as modern Yugoslavia.

4. *Argument from the standpoint of practical strategy and present need (vv 22-33):* Some authors have pronounced all of Rom 15:14-33 an epilogue, his instructions and exhortations being now complete. Others, certainly correct, assert that herein he "comes to the last design of his Epistle, which is, to make Rome the principal station for his missionary labors in the West."[6] Since we have read this climactic practical main design of the letter we may use it to guide us in interpreting the previous parts—something the first recipients could not do when they first heard it read in their assembly. They could do so the second time over.

I shall not cite this lengthy section in full and shall not attempt consecutive exposition. Rather I shall summarize in several propositions what Paul seems to be saying and relate it to the going and sending mission of world evangelism as related to his time.

(1) A new missionary venture is about to be launched: Paul is going to move his missionary activity to Spain. There is even a hint in Luke's report just a bit later (Acts 19:21). Reasons have already been given in the earlier parts of the chapter. He summarizes by claiming he has run out of space for his effort in the east: "having no more any place in these regions" (v 22). "Whensoever I go unto Spain" (v 24) states the intention. "When therefore I have accomplished this and have sealed to them this fruit, I will go by you unto Spain" (v 28) sets the schedule as far as Paul could determine it. Of

[6]Ibid., p. 439.

course as every reader of Acts 21-28 knows, Paul lost all personal control of his travels and work for several years. When he finally did get to Rome it was under guard as a prisoner of the empire. Whether he ever got to Spain is not known for certain, though there are strong local traditions in various parts of Spain that he did. These are credited sufficiently in Spain today that "in the early 1960's several Spanish communities celebrated the 19th centenary of the arrival of the Apostle Paul in Spain, and in 1961 the Spanish postal authorities issued a 1-peseta commemorative stamp showing El Greco's Apostle Paul with the text: 'XIX CENTENARIO DE LA VENIDA DE SAN PABLO A ESPANA'."[7] Early Christian documents support the tradition of Paul's missionary travel about the empire later than the two years of Acts 28:30 and therefore after his release from the Roman prison: *Epistle of Clement of Rome to the Corinthians* (A.D. 96), *Canon of Muratori* (ca. A.D. 170), *Apocryphal Acts of Peter* (chap. 3).

(2) Evidently the missionary party had already been formed. I assume this on the correlation of certain statements here with data of the later chapters of Acts. The Christians of Macedonia and Achaia (Athens and environs in Greece) have given money for the relief of poverty-stricken and oppressed believers (Jewish) of the mother Church of Christendom at Jerusalem (v 26). This is a duty (Paul used the word "debtors," *opheiletai*, v 27) of the Gentile believers—of which more later. He is about to carry this gift personally to Jerusalem, but he is apprehensive that the anti-Gentile sentiments of the Jewish Christians at Jerusalem may prevent him from delivering it. He asks the Roman believers to pray that they will receive it. He is also apprehensive that he may come to harm from the jealous non-Christian Jews of Palestine (v 31). Now all this appears in the reports of the book of Acts. We know also that Paul was not traveling alone. Chapter 20 onward in Acts is reported by Luke in first person plural—the well-known "we" device. Evidently Luke stayed with Paul right on through the two years' imprisonment at Caesarea and the voyage to Rome (see Acts 27:1; 28:1; and so on). It seems safe to suppose that others of the well-known associates of Paul, veterans of the eastern campaigns, were to join him at Rome. The tradition, however, is that his companions were two young believers of Rome and that they sailed with him from Ostia (*Acts of Peter*, chap. 3).

(3) The principle of universal (ecumenical, if you please) Christian support for the common cause of the Christian mission is assumed without being stated. There is first of all the cooperative collection itself, to which Paul alludes. He argues that Gentiles have a special duty in this regard (v 27): "Their debtors they are. For if the Gentiles have been made partakers of their spiritual things, they owe it to them also to minister unto

[7]O. F. A. Meinardus, "Paul's Missionary Journey to Spain," *BA* 41/2 (June 1978) 63.

them in carnal things." This principle could extend to support of missions in distant places where the ordinary believer cannot go. It links neatly with "how shall they preach except they be sent" (10:15) and the argument for support of apostles and other missionary "professionals" elsewhere by Paul: "What soldier ever serveth at his own charges?" (1 Cor 9:7; cf. entire chapter).

(4) The apostle has selected Rome and the Roman Church as base for this new missionary thrust. He has just expressed his long-deferred desire to come "to you [Romans]" (v 23), and now Paul plainly if indirectly places his mission before their Christian consideration: "Whensoever I go unto Spain (for I hope to see you in my journey, and to be brought on my way thitherward by you, if first in some measure I shall have been satisfied with your company). . . . I will go on by you into Spain. And I know that, when I come unto you, I shall come in the fullness of the blessing of Christ. Now I beseech you, brethren, by our Lord Jesus Christ, and by the love of the Spirit that ye strive together with me in your prayers to God for me" (vv 24, 28, 29, 30). He makes his appeal for support somewhat indirectly (as is still common today) but none the less distinctly. He wants their friendship; he calls it "company" (v 24). He desires their material support; it is surely more than an escort "thitherward by you" (v 24). The offering for the poor believers at Jerusalem, in which they had no part, would surely further incline them to see the propriety of giving money to pay for Christian efforts outside their local congregation. This aspect of his advance publicity (like mention of money by missionary publicists today) may be only a broad hint, understandably so in each case. He also desires their prayers. He is specific about prayer for a reception of his mission on the detour to Jerusalem and for physical safety there. Though he does not specifically mention prayer in connection with his great project in Spain, we cannot doubt that they did think about it and that once in Rome he intended to spell this out fully.

The early Church was convinced that Paul's appeal to Caesar was successful, and being freed again he entered on another rather lengthy ministry of "itinerant evangelism." Many modern scholars have been convinced that 2 Timothy and Titus come from this later period. The greatest of the early Church historians, Eusebius, wrote that "after pleading his cause, he is said to have been sent [note the word "sent" in connection with the theme of this essay] again upon the ministry of preaching, and after a second visit to the city [Rome], he finished his life with martyrdom."[8] If this is true, then the book of Romans just may be the first bit of successful literature of what until very recently was called foreign mission propaganda.

[8] Eusebius *Hist. eccl.* 2.22.

Textual Variants of the
"Apostolic Decree"
and Their Setting in the Early Church

J. JULIUS SCOTT, JR.

MOST serious students of the NT are aware of variants to the traditional text of the so-called "apostolic decree" of the Council of Jerusalem (Acts 15:20, 29; cf. 21:25). Less well known is the extent of these variations.

The traditional text, represented by the Alexandrian and Byzantine traditions, states that Gentile Christians should abstain (or "keep away") from four things: (1) the pollution of idols; (2) fornication (or "unchastity"); (3) things strangled; and (4) blood. The Western text (including D and Irenaeus *Against Heresies* 3.12, 14) omits "things strangled" but adds a negative form of the "golden rule": "And whatever you do not wish to be done to you, do not to others." Tertullian (*On Modesty* 12) not only follows D by omitting "things strangled"[1] but also omits the negative rule.[2] P45 (the Chester Beatty papyrus) supports quotations by Origen (*Against Celsus* 8.29) and the Rendel Harris manuscript of the Didascalia[3] by retaining "things strangled" but omitting "fornication."[4]

---

[1] Without making specific reference to the decree Tertullian affirms that Christians abstain from eating "things strangled" in *Apology* 9.

[2] Tertullian knows and quotes the negative rule in *Against Marcion* 4.16, a context in which the decree is not mentioned.

[3] Cited by E. Preuschen, *Die Apostelgeschichte* (HNT; Tübingen: 1912) 97.

[4] P. H. Menoud, "The Western Text and the Theology of Acts" (Bulletin 2 of the Society of New Testament Studies; Oxford, 1951) 19 ff., argues that the original text must have included only prohibitions against the pollution of idols and from blood. The rest, he says, were added later. Although there is no manuscript evidence for a two-part decree, Menoud argues that such a thesis is required on the principle that within the history of the growing Church we have no examples of a constricting development. Always the reverse is true.

This is a common argument but not always true. Passages in *T. Levi* and *T. Naph.* have been discovered at Qumran that are longer than the previously known and later Greek texts (cf. M. Burrows, *More Light on the Dead Sea Scrolls* [London, 1958] 179). The Latin translation of the epistle of Barnabas is shorter than the Greek text. Jerome both fills out and shortens the commentary on the Apocalypse by Victorinus of Petau.

In addition to actual wording, the order of the decree differs. The order given above is that of Acts 15:20. In the Alexandrian-Byzantine text the order of 15:29 is 1, 4, 3, 2; in 21:25 it is 1, 4, 2, 3. The second time Tertullian lists the decree (*On Modesty* 12) his order is 2, 4, 1.

It is obvious that there was a textual fluidity in the traditions about the decree in the early Church. This investigation is an attempt at historical reconstruction, not an exercise in textual criticism.[5] It seeks to suggest the possible life-situations that encouraged the emergence and development of these textual variations.

I. THE RELATION OF THE DECREE TO THE COUNCIL OF JERUSALEM (Acts 15)

The subjects considered at the Council of Jerusalem described in Acts 15 and the nature of the actions taken are points of disagreement among students of Acts. There are also differences of opinion regarding the relation of the meetings Paul had with Jerusalem officials according to Acts 9, 11 and 15 and the meetings described in Galatians 1 and 2. Investigations of the last two centuries have cast doubt on the convening of the council, on Paul's participation in such a meeting, and on the authenticity of the decree as now associated with the account in Acts 15.[6]

I hold that the council was convened to deal primarily with the questions of the relation of circumcision and observance of the Mosaic customs and laws to Christian salvation (Acts 15:1, 5). This matter was settled by noting evidences of God's work both in Palestine (the Cornelius incident) and elsewhere that made it clear that God made "no distinction" between Jews and uncircumcised Gentiles "but cleansed their hearts by

---

[5] For an investigation of the textual problem see J. H. Ropes, *The Text of Acts*, Vol. 3 of *The Beginnings of Christianity* (ed. F. J. Foakes-Jackson and K. Lake; London, 1926) *ad loc.*; C. S. C. Williams, *Alterations to the Text of the Synoptic Gospels and Acts* (Oxford, 1951) 72 ff.; F. F. Bruce, *The Acts of the Apostles* (2d ed.; Grand Rapids, 1952) 299-300; and B. M. Metzger, *A Textual Commentary on the Greek New Testament* (New York, 1971) 429 ff.

[6] For a summary of these discussions see relevant sections in commentaries on Acts, esp. F. F. Bruce, *Acts of the Apostles*, 287 ff.; *Commentary on the Book of the Acts* (NICNT; Grand Rapids, 1954) 298 ff.; E. Haenchen, *The Acts of the Apostles* (Eng. trans.; Oxford, 1971) 440 ff. Cf. also J. C. Hurd, Jr., *The Origin of I Corinthians* (London, 1965) 240 ff.; M. Simon, "The Apostolic Decree and its Setting in the Ancient Church," *BJRL* 52/2 (1970) 437 ff.

Elsewhere I have dealt with the Jerusalem Council as a whole, including the historical and critical problems that arise from a comparison of the accounts in Acts with those in Galatians. I have also discussed the purpose, setting and text of the decree. See "The Church of Jerusalem, A.D. 30-100: An Investigation of the Growth of Internal Factions and the Extension of its Influence in the Larger Church" (unpublished Ph.D. dissertation; Manchester, England: University of Manchester, 1969) 15 ff., 169 ff.

faith" (15:9). This evidence from experience was supported by OT Scriptures that had predicted that God would accept Gentiles who sought him and called upon his name (15:15-18 citing Amos 9:11-12 LXX). Thus the council recognized that for both Jews and uncircumcised Gentiles alike Christian salvation was "through the grace of the Lord Jesus" (15:11), appropriated "through faith" (15:9).

This decision raised at least two distinct practical problems. Jewish Christians who desired to continue living by the Torah, either from habit or nationalistic motives, faced a dilemma. On the one hand, how could they accept and associate with their Gentile brother-Christians as the Church required and at the same time abstain from contact with ceremonially unclean persons and objects as at least some interpretations of the Torah required?[7] On the other hand, Jewish Christians knew well that paganism involved a whole way of life and culture. As a matter of course, many Gentiles accepted attitudes and practices that were abhorrent to Jewish sensitivities and unacceptable in the Christian life. Hence some framework was needed to assure that those who entered the Christian community from pagan backgrounds would maintain at least minimum standards of decency and morality. It was to this issue, it seems to me, that James and the council with him turned after clarifying the prior question of the Christian way of salvation.

There was within Second-Commonwealth Judaism the machinery for dealing, at least in part, with these difficulties.[8] The Pentateuch made provision for the "stranger" (gēr) who desired to live within the geographical boundaries of Israel, but it placed certain restrictions and obligations upon him (cf. Leviticus 17-18). Both Josephus Ag. Ap. 3.39 (282) and Sib. Or. 3:24 ff., 162 ff. allude to observances which, if kept by Gentiles, permitted them some intercourse with pious Jews. In the post-NT period the Talmud assumes that the so-called "Laws of the Sons of Noah"[9] were obligatory for the whole human race, but in practice their restrictions may have only provided a framework for Jewish-Gentile contacts. All this appears to point toward the existence of some generally understood requirements for that unofficial class known as "God-fearers"—Gentiles

---

[7]But A. Büchler, "The Levitical Impurity of Gentiles in Palestine Before the Year 70," JQR NS 17 (1926-27) 1-81, argues that Judaism did not regard contact with Gentiles to be a cause of defilement until after A.D. 70.

[8]See also the general discussion of Jewish elements behind the decree in Str-B, 2. 729 ff.

[9]The Talmud frequently speaks of the "seven laws of the sons of Noah," but lists of these differ in context, order, wording and actual number. Sanh. 56b (cf. Gen. Rab. Noah 34) commands Jews (1) to obey those in authority, (2) to sanctify the name of God, (3) to abstain from idolatry, (4) to commit no fornication, (5) to do no murder, (6) not to steal, and (7) not to eat living flesh—i.e., flesh with blood in it. Cf. J. H. Greenstone, "Laws, Noachian," Jewish Encyclopedia, 8. 648 ff.

who revered Yahweh, attended synagogue worship and had some contact with Jews but stopped short of becoming proselytes. I believe that it was from such a background and spirit as this that the decree of the Jerusalem Council originated.

However, to understand better what is involved in both these Second-Commonwealth Jewish requirements and in the decree of Acts 15 we must note more precisely just what caused the pious Jew to recoil from unnecessary contact with Gentiles. Second-Commonwealth Jewish hatred of Gentiles and/or aversion to contact with them was a complex and many-sided phenomenon. Three factors seem to predominate. Jews abhorred and were suspicious of Gentiles because of their (1) idolatry and all associated with it, (2) low ethical and moral standards, and (3) disregard of and often animosity for Jewish dietary restrictions and other regulations for ceremonial purity.[10] These Gentile practices and attitudes were often interrelated as parts of the life-style of the paganism from which Gentile Christians had come. Jewish Christians knew all too well that the "side effects" or "pollutions" of idolatry might remain as ingrained habits long after the Gentile believer had given up actual worship of idols.[11] However, not all Gentile sexual irregularities, abortions, murder of slaves, infanticides, and so forth were performed as acts of pagan worship. Jewish aversion to table fellowship with Gentiles was based upon more than simple fear of meats that had been dedicated in a pagan temple. Unregulated contact with Gentiles might endanger the whole system of ceremonial and ritual observances that had become an emblem of national identity and instruments of a protective exclusivism within some branches of Second-Commonwealth Judaism.[12]

With this in mind it appears likely that the decree was directed toward genuine, specific problems that Jewish Christians faced in an interracial but

---

[10]In the Midrash collection *Gen. Rab.* 31:6 some light is shed on the question, "What are the cardinal sins in Judaism?" The passage comments on Gen 6:11, which states that God's wrath fell on the world of Noah "because the earth was filled with *ḥāmās* (violence)." R. Levi says that *ḥāmās* means "bloodshed" (= murder; prooftext Joel 4:19), "sexual abominations" (prooftext Jer 51:35) and "idolatry" (prooftext Ezek 8:17, which in fact is a quotation of Gen 6:11). *T. Sanh.* 74a says that every Jew must be willing to martyr himself to avoid committing these three sins. For these rabbinic references I am indebted to T. S. Frymer-Kensky, "The Atrahasis Epic and its Significance for our Understanding of Genesis 1-9," *BA* 40/4 (December 1977) 147-155.

[11]We have but to observe the "negative" ethical lists in some NT epistles to realize the enormity of the problem faced by the early Church. Evidently the writers had reason to believe that such sins as those mentioned in Gal 5:19-21; Col 3:5-9; 1 Pet 4:3, to say nothing of the specific situations dealt with in 1 Corinthians, were being practiced by some Gentile Christians.

[12]Cf. W. Forster, *Palestinian Judaism in New Testament Times* (trans. G. E. Harris; Edinburgh, 1964) 5 ff.

predominantly Jewish-oriented Church. At the same time that the council asserted the principle of Gentile freedom from the Torah it requested that this freedom be exercised within the limits of responsibility, including the purity inherent within Christian morality and sensitivity and with concern for the consciences of other members of the body of Christ.[13]

II. THE MEANING AND INTENT OF THE TEXTUAL VARIANTS OF THE DECREE

It is often difficult to determine the precise shade of meaning and emphasis given the decree as a whole by the inclusion or omission of one or another element. It is generally agreed that the forms of the text indicate that the decree was apparently understood as relating to food and ceremonial restrictions in the east and was interpreted as a moral injunction in the west.[14] I believe this to be an oversimplification.

The investigator who attempts to probe more deeply faces the difficulty of determining the precise referent of the individual elements of the decree. For example, is the prohibition of "fornication" primarily a ceremonial command against consorting with sacral prostitutes in pagan temples, or does it relate to marriage within restricted bounds (cf. Lev 18:6 ff.), or is it a moral injunction against any form of sexual irregularity? Is the prohibition of "blood" to be equated with "things strangled" as dual enjoinders against drinking blood (cf. Gen 9:4; Lev 3:17; 7:27; 17:10-14) or/and eating flesh not properly drained (cf. Lev 19:26), or does "things strangled" convey a ceremonial-dietary prohibition while "blood" is a moral injunction against murder?

All forms of the decree contain *tōn alisgēmaton tōn eidōlōn* (or *apechesthai eidōlothytōn* in 15:29) which, with Lake[15] and the *RSV*, I have translated "abstain from the pollution of idols." This translation assumes that this part of the decree included not only the prohibition of actual worship of false gods but also all that was associated with it. There is of course more than simple Jewish preference or sensitivity behind this element of the decree. Monotheism is as much an inherent part of Christianity as it is of Judaism. Threats against it were always present in

---

[13] I suggest that the decree was a compromise characteristic of the spirit of the "Moderate Hebrew Christians" (one of at least three factions in the Jerusalem Church). It was intended to safeguard Jewish consciences and hopefully to further peaceful relations between Jewish and Gentile Christians. See my "The Church of Jerusalem," 165 ff.; "Parties in the Church of Jerusalem as Seen in the Book of Acts, " *JETS* 18/4 (Fall 1975) 224 ff.

Compare the conclusions of M. Simon who says, "The purpose of the Decree is precisely to establish between Jewish Christians and Gentile Christians an effective community, in particular as regards meals, and thus to make possible a common celebration of the Lord's Supper." "Apostolic," 459.

[14] For a summary of interpretations and opinions see Haenchen, *Acts*, 449 n. 1.

[15] Lake, *Beginnings*, 5. 205; cf. "*eidōlon*," *TDNT* 2 (1964) 375 ff.

the world and culture within which first- and second-century Gentile Christians lived.

The invitation of early Christian witnesses to accept Jesus as Savior and Lord would not necessarily have been strange to many pagans. They would have seen no difficulty in worshiping this God along with other gods. It was the Christian insistence upon the existence of and call for commitment to only one God, he who had revealed himself through Jesus Christ, that was a unique feature of Christianity. Many Gentile Christians seem to have been slow or reluctant to recognize this fact. There was a constant need to guard against syncretism. The consistent occurrence and priority of place given this prohibition in all versions of the decree is an eloquent reminder of the magnitude and gravity of this problem in the early Church.

But what is the significance of the inclusion or omission of one or more of the other elements of the decree? The Alexandrian-Byzantine four-element version of the decree could be interpreted in at least one of three ways: (1) If the prohibition against fornication has reference to sacral prostitution and/or marriage restrictions and the mention of "blood" is intended to enforce the Levitical regulations against drinking blood, then the primary concern of the decree is with ceremonial and dietary matters. (2) If "fornication" is meant to enjoin all forms of sexual irregularity and the prohibition against blood a restatement of the sixth commandment, then the wide difference between Jewish and Gentile moral codes and practices may be the major concern behind this form of the decree. (3) It is also possible that the fourfold form of the decree intends sanctions of equal emphasis against each of the categories of Gentile sins from which Jews recoiled.[16]

The omission of "fornication" in the P45-type text probably suggests primary emphasis upon ceremonial matters, especially food laws. This is surely the case if "blood" is interpreted as a dietary restriction.

The absence of "things strangled" from the D-text and Tertullian seems to give the decree a decided moral and ethical emphasis. The negative form of the golden rule strengthens the ethical orientation of those representatives of the Western text in which it is included.

---

[16]Thus the mention of particular sins in the decree (representing religious, moral and ceremonial matters) may be a case of citing specific members of a class or group although the whole category is intended. This appears to have been an accepted Jewish interpretative practice (see no. 18 of the thirty Middoth of the Talmud). Cf. H. L. Strack, *Introduction to the Talmud and Midrash* (Eng. trans.; Philadelphia, [1931] 1959) 95 ff.

III. The Citation and Interpretation of the Decree by Early Christian Writers

All forms of the decree address the problem of the religious idolatry that permeated the ancient Gentile world. But this was not the only difficulty encountered by believers who lived in the Roman empire. The early Christian leaders who cite the decree also found themselves in societies and cultures with other customs, attitudes, ethical practices, and problems concerning which their readers needed guidance.

The incident precipitating Paul's sharp words to Peter in Antioch over eating with Gentiles (Gal 2:11 ff.) reminds us of how serious ceremonial-dietary matters were to some Jewish Christians.[17] However, a ceremonial interpretation of at least some parts of the decree seemed to be assumed among some Gentile Christian groups as well. At least one instance of a ceremonial-dietary application is found in the west, where it is usually assumed that the decree was understood as a moral guideline. Biblias, a martyr in the Rhone valley, along with other Christians had evidently been accused of cannibalism. She protested, "How can such as these [Christians] eat children who are forbidden to eat the blood of irrational animals?" (Eusebius *Hist. eccl.* 5.1.26).[18]

Origen cites the three-part version of the decree, which is also found in P45. He clearly interprets it as a ceremonial-dietary regulation. But the context and the way in which Origen uses the decree shows he believed that it referred to more than simply the Jewish ceremonies and laws that were its original referent.

Jewish food laws, including the prohibition against eating blood and bloody meats, is the subject with which Origen is dealing when he quotes the decree in *Against Celsus* 8.29. Earlier he cites Matt 15:11, 17-19 to show that Jesus substituted ethical for dietary considerations as standards for true cleanliness or actual pollution. Further, he notes Paul's attitude that food is a matter of spiritual indifference (cf. 1 Cor 8:8). Then Origen continues:

> Therefore since without some explanation, there is some obscurity about this matter, it seemed good to the apostles of Jesus and the elders gathered together at Antioch (*sic!*[19]) and also, as they themselves say, to the Holy

---

[17]Note also the refusal of the Christians of the Pseudo-Clementine sect to eat with unbaptized persons: *Recognitions* 1:19; 4:34; *Homilies* 7:8; 8:19.

[18]This apparent ceremonial interpretation of the decree comes from the same geographical area and only slightly earlier in time than Irenaeus. Irenaeus seems to have known the decree in the Western text-form and interpreted it accordingly.

[19]Origen may have located the council at Antioch rather than Jerusalem because (1) he was quoting freely and accidentally wrote "Antioch" (and possibly

> Spirit, to write a letter to those of the Gentiles who are believing, forbidding
> them to partake only of those things from which they say it is necessary to
> abstain, "idolatrous things (*eidōlothyta*), things strangled, and blood."

Then in the following chapter (*Against Celsus* 3.30)—and modern commentators seem to have overlooked this point—while Origen makes clear that he believes the latter two elements of the decree do indeed refer to foods, he does not restrict them to just Jewish food laws. Rather he applies them to some pagan, idolatrous and occult practices with which he seems to be familiar. "Blood," says Origen, "is said to be the food of demons." To drink blood or to eat meat with blood in it might put Christians in the position of having evil "spirits feeding along with us." Thus the pagan practices and notions of the geographical area and cultural setting within which Origen used the decree caused him consciously to shift the application of it from the Jewish ceremonial problem to which they were first applied by the early Christians to the Gentile, pagan ceremonial problems of his own time and locale. I would not suggest that Origen himself altered the text by omitting "fornication." But his use of a form of the decree that does omit it probably reflects the type of thought, use and setting that accounts for the form of the text found in P45.

In Tertullian's *Apology* he also notes that Christians abstain from eating "things strangled." Yet he does so without the type of direct reference to the decree he makes in his treatise *On Modesty*. In *Apology* 9 Tertullian contrasts the Christian way of life with the moral degradation of the Gentile world. He rails against child sacrifice, abortion (which Tertullian equates with murder), oaths sealed by parties eating each others' blood, gladiatorial fights, infanticide, and forms of cannibalism practiced in pagan society. Tertullian continues:

> Blush for your vile ways before the Christians, who have not even the blood
> of animals at their meals of simple and natural foods; who abstain from
> *things strangled*.... You tempt Christians with sausages of blood, just
> because you are perfectly aware that the thing by which you thus try to get
> them to transgress they hold unlawful (italics mine).

Although this is not a clear reference to the apostolic decree, there are three features of this passage in Tertullian's *Apology* that are important for this study. Tertullian here reveals some of the moral and social customs and attitudes of non-Christians in the area in which he lived. Secondly, he confirms that the refusal of Christians to eat blood was well known and that attempts were made to entice them to do so. Finally, Tertullian

---

for the same reason omitted "fornication" from the text of the decree) or (2) he may have been familiar with a tradition independent of Acts that located the council in Antioch and also gave a three-part version of the decree.

regards abstinence by Christians from "things strangled" as a moral, not a ceremonial, issue.

When Tertullian makes direct reference to the decree in *On Modesty* 12, with the D-text he transforms it into what Harnack calls "an abstract of an ethical catechism."[20] This is evident from the omission of "things strangled," from the context in which Tertullian quotes the decree, and in his commentary upon it. Tertullian makes reference to the decree to support his argument against moral laxity. He says, "In this place [the decree] there has been preserved for adultery and fornication a position of their own honor between idolatry and murder." In the same chapter he clarifies that "blood" is here "an interdict . . . upon human blood."

Tertullian's discussion provides further light on the question of how he understood the original setting of the decree. He says it was introduced

> when first the Gospel thundered and shook the old system to its base, when dispute was being held on the question of retaining the law or not; this is the first rule which the apostles, on the authority of the Holy Spirit, sent out to those who were already beginning to be gathered to their side out of the nations.

He calls the decree the "pristine law" and the "compendia of discipline" that relaxes the OT law but binds "from the more noxious" actions that were also prohibited by the OT. He believes the decree is "ever immutable" and exists "in perpetuity." Tertullian affirms that it "will cease [only] with the world."

Does Tertullian interpret the decree as the basis of a new, Christian legalism? If by "legalism" we mean becoming a Christian, earning God's favor by observing laws, the answer is negative. It would be a mistake to interpret any version of the decree, including Tertullian's, as legalism in this sense. The thrust of the earlier part of the record of the Jerusalem Council in Acts 15 rejects that possibility. Salvation is clearly defined as a state received "by faith" (v 9) "through grace" (v 11). It is true that the provisions of the decree are called "necessary things" (15:28), but the letter containing them concludes with the statement that they are "necessary" in order that the Gentiles "will do well" (15:29). There is no hint in Acts that the decree was considered necessary for salvation, and Tertullian does not appear to introduce any such idea into his discussion of it.

"Legalism" may also refer to precise definition and regulation of the conduct of one already a Christian through stated ordinances. Tertullian's insistence upon the decree as a "compendium of discipline" and an irrevocable law for believers seems to indicate that he did regard it as the standard for a Christian legalism of this sort.

[20] A. Harnack, *The Acts of the Apostles* (trans. J. R. Wilkinson; London, 1909) 251 ff.

Some type of legalistic interpretation of the decree may also be intended in the version found in Codex Bezae (D) and Irenaeus, which, with Tertullian, omits "things strangled" but differs from the Latin father by adding a negative form of the golden rule.[21] The rule is not indigenous to this context for it is also found in moral catechisms of both Jewish and Christian origin.[22] Its significance here must be considered along with another D-text feature. Following the phrase "you will do well" in Acts 15:29, Codex Bezae and other Western witnesses add "being sustained (or "borne along") by the Holy Spirit." Eldon Epp demonstrates convincingly that the variants of the D-text of Acts disclose a general widespread anti-Jewish tendency and accentuate the differences between Judaism and Christianity.[23] More particularly he observes that the addition to 15:29 serves "to counteract any legalistic overtones which might accompany the apostolic letter as a result of the Judaizing controversy."[24]

Thus when all the peculiarities of Codex Bezae (including the omission of "things strangled," the addition to 15:29, and the inclusion of the negative rule) are taken into consideration, Epp concludes, the

ethical interpretations of the "decree" and its pneumatic setting in the "Western" text not only reveal a Christian emphasis over against Judaism, but also minimize the seriousness of the Judaizing dispute and, more important, nullify the Judaizing contention, for the apostolic decision, understood in this way, yields nothing to their position and enjoins upon the Gentile Christians none of their demands.[25]

In this Epp agrees with P. H. Menoud that, with the addition of the negative rule, the decree becomes "a standard for Christian belief and practice . . . [which] . . . cannot be practiced except in Christ and in the Spirit."[26] When compared with the decree as cited by Tertullian, the D-text version appears to have a stronger anti-Jewish tone and a less legalistic flavor.

In Irenaeus *Against Heresies* 3:12, 14 the D-text form of the decree appears as part of the summary of a report on the Jerusalem Council of

[21]Williams, *Alterations*, 72, thinks the presence of the negative form of the golden rule is a characteristic of the Western European form of the Western text in contrast to the West African Western text tradition represented by Tertullian, which omits it.

[22]The best known Jewish citations are Tob 4:15 and *t. Šabb.* 31ₐ (quoting Hillel). In Christian literature the negative rule is found in *Did.* 1:2 and *Didascalia* 1. For discussion see Bruce, *Acts of the Apostles*, 299 n. 1.

[23]E. Epp, *The Theological Tendency of Codex Bezae Cantabrigiensis in Acts* (SNTSMS; Cambridge, 1966) 165 ff.

[24]Ibid., pp. 110-111.

[25]Ibid., p. 111.

[26]Menoud, "Western Text," 26-27; Epp, *Bezae*, 110-111.

Acts 15. Irenaeus does not comment on the decree as such. For him the Acts account supports the Christian doctrine of the deity of Jesus and demonstrates that the God of the OT is the same as the God of the NT. He emphasizes the nonlegal character of Christian salvation and specifically mentions that the argument for circumcision was disallowed. This latter point indicates that from his familiarity with Acts Irenaeus was aware of the ceremonial questions that prompted the formulation of the decree, but this was not a major part of Irenaeus' concern. Rather than supporting a new legalism on the basis of the decree, as Tertullian appears to do, Irenaeus specifically says that the Acts 15 council recognized that God has given "the new covenant of *liberty* to those who had lately believed in God by the Holy Spirit" (italics mine).

The writer to the seven churches of Asia seems to allude to the decree in addressing situations at Pergamum and Thyatira (Rev 2:14, 20). Here, as elsewhere in the early Church (cf. 1 Cor 8:1 ff.; 10:19 ff.), the problem involved a combination of foods and idolatry. Some Christians were at least indirectly seeming to participate in pagan rites as they were enticed to "eat things sacrificed to idols."

The Apocalypticist also specifically mentions fornication as a problem in Pergamum and Thyatira. Although both the Alexandrian-Byzantine and Western textual traditions include fornication as an element of the decree, only Revelation applies it to a particular situation. This is surprising, for from the Thessalonian and Corinthian correspondence and such ethical lists as Gal 5:19; *Did.* 2:2; 3:3; *Barn.* 19:4 (cf. Rom 1:26 ff.) we know that sexual problems were widespread in many Gentile churches. It is almost inconceivable that sexual abuses were absent from the Christian societies in which Tertullian, Irenaeus and others lived or that these writers would not have thought of the decree in confronting these problems. There is no conclusive explanation at hand for this lack of specific application of the prohibition against fornication by any writer immediately after the NT period. The best guess may be that early Christian leaders might have tended to assume that simply to report the prohibition as a part of the apostolic decree was sufficient to remind their readers of this injunction, which they may have considered self-explanatory and self-applying.

It is apparent that the various editions of the decree reflect more than general categories of ceremonial restrictions and moral commands. Within these major categories we may detect specific concerns and a willingness to apply the prohibitions to prevailing local, cultural situations. The several editions of the decree contain references to one or a combination of such matters as idolatry in general, Jewish ceremonial-dietary concerns, pagan rites, or moral directives. In some locales they seem to have held the status of at least semi-legalistic rules. In other areas they appear to have been regarded as general guidelines for Christian ethics.

IV. The Textual Variants and Their Settings in the Ancient Church

I suggest that the differences of emphasis and interpretation noted in this survey arose because of the need to apply what the early Christians understood to be the original purpose and intent of the decree to changing needs in different locations. Evidence for this proposal may be drawn from the use made of the decree by early Christian writers whose geographical areas can be located.

Unfortunately, representatives of some of the text-forms are not numerous. Citations can only rarely be associated with a particular geographical area with certainty. We lack precise information about the original province of most individual manuscripts (such as P45) or manuscript groups (such as the Alexandrian "family"). Nevertheless, I feel that there is sufficient basis for suggesting that particular types of emphases found in the several text-types may be related to the cultural, social and theological settings and to the practical problems present in different sectors of the early Church.

Previous investigations have already recognized that idolatry was a universal problem for early Christian communities and individuals. Its influences were so widespread and insidious that there was need for constant warning against it. Consequently every extant form of the decree contains the prohibition against the pollution of idols. Moreover, our investigation reminds us that Christians faced sets of problems peculiar in fact or in emphasis to their geographical area. It is scarcely accidental that textual traditions more closely associated with the western parts of the early Church (e.g., D, Irenaeus and Tertullian) tend to emphasize the ethical interpretation of the decree, whereas ceremonial concerns remain strong in those text traditions (e.g., the Alexandrian-Byzantine tradition, P45 and Origen) from areas closer to Syro-Palestine, where Jewish influence was strong. However, it is necessary to reiterate that neither ethical nor ceremonial concerns were totally absent from any area or text-form.

The point raised by this study is that a sociological consideration of the decree must accompany a legitimate concern to recover the earliest form or forms of the text. If the problems faced by Christians in a particular area are reflected in at least a general way in the textual variants of the decree of the Jerusalem Council, then the variants may provide an indispensable clue to the social and cultural, as well as the theological, dynamics of that area.[27] It may be assumed that the issues and situations faced by various groups of early Christians may at least partly be responsible for the variety of text-forms in which the decree is found.

It is my contention that the remembrance of the situation and concerns that prompted the issuance of the decree in the first place—namely, Jewish

[27]Cf. C. H. Turner, "Textual Criticism as a Branch of Church History," *JTS* 10 (1909) 13 ff.

fears springing from a general distrust of Gentile propensity toward idolatry, moral laxity and disregard for the implications of certain Jewish ceremonial rites—persisted in the early Church well into the second century. When at later times and in different cultural settings issues arose that were related or similar to the original concerns of the Jerusalem Council, Christians turned for directives to the apostolic summary of "necessary things." In the course of time the decree became a guideline for relations between Christians in general or were used to enforce some interpretation of proper Christian attitudes toward idolatry and its pollutions, moral conduct, and matters that might prove offensive to some group of fellow Christians (especially those relating to table fellowship).

These directives, it seems, were applied in accordance with early Christian memory and understanding of (1) the original setting and intent of the decree and (2) the needs of the particular situation faced by their users. This interaction between memory of the past and different changing circumstances of the present caused emphases to shift from one to another element of the decree. These shifts of emphasis provide evidence of phases of interpretation and application of the decree that can be seen in the history of the transmission of the text of Acts 15:20 and parallel passages.[28]

[28] I gratefully acknowledge many helpful comments and suggestions on this paper by E. M. Howe, W. L. Lane and R. A. Veenker, my former colleagues at Western Kentucky University.

The Theism of the Apocalypse

Merrill C. Tenney

THE Apocalypse of John has been a fruitful source for eschatological data ever since its acceptance into the canon of the NT. Its odd construction and its symbolic language have evoked all kinds of speculation concerning its real meaning, and in the minds of many it has been regarded as irrelevant to modern theological thinking. Controversy has abounded, and the various schools of interpretation disagree both charitably and uncharitably about it. There is one approach, however, that has received considerably less attention and on which there is a far better chance of accord: its theism.

The theism of the Apocalypse, whether drawn from its positive statements or from its symbolic representations, is more instructive than controversial. Its picture of God is closely akin to the general doctrine of God in the rest of the Bible, though it has its own peculiar emphases. This theism is based on that of the Jewish Scriptures interpreted through the person of Christ, whose redemptive action portrays the work of God in history by the representation of the sacrificial Lamb of God.

The date of the Apocalypse has by most conservative authorities been placed toward the end of the first century in the reign of Domitian, the elder son and immediate successor of Vespasian (A.D. 81-96). To what extent there was a general persecution during his reign is somewhat debatable. Although several of Domitian's predecessors had been elevated to the rank of deity at the time of their deaths by the Roman senate, they had not dared to claim the title for themselves during their lifetime. Domitian, however, would not be satisfied with posthumous glory and demanded to be hailed as *Dominus et Deus* (Lord and God) while still living.[1] The oldest external witnesses to the Apocalypse assert that, subsequent to Nero, the first persecution of the Christians occurred during the reign of Domitian,[2] and Irenaeus (c. 180) definitely ascribed it to that period, "almost in our day, toward the end of Domitian's reign."[3] If this date be accepted, the theological teaching of the Apocalypse represents the theistic aspect of Christian theology by the end of the first century as it related to the world conditions prevalent at that time.

---

[1]Suetonius *Domitian* 13.
[2]Melito of Sardis, quoted in Eusebius *Hist. Eccl.* 4.26.9.
[3]Irenaeus *Against Heresies* 5.30.3.

It was therefore a protest against the deification of a human being in the place of God and the consequent ascription to him of power that is not rightfully his. It is essentially the contrast between theism, which recognizes man as the creation and servant of God, and humanism, which makes man his own god. It represents the clash of two diametrically contrasting philosophies that may take different shapes from time to time but that in reality are essentially the same.

This theism was not the invention of the period. Behind it lay the long traditions of the OT revelation through the Law and the Prophets. This conclusion is not based merely on a chance comparison of texts but on obvious quotations or allusions drawn from the OT. For instance, the definitive assertion of Revelation, "I am the Alpha and the Omega, saith the Lord, who is and who was and who is to come, the Almighty" (Rev 1:8; 21:6; 22:13), is a clear allusion to Isa 41:4, a part of the prophecy of hope that comprises Isa 40:1-45:25. This passage is the declaration of Israel's hope in God, counter to the misfortunes and calamities that threatened the last phase of the Judean kingdom during which Isaiah prophesied. The sovereign power of God, which was the last resort of the faithful remnant and which ultimately brought the restoration of the commonwealth under the Persian empire, insured hope for the exiles who would otherwise have been plunged into frustration and despair.

Similarly the effect of the unchangeable eternity of God, "who is, and who was, and who is to come" (Rev 1:4, 8), is an echo of Exod 3:14, "I Am That I Am," or, in the LXX, "I Am The One Who Is." The fact that a number of these allusions are not given as separate quotations but are combined for purposes of teaching indicates that they had become a groundwork accepted as foundational in Christian thinking.

Some of the figurative passages have their parallels in the OT. The description of deity in Revelation 4 bears a strong resemblance to Isaiah's vision (Isaiah 6). Both speak of a throne, both refer to the Presence on the throne as fearful and glorious (yet without attempting any linear description), both mention the celestial attendants, and both emphasize the chant of adoration, "Holy, Holy, Holy is the LORD Almighty" (or "Yahweh of Hosts"). Whether these represent the coincidental similarity of two visions of the same Reality, or whether the Revelation is a literary description based on the former (as some contend), the agreement still remains and demonstrates the permanence of the truth for which the vision stands.

Noteworthy also is the fact that these allusions and figures belong in a common sequence of prophetic declaration. The theism of Revelation is not the result of human reaction to a single emergency but is the repetitive assertion of an abiding truth to meet recurring emergencies. There may be a fresh expression of the truth, but the truth itself is not a novel discovery. The theistic theme is the common and continuing foundation for the faith of God's people when they are confronted by the stress of untoward circumstances or by the pain of persecution.

I. THE PLACE OF THEISM IN THE APOCALYPSE

The theistic teaching of Revelation has three major aspects: (1) the sovereignty of God, (2) the justice of God, and (3) the grace of God. All of these are related to the person of Christ in keeping with the initial statement: "The revelation of Jesus Christ, which God gave unto him to shew unto his servants the things which must shortly come to pass" (Rev 1:1). The purpose of the book is not so much to describe the details of future occurrences as to declare God's purpose in them and to prepare his people to meet them. The character and intentions of God are more important than the events themselves. For this reason the Revelation stresses the sovereignty of God in contrast to a philosophy of a world of random and generally calamitous accidents, the justice of God in contrast to a universe that has neither righteousness nor retribution in its constitution, and the grace of God in contrast to an unthinking and unfeeling universe that remorselessly crushes its victims as it rolls on its fatalistic way. To a suffering Church that is crying out for answers to the questions that persecution and injustice have raised, the theistic response gives a word of encouragement.

1. *The sovereignty of God.* Primary to all theism is the truth of God's sovereignty. He is the Center and Ruler of the universe, and nothing in it occurs without his knowledge and control. The Apocalypse demonstrates this sovereignty by the symbolism of the throne of God, which is mentioned not less than 39 times. Of this number, eleven identify Deity as "the one seated on the throne" (4:2, 9, 10; 5:1, 7, 13; 6:16; 7:10, 15; 19:4; 21:6). In two or three instances "throne" refers to the seat of Satan's power (2:13; 13:2; 16:10). In such instances the throne denotes the center of authority, for the throne is for any king the place from which he issues his decrees and pronounces his judgments. The very structure of the book confirms this principle, for beginning with the narrative vision of Rev 4:1 and continuing through to its conclusion the throne is the focus of worship (4:8-11; 7:11-12), action (5:1-14), judgment (7:9; 20:11-12) and the gathering of the redeemed (7:14-17; 14:3) as well as the source of future blessing (22:1). The final rule of God and of Christ emanates from the throne (22:3).

Insofar as the sovereignty of God can be represented by a material symbol, the throne is that symbol. It is the one fixed and unchanging center of the kaleidoscopic visions of the Apocalypse. It indicates that however the events of the world change for better or for worse the will and purpose of God remain unaltered and undefeated.

Moreover, this is not the sovereignty of an arbitrary whim or of a mechanical fatalism. The Apocalypse indicates that God's purpose is eternal in character. It is established not by the sudden pressure of expediency but rather by his holy nature and moral laws. The entire procedure of the book is determined by the scroll that contains his stated plan and is executed by "the Lamb in the midst of the throne" (Rev 5:6-7). By the execution of that redemptive purpose the judgments are pronounced, evil is defeated, and the kingdom of God is inaugurated.

This plan provides purposefully for the option of repentance. At the end of the first catalog of plagues in the trumpet judgments, the statement appears that "the rest of mankind, who were not killed with those plagues, repented not of the works of their hands, that they should worship demons, and the idols of gold and of silver and of brass and of stone and of wood . . . and they repented not of their murders, nor of their sorceries, nor of their fornications, nor of their thefts" (Rev 9:20-21). Two similar notes conclude the final judgment of the "bowls": "They repented not to give him glory" (16:10), and "they repented not of their works" (16:11). The implication seems to be clear that if they had repented God would have withheld further judgment, but their obstinate disobedience brought the inevitable penalty of a broken law. The offenses listed in these two series of retributive actions are direct violations of the basic ethics contained in the Ten Commandments, which were the essence of God's requirements for Israel and the concentrated sample of his moral standards for all men. If men suffer the judgments of God, it is because they have rejected his known will and have been swayed by their own evil desires rather than obeying his precepts.

2. *The justice of God.* Inherent in the divine government of the world is the concept of justice. On the one hand, God is the Deliverer of his people. The very fact that they have been summoned to his service separates them from the general current of the world at large. His favor to them is not arbitrary but is rather his purpose to create an instrument through which he can communicate with all men by precept and example that will be comprehensible to them. When he called Abraham, he told the patriarch that "in thy seed shall all the families of the earth be blessed" (Gen 12:3; Acts 3:25). The same concept appears later in the prophecy of Isaiah: "I the LORD will keep thee, and give thee for a covenant of the people, for a light to the Gentiles, to open the blind eyes, to bring out the prisoners from the dungeon, and them that sit in darkness out of the prison house" (Isa 42:6-7). The same concept appears again: "I will also give thee for a light to the Gentiles, that thou mayest be my salvation unto the ends of the earth" (Isa 49:6). In similar fashion God summons his Church to the same missionary calling. It involves suffering, for the salvation of others always necessitates the assumption of responsibilities and perils, but the

justice of God requires that he shall deliver his servants from fear and preserve them for his work.

Conversely, the justice of God demands judgment on those who have broken his laws and refused his offer of reconciliation. The calamitous crisis described in Revelation is not God's favorite occupation. It is the logical consequence of sin and operates in accord with fixed moral law, the law of God's being. Sin withers in his presence as germs die in sunlight. Were there no judgment for sin there could be no reason or order in the universe, and righteousness would be a mockery or a futility or both. The character of God demands a point of reckoning beyond which the moral debt of humanity cannot be extended. God awaits repentance, but there must be a time when he will call all men to account for their attitude and actions. The justice of God must be vindicated in the destruction of evil. The heavenly worship at the time of the crisis declares this truth: "True and righteous are his judgments, for he has judged the great harlot, her that corrupted the earth with her fornication, and he hath avenged the blood of his servants at her hand" (Rev 19:2).

3. *The grace of God.* The doctrine of sovereign grace is not stressed in Revelation since the prevailing theme of the book is judgment, but the concept appears in the allusions to the preservation of God's people. They have been redeemed "out of every nation, and of all tribes and peoples and tongues" (7:9). The expression of this grace is defined by the song of the elders: "Worthy art thou to take the book and to open the seals thereof: for thou wast slain, and didst purchase unto God with thy blood every tribe, and tongue, and people, and nation, and madest them to be unto our God a kingdom and priests; and they reign upon the earth" (Rev 5:9-10).

The manifestation of God's sovereign grace is effected through the redemptive sacrifice of Christ, symbolized by the Lamb that had been slaughtered for sacrifice (Rev 5:6). The resurrection is implied by the fact that he lives and is asserted by the title given to him, "the firstborn of the dead" (1:5) and by the declaration, "I was (became) dead, and behold, I am alive forevermore" (1:18). The intervention of God in providing salvation and the option of the offer of repentance are the proofs of the grace that is more potent than the law that death is the necessary consequence of sin. The power of God is manifested in producing a new creation that excels and supersedes the older one, which was ruined by man's disobedience and shattered by divine judgment (Rev 21:5).

II. THE ACTS OF GOD

The theism of the Apocalypse is related particularly to the interpretation of the future. The total focus of Revelation beginning with the fourth chapter and continuing through the rest of the book to the epilogue concerns "the things which must shortly come to pass hereafter" (4:1). This does not mean that all future events are described in detail nor that all the symbolism included in the following text is necessarily confined to any one cluster of acts. Furthermore, the descriptions are symbolic at least to some extent, and there may be legitimate difference of opinion in interpreting them. It is clear, however, that these symbols or events presuppose a divine pupose and a progressive method of achieving it that concludes with a definite crisis. Three stages in this progress may be discerned.

1. *The opening of the scroll.* The vision of chaps. 4 and 5 depicts a scene that portrays the delegation of authority to Christ. In the hand of the awesome Figure on the throne is a scroll, folded and sealed with seven seals. Although its content is not identified explicitly, it is plainly a document that outlines some procedure that can be administered only by proper authority. Its form resembles that of a deed or will that authorizes the possessor to undertake some specific commission. It was available only for one properly qualified, and at the outset no suitable candidate appeared to take charge of the divine appointment. Finally the Lamb, the One who had been sacrificed and who had lived again, came forward and was declared worthy to become the executor of its purpose. As he opened the seals one after the other, the judgments of God followed in logical order. Redemption and judgment thus are concomitant: The redeemed find their safety in the midst of judgment and can appreciate their privilege only when confronted with the opposite. The judgments fell on those who had sinned and who are indifferent or unrepentant. In the present age divine history begins with the incarnation, in which the revelation of God's person and purpose, the offer of reconciliation through Christ, and the provision for fulfillment through the resurrection are combined in one tremendous act of God. His purpose is dual: to offer redemption to men and to make it effective in their lives, and to eliminate sin from his world by a process of judgment that will ultimately destroy it completely.

2. *The process of history.* History at present is the arena in which God is working. To identify each of the symbolic events of the Apocalypse with a specific sequence of known occurrences is probably impossible. It may be wiser to regard them as descriptive trends, or perhaps in many instances as crises that are impending but that have not yet come to fulfillment. Of one thing the interpreter can be certain: The Apocalypse is not a disorganized collection of grotesque images that have no particular meaning. It is rather an interpretation of the trends of history as they move toward a conclusion. God is neither frightened nor indifferent. He has a work to finish and a kingdom to establish, and he will do both. In spite of apparent reverses and seeming impossibilities he is moving toward his ultimate goal, and nothing can impede his progress. The demonic powers, the corruption of evil men, the gross materialism of human civilization, and the decline of human

culture will not hinder nor avert the final manifestation of judgment and the ultimate establishment of the City of God.

3. *The conclusion of history.* Process does not mean an indefinitely long extension of a conflict but rather the progress in its resolution. There is unmistakable evidence in Revelation that a definite point must come when God will act decisively. The wrath of God, his fixed displeasure against sin, must be "finished" (Rev 15:1); Babylon "is fallen" (18:2); the "beast" and the "false prophet" were cast alive into "the lake of fire that burneth with brimstone" (19:20); "the devil that deceived them" suffered the same fate; and "the kingdom of the world is become the kingdom of our Lord and of his Christ: and he shall reign forever and ever" (11:15). The vindication of God and of his people is conclusive. God's final intervention will mark an irreversible turning point in the course of history.

III. THE RELATION OF GOD TO MEN

Revelation is more than a map of coming events. It is a disclosure of the relation of God to humanity in terms of his purpose for them. The dual trends of redemption and retribution reveal both his mercy and severity, his love for sinners and his hatred of sin, his compassionate prolongation of man's opportunity for repentance and his decisive determination to execute judgment on evil. These relationships appear in three different forms.

1. *God's relation to the world in general.* This relationship is pictured in the song of the "elders" who offer their adoration to the Figure on the throne. As they prostrate themselves and cast their crowns before the throne, they say: "Worthy art thou, our Lord and our God, to receive the glory and the honor and the power, for thou didst create all things and because of thy will they were and are created."

As the Creator, he holds the ownership of the universe and the consequent right to control it. Obedience to him is obligatory and proper. Anyone who creates something has a right to possess it. One might say that God has copyright laws on the universe in general and on men in particular. Independence of God is an insult to our Maker. He has no desire to enslave us, but he does have the right to direct us. The world of humanity is in a state of revolt against its Creator and must be recovered if God's original plan is to be perfected. The "new creation" (Rev 21:5) is the consummation of that creative purpose and the final masterpiece of God's work in bringing order out of chaos and perfection out of ruin.

2. *God's relation to the people of God.* The book of Revelation was written to explain God's purpose to his own people, "to shew unto his servants the things which must shortly come to pass" (1:1). To them he is, through Christ, the Redeemer who has "loosed [them] from [their] sins by his blood, and made [them] a kingdom" (1:7). The letters to the churches

contained in chaps. 2 and 3 reveal the divine concern for those small bodies
of believers who were attempting to combat the temptations and opposition of an evil world. To each one of the specimen churches words of counsel
and correction were offered that they might avert failure and the loss that
accompanies it. Each was given a promise of reward for faithfulness. There
was no relaxation of spiritual standards, but there was every encouragement to maintain a struggle for holiness as a witness to the power of God.
God is not an impersonal and unapproachable judge but is essentially a
Savior.

3. *God's relation to the rebellious.* God is eager to see men repent, but
if they will not he becomes their adversary. The world is organized against
those who oppose him. As the book of Judges states the principle, "The
stars in their courses fought against Sisera" (Judg 5:20). For the unrepentant there can be only destruction and death. As the plagues of Egypt
demonstrated, the longer Pharaoh refused to listen to God's message the
more severe the plagues became, until he was forced to accept either
accession to God's desire or the extinction of his nation. In similar fashion
the increasing severity of the judgments pictured in the Apocalypse illustrate God's inflexible insistence on righteousness as the standard for the
universe and the hopelessness of resisting him.

IV. CONCLUSION

The Apocalypse makes a contribution of its own to the theistic
teaching of the NT. Against its background of eschatology it depicts a God
of holy character who has created the universe, who has a definite purpose
for his creation, and who will accomplish this purpose by redemption. He
has undertaken to solve the dilemma of destiny that man has initiated:
either to let man perish as a result of his sins and thus to see the creation
dissolve into futility, or to offer redemption from judgment at infinite cost
to himself. By adopting the latter alternative God has manifested both his
severity and his goodness. He is a being of inflexible righteousness who
cannot be compromised, and he is also the compassionate Savior who
assumes the cost of forgiving those who repent of their sins and trust him
for salvation. For the redeemed, "the Lord God shall give them light, and
they shall reign for ever and ever" (Rev 22:5).

SECTION III
How God's Word Abides With Us

Immanence, Transcendence, and the Doctrine of Scripture

MILLARD J. ERICKSON

THEOLOGIANS are becoming increasingly aware of the role that pre-suppositions play in theological conclusions. The differences between the doctrinal positions of two theologians may be less a result of what data they consult (in many cases they are using the same data) than of their methodologies or their conceptions of the nature of reality or of truth.

Two types of presuppositions are brought to the formulation of any particular doctrine. The first type is external to the system in the sense that it is broader than a merely theological conception. Here are the philo-sophical conceptions that underlie one's whole world-view. The theology of Augustine was built upon Platonic philosophy, that of Thomas Aquinas upon Aristotelianism. Emil Brunner and the early Karl Barth drew heavily upon the existentialism of Soren Kierkegaard.

In a chapter on "The Church Doctrine of Biblical Authority," Jack Rogers relates the theology of the "Old Princeton" school to Scottish common-sense realism. He says that "the principles of Scottish Common Sense philosophy are directly reflected in the principles of biblical inter-pretation of the Princeton theologians."[1] It was this, and not a difference of data, that differentiated the view of Scripture held by Warfield and the Hodges from that of the higher critics. The influence of one of these "axioms" is spelled out by Rogers:

> This principle of universality pitted the Princeton theologians against the higher critics, who maintained that the ancient world view of biblical times was different from a nineteenth-century view. The critics assumed, as the Princeton theologians did not, that presuppositions and world views varied with historical periods and cultures.[2]

Rogers has correctly noted the presuppositions of the Warfield-Hodge positions. Unfortunately, however, he and the authors of the other chapters in the volume he has edited show little inclination to identify their own presuppositions in similarly specific ways.

---

[1] J. Rogers, *Biblical Authority* (ed. J. Rogers; Waco: Word, 1977) 39.
[2] Ibid., p. 40.

The other type of presupposition is internal to the theology itself. By this is meant that the various parts of a theology—i.e., the beliefs and teachings about the different doctrines—are interconnected and affect one another. One way of identifying this is the "organic" character of theology. Theology is a unitary whole rather than a collection of unrelated parts. Thus the view one has of the nature of God will color his understanding of the nature, extent and consequences of sin. Similarly the belief about the deity and humanity of Christ will strongly affect the belief about the type of work of atonement that he could make.

James I. Packer makes this point quite emphatically in his essay, "Encountering Present-Day Views of Scripture":

> First, *when you encounter a present-day view of Holy Scripture, you encounter more than a view of Scripture.* What you meet is a total view of God and the world, that is, a total theology, which is both an ontology, declaring what there is, and an epistemology, stating how we know what there is. This is necessarily so, for a theology is a seamless robe, a circle within which everything links up with everything else through its common grounding in God. Every view of Scripture, in particular, proves on analysis to be bound up with an overall view of God and man.[3]

Despite this declaration, however, there does not seem to be much application of this insight in the chapter that follows.

Certainly in dealing with the question of Scripture the understanding of God's nature is especially significant if the issue is the sense in which the Bible is God's self-revelation. One particular facet of this is the immanence and transcendence of God. Shifting convictions on this continuum have been reflected in varied views of the nature of Scripture as well. It will be the aim of the remainder of this essay to examine several twentieth-century theological movements and to note their conceptions of the immanence and transcendence of God as well as the implications of this for their views of Scripture. By divine transcendence is meant that God is separate from and superior to man and the rest of creation. By immanence we mean that God is present and active within his creation and is close to man. Views that emphasize immanence see God within the commonplace everyday experiences and see him working within natural processes of reality in a somewhat more diffused fashion. Those views that emphasize transcendence see God working in more unusual, extraordinary ways. Miracles, direct interventions, are more the mark of divine activity here.

For most of its history the Christian Church has held to a rather transcendent view of God. Drawing and building upon the Jewish belief, Christian theologians saw God as high and lofty, far beyond man in his

---

[3] J. I. Packer, *The Foundation of Biblical Authority* (ed. J. M. Boice; Grand Rapids: Zondervan, 1978) 61-62.

power and knowledge. Because man could not discover God or even comprehend him, it was necessary for God to make himself known to man and to give understanding of the revelation. This revelation has been preserved in the Bible. Although written by human authors and in human language, it has been produced by such an intensive working by God that it is fully the message that he wished to have conveyed. As such it is fully authoritative and free from error.

When theological liberalism became a powerful force in Christianity, its view of God strongly influenced its understanding of the Bible. In varying degrees liberalism conceived of God as immanent. He was closely identified with nature and the processes within it. Evolution was seen not as a neutral mechanical process but as the actual presence of God himself working through "natural" laws and mechanisms to accomplish his ends. He was not totally distant and different from man, but rather a spark of the divine is found in all men. Thus God is not restricted to working through the Church but can do his tasks through all persons, including those who do not confess belief in him.

Accordingly the Bible was seen as a much more natural book than had been believed earlier. In one version of this, the Bible was considered to be a record of the religious experience of the people of Israel. This view did not even presuppose a belief in any kind of God at all, although ordinarily such a belief was included. Here were to be found a variety of materials drawn from the culture of the Jewish people: poems, sagas, visions, and so forth. The OT was the "Jewish national religious scrapbook." Another variety saw the Bible as the record of the progressive discovery of God by the Jewish people, who must be regarded as religious geniuses. What is found in the Bible is actually natural theology. A third variety said that God takes the initiative in revealing himself to man. Because he respects man's personality he reveals himself only to the degree that man is willing and receptive. Hence the revelation comes through human personality and is of necessity somewhat distorted.

Note in all of these views the presupposition of divine immanence. In many ways, liberalism emphasized this. All men contained within them a spark of divinity. There was within them such a natural affinity for God that they could assimilate his truth. Further, God worked through natural processes of communication rather than simply dropping the Bible to man in some direct or unmediated fashion.

In many ways Borden P. Bowne represents well this aspect of liberalism as he develops the idea of God working through processes to accomplish his ends. This is true of the works of God, which are on a supernaturalistic understanding termed "miracles." It is also true with respect to God's word or revelation. He notes that God's way is one of growth and slow development out of the natural into the spiritual. Thus he says that

we are not surprised to find him using the legends and picture-stories and
naive interpretations of early men as vehicles for communicating to them
deeper and higher conceptions of himself. In themselves these things were
imperfect and crude enough, but as vehicles of revelation they nevertheless
revealed. Why should not God begin with men where they are, intellectually
and morally, and use even their myths and imaginings to lift them to higher
insight? No one who has not first banished God from both history and the
world need be offended by such a method, if investigation should show it to
have been the fact.[4]

Bowne insists on the importance of distinguishing between the contents of
revelation and the method of revelation. All that faith is really concerned
with is the divine contents. It is willing for the method to be whatever
investigation shows it to have been.[5]

William Temple develops a similar idea. He notes that revelation as
found in the Bible is not in the overwhelming of man with some esoteric
truths that he could not otherwise have known or understood. God does
not make himself known only through certain of his works, with the others
not serving at all as a revelation of him. This would make the world for the
most part independent of God. God is involved in the whole of what
happens, and the entire process is to be considered revelation. Temple says
that

> this leads us to the conviction that the process itself and all occurrences
> within it—including the intelligences of men—are due to the purposive action
> of that Person whose reality has been established as the governing fact of
> existence. *He guides the process; He guides the minds of men; the interaction
> of the process and the minds which are alike guided by Him is the essence of
> revelation.*[6]

God's action in guiding the world is not the impersonal dead action of an
immanent principle, however. It is the dynamic or living action of a person.

To be sure there are, according to Temple, some elements or events
within this process that are especially appropriate to serve as revelation of
God. These, however, do not impart truth as the intellect apprehends truth,
in some abstract, rationalistic seizing of concepts. Rather revelation consists of the coincidence of event and appreciation. And because God is so
fully involved in all parts of his creation and in all that occurs within it,
both of these are his doing.[7]

[4]B. P. Bowne, *The Immanence of God* (Boston: Houghton, Mifflin, 1905) 95-
96.

[5]Ibid., p. 96.

[6]W. Temple, *Nature, Man, and God* (London: Macmillan, 1953) 312.

[7]Ibid., p. 314.

Similarly L. Harold DeWolf calls into question the familiar distinction between general and special revelation on the ground that the events generally designated by the former term are no less acts of God than are the latter. God is at work in our knowing of the ordinary events of life through sense experience just as in the special events related in the miracle accounts. He is everywhere present and active. DeWolf says:

> It is God who feeds the birds of the air and clothes the grass of the field in flowering glory. If God does these things which are plainly parts of the regular natural order, then no dividing of a sea nor halting of the sun in its visible march across the sky could be more completely a divine act.[8]

This applies as well to the question of revelation. Bracketing for the moment the question of whether such miracles can occur, he writes that

> if a miracle were to be called a special revelation it could not be so-called because of its being any more an act of God than are the ordinary processes of nature, but only because it was more revealingly meaningful to men.[9]

Neo-orthodoxy makes directly the opposite presuppostion regarding God's relationship to the created order. Here God is "wholly other," so far off that there is a vast chasm between Creator and creature, and man can do nothing to bridge the gap from his side. Not only can he not work his way up to God by thinking or doing; he cannot comprehend God when he reveals himself to him.

On this basis God's revelation does not come at all through general culture. It comes "vertically from above," or in a fashion perpendicular to human knowledge. So transcendent is God, however, that although man produces the Bible out of the encounter with God no part of God is retained in the Scripture. God cannot be captured in the concepts and logic of human beings. He touches the human consciousness much as a tangent touches a circle. When he withdraws, no "residue" remains, no deposit of "truths."

The Word of God is never to be simply identified with any collection of words, specifically the Bible. It is only when the transcendent Word of God comes that we can speak of the Bible as the Word of God. This is a dynamic occurrence, not a permanent, resident quality of Scripture. Karl Barth put it thus:

> Why and in what respect does the Biblical witness possess authority? In that it claims no authority whatsoever for itself, that its witness amounts to letting

[8] L. H. DeWolf, *A Theology of the Living Church* (New York: Harper, 1960) 66.

[9] Ibid.

the Something else be the authority, itself and by its own agency. Therefore
we do the Bible a poor honour, and one unwelcome to itself, when we
directly identify it with this something else, with revelation itself.[10]

While emphasizing the difference, Barth also indicates the circumstances
under which the two coincide.

Such direct identification of revelation and the Bible, which is the practical
issue, is not one to be presupposed or anticipated by us. It takes place as an
event, when and where the Word of the Bible becomes God's Word, i.e.,
when and where John's finger points not in vain but really pointedly, when
and where by means of its word we also succeed in seeing and hearing what
he saw and heard. Therefore, where the Word of God is an event, revelation
and the Bible are one in fact, and word for word one at that.[11]

Note that in this view the presence of God's Word in the Bible is not unlike
the presence of God in nature in miraculous working. There is no permanent dwelling there, merely a temporary but very dramatic and effective
presence.

The words of the Bible are the words of Samuel, Isaiah or Luke. They
are not the words of God. Somehow God's Word always remains transcendent to these human words. It is only when God comes upon man in a
perpendicular fashion that one can in any meaningful way speak of this as
God's Word.

When we come to the present time the scene is very interesting. It is
my contention that within contemporary evangelicalism we have much the
same type of issues as were present in the earlier disagreements between
fundamentalists and modernists, and with positions being taken that in
some respects resemble those earlier stances, although with a less sharp
separation and more moderate positions being occupied on the theological
continuum with respect to any specific issue. Two clusters, which represent
general consensuses, are beginning to emerge.

One group could be called, for want of a better term, the "Amsterdam
School," since many of its adherents identify with the stance of G. C.
Berkouwer, who for many years taught at the Free University of Amsterdam. Although he himself appears to be somewhat more moderate than
some representatives of this group, a number of them credit him with
enunciating their position, and several studied with him. Many but not all
of the faculty of Fuller Theological Seminary hold this view of the Bible.
The editorial position of William B. Eerdmans Publishing Company largely
supports this view. The position is presented in such contemporary writings
as *The Authority of the Bible* edited by Jack Rogers, G. C. Berkouwer's

[10]K. Barth, *Church Dogmatics: The Doctrine of the Word of God* (Edinburgh:
T. & T. Clark, 1936), 1/1. 126.
    [11]Ibid.

Holy Scripture, and H. M. Kuitert, *Do You Understand What You Read?* In relationship to the evangelicalism of the earlier part of this century, this view approximates that of James Orr in contrast to the theology of B. B. Warfield. A brief description of the major characteristics of the movement will help us assess its stance on the question of immanence and transcendence.

1. The function of the Bible is emphasized rather than the nature of the Bible per se. This is seen even in the statement that appears above the title on the dust jacket of *Biblical Authority*: "Turn your Bible from a Battlefield into a Source for Spiritual Strength." More important than one's precise theory about the Bible and its authority is his attitude toward it.[12]

2. The Bible is approached more from the perspective of the Biblical disciplines than from that of theology. One finds the Biblical (and currently especially the NT) faculty in some evangelical schools setting the pace in defining the view of Scripture from the phenomena with which they are dealing in their study of the Bible without really posing the epistemological question: Can such a Bible really give us a knowledge of God? Much is made of the problems of the parallel accounts of the synoptic gospels and of Samuel, Kings and Chronicles.[13]

3. There is a considerable positive attitude toward the utility of critical methodology in the study of the Bible. As a book that shares many characteristics with other books authored by humans, understanding of the Bible can be advanced by the use of methodologies commonly applied to them. Not merely textual criticism, but also such techniques as form criticism and redaction criticism, are legitimate and desirable methods of determing the correct meaning of the Bible.[14]

4. There is a distaste for the word "inerrancy." This is partly because this is a negative term, partly because it refers to originals that we no longer have, and partly because it misleads as to the real nature and function of the Bible. At least ostensibly these persons prefer not to discuss the issue at all. David Hubbard says:

We break with the basic Reformed teaching on the sufficiency of the Bible, both when we claim it to be inerrant on the basis of minute details of chronology, geography, history, or cosmology or when we attack its authority by pointing to alleged discrepancies. The false alternatives often posed between biblical inerrancy and biblical errancy are not themselves biblical

[12] B. Ramm, "Is 'Scripture Alone' the Essence of Christianity?", *Biblical Authority* (ed. J. Rogers) 115-116.

[13] H. M. Kuitert, *Do You Understand What You Read?* (Grand Rapids: Eerdmans, 1970) 14-15.

[14] D. Hubbard, "The Current Tensions: Is There a Way Out?", *Biblical Authority* (ed. J. Rogers) 175.

choices. They are imposed from without in a way that tries to force the Bible to give answers that God, who inspired the Book, apparently had no intention of giving.[15]

The other position is one that finds its theological heritage in the Princeton Seminary of the nineteenth century, in the writings of Charles Hodge, A. A. Hodge and Benjamin B. Warfield. It is identified with moderates within the International Council on Biblical Inerrancy. It is represented by such writings as *The Foundation of Biblical Authority*, edited by James M. Boice, James Packer's *Fundamentalism and the Word of God*, and Francis Schaeffer's *No Final Conflict*. Institutionally it is perhaps best exemplified by the position of the faculty of Trinity Evangelical Divinity School. The editorial practices and policies of Zondervan Publishing Company approximate this position. We may designate it as the "Council" position, an abbreviation for the International Council on Biblical Inerrancy. In several basic characteristics and tenets it contrasts with the Amsterdam school.

1. There is a concern to define rather clearly the nature of Biblical inspiration and authority. While not degrading the importance of the Bible's use, these people believe that the use will be determined or at least strongly influenced by the understanding of its nature. Thus it is important to define the nature and extent of Biblical authority quite precisely. To fail to do so is to drift into deviations in other areas of doctrine as well. History is cited to demonstrate that this is the effect of any softening of a "strong" view of Biblical authority.[16]

2. This view of the Bible approaches the doctrine of Scripture from a theological perspective rather than purely from the details of the Bible itself. That is to say, the issues posed include epistemological questions such as: How do we know? How does language present truth? What is necessary for an authority to be a dependable source of knowledge? How can we distinguish between false and true claims to knowledge? An example is their pointing out the implications of affirming the complete truthfulness of statements about supraempirical realities while not extending such an affirmation to those statements that are susceptible of verification or falsification.[17]

3. This view of Scripture is quite negative about the employment of critical methodology. While practicing "lower" or textual criticism, this group sees serious problems with the different varieties of "higher" criticism. In particular, these thinkers object to the philosophical presupposi-

---

[15]Ibid., p. 168.

[16]J. Gerstner, "The Church's Doctrine of Biblical Inspiration," *Foundation* (ed. J. M. Boice).

[17]R. C. Sproul, "*Sola Scriptura*: Crucial to Evangelicalism," *Foundation* (ed. J. M. Boice) 23.

tions underlying or incorporated into the method. The negative criticism rests upon the premise of naturalism rather than supernaturalism. Consequently, instead of letting criticism judge the Bible they propose that higher criticism must be judged and corrected by the Biblical revelation. While not categorically rejecting higher criticism, they insist that it must be carefully scrutinized and evaluated.[18]

4. The concept and the term "inerrancy" is important and needs to be retained. It is the only way really to guarantee that the full authority of Scripture will be preserved. While at times willing to acknowledge that the word is not the *sine qua non* of orthodoxy, they nonetheless insist on the concept and method designated by the term.[19]

Having thus described the two positions and distinguished them from one another, the question remains regarding the presuppositions of the views. Can we detect here indications of assumptions or beliefs regarding the immanence and transcendence of God that may be correlated with the differences in their views of Biblical inspiration?

It is my contention that the view that I have here labeled the "Amsterdam" position gives indications of a somewhat more immanent view of God than does the "Council" position. By that I mean that God in producing the Bible worked to a considerable extent through natural processes, developing it over a long period of time and employing the personalities and activities of the writers.

One indication of this is the emphasis upon the Bible as the result of a process of development rather than something that simply dropped ready-made from heaven. It has human components and a human history. Dewey Beegle apparently approves of the view of Bruce Vawter, as he notes that the composition of the Bible included the work of numerous editors:

> This fact, of course, raises the question as to which editor of the book was the most inspired one. The easy answer is to regard the final editor as the truly inspired person. But as Bruce Vawter, the Roman Catholic scholar, accurately observes, "The final-redactor theory can hardly be the answer to our problem. We have come to realize that the full meaning of the Scripture must be sought in its total literary history, and even in whatever pre-literary history may underlie it. The final redactor must be heard, certainly, but he is only one voice of many speaking in the Bible."[20]

There is further indication of this leaning toward immanence in references to God's working through the activities of men. There is here

[18] J. M. Boice, "The Preacher and God's Word," *Foundation* (ed. Boice) 135-139.

[19] Packer, *Foundation* (ed. Boice) 79-80.

[20] D. Beegle, *Scripture, Tradition, and Infallibility* (Grand Rapids: Eerdmans, 1973) 203.

what older theological debates referred to as synergism: that God works together with and through the working of men. Thus God is seen as working not only in the manifestations of himself to human beings but also in their response, their understanding, their insight into his actions.

> In the third place, in and through all that men do, the work of the Holy Spirit is being done. Unfortunately, in the church's history, the Spirit has sometimes been segregated from the work of man.
>
> But we must never suppose that where the Holy Spirit does things, we have nothing to do. The Spirit does not crowd out the work of men; the Spirit always enlists men in His work.[21]

A third indication of this immanentism is the belief that certain segments of Scripture represent non-Biblical, nonrevelational, or even "secular" sources, which have been incorporated by Biblical writers. Thus some of the interpretations given by Paul to OT passages are to be understood as the rabbinical views that he had been taught. Some references to events that have supposedly occurred in OT times will be seen to have been taken from the Apocrypha. Scientific and historical references were simply the views commonly held in that day. God did not somehow give these materials through a miraculous direct communication to the writer. He guided him to utilize insights readily at hand. In so doing, however, he did not purge these materials of all imperfections. These were incorporated into the end product. Kuitert's discussion of Paul's allusion to the rock that traveled through the wilderness with Israel illustrates this (1 Cor 10:4). There was no such reference in the OT. We do find, however, a rabbinic tradition of a rock that traveled along with Israel and out of which they received drinking water. Paul was familiar with this tradition from his childhood, and it is likely that he simply adopted it. Kuitert says:

> Perhaps the question of its historical or nonhistorical character was not real for Paul; perhaps he simply took the story and used it in the service of his teaching about Jesus? This must surely have been the case. Paul makes use of rabbinic wisdom, this we understand quite well. He used concepts, arguments, and sometimes even a kind of logic that were typical of a particular time and a particular culture, in his case the rabbinic. He also uses the stories that Rabbis told. But no one has to become a Rabbi in his thinking in order to become a Christian.[22]

Finally, we note the willingness and even eagerness to apply to the Bible the same methods of literary and historical analysis used on other writings. Berkouwer engages in a lengthy discussion of the legitimacy of employing critical methodology in the study of Scripture. He notes that

[21]Kuitert, *Understand*, 20.
[22]Ibid., p. 42.

because of the human aspect of Scripture, the fact that God's Word has come through human words, it may now be scrutinized by human activity or study. He says:

> This is indeed an important aspect of the entire doctrine of Scripture, for it is inseparably related to the way God speaks to us in his Word—in the form of a witness through human words. God's Word does not break through or undo this human aspect; it comes to us in such a way that it can become the "object" of human research. The Word does not come to us by way of a supernatural evidence that makes every human activity superfluous and even dangerous. . . . A supernaturalistic view of revelation would consider any human "research" puzzling and inconceivable.[23]

When we look at the Council position we see indications of belief in the transcendent working of God in producing the Bible. We shall note these in turn.

First, there is a rejection of a particular idea of accommodation. By this is meant that God, in communicating his truth to man, worked in such a way that when references to scientific and historical matters were made they were merely the unsophisticated and even mistaken beliefs generally held by people of that time. Similarly the accommodation view teaches that Jesus did not correct the mistaken beliefs of people in these matters but for the sake of effective communication simply assumed and repeated them, or even that as a condition of his humanity he became subject to the same limitations as his hearers. The Council position, however, is that even in such matters God so intervened that all that was taught was preserved from the limitations and imperfections of human knowledge. Any use of the concept of accommodation in this sense must be emphatically rejected, for

> it plainly implies that God was somehow constrained, hampered and indeed frustrated in His revelatory purpose by the quality of the human material through which He worked. But this is to deny the biblical doctrine of providence, according to which God "worketh all things after the counsel of his own will." The Bible excludes the idea of a frustrated Deity. "Whatsoever the Lord pleased, that did he in heaven, and in earth." He was well able to prepare, equip and over-rule sinful human writers so that they wrote nothing but what He intended; and Scripture tells us that this is what in fact He did.[24]

A second sign of this transcendence is found in the significance that these theologians attach to minute points of Scripture and that they see NT writers attaching to specifics of OT writings. This suggests that God must have so worked that every word and grammatical detail was just what he

[23]G. C. Berkouwer, *Holy Scripture* (Grand Rapids: Eerdmans, 1975) 358.

[24]J. I. Packer, *"Fundamentalism" and the Word of God* (Grand Rapids: Eerdmans, 1968) 80.

intended. Yet this is not to be understood as committing one to a literalistic interpretation of Scripture.

> In some instances Christ based his teaching on a careful exegesis of the exact reading in the Torah. For example, he pointed out in Matthew 22:32 the implications of Exodus 3:6 ("I *am* the God of Abraham, and the God of Isaac, and the God of Jacob") on the basis of the present tense implied by the verbless clause in Hebrew. He declared that God would not have spoken of himself as the God of mere corpses moldering in the grave ("He is not the God of the dead, but of the living"). Therefore Abraham, Isaac, and Jacob must have been alive and well in the life beyond at the time when God addressed Moses at the burning bush four or five centuries after they had died. Similarly his discussion with the Pharisees concerning the identity of the one referred to as "my lord" in Psalm 110:1 really turned upon the exact terms used in that clause or sentence. He therefore asked them, "If David thus calls him Lord, how is he his son?" (Matt. 22:45). In other words, the Messiah must not only be David's lineal descendant, but he must also be his divine Lord (kyrios)![25]

A third indication is found in the view of the unity and harmony of the Scriptures. Whereas some theologians and Biblical scholars have emphasized a development or progression within the Bible, with earlier ideas being superseded or even contradicted by the later ones, these theologians emphasize the continuity of the several portions of the Bible. Great themes such as the wrath of God and the sacrificial system run throughout the Bible. Boice says:

> It is true that the detailed sacrifices of the Old Testament system are no longer performed in the New Testament churches. But this is not because a supposed primitive conception of God has given way to a more advanced one, but rather because the sacrifice of Jesus Christ of himself has completed and superseded them all, as the Book of Hebrews clearly maintains. For this person the solution is not to be found in an evolving conception of God, for God is always the same—a God of wrath toward sin, a God of love toward the sinner. Rather, it is to be found in God's progressing revelation of himself to men and women, a revelation in which the sacrifices (for which God gives explicit instructions) are intended to teach both the dreadfully serious nature of sin and the way in which God has always determined to save sinners.[26]

The foregoing suggests that there is a positive correlation between one's view of the relationship of God to his creation and one's conception of revelation. If one believes that God is immanent and works through the natural processes of his world, then the Bible will be a somewhat more

---

[25]G. Archer, "The Witness of the Bible to Its Own Inerrancy," *Foundation* (ed. Boice) 97-98.

[26]Boice, *Foundation* (ed. Boice) 138.

natural book, having many similarities to other literature and bearing many marks of human authorship. If on the other hand one sees God as transcendent and working outside of nature and man, then revelation will be very supernatural and even miraculous in its nature and appearance. In the case of the neo-orthodox, revelation is not identified with words, but the personal encounter that constitutes revelation remains beyond man's ability to produce or even to comprehend, while the Bible, as man's attempt to elucidate the revelation, is a thoroughly human book. In the case of the conservative evangelicals whose views are referred to herein as the Council position, however, the Bible is identified with God's revelation and so is a supernatural treatise.

It should of course be realized that even theologians do not always move logically from presuppositions to conclusions and that there may be a reciprocal influence among presuppositions. Nonetheless, scrutinizing the presuppositions of a view should have a fruitful effect on one's understanding of it.

The purpose of this paper has been to elucidate rather than arbitrate. In particular, it has been the hope of the author that this writing might contribute to progress in the current discussions going on within Christianity and especially within evangelicalism. This would be done by focusing upon one set of presuppositions that lead to differing selections of data and differing interpretations of the data. In so doing, perhaps one step has been taken along the lines suggested by Kenneth Kantzer:

> The presuppositions of the opponents of a full-fledged orthodoxy must be spelled out explicitly, and these must be set forth in contrast to sharply and clearly delineated presuppositions of evangelical faith.[27]

Without such delineation, the arguments of the discussants may simply pass by each other without really coming to grips. Or, worse than that, instead of being the watershed of evangelicalism the doctrine of Scripture and of inerrancy could become the cause of its bloodshed.

[27]K. Kantzer, *Foundation* (ed. Boice) 152.

The Inspiration of Scripture Among the Seventeenth-Century Reformed Theologians

BONG RIN RO

THE renewed discussion on the inspiration, infallibility and inerrancy of Scripture among evangelical theologians in the late 70s has once again focused attention on the historical perspective of this topic. Although it is important to consider what God has revealed to us in the Scriptures about his Word, the major thrust of this paper is to concentrate on the history of how Reformed theologians in the seventeenth century have regarded Scripture. The controversies on the inspiration of Scripture in the Roman Catholic Church, the Lutheran and the Reformed Churches in Europe during the seventeenth century laid the foundation for the more complicated science of Biblical criticism of the succeeding centuries. In reaction to the rising intellectual climate and Biblical criticism during the seventeenth century, orthodox theologians were compelled to defend the authority of Scripture and began to emphasize the inspiration and infallibility of the Scriptures.

Lutheran scholars in recent years have concentrated much effort in tracing the Lutheran orthodox movement of the seventeenth century. Robert Preus' *The Inspiration of Scripture: A Study of the Theology of the Seventeenth Century Lutheran Dogmaticians* is an excellent example. However, in the Reformed school of theology there has been comparatively little scholarly accomplishment concerning the Reformed orthodox movement during the same period. This paper traces the historical background of the seventeenth century that fermented the rise of Biblical criticism and also displays the views of Scripture of the Reformed orthodox theologians in their defense of Scripture.

I. HISTORICAL BACKGROUND

In the post-Reformation period the Church met diverse challenges from the new intellectual climate at the dawn of the Age of Reason.

Politically, the Thirty Years' War, a religious battle between the Catholics and Protestants in Europe, brought devastation to both Churches. Protestants were longing for religious freedom and succeeded at the Peace

of Wesphalia in 1648. But in a few years under Louis XIV in France wars
continued one after another in Europe until 1763.

Theologically, Reformers in the seventeenth century were under heavy
attack from all sides. The Roman Catholic Church vigorously demanded
the recognition and authority of the Church and papacy over all Christendom. Some Catholic theologians, particularly Richard Simon, applied
historical criticism to Scripture from the last two decades of the seventeenth
century.[1] Socinians attacked the historical accounts of the Scriptures in
relation to Christology. Arminians (Remonstrants), Schwenkfelders and
Weigelians were willing to accept errors in the Bible and took a position
of compromise on Scripture. Revived Montanism shifted its emphasis from
the objective revelation of the Bible to the subjective illumination of the
Spirit of God.[2] Reacting against scholastic Biblical dogmatism, German
pietism arose under the leadership of John Arndt, Philip Jacob Spener and
August Hermann Francke and established the University of Halle in 1694
as the center of German pietism.

With the rise of the new rationalism, which marked the beginning of
the Age of Reason from the middle of the seventeenth century, idealists such
as Rene Descartes, Baruch Spinoza, Gottfried Leibnitz and the empiricist
John Locke brought a tremendous blow to the traditional beliefs of the
Church. Aristotelian or Cartesian principles and approaches made the
scriptural claims ambiguous. English deists, such as Lord Herbert of
Cherbury and Thomas Hobbes, applied higher critical thought to Scripture.
Scientists tried to reconcile their discoveries with the official beliefs of the
Church and brought challenge to the Church. Johann Kepler's planetary
motion and Galileo's reaffirmation of Nicolaus Copernicus' (1473-1543)
heliocentric theory had given new insight in understanding the universe.
Galileo tried to reconcile his theories with Scripture and met opposition
from the Church.[3]

II. CONTROVERSY WITH CARTESIAN PHILOSOPHY

Among various elements of influence borne upon the Reformed
Church during the seventeenth century, the controversy between Reformed
orthodox theologians and Cartesians was very significant. The philosophy
of Descartes with its radical doubt in correspondence with natural science
undermined the validity of the Scriptures.[4]

[1]S. L. Greenslade, ed., *The Cambridge History of the Bible: The West from the
Reformation to the Present* (Cambridge: University Press, 1963) 194.

[2]G. W. Bromiley, "The Church Doctrine of Inspiration," *Revelation and the
Bible* (ed. C. F. H. Henry; Grand Rapids: Baker, 1958) 214.

[3]Greenslade, *Cambridge*, 225-226, 255.

[4]E. Bizer, "Reformed Orthodoxy and Cartesianism," *Translating Theology into
the Modern Age* (ed. R. W. Funk; New York: Harper, 1965) 21-82.

Cartesian philosophy developed rapidly and affected theologians of the day at both the universities of Utrecht and Leiden. Three important theologians can be named in this category who approached the Scriptures with new hermeneutical principles: Ludwig Meyer, Ludwig Wolzogen and Christoph Wittich. Meyer, a "Spinozian Cartesian," realized the doctrinal disunity among the orthodox who believed in Scripture and developed a new hermeneutical methodology. His followers claimed that neither the Church nor Scripture nor the Holy Spirit can help to expound Scripture rightly because of the ambiguity of Biblical language. He tried to emphasize the philosophical element in the interpretation of Scripture.[5] Wolzogen also applied his confident philosophical method to interpret the Bible. He said nothing is needed beside reason and the familiarity of the Biblical languages for an exegete, because Scripture is like any other book.[6]

In the controversy, Gijsbert Voetius, who became a professor of theology at Utrecht from 1634 to his death in 1669, attacked Cartesianism vigorously and charged its followers as atheists. In his *Disputations Concerning Atheism* Voetius condemned Cartesians for rejecting the divinity and certainty of Scripture and for denying God himself.[7]

In an intellectual defense of orthodoxy Voetius adopted the method of scholasticism. As to the question of whether Scripture alone bears sufficient proof for the knowledge of God against atheists, he answered in the negative. He believed that Scripture did not give enough proof for the existence of God, especially to non-Christians such as Jews and pagans.[8] He strongly defended natural theology to prove the existence of God and revived scholasticism.

The Cartesian theology created a strong reaction from the Reformed orthodox theologians such as Peter Van Mastricht and Melchior Leydekker. They charged Cartesians for making faith into knowledge upon which dogmas can be built. For the defense of Scripture the Reformed orthodox theologians developed a more scholastic approach to the whole matter. Charles Briggs also pointed out that there was a change of emphasis from the exegetical into the scholastic approach among the Reformed theologians after Calvin and Zwingli.[9] According to Bizer the "traditional" view of verbal inspiration started from this period among the Reformed orthodox theologians against Cartesian philosophy. They wanted to explain the whole matter of inspiration on a more tangible and earthbound form, and

---

[5]Ibid., pp. 41-45.
[6]Ibid., pp. 45-46.
[7]Ibid., p. 28.
[8]Ibid., p. 32.
[9]C. A. Briggs, *General Instruction to the Study of Holy Scripture* (New York: Scribner's, 1899) 458-459.

consequently their doctrine of inspiration deviated from the scriptural one.[10]

Barth had the same explanation as Bizer as to the origin of the doctrine of traditional verbal inspiration during the post-Reformation period. They closed the mystery of inspiration of Scripture, which was reopened by the Reformers and gave rise to the "newer Protestantism"[11]— so-called "orthodoxy"—which first became visible in 1700. The orthodox, strict supernatural approach to the Bible created "an optical illusion."[12] While these high orthodox theologians—Calov, Heidegger, and Voetius— became increasingly lax toward natural theology, they took a stricter view of inspiration. For them the Bible became the "paper Pope."[13]

The charge of Barth and Bizer against the Reformed orthodox theologians during the seventeenth century for the creation of a new traditional doctrine of inspiration of the Bible demands a careful study of the writings of these orthodox theologians. That Cartesianism and other intellectual stimuli greatly influenced these theologians for their theological methodology can be understandable, but that their doctrine of inspiration of Scripture differed from that of Scripture is objectionable. The following material of this paper specifically deals with this doctrine from the writings of the Reformed orthodox theologians.

III. Reformers' Views of Scripture

Luther's doctrine of *sola scriptura* was fully accepted by other Reformers. For Calvin the Scriptures were God-inspired books that were given to the prophets and the apostles and that demand our submission:

> The prophets and apostles boast not their own acuteness or any qualities which win credit to speakers, nor do they dwell on reasons; but they appeal to the sacred name of God, in order that the whole world may be compelled to submission. . . . Our conviction of the truth of Scripture must be derived from a higher source than human conjectures, judgments, or reasons; namely, the secret testimony of the Spirit.[14]

He also emphasized the testimony of the Holy Spirit in the heart of a believer to make his word true.[15]

[10]Bizer, "Reformed," 42.

[11]K. Barth, *Church Dogmatics: The Doctrine of the Word of God* (trans. G. T. Thomson and H. Knight; Edinburgh: T. & T. Clark, 1956), 1. 522.

[12]Ibid.

[13]Ibid., p. 525.

[14]J. Calvin, *Calvin's Institutes* (trans. H. Beveridge; Grand Rapids: Eerdmans, 1962), 1. 71.

[15]Ibid., pp. 71-72.

Zwingli of Zurich also regarded the importance of Scripture as Luther and Calvin. He commented, "None the less, the central principle of the Reformation is enshrined in the will to heed the divine word of Scripture. ... God was in the very words of Christ, of the apostles and of the prophets."[16] Heinrich Bullinger, the successor of Zwingli, followed the same emphasis when he said, "Briefly, since Scripture is the Word of God, it must be believed without doubt."[17] He was the first one among the Protestant theologians who tried to defend in a monograph the inspiration of the Scriptures in detail.[18]

Summarizing the Reformers' view on the Scriptures, Karl Barth agrees that they held to the verbal inspiration of the Bible with the idea that God is the author of the Bible, and sometimes with the view of dictation.[19] But Barth also observed in the Reformers that their idea of inspiration of Scripture by the Holy Spirit was different from the distorted view of inspiration that had been held by the early Church fathers from Clement of Alexandria who developed the Biblical mystery of inspiration into a more tangible form with grammatical emphasis.[20] So the Reformers viewed inspiration not as a kind of miracle but as man's witness to God's revelation. Barth says:

> For them [the Reformers] the literally held inspired Bible was not at all a revealed book of oracles, but a witness to revelation, to be interpreted from the standpoint of and with a view to its theme, and in conformity with that theme.[21]

Another point of the Reformers that Barth praised was their belief that the Holy Spirit was working in believers to make the Biblical witness as the Word of God:

> As Luther insisted in innumerable passages the word of Scripture given by the Spirit can be recognised as God's Word only because the work of the Spirit which has taken place in it takes place again and goes a step further, i.e., becomes an event for its hearers or readers.[22]

---

[16] J. Rilliet, *Zwingli, Third Man of the Reformation* (trans. H. Knight; Philadelphia: Westminster, 1959) 57.

[17] H. Heppe, *Reformed Dogmatics* (trans. G. T. Thomson; London: George Allen & Unwin, 1950) 25.

[18] J. L. Neve, *A History of Christian Thought* (Philadelphia: Fortress, 1946), 1. 318.

[19] Barth, *Dogmatics*, 1. 520.

[20] Ibid., p. 517.

[21] Ibid., p. 521.

[22] Ibid.

Barth here is trying to prove his point that the Bible becomes the Word of God in a believer as the Spirit interprets the Bible to him. This view has been discussed extensively both in the theological liberal, neo-orthodox and orthodox camps.

IV. INSPIRATION OF SCRIPTURE

In the area of the inspiration of Scripture many questions arose as to the nature of inspiration, the inerrancy on the part of the writers of Scripture, the possible guarantee of nonerroneous reading, degrees of inspiration, the relation of inspiration to language, the act of writing, and other problems that created contentions and anxieties within the Church.

We will first consider what elements were involved in the constitution of Scripture. The dogmaticians divided Scripture into two main categories, *materia* and *forma*. The *materia* of Scripture is further subdivided into *ex qua* and *circa quam*. The *materia ex qua* of Scripture is the letters, syllables, words and phrases, and the *materia circa quam* is specific doctrines contained in Scripture. The *forma* is also divided into the external and internal *forma*. The external *forma* is the idiom and style of writing according to each writer's personal particular background, and the internal *forma* is God's thoughts revealed to us in Scripture.[23]

1. *Divine element.* This was what Reformed orthodox theologians believed: that God was the author of Scripture as Luther and Calvin held.[24] Cocceius said, "The author and giver of these books is God (not the Father only but also the Son), who ordered them to be written, and by His Spirit inspired. . . ."[25] Mastricht expressed the same idea:

> God made Scripture (a) partly by revelation, which was carried out; (1) by writing, as is clear in the decalogue; (2) by a behest that it should be written . . . (3) by inspiring it . . . i.e. by suggesting the things to be written and by infallibly directing the writing, so that in everything, whether they were occupied in the law or in deed, He not only inspired the actual things but also dictated the separate words: (b) partly by canonisation, by which inspiration the writings were transmitted to the Church.[26]

This view is quite similar to Gerhard's view that the Triune God is the author of Scripture.[27]

Rijssen said that

---

[23] R. Preus, *The Inspiration of Scripture* (Edinburgh: Oliver & Boyd, 1955) 14-15.

[24] Barth, *Dogmatics*, 1. 520.

[25] Heppe, *Reformed*, 17.

[26] Ibid., p. 20.

[27] Preus, *Inspiration*, 28.

Scripture is the collection of books written through the Spirit by men of God concerning the things which men must know, believe and do for the glory of God and their own salvation.[28]

Marcus Wendelin of Speyer in the fifteenth century believed that the writers of Scripture were either prophets or apostles and that books not written by either were apocryphal books.[29] On the other hand, Voetius said that since writers such as Luke and Mark were not apostles one should not limit the office of Biblical writers to apostles only.[30]

These Reformers, like the Lutheran orthodox dogmaticians, believed that God commanded the prophets and the apostles to write Scripture. Heidegger declared in *Corpus Theologiae* (1700):

The compulsion to write was enjoined upon them, not by a direct calling to the prophetic and apostolic—not on chance occasions only—not by the will of man—but alike by God's mandate both general (by which they were commanded to teach all nations), and special—and by inspiration or the divine inward mandate.[31]

Turretini also said that the writers of Scripture were commanded by the Spirit to write the Scriptures.[32] However, as to the question of whether the Spirit's command or compulsion upon the writers forced them to write in spite of their unwillingness, Voetius answered negatively.[33] Cardinal Bellarmine, a professor at Louvain, taught that God did not sometimes order the apostles to write specifically but that they wrote out of their own occasion. Turretini agreed that not all scriptural passages had God's specific command to write but that some wrote under general command. He divided the divine command into two categories: *implicitum* (general) and *explicitum* (explicit). Sometimes there was a definite command to a man of God to write his message in numerous passages such as Exodus 17; Deut 31:19; Isa 8:1; Jer 36:2; Hab 2:2. But at other times the apostles wrote under immediate inspiration (*inspiratio immediata*; 2 Tim 3:16; 1 Pet 2:1). For example, John and Jude had the inward assurance by God's Spirit without his definite command to write Scripture.[34] Even though not every apostle was called upon to write, every apostle was called upon to preach. The apostles who wrote Scripture commended themselves to divine inspiration, and their writings were equally respected with any other book of the Bible.

[28] Heppe, *Reformed*, 12.
[29] Ibid., pp. 12-13.
[30] Ibid., p. 19.
[31] Ibid., p. 18.
[32] F. Turretini, *Opera* (Edinburgh: University Press, 1847) 57-58.
[33] Heppe, *Reformed*, 19.
[34] Turretini, *Opera*, 58, III and IV.

These writers of Scripture were the men of God to whom the revelation of God descended for their writings.

2. *Human element*. Although emphasizing the divine element in the inspiration of the Bible, these Reformed orthodox theologians did not neglect the human element. First of all, the will power of the prophets and apostles was recognized as they were compelled to write Scripture. *Leyden Synopsis* maintained that the Biblical writers were not passive but active to a certain extent.

As the Lutheran orthodox theologians such as Quenstedt, Calov and Gerhard taught the "dictation theory" (which was misinterpreted by Sasse as mechanical dictation),[35] the Reformers from Calvin also taught the dictation theory. In explaining the inspiration of Scripture Calvin used words like "dictation," "clerks," "penman," "sure and authentic amanuenses of the Holy Spirit," "mouths for God."[36] Yet he did not think of the mechanical theory because he also said that the writers of the Bible were not "carried away" by a "heavenly afflatus" and that "God illumined their senses" and they "wrote freely and honestly."[37] Similarly B. B. Warfield understood Calvin's view of inspiration as not a mechanical dictational theory.[38]

As early as the end of the sixteenth century Cocceius taught the amanuensis theory of the Biblical writers:

> The men of God called prophets in general parlance, were God's assistants and amanuenses, who wrote exactly as they spoke, not by their own will but driven by the Holy Spirit.[39]

Barth stated that W. Bucan in his *Institutiones Theologicae* (1602) also taught the amanuensis theory,[40] and Barth interpreted these post-Reformation theologians' conception of inspiration as mechanical dictation.[41]

The question of whether the use of words like "amanuenses" and "dictation" by the Reformers meant the mechanical theory of inspiration needs to be carefully studied. In the Lutheran orthodox view of inspiration, Robert Preus wrote succinctly that their view of *dictatio* cannot carry the

---

[35] Preus, *Inspiration*, 57, 71-72.

[36] K. Kantzer, "Calvin and the Holy Scripture," *Inspiration and Interpretation* (ed. J. F. Walvoord; Grand Rapids: Eerdmans, 1957) 137.

[37] Ibid., p. 139.

[38] Ibid., p. 140.

[39] Heppe, *Reformed*, 42.

[40] Barth, *Dogmatics*, 1. 523.

[41] R. L. Harris, *Inspiration and Canonicity of the Bible* (Grand Rapids: Zondervan, 1957) 174-175.

mechanical interpretation of inspiration. In the Reformed circle mechanical inspiration was unknown in D. Ursini's *Loci Theologici* (1562), but later at the end of the seventeenth century Heidegger denied the pure mechanical theory of inspiration[42] and viewed the differences in style of the Bible as not hampering the doctrine of inspiration.[43] Geoffrey Bromiley feels that there was a definite development of the dictation theory from Calov's ambiguous use of the word *dicto* to the idea of "assistants and amanuenses" by Gerhard and Bucan and the "flute-player" of Heidegger.[44]

3. *Scripture and the Word of God.* In discussing the relationship of the Word of God to the Scriptures, the Reformed orthodox theologians made a quantitative rather than a qualitative distinction between the Word of God and Scripture. Polanus distinguished the Word of God into two categories. The "internal Word of God" is the revelation of God to man through the Holy Spirit, and the "external Word of God" is through a living voice, angels, men or written symbols. The internal and external Word of God are the same Word, and both are necessary for saving faith. But only the second, particularly Scripture, constitutes faith and theology.[45]

Des Marets brought out the historical aspect of the Word of God. During the patriarchal period in the OT, revelation of God came in its unwritten form. But from the Mosaic time God's revelation in part was provided in the written Word.[46] Nevertheless, written Scripture, which contains a part of God's revelation, was considered as the Word of God. Heidegger stated that

> Holy Scripture is the Word of God described on the authority of Holy Scripture through Moses and the prophets in the Old Testament, through the evangelists and apostles in the New Testament, and made up into canonical books, in order to teach the Church fully and plainly about God and things divine and to be the single norm of faith and life unto salvation.[47]

Wolleb insisted that Scripture shared the essential nature of God and shifted the terminology from "Word of God" to "written Word of God."[48] The distinction therefore between the Word of God and Scripture is that of form rather than of substance, and the "basic and organic principle" of

---

[42] Bromiley, "Church," 213.

[43] Heppe, *Reformed*, 18.

[44] Bromiley, "Church," 213.

[45] J. F. Robinson, "The Doctrine of Holy Scripture in the 17th Century Reformed Theology" (unpublished Ph.D. thesis; Univercite de Strasbourg, 1971) 20. Polanus, *Syntagma*, Book 1, chap. 14, 28-29; Book 1, chap. 15, 29.

[46] Robinson, "Doctrine," 21. Des Marets, *Systema Breve*, Loc. 1, sec. 25, 12-13.

[47] Heppe, *Reformed*, 12.

[48] Robinson, "Doctrine," 21. Wolleb, *Compendium*, Prol., secs. 3-5, 3-4.

theology could be applied to both the Word of God and Scripture without any contradiction.[49]

4. *Was revelation necessary?* Was it for the Word? Turretini answered affirmatively. For him the Word of God was the only foundation for theology and had to come before everything. And, in fact, it was necessary for God to reveal to believers his truth.[50] The old orthodox Church had always taught that the Word of God stood absolutely and was a simple necessity for God's revelation for man's salvation because "it is the seed (semen) whereby we are regenerated (I Pet. 1:23), and light (lux) by which we are directed (Ps. 119:105), [and] the food (cibus) by which we are fed (Heb. 5:13, 14)."[51]

For Turretini the Word of God was absolutely necessary in order that God could reveal himself and his desire for man. This Word of God showed three main facts: (1) the communicative "sum of God's goodness" (*summa Dei bonitas*); (2) "extreme human blindness and corruption" (*extrema hominis coecitas et corruptio*); and (3) correct reasoning (*recta ratio*), which teaches us of God. He believed in total depravity (*depravitus*) of man by which man cannot know God unless God reveals himself to man (1 Cor 2:14; Eph 5:8). To Turretini, finding God by human reason was impossible. Man was not able to understand God without the divine light, just as the sun was not capable of being seen without its own light (Ps 36:10).[52] Therefore the importance of Scripture was based on the fact that God had revealed himself supernaturally to man through the Word.

According to Turretini, Scripture confirmed two desires (*appetitus*) implanted in natural man: One is the old truth (*veritatis*) and another is immortality (*immortalitatis*) of man. Concerning this truth, the author tried to show man's total inability to find the prime truth and highest good in nature of himself. With regard to immortality, here again Scripture alone postulated the glory of God and man's salvation, because the school of nature (*schola naturae*) cannot make the truth of God known to man. The Reformer's conclusion is that God's Word is necessary as the higher grace or gift (*superior gratiae*) for his truth, and neither philosophy nor reason can assure this.[53] He goes into detail concerning the place of natural theology, and even though he accepts God's revelation in nature he denies the sufficiency of natural theology for man's salvation through Christ.[54]

---

[49] Robinson, "Doctrine," 22. F. Gomar, *Disputationes Theologicae*, in *Opera Theologica Omnia*, Vol. 2, Disp. 2, p. 3.

[50] Turretini, *Opera*, 1. 53.

[51] Ibid., 2.

[52] Ibid., 3.

[53] Ibid., 4. 54.

[54] Ibid., 5 and 6.

There is no doubt that the Reformed orthodox Church was fully alerted by the rational and Cartesian attacks on the Scriptures from within and outside of the Church. Against such attacks the orthodox tried to defend the authenticity of Scripture. Sometimes their enthusiastic effort in defending the doctrine of inspiration was carried out too extremely over what the Scriptures themselves said. For example, Voetius taught that the NT was inspired only in Hellenistic Greek and not in the Aramaic or Syrian language that was their native language. Because the NT was written in Greek, the Holy Spirit must have inspired their thought in Greek.[55] As to the question of the authenticity of the accents of Hebrew and Greek in the Bible, Voetius distinguished the musical from the tonal accents and said:

> As regards the euphonic or musical accents of the Hebrews according to which they chant when reading, I do not see why they should be affirmed. As for the tonics I fail to see why they should be rejected.[56]

Nevertheless, Voetius did not believe that the titles of Scripture were authentic.[57]

In spite of some differences that are found among some Reformed orthodox theologians, the doctrine of inspiration held by them, in general, was the scriptural view of inspiration. Since the Reformed churches in Europe were not localized in one part of Europe like the Lutheran Church in Germany, any Reformed orthodox movement in one place cannot speak for the whole Reformed Church. In other words, the Cartesian influence that was so dominant at Utrecht and Leiden might not be so in other Reformed churches in Zurich, Geneva, Scotland and other places.

5. *Was it necessary for the Word of God to be recorded?* This was one of the common questions raised by the Reformed theologians. Turretini elaborated on this question in his *Institutio theologiae elencticae*. He argued with the Roman Catholics on the question of whether the written Word of God (*Dei Verbum Scripto*) was necessary. The Roman Church attempted to weaken the position of the written Word in order to bring out the importance of tradition (*agraphon*) and the papacy.[58]

Cardinal Bellarmine contended that the written Word would be helpful but not absolutely necessary and that it would be better off for the Church if nothing had been written. God, according to the Roman Church, gave Scripture in two fashions, either material (*materialiter*) or formal (*formaliter*). The former, which is handed down to us in the written form, is so

---

[55] Heppe, *Reformed*, 19; Barth, *Dogmatics*, 1. 524.
[56] Heppe, *Reformed*, 20.
[57] Ibid.
[58] Turretini, *Opera*, 2. 55.

absolute and simple that the Church cannot change it. But the latter, which shows the way God handed it down to the scriptural writers, is not clear and therefore not absolutely necessary.[59]

The papacy brought in the Biblical conception that God spoke before Moses for two thousand years concerning the institution of the Church. In other words, the papacy was saying that the OT Church went along well even before Moses actually received the written Word from God. "Therefore, God indeed is not bound by the Scripture, but He binds us to the Scripture."[60] The real question is not whether the written Word is absolutely necessary, but whether it is related to God's economy of dealing with man now. Therefore it is a more existential question. To this question the Church (Roman) gives the answer (Eph 3:10).[61]

From this argumentation the distinction of *agraphon* and *egraphon* came into existence. For the Roman Church this distinction is not in substance but in accidence (*accidentia*). Since God was able to teach his people without the written Word in the past, the Church is able to lead its people. This was a subtle argument against the *sola scriptura* of the Reformation.

In replying to the papal attack on this matter, Turretini emphasized the importance of Scripture as our constant guide. He said that there are three powerful necessities that Scripture itself confirms. First is the conservation (*conservatio*) of the Word by which Scripture has been carefully preserved from infirmity, human perversion or willful abbreviation. Secondly, the certitude is vindicated against the falsity and corruption of Satan. Thirdly, the Word of God has to be propagated and transmitted to the world.[62]

Both Cappel and Des Marets also stressed the danger of forgetting and adulterating the heavenly voices and visions by Satanic powers and corrupt men unless they were recorded.[63] The constantly changing historical situation could further distort the revelation of God.[64]

Rijssen emphasized the written Word in order that man might be able to read it and confirm his faith and pointed out that the NT was confirmed by the OT.[65] Scripture was absolutely crucial not only for the well-being of the Church but also for the very existence of it.[66]

[59] Ibid.

[60] Ibid.

[61] Ibid., 3.

[62] Ibid., 4. 56.

[63] Robinson, "Doctrine," 24. Cappel, "De Necessitate Scripturae," 1. 4, 17, p. 39. Cf. Des Marets, *Systema Breve*, Loc. 1, sec. 28, 14.

[64] Robinson, "Doctrine," 24. Spanheim, *Disputationes*, Part 2, sec. 4, cols. 1190-1191.

[65] Robinson, "Doctrine," 25. Rijssen, *Summa*, Loc. 2, sec. 4, 9.

[66] Robinson, "Doctrine," 23. Turretini, *Opera*, 1. 2.2.2, 60. Cf. In Momma's *Praelectiones Theologicae*, Loc. 2, 10.

V. INFALLIBILITY OF SCRIPTURE

The authority and infallibility of Scripture was challenged by three groups. The first consisted of atheists and rationalists. The second— Socinians, Remonstrants, Schwenkfelders and Weigelians—admitted errors in Scripture. Third, some Roman Catholics, in order to strengthen the tradition of the Church, acknowledged contradictions, absurdities and corruptions in Scripture.

Calvin had no difficulty in accepting the infallibility of Scripture, although he found some difficult textual problems such as Acts 7:14 compared with Gen 46:27 and a wrong name in Acts 7:43. In his commentaries Calvin tried to exegete the passages to harmonize them. His main concern was not textual infallibility but rather the faithful transmission of God's revelation through the Holy Spirit to Scripture without errors.[67]

Referring to Calvin's and Luther's views of Scripture, Harold Lindsell said:

> Anyone who reads Calvin and Luther and compares them with modern writers who deny biblical infallibility cannot fail to note the difference between the attitude of the Reformers and that of the modern objectors to infallibility. The latter unfailingly seek to denigrate Scripture, to harmonize it, to swallow a camel and strain out a gnat. The Reformers did not react in this way. Their attitude toward the Word of God was one of reverence, humility, and positive acceptance of it as both authoritative and infallible.[68]

For most Reformed theologians the concept of infallibility was understood in terms of "inerrancy." DuMoulin viewed Scripture as the "sovereign and infallible judgments" for man.[69] Spanheim denied any errors in Scripture in its doctrine and narrative stories because the writers "were led by the Holy Spirit in everything, were led by him alone and always."[70] Louis Tronchin in Geneva and Rijssen also declared the infallible writings of Biblical writers free from error.[71] Voetius extended infallibility to the form of Scripture (style and words).[72] Pierre Jurieu made God fully responsible for infallible Scripture.

> Besides, it is clear that God should not and could not have had written the oracles which he Himself pronounced and the miracles which he performed except by pens directed by his Spirit, in order that his words and his actions

---

[67] Calvin, *Commentary*, Acts 7:14.
[68] H. Lindsell, *The Battle for the Bible* (Grand Rapids: Zondervan, 1976) 12.
[69] Robinson, "Doctrine," 39.
[70] Ibid. Spanheim, *Disputationes*, Part 3, sec. 6, col. 1192.
[71] Robinson, "Doctrine," 39; L. Tronchin, *Theses Theologicae* (Geneva, 1663) 3.
[72] Robinson, "Doctrine," 39; Voetius, *Disputationes*, 1. 32-33.

be reported with a perfect exactitude, without any omission and without any addition.[73]

The Westminster Confession (1647) declared that Scripture is "our only infallible rule of faith and practice" in spiritual matters.

Turretini admitted that the prophets and apostles were not perfect in their personal lives and proved this point by using the story of David with Uriah and Peter's hypocrisy in Gal 2:12. Nevertheless, when they wrote Scripture they made no mistakes.

> The Prophets did not fall into mistakes in those things which they wrote as inspired men and as prophets, not even in the smallest particulars; otherwise faith in the whole of Scripture would be rendered doubtful.[74]

Turretini furthermore affirmed the historicity of Moses and his authorship of Scripture. He warned Christians that they should not have negotiation with those who deny the truth about Moses. Not only Jews but also Christians believed in Moses' existence and writings, and he could not be denied unless other ancient figures such as Plato, Aristotle and Cicero were denied.[75]

Even when confronted with difficult textual problems in Scripture, orthodox theologians emphatically affirmed the infallibility of Scripture. Des Marets admitted problematic passages but denied the possibility of admitting errors in Scripture.[76] Voetius dealt with the "insolubles" in Scripture that the critics brought out, such as minor and insignificant errors not necessary for salvation, but he denied the possibility of such minor errors in Scripture.[77]

Hoornbeek in supporting the trustworthiness of Scripture declared, "All Scriptures are divinely inspired; nothing at all was written except what the Holy Spirit himself included; thus nothing whatsoever was in fact able to be in error." He quoted excerpts from a number of prominent Dutch theologians of the late sixteenth and early seventeenth centuries.[78]

The beginning of extensive Biblical criticism on the basis of literary and historical accounts did not come until the end of the seventeenth century. In 1678 the Catholic theologian in France, Richard Simon, who was called the "father of Biblical criticism," published his most important book on OT criticism. It was called the *Critical History of the Old Testament* and was translated into English in 1682. Simon elaborated on

---

[73]Robinson, "Doctrine," 39; P. Jurieu, *L'Esprit de Mr. Arnaud* (Deventer, 1684) 170.

[74]Robinson, "Doctrine," 39-40; Turretini, *Institutio*, 1. 2.4.5, 66; 1. 2.4.23, 73.

[75]Turretini, *Opera*, 18. 63.

[76]Robinson, "Doctrine," 40; Des Marets, *Systema Breve*, Loc. 1, sec. 29, 15.

[77]Robinson, "Doctrine," 40; Voetius, *Disputationes*, 1. 49-50.

[78]Hoornbeek, *Institutiones Theologicae*, Sec. 2, 6, 18.

the criticism of the Pentateuch by previous Catholic theologians such as Andreas Masius, Bento Pereira, Jacques Bonfrere, Jean Morin and Isaac de la Peyre. Simon was consequently dismissed from the Oratory, and the King's Council ordered the book confiscated and placed on the *Index*. Theological polemics over historical criticism also arose between Simon and the Protestant theologians, particularly with Isaac Voss, canon of Windsor, and Jacques Basnage, pastor at Rouen and later at Rotterdam. Simon subsequently published a number of other books: *Histoire critique du texte du Nouveau Testament* (1689), *Histoire critique des versions du Nouveau Testament* (1690), *Histoire critique des principaux commentateurs du Nouveau Testament* (1693) and *Le Nouveau Testament de Notre-Seigneur Jesus Christ* (1702).[79]

In line with Simon's historical criticism Hugo Grotius of the Netherlands, English deists such as Lord Herbert of Cherbury, Thomas Hobbes and John Locke, and the philosopher Benedict Spinoza also fanned the flames of higher criticism of Scripture. These critical approaches to Scripture therefore laid the foundation at the end of the seventeenth century for the further development of the science of Biblical criticism from the eighteenth century onward.

VI. CONCLUSION

The Reformed orthodox theologians of the seventeenth century were mainly occupied with problems of vowel points and textual variants and the defense of Scriptural infallibility in the original texts. In 1680 the nature of the battle shifted from textual authenticity to literary and historical criticism. Church history teaches us that the sovereign God of history, the author of the Book, has raised up men of God in each generation to defend Scripture against various attacks on it. The seventeenth century was no exception, and the Reformed orthodox theologians performed their part in the defense of the infallible Scriptures.

[79]Greenslade, *Cambridge*, 194, 218-219.

APPENDIX: BIOGRAPHICAL DATA
ON THE SEVENTEENTH-CENTURY REFORMED THEOLOGIANS

1. Polanus von Polansdorf, Amandus (1561-1610)
   Polanus studied at the universities of Tübingen and Basel and became professor of OT at the universities of Heidelberg and Basel. He had correspondence with Theodore de Beza. His main work was *Syntagma theologiae christianae* (Basel, 1609).

2. Wolleb, Johannes (1586-1629)
   Wolleb studied philosophy and theology in Basel and later became professor of OT at the University of Basel. He wrote *Compendium theologiae Christianae* (Basel, 1626).

3. Cappel, Louis, Younger (1585-1658)
   Cappel studied in Sedan, England, Belgium and Germany and became professor of Hebrew and theology at Saumur. His works were *Arcanum punctationis revelatum* (Leiden, 1624); *Critica Sacra* (Paris, 1634); *Diatriba de veris et antiquis Hebraeorum literis* (Amsterdam, 1645); *Syntagma thesium theologicarum in academia salmuriensi ... disputatarum* (Saumur, 1641).

4. Gomar, Francis (1563-1641)
   Gomar studied in Strasbourg, Neustadt, Cambridge (England) and Heidelberg and became professor of theology at Leiden. His main work was *Opera theologica omnia* (Amsterdam, 1645).

5. Voetius, Gijsbert (1589-1676)
   Voetius studied at Leiden, Netherlands, and became professor of theology and oriental languages at the University of Utrecht. He was against the Remonstrants and attended the Synod of Dordrecht in 1619. His main work was *Selectae disputationes theologicae* (5 vols.; Utrecht, 1648-1649).

6. Cocceius, Johannes (1603-1669)
   Cocceius was known as the originator of "federal theology," which promotes a personal covenant between God and man. He studied Hebrew and rabbinic studies at Hamburg and later at Franeker, Netherlands, and became professor of theology at Leiden. His works were *Summa doctrina de foedere et testamento Dei* (Leiden, 1648); *Summa theologiae ex Sacris Scripturis repetita* (Leiden, 1662); *Opera omnia* (8 vols.; Amsterdam, 1673-1675).

7. Hoornbeek, Johannes (1617-1666)
   Hoornbeek studied both at Leiden and Utrecht and later became professor at Leiden and Utrecht. He was one of the chief opponents of Cocceius' federal theology. He wrote *Socinianismus confutatus* (Utrecht, 1650-1654); *Summa controversiarum religionis* (1653); *Institutiones theologicae ex optimis auctoribus concinnatae* (1653).

8. Des Marets, Samuel (1599-1673)

   Des Marets studied in Paris, Saumur, Geneva and Leiden and served as pastor in several churches in the Netherlands, teaching also at Bois-de Duc (1636-43) and at Groningen from 1643 onward. He wrote more than a hundred works against Roman Catholics, Socinians, Arminians and Chiliasts. His main work was *Collegium theologicum* (Groningen, 1645).

9. Spanheim, Friedrich, Younger (1632-1701)

   Spanheim studied at Leiden and Heidelberg and became professor of theology and Church history at Leiden. His works were *Summa historiae ecclesiasticae* (1689); *Brevis introductio ad historiam sacram utriusque Testamenti ac praecique christianam* (1694); *Opera* (3 vols.; Leiden, 1700-1703).

10. Rijssen, Leonard Van (1636-ca. 1700)

    Rijssen studied at Leiden under Voetius and served several churches in the Netherlands. His main works were *Dootstuypen der Cartesianen en Coccejanen* ("The Mortal Convulsions of the Cartesians and Cocceians") (2 vols.; Utrecht, 1675-1676); *Synopsis impurae theologiae remonstrantium* (Utrecht, 1661); *Summa theologiae elencticae* (Deventer, 1671).

11. Turretini, Francois (1623-1687)

    As the son of a pastor and professor of theology, Benedict Turretini, in Geneva, Francois studied in Geneva, Leiden, Utrecht, Paris, Saumur, Montauban and Nimes. He became the pastor at the French and Italian church in Geneva in 1648 and later in Lyon in 1650 for a short period. Three years later he became professor of philosophy in Geneva and had extensive correspondence with many Reformed theologians in Europe. His main work was *Institutio Theologiae Elencticae* (Geneva, 1688), and his writings were collected later in his *Opera* (4 vols.; Edinburgh, 1847).

12. Tronchin, Louis (1629-1705)

    As a son of German theologian Theodore Tronchin, he studied at Saumur and became professor of theology in Geneva. His writings were *Theses Theologicae* (Geneva, 1663); *Disputatio de providentia Dei* (1670); *Disputatio theologica de authoritate Scripturae Sacrae* (1677).

13. Heidegger, Johann Heinrich (1633-1698)

    Heidegger studied in Zürich, Marburg and Heidelberg and taught Hebrew, philosophy and Church history in Steinfurt and later Christian ethics and theology in Zürich. He wrote *Corpus theologiae Christianae* (2 vols.; Zürich, 1700); *Ethicae Christianae elementa* (Frankfurt, 1711).

14. Jurieu, Pierre (1637-1713)

Jurieu was a French Calvinist and opposed Catholic theology. He studied philosophy at Saumur and theology at Sedan and taught at Sedan until 1681 when the academy was dissolved by Louis XIV. His works were *Ratterdam* (1681-1713); *Histoire du Calvinisme et du papisme mis en parallele* (2 vols.; 1683); *Histoire Critique de dogmes et des cultes* (1704-1705).

The Concept of Truth in the Contemporary Inerrancy Debate*

Norman L. Geisler

How is it that evangelicals on both sides of the inerrancy debate can claim that the Bible is wholly true while one side believes that there can be minor mistakes of history or science affirmed by the Biblical authors[1] and the other denies that there any mistakes whatever? Some even claim to believe in inerrancy to the point that every word of the Bible is true[2] and yet hold that Jesus' statement that the mustard seed is the "smallest of all seeds" is scientifically incorrect.[3] Some claim that the Bible is "the only infallible rule of faith and practice"[4] but hold that Paul was wrong when he affirmed that the husband is the "head" of the wife.[5] One errantist put it bluntly when he wrote, "We can speak of the Bible as being inspired from cover to cover, human mistakes and all."[6] Is this duplicity? Are these men intentionally deceiving their constituencies? Do they hold a

---

*Apart from minor editorial differences, this chapter is substantially the same as the article in *BSac* (October-December 1980) 327-339.

[1]See W. S. LaSor in *Theology, News and Notes* (special issue for Fuller alumni; 1976) 7, where he admits that "those portions where one passage is clearly in disagreement with another (such as the thousands in Kings compared to the ten thousands in Chronicles)" cannot be explained as "textual corruptions." Otherwise "we could never again use the canons of criticism to support any text against the conjectural reading of liberal critics." This means that clear contradictions (such as 4,000 stalls [2 Chr 9:25] and 40,000 stalls [1 Kgs 4:26]) should be accepted as part of the autographa.

[2]In a letter to a radio listener (April 26, 1978) D. Fuller wrote, "*I believe that every statement in the Bible is totally without error* and every word is equally inspired" [italics mine].

[3]D. Fuller claims that "although the mustard seed [see Matt 13:32] is not the smallest of all seeds, yet Jesus referred to it as such . . ." because "to have gone contrary to their mind on what was the smallest seed would have so diverted their attention from the knowledge that would bring salvation to their souls that they might well have failed to hear these all-important revelational truths." *BETS* 2/2 (Spring 1968) 81-82.

[4]From Fuller Theological Seminary's "Statement of Faith," Article III.

[5]See P. K. Jewett, *Man as Male and Female* (Grand Rapids: Eerdmans, 1975) 139.

[6]D. Beegle, *The Inspiration of Scripture* (Philadelphia: Westminster, 1963) 138.

double standard of truth? As a matter of fact it is not necessary to come to any of these conclusions. It may be that they do not hold a double standard but rather a different theory of truth. In point of fact it is precisely the case that some evangelicals who admit to errors in Scripture do hold a different theory of truth from those who do not admit to any errors in Scripture.

Could it be, then, that the real problem is that a fundamental issue that occasions the difference between the two major camps of evangelicals on inerrancy is that they are presupposing different theories of truth? I propose that this is indeed the case. One thing is certain: Different theories of truth will make a significant difference in what one considers to be an "error" or deviation from the truth. In fact, what counts as an error on one definition of truth is not an error on another definition of truth.[7]

I. Two Theories of Truth

Let us elaborate two different theories of truth and see what difference it would make in one's view as to whether the Bible's writers ever affirmed what is actually incorrect.

1. *A Correspondence Theory of Truth.* According to this view, truth is "that which corresponds to the actual state of affairs," to the way things really are. If this theory of truth is correct, then an "error" is that which does not correspond with the facts, with what is really the case.[8]

(1) The first corollary of a correspondence view of truth is this: A statement is true even if the speaker (writer) intended not to say it, providing that the statement itself correctly describes a state of affairs.

(2) The second corollary is that one can make a true statement that is actually *more* than he intends to say. Everyone has had the experience of accidentally revealing more by his words, to his own embarrassment, than he intended to say. I once heard a bad (I think, unfair) umpire say, "I umpired *against* that team once." He obviously meant, "I umpired a game *for* that team." Judging by his highly questionable calls, what he actually said was true even though he did not mean to reveal as much.

[7]That the noninerrantists recognize this is clear from their writings. D. Hubbard wrote, "The nub of Lindsell's quarrel with many of us who have been his colleagues is the interpretation of the word 'error.' . . . Many of us signed, and still could sign, Fuller's earlier Statement without buying Lindsell's definition of error." *Theology, News and Notes* (1976) 8. See also J. Rogers, *Biblical Authority* (Waco: Word, 1977) 43, who approvingly quotes Bavinck that "the purpose, goal, or 'distinction' of Scripture was 'none other than that it should make us wise to salvation.' According to Bavinck, Scripture was not meant to give us technically correct scientific information." In other words, since the Bible accomplishes this salvific intention it is true.

[8]On a correspondence view of truth see Aristotle, *Categories* 4a10-4b19; *On Interpretation* 16a10-19.

(3) The third corollary of a correspondence view of truth is that, properly speaking, truth is a characteristic of propositions (or other expressions) about reality, but truth is not a characteristic of the reality itself.

(4) The fourth corollary is that reality, or that which is, is neither true nor false as such—it simply is. For instance, a lie can be real but the lie is not true. That is, that someone is lying to you can be the actual state of affairs. One would not say that the lie is therefore true. It is simply true that he is actually lying.

Therefore, strictly speaking, it is propositions about states of affairs that are true or false. Properly speaking, truth is found in the affirmation (or denial) about reality, not in the reality itself.

Of course "reality" or states of affairs referred to by propositions can be mental states of affairs (thoughts, ideas, and so on) or even another proposition. But strictly speaking, on a correspondence theory of truth only affirmations (or denials) are true or false, not the reality about which the affirmations are made. Persons can be called true in the secondary sense that what they say can be trusted to come to pass or to correspond to reality. So they can be called true or trustworthy persons because their statements can be trusted to come to pass or to correspond with reality.[9]

2. *A Noncorrespondence Theory of Truth.* For the sake of simplicity of discussion let us narrow the field of relevant noncorrespondence views of truth to one use by noninerrantists that we will call an intentionality view of truth.[10] According to this view of truth a statement is true if "it accomplishes what the author intended it to accomplish"[11] and, of course, false if it does not. There are several corollaries of this view of truth as well.

(1) The first corollary is that a statement is true even if some of its factual assertions do not correspond with reality, so long as the statement

---

[9]The article on "Truth" in *The New International Dictionary of New Testament Theology* (ed. C. Brown; Grand Rapids: Zondervan, 1971), Vol. 3, gives an excellent discussion of the various theories of truth and of the Biblical usage of "truth" (*alētheia*).

[10]It could also be called a "functional" view of truth since it centers in the saving function of the Bible. J. Rogers writes, "The authority of Scripture in these [Reformed] confessions resided in its saving function, not in the form of words used." Again, "it is significant to note . . . that for the Reformation concept of the reliability" of Scripture in achieving its function of salvation, Turretin substituted a discussion of the formal 'necessity' of Scripture." *The Authority and Interpretation of the Bible* (New York: Harper, 1979) 125, 175.

[11]D. Fuller (*BETS* 2/2, 82) and D. Hubbard hold this same functional view of truth—namely, that the Bible is true in that it is "able to make us wise unto salvation." Hubbard contends that error in the Bible means "that which *leads astray* from the truth God is teaching" [italics mine], *Theology*, 8.

accomplishes its intended purpose.[12] This means that factually incorrect statements can be true providing they accomplish their intended results. For instance, the parental exhortation to a young child, "If you are good, Santa Claus will bring you presents," is factually incorrect, but according to this view of truth it could be actually true if it helps produce the intended good behavior in children before Christmas.

(2) A second implication of this point is that factually correct statements can be false if they do not accomplish their intended goals. Some parents are driven to the negative psychology of saying, "That is bad; do not do that," because their factually correct statement, "That is good," was not accomplishing its intended result.[13]

(3) A third corollary of the intentionalist view of truth is that persons, not merely propositions, can be properly characterized as true.[14]

A person is true if he accomplishes or lives up to someone's intentions for him. Persons are not true if they fail to measure up to someone's expectations (whether the intentions are their own or another's).

II. Some Implications for Inerrancy

It seems apparent that if one adopts the intentionality view of truth he could easily (and consistently) hold that the Bible is wholly true (as God intends it) and yet could have many errors in it. For if truth means only that the Bible (or Word of God) will always accomplish its intended purpose (regardless of factual incorrectness)—for example, "to make men wise unto salvation"[15]—then surely it can do that with or without minor

[12]Berkouwer makes it clear that he holds this same intentionalist or functional view of truth when he wrote approvingly of Kuyper that "he was not at all troubled by the absence of accuracy and exactness precisely *because* of the God-breathed character of Scripture: the reliability of the Gospels was guaranteed by this *purpose* of the Spirit." Elsewhere he added that "the authority of Scripture is in no way diminished because an ancient world view occurs in it; for it was not the *purpose* of Scripture to offer revealing information on that level." *Studies in Dogmatics: Holy Scripture* (Grand Rapids: Eerdmans, 1975) 250, 181 [italics mine].

[13]See Rogers, *Authority and Interpretation*, who claims that the redemptive function of the Bible is the locus of truth rather than the verbal form. Broadly speaking, the intentionalist (functional) view is a species of the "pragmatic" theory of truth, along with its sister "personalistic" and "existential" theories of truth.

[14]That revelation is personal, not propositional, is of course the contention of neo-orthodox theologians such as E. Brunner (see his *Revelation and Reason* [Philadelphia: Westminster, 1946] 369-370), which bears a strong kinship with the neo-evangelical views of Berkouwer, Rogers and others.

[15]In personal correspondence with D. Fuller he stated this point very clearly (March 29, 1978): "I believe it is a necessary implication of II Tim. 3:15 that the Bible's truth depends on how well it lives up to this intention, stated explicitly here. I know of no other verse which states the Bible's purpose so succinctly as II Tim. 3:15."

errors. Even incorrect maps can get one to the intended destination. There can be unintentional Biblical errors in the minor matters without affecting the author's main intention to save sinners. These minor errors do not reflect badly on the author's (God's) character, since they are not pernicious. On an intentionalist view of truth one does not need an inerrant Bible. All one needs is a "reliable" and "trustworthy" Scripture.

In short, different implications for the doctrine of inerrancy follow from each of these theories of truth. Let us briefly examine some of them.

1. *On the Correspondence View*. Inerrancy means "without error" or "wholly true." On the correspondence view of truth, several implications are involved. First, it would mean that whatever the writer of a scriptural book actually affirmed is to be taken as true, even if he personally did not intend to affirm it. That is to say, the Bible could say more than its human author intended it to, since God could have intended more by it than the author did.[16] Psalm 22 may be an example of this: David may not have intended to affirm the crucifixion (but merely describe his own persecution), whereas God did intend to affirm the cross in this passage. This is indeed what many scholars think happened to the prophets (1 Pet 1:10-11) when they wrote of things that seemed to go beyond them (cf. Dan 12:4). Of course the fact that the authors could say more than they intended does not mean they did. One might hold that God supernaturally restrained the Biblical writers from doing so in order that there would always be an identity between God's intentions and the author's intentions.[17] In any case, an implication of the correspondence theory of truth is that one knows an author's intentions by his affirmations and not his affirmations by his intentions. This is so because there is no way for us to get at the Biblical author's intentions apart from his expressions of them. We cannot read his mind apart from reading his writings.[18]

Second, on the correspondence view of truth an error can occur even when an author intended otherwise, because error has to do with his affirmations and not simply with his intentions apart from his affirmations.

---

[16]Even E. D. Hirsch, Jr., who placed strong emphasis on the intention of the author in interpretation, admitted that "the human author's willed meaning can always go beyond what he consciously intended so long as it remains within the willed type, and if the meaning is conceived of as going beyond even that, then we must have recourse to a divine author speaking through the human one. In that case it is His willed type we are trying to interpret, and the human author is irrelevant." *Validity in Interpretation* (New Haven: Yale University Press, 1967) 126 n. 37.

[17]W. Kaiser places great weight on this point. See his chapter on "Legitimate Hermeneutics" in *Inerrancy* (ed. N. L. Geisler; Grand Rapids: Zondervan, 1980).

[18]P. B. Payne makes an interesting point of this in an article entitled "The Fallacy of Equating Meaning with the Author's Intention," *Trinity Journal* 6/1 (Spring 1977) 23-33.

In short, mistakes are possible even if they are unintentional. Therefore to prove the Bible in error one need not prove wrong intentions of the author (which is virtually impossible to do) but simply show that he made an incorrect affirmation.[19] Hence any proposition affirmed as true by any writer of Scripture which does not (or did not) correspond with the reality to which it referred would be false and in error even if the author did not intend to so affirm. For instance, if the Bible actually affirms that hell is geographically down and heaven is up, and if this is contrary to fact, then the Bible would be wrong regardless of what the author may have intended by the passage. Further, if the Bible affirms that God directly created all basic forms of life, and if this is contrary to scientific fact,[20] then the Bible would err. Likewise, if Paul affirmed that a husband is the "head" of his wife, and if in fact God does not intend this to be so, then the Bible would be in error here. The same is true of Jesus' statement that the mustard seed is "the smallest of all seeds." If this is factually incorrect then Jesus would have erred, regardless of how true or good his intentions were.[21]

It should be noted in passing that the correspondence view of truth does not have any direct implications as to the *beliefs* of the Biblical authors. They may have believed many false things just so long as they did not *affirm* any of these false beliefs in Scripture.[22] For on this view of truth "whatever the Bible affirms, God affirms," and God cannot affirm as true what is false.

---

[19]Hirsch (*Validity*, 58) contends that there is no meaning apart from the author's intention of that meaning. But if this claim is not false it is at least in need of serious qualification. First, it would seem to make all unintentional falsehoods meaningless statements, whereas it seems evident that unintentionally false directions can be clearly understood even though they are wrong. Second, why cannot a statement be meaningful even if no human has affirmed it? As long as someone could affirm it, even as he reads it, it would seem to be a meaningful statement. In other words, is not its affirmability (not whether it has been affirmed) a sufficient condition for its meaning?

[20]I personally believe that the Bible does affirm creation and oppose evolution. See the excellent book by W. Smith, *Man's Origin, Man's Destiny* (Wheaton: Harold Shaw, 1968).

[21]In this sense inerrancy as held by a proponent of the correspondence view of truth is a truly falsifiable position. All one needs to do to falsify the Biblical affirmation that "Christ rose from the dead" is to produce the body of Christ or good evidence of witnesses who saw it in decay sometime after the first Easter morning (see 1 Cor 15:12).

[22]It may even be possible for an author to reveal some of his beliefs through his affirmations without necessarily affirming those beliefs. 1 Thess 4:15 may be an example ("we who are alive"). Paul did not affirm that he would be alive when Christ returned, but he seemed to believe (or hope?) that he would be alive at the Lord's return.

2. *On the Intentionalist View.* According to this view several different implications follow for inerrancy. We will concentrate on two of them.

First, factual incorrectness in affirmations is not necessarily an error unless the author intended to affirm it.[23] Accordingly, the so-called "three-storied universe," the "mustard seed," and affirmation about creation (versus evolution) are not really errors, even if they are factually incorrect statements. For example, as long as Genesis 1 and 2 fulfills its intention—namely, to evoke worship of God—then any incorrect scientific affirmations notwithstanding, it could still be wholly true and without error. The same could be true of Noah's flood, Jonah and the great fish, Paul's view of male "headship" and other Biblical affirmations of this kind. On an intentionality view of truth these could all be factually wrong and yet the Bible would still be without error.[24] As long as the intention of God is being fulfilled through these passages—that is, his redemptive function—it does not matter whether some aspects affirmed in them correspond with reality.

Second, properly speaking, on an intentionalist view, truth can be personal and not merely propositional. Persons who fulfill someone's intentions are true or genuine. In this sense Jesus' claim, "I am the . . . truth" (John 14:6), could mean that he is the one who perfectly fulfills the Father's intentions for him.

It should be noted in passing that proponents of this view cannot claim that something is not true simply because it was intended by someone. If this were so, then almost everything ever written would be true since surely almost every author intended to tell the truth even though most of them made many mistakes. In any event, the intentionalist view of truth discussed here holds that true statements are those that faithfully fulfill their author's intentions. That is to say, it is not simply a matter of intention but of accomplished intention that makes something true.[25] In the

---

[23] A thoroughly consistent intentionalist view of truth, by contrast with a correspondence view, is factually unfalsifiable. For no matter what facts are presented contrary to the affirmation, it is always possible that the author's intentions were true.

[24] S. T. Davis is more forthright than most noninerrantists in admitting errors in the Bible (see his *The Debate About the Bible* [Philadelphia: Westminster, 1977]). He tries to preserve the "infallibility" of the Bible in moral matters while denying its inerrancy in historical and scientific matters. But even here he runs into difficulty since some of his illustrations are "errors" and have decidedly moral aspects—for instance, the slaughter of the Canaanites (see p. 97).

[25] In this sense the intentionalist or functional view of truth is akin to or a kind of subspecies of a pragmatic view of truth (see W. James, "Pragmatism's Conception of Truth," *Essays in Pragmatism* [New York: Hafner, 1968] 159-176)—namely, "truth happens to an idea. It becomes true, is made true by events." That is, "truth" is only the expedient in the way of our thinking, just as "the right" is only the expedient in the way of our believing (pp. 161, 170).

case of God's truth one could say that it always accomplishes what God intends (Isa 55:11). The Bible, then, would be inerrant so long as it always accomplishes its purpose to "make us wise unto salvation" (2 Tim 3:15).

III. What Is Truth?

At first blush one might think that the resolution of the problem as to which view of truth is correct could be achieved by a simple appeal to Biblical usage of the terms for "truth"—namely, *alētheia* and *ʾĕmet*.[26] However, these and kindred terms are used both ways in Scripture. "Truth" is used of correspondence in Eph 4:25; John 8:44-45; Prov 14:25; Acts 24:8, 11 and many other places. On the other hand, God is said to be truth(ful) (Rom 3:4), and Jesus said, "I am ... the truth" (John 14:6), so "truth" is used of persons.

How then can the problem of the two views of truth be resolved? Is there an irresolvable impasse? I think not. For one view of truth is broad enough to include the other but not the reverse. For example, a true statement will always accomplish its intention, but what accomplishes its intention is not always true. Lies and falsehood sometimes accomplish their intentions too. Hence only the correspondence view is adequate as a comprehensive view of truth. Further, if truth is only personal but not propositional, then there is no adequate way of explaining the numerous Biblical passages where truth means propositional correspondence.[27] In fact, of the some 100 NT occurrences of the word "truth" (*alētheia*) only one passage indisputably uses truth of a person as opposed to propositions or expressions about reality (John 14:6). Some other passages speak of truth as being (or not being) in a person (e.g., John 1:14, 17; 8:44; 1 John 2:4), but the latter passage makes it clear that a person is not considered

---

[26]The Hebrew word for truth (*ʾĕmet*) is used in roughly the same way as the NT words. It occurs some 127 times. Often it is used of propositional truth. The OT, e.g., speaks of true laws (Neh 9:13), words of men (1 Kgs 17:24), words of God (2 Sam 7:28; Ps 119:160), commandments (119:151), Scripture (Dan 10:21) and the factually correct (Deut 17:4; 22:20; 1 Kgs 22:16; 2 Chr 18:15). Also "truth" is used of God (15:3; Jer 10:10), of value judgments (Ezek 18:8) and of actions (Gen 47:29: Judg 9:16). But even these can be understood in the sense of correspondence to what is or what ought to be. In short, truth is what can be spoken (Jer 9:5), known (Isa 10:19), declared (Ps 30:9), factually investigated (Deut 13:14), written (Neh 9:13) or expressed in some way (2 Sam 2:6) and that would correctly represent that to which it refers.

In view of this it is strange to read authors who say that "truth is not measured in the Old Testament by correspondence to a theoretical norm but by its ability to achieve its goal." B. Childs, *Introduction to the Old Testament as Scripture* (Fortress) 535.

[27]See n. 26 above for OT examples and the following discussion for NT examples.

true because he "is a liar," which involves false propositions (or expressions). 2 John 4 speaks of "walking in the truth" or to "continue in his teachings" (v 8) as though truth were personal, but then (v 6) proceeds to explain that this means to "walk in obedience to his commands," which are propositional. Most other passages using truth in a personal sense employ words for truth in the adverbial sense of "truly," not in the substantival sense of "truth." At least one can safely say that the normal and consistent NT usage of "truth" is of truth in the normal cognitive propositional sense. Truth is what can be known (Rom 2:20), what can be thought (2 Tim 6:5), what can be spoken (Eph 1:13), what can be heard (2 Tim 4:4), what can be believed (2 Thess 2:12)—in short, it is used of propositions. And any passage where truth is used in reference to a person can be understood as meaning a person who speaks the truth or one whose word can be trusted (cf. Rev 3:14; 21:5). But even if some passages are best understood as meaning truth in a personal or practical sense, they still entail a correspondence view of truth. For the person or action must correspond to God's expectations in order to be true. Furthermore, the passages where truth is used propositionally cannot all be explained as truth in a strictly intentional or personal sense—that is, one that is not necessarily factually correct. Hence truth—Biblical truth—understood as primarily (or exclusively) personal or intentional does not represent the teaching of Scripture about the nature of truth.

IV. In Defense of a Correspondence Theory of Truth

There are two basic lines of argument for a correspondence view of truth, the Biblical and the philosophical. First we will offer a few Biblical arguments.[28]

1. *The ninth commandment is predicated on a correspondence view of truth.* "Thou shalt not bear false witness against thy neighbor" depends for its very meaning and effectiveness on the correspondence view of truth. This command implies that a statement is false if it does not correspond to reality. Indeed this is precisely how the term "lie" is used in Scripture. Satan is called a liar (John 8:44) because his statement to Eve, "You shall not surely die" (Gen 3:4), did not correspond to what God really said— namely, "You shall surely die" (2:17). Ananias and Sapphira "lied" to the apostles by misrepresenting the factual state of affairs about their finances (Acts 5:1-4).

2. *There are numerous Biblical examples of the correspondence view of truth.*

[28]These arguments are basically an elaboration and expansion on some of the same points made by R. Preus, *The Inspiration of Scripture* (London: Oliver and Boyd, 1955) 24.

(1) Joseph said to his brothers, "Send one of your number to get your brother; the rest of you will be kept in prison, so that your words may be tested to see if you are telling the truth" (Gen 42:16).

(2) Moses commanded that false prophets be tested on the grounds that "if what a prophet proclaims . . . does not take place or come true, that is a message the LORD has not spoken" (Deut 18:22).

(3) Solomon prayed at the dedication of the temple, "And now, O God of Israel, let your word that you promised your servant David my father [that there would be a temple] come true" (1 Kgs 8:26).

(4) The prophecies of Micaiah were considered "true" and the false prophets' words "lies" because the former corresponded with the facts of reality (22:16-22).

(5) Something was considered a "falsehood" if it did not correspond to God's law (truth) (Ps 119:163).

(6) Proverbs tells us, "A truthful witness saves lifes, but a false witness is deceitful" (14:25), which implies that truth is factually correct. Intentions alone will not save innocent lives in court. Only "the truth, the whole truth, and nothing but the truth" will do it.

(7) In Daniel 2 the king demanded to know the facts and considered anything else "misleading" (2:9).

(8) Jesus' statement in John 5:33 entails a correspondence view of truth: "You have sent to John, and he has testified to the truth."

(9) In Acts 24:8 there is an unmistakable usage of the correspondence view. The Jews said to the governor about Paul, "By examining him yourself you will be able to learn the truth about these charges we are bringing against him." They continued, "You can easily verify the facts" (v 11).

(10) Paul clearly implied a correspondence view of truth when he wrote, "Each of you must put off falsehood and speak truthfully to his neighbor" (Eph 4:25).

3. *The Biblical use of the word "err" does not support the intentionality theory of truth, since it is used of unintentional "errors"* (cf. Lev 4:2, 27, and so forth). Certain acts were wrong whether the trespassers intended to do them or not, and hence a guilt offering was called for to atone for their "error."[29]

To summarize, everywhere the Bible employs a correspondence view

---

[29]Of the five times *šāgag* ("to err") is used in the OT (Gen 6:3; Job 12:16; Ps 119:67; Lev 5:18; Num 15:28) the last two are clearly of unintentional error. Further, the cognate term *šᵉgāgâ* is used 19 times, and all but two are of unintentional errors (see Lev 4:2, 22, 27; 5:15, 18; 22:14; Num 15:24, 25 (2), 26, 27, 28, 29; 35:11 (2); Josh 20:3, 9; only Eccl 5:6; 10:5 could be understood as intentional errors).

of truth. A statement is true if it corresponds to the facts and false if it does not. Rarely are there even apparent exceptions to this usage.[30]

If the Biblical arguments are this strong for a correspondence view of truth, why is it that many Christians—even some who believe in inerrancy—claim to hold a coherence view of truth, or a pragmatic view, or some other view? Actually the reason is often quite simple: There is a confusion between *theory* of truth and *test* for truth. That is, often both parties hold the correspondence theory of truth but differ in their claims that truth is tested by correspondence, by results, or by some other method. In short, truth should be defined as correspondence but defended in some other way.

In summation, there are good reasons for insisting that we should all accept a correspondence theory (definition) of truth whatever the apologetic debate about how Christian truth is to be tested.

There are several philosophical arguments outside Biblical usage in support of a correspondence view of truth. We will mention only four of them here.

1. *Lies are impossible without a correspondence view of truth.* If one's statements need not correspond to the facts in order to be true, then any factually incorrect statement could be true. And if this is the case, then lies become impossible because any statement is compatible with any given state of affairs.[31]

2. *Without correspondence there could be no such thing as truth or falsity.* In order to know something that is true as opposed to something

---

[30] John 5:31 (*RSV*) appears to be one. Jesus said, "If I bear witness to myself, my testimony is not true" (*alēthēs*). This would seem to imply that Jesus' factually correct statements about himself were not "true." This, however, would be nonsense on even an intentionalist's definition of truth, for surely Jesus intended truth about himself. What is meant here is that a self-testimony was not established as true. Or, as the *NIV* puts it, such "testimony is not valid," despite the fact that it is true, since it is only "by the mouth of two or three [other] witnesses that every word is established" (Matt 18:16; cf. John 8:17) and not by one's own word. Elsewhere Jesus clearly said, "Even if I testify on my own behalf, my testimony is true" (John 8:14), meaning that it is factually correct even if they did not accept it.

[31] Part of the confusion rests in the fact that noninerrantists sometimes confuse "lying," which is always an intentional falsehood, and "error," which is just a plain falsehood. Rogers seems to make this mistake when he said that "error, for Augustine, had to do with *deliberate and deceitful* telling of that which the author knew to be untrue" (*Authority and Interpretation*, 30; italics mine). Beside the fact that Augustine is not speaking of a mere error but a lie in this context—a crucial fact that Rogers mistakenly overlooks—Rogers' use of the word "untrue" in the last part of the sentence belies a correspondence view of truth that is at odds with the intentional view he is proposing in the first part of the quotation.

that is false, there must be a real difference between things and the statements about the things. But this real difference between thought and things is precisely what is entailed in a correspondence view of truth.

3. *Factual communication would break down without a correspondence view of truth.* Factual communication depends on informative statements. But informative statements must be factually true (that is, they must correspond to the facts) in order to inform one correctly.

Further, since all communication seems to depend ultimately on something being literally or factually true, then it would follow that all communication depends in the final analysis on a correspondence view of truth.

4. *Even the intentionalist theory depends on the correspondence theory of truth.* The intentionalist theory claims that something is true if it is accomplishing what it intends. But this means that it is true only if the accomplishments correspond to the intentions. So without correspondence of intentions and accomplished facts there is no truth.

V. CONCLUSION

There is a certain irony involved in the present debate about inerrancy that illustrates this point. David Hubbard, who is apparently an intentionalist and noninerrantist, recently criticized Harold Lindsell (who is an inerrantist and correspondentist) for misrepresenting the facts about the situation at Fuller Theological Seminary. He provides Lindsell with "a handful of errors"[32] in Lindsell's treatment of the Fuller situation. But why should these be called "errors" on an intentionalist view of truth? Surely Lindsell intended well and even accomplished his intentions in arousing awareness of the drift from inerrancy at Fuller. But this is all that one can expect on an intentionalist view of truth. In short, why should Hubbard complain about factual misrepresentation unless he really holds a correspondence view of truth? And if he holds a correspondence view of truth, then why should he reject the factual inerrancy of the Bible? The least we can expect is that one be consistent with his own view of truth.

There is more, however, that we must expect (even demand) as Biblical Christians. It is this: We should expect that every Christian get his view of truth about the Bible from the Bible. And if this is the correspondence view of truth, as the foregoing discussion indicates, then it follows that the factual inerrantists are right. That is to say, the Bible is inerrant in whatever it affirms from mustard seeds to major doctrine, from geology to theology.

---

[32]See *Theology* (1976) 26. Hubbard's comment is especially strange in view of the fact that he explicitly rejected Lindsell's view of an "error" or untruth (p. 8).

The Clarity of Scripture

ROBERT T. SANDIN

M Y purpose in this article is to consider some hermeneutical implications of the historic Protestant view of the authority of the Bible as the Word of God. Within the compass of these pages it is not possible, of course, to develop a complete argument in support of this view of the Bible. I simply wish to accept it as my point of departure and then to trace some of its implications for the theory of Biblical interpretation. In particular I wish to suggest that some recent approaches to Biblical hermeneutics (as inspired by the writings of Dilthey, Heidegger, Bultmann and Gadamer) are in fundamental conflict with the historic Protestant principles of *sola scriptura* and *claritas scripturae*.

In the history of Christian thought, philosophy has served theology in two ways. On the one hand, philosophical argumentation has been employed for the purpose of establishing sufficient reasons for Christian belief—or at least for certain tenets of Christian belief, such as belief in the existence of God. On the other hand, philosophical analysis has been applied in the investigation of the meaning of theological discourse. In what follows I shall be concentrating on this latter view of the relevance of philosophy for theology.

The philosophical analysis of the meaning of theological discourse stems from a perfectly justifiable concern to avoid the isolation of theology from other branches of learning. The language of faith is not some kind of ghetto language, impervious to the analysis that is appropriate for language in general.[1] On the contrary, the theologian too must make responsible use of language and must follow rules that govern verbal communication generally.

In the twentieth centrury the analysis of the meaning of religious language in the English-speaking world has often been preoccupied with the question of the applicability of the so-called verification criterion of meaning. A substantial literature has grown up, dedicated to examining the implications of the requirement that meaningful theological discourse, like all other meaningful utterance, must be subject to the test of verifiability (falsifiability). Increasingly, as the verification theory of meaning has fallen into discredit, interest has shifted to the continental literature that has

[1] Cf. G. Ebeling, *Introduction to a Theological Theory of Language* (Philadelphia: Fortress, 1971).

developed out of the work of Schleiermacher, Dilthey and Heidegger. Within these two traditions in contemporary philosophy there has been an extraordinary convergence of hermeneutical concerns (which are so obviously central to theology) and the philosophical analysis of meaning.

Among the cardinal declarations of Christian theology is the contention that the Word of God comes to man by way of a divine accommodation to the human condition. The revelation of God is mediated by the incarnation—by the humiliation of Christ. And a coordinate condescension is manifest in the appearance of the Word of God in the form of human language. When the gospel comes to man it comes as something conveyed in language, and the structure of this language establishes limits within which the divine-human communication occurs.

My purpose here is to explore some implications of this divine accommodation to human language with particular reference to the Protestant view of the Bible as the Word of God. I wish to consider some consequences of the Protestant principle, "Through God alone can God be known," when that principle is combined with recognition of the limitations of the Biblical revelation of God as language-bound.

I. Meaning and Clarity

I wish to begin with a proposition of Wittgenstein: "Everything that can be thought at all can be thought clearly. Everything that can be said can be said clearly."[2] I wish to accept this declaration as a valid formulation of a necessary condition for all thought and for all meaningful communication.

It is not, of course, a proposition about reality. Wittgenstein is not propounding the quite dogmatic contention that all reality must conform to the limitations of human thought and speech. He is only stipulating a necessary condition under which it becomes possible to speak meaningfully of anything.

I am not here recommending the general framework for the analysis of meaning that apparently dominates Wittgenstein's thought in the *Tractatus*. His interpretation of meaning as "referring" and of words as "signs" is not essential to the analysis that I wish here to undertake. I take my point of departure only from his simple declaration that if any assertion has a meaning its meaning is something self-identical and determinate.

The paradigm of a communication situation is expressed in the formula: "I am saying something to you." The analysis of the polarities and processes of the communication situation is extremely complex and cannot detain us here. I wish to emphasize, however, that one of the elements of

---

[2]L. Wittgenstein, *Tractatus Logico-Philosophicus* (trans. Ogden; London: Routledge and Kegan Paul, 1922) 4.116.

the communication process, as expressed in the paradigmatic formula, is a "something" that is communicated. But this "something" is what it is and not some other thing (as G. E. Moore would say). Without the assumption that something determinate is communicated, it is impossible to conceive of communication by means of language. I wish to begin therefore from the assumption that all communication by means of language presupposes the self-identity and determinateness of what is spoken/heard (written/read).

This general requirement of meaning is advanced by Wittgenstein not only in the *Tractatus* but also in the *Investigations*: "The sense of a sentence . . . may, of course, leave this or that open, but the sentence must nevertheless have *a* definite sense (*einen* bestimmten Sinn). An indefinite sense—that would really not be a sense at all." To say that a sentence has a meaning but not a definite one would be, Wittgenstein explains, like saying that a boundary was a boundary even though it was not a definite boundary. It would be like saying, "I have locked the man up fast in his room—there is only one door left open."[3]

"One wants to say," says Wittgenstein, that "a significant (*sinnvolle*) sentence is one which one cannot merely say, but also think."[4] A clear expression, Wittgenstein says, is coordinate with a clear understanding. By contrast a vague or unclear expression is indicative of a thought that is still struggling to be born.[5] What thought can be said to occur, asks Wittgenstein, when one contemplates a series of undecipherable marks on a page? Similarly, when the Ethiopian who is "reading" the prophet confesses in all honesty that he does not understand what the prophet says[6] we would say not that he is truly "reading" but rather that he is "trying to read" the text.

There is a school of religious thought that concentrates on considering how vague or even self-contradictory utterances might be religiously meaningful, on showing how the inexpressible might be expressed or the ineffable described. Such an approach to the analysis of the meaning of religious discourse is misplaced from the point of view of both linguistic philosophy and Christian theology. Wittgenstein says:

> The right method of philosophy would be this: To say nothing except what can be said . . . and then always, when someone else wished to say something metaphysical, to demonstrate to him that he had given no meaning to certain signs in his propositions. . . . Whereof one cannot speak, thereof one must be silent.[7]

---

[3]L. Wittgenstein, *Philosophical Investigations* (trans. Anscombe; Oxford: Blackwell, 1953), Sec. 99.

[4]Ibid., Sec. 511.

[5]Cf. Ebeling, *Introduction*, 119.

[6]Acts 8:30-31.

[7]Wittgenstein, *Tractacus*, 6.53, 7.

Of course we might admit of a self-contradictory statement that it was meaningful if it were so only apparently or superficially—i.e., if closer analysis exposed the consistent meaning that lay behind the apparent contradiction. But in that case the contradictoriness of the expression would give way as its meaning was exposed. On the other hand, if an expression were of the form $p \cdot \sim p$, it would be simply impossible to understand what thought was communicated by means of that expression. "Nothing meaningful can be said," as Schillebeeckx says, "unless the logical law $p \equiv \sim(\sim p)$ is accepted."[8]

Applying Wittgenstein's general criterion of meaning to the case of the Bible, we may say that if there is a meaning in Scripture such meaning is clear. How then does it become necessary on occasion for the meaning of Scripture to be explained? The necessity of such explanation stems from the self-limitation of the Word of God in addressing itself to human understanding under the form of language. To say that whatever can be said can be said clearly does not imply, of course, that whatever is clear to the speaker will also be clear (in the same way) to the hearer. A word that is clear in itself may not be clear to us. The necessity of interpretation arises from the need to remove hindrances to communication that may prevent the intention of the speaker (author) from being realized in the understanding of the hearer (reader). Apart from these hindrances the meaningful expression (with its inherent clarity) would be an effective and sufficient means of communication. The clarity of a meaningful expression, however, cannot guarantee the successful completion of the communication process. On the other hand, the very possibility of misunderstanding an expression presupposes the determinacy (clarity) of what the speaker means.

It is to be emphasized that the task of interpretation is not to lend meaning to verbal statement but to expose the meaning that it possesses in its own clarity. The task of interpretation is to remove obstacles to the effective functioning of meaningful discourse, not to give meaning to an expression that is itself meaningless or vague. Consequently, hermeneutics begins not with the author or the text or even the interpreter, but with the reader. It considers what hindrances stand in the way of the reader's understanding. As stated in Terry's classic formulation, hermeneutics "aims to remove the supposable differences between a writer and his readers, so that the meaning of the one may be truly and accurately apprehended by the others."[9]

The removal of obstacles to communication itself takes place by means of language. Accordingly the explanation by which the meaning of a text is

[8] E. Schillebeeckx, *The Understanding of Faith* (trans. N. D. Smith; New York: Seabury, 1974) 33.

[9] M. S. Terry, *Biblical Hermeneutics: A Treatise on the Interpretation of the Old and New Testaments* (New York: Eaton and Mains, 1883) 17.

clarified for the reader must itself be clear and understandable. The interpreter can hardly expect to clarify the meaning of an obscure text by an account that his readers will find equally or more obscure. A responsible interpreter will not make the meaning of a text clearer than it really is, nor will he make it more obscure than it really is.[10] The interpreter's language is bound by the same requirement as applies to all meaningful discourse. He too must speak clearly. Hence, as Ebeling puts it, the process of interpretation is primarily a matter not of establishing an understanding of language but of establishing understanding by means of language.[11] The interpreter of a text, that is, depends not on some type of creative impulse or inspiration in the reader that will miraculously disclose the meaning of the text but on clarifying discourse that is itself clear and understandable.

The method of hermeneutics is therefore, as Terry says, a rational one.

> When one rational mind desires to communicate thought to another it embodies such conventional means of intercourse as are supposed to be understood by both. . . . It is the province of interpretation to observe the laws of human thought as exhibited in the ordinary processes of speech.[12]

Biblical hermeneutics is an application of general hermeneutical principles. And these principles are eventually derived from the assumption that the meaning of a text is something determinate and specifiable in the sense of Wittgenstein's dictum.

II. THE FORCE OF SOLA SCRIPTURA

If we begin by assuming that every meaningful utterance is clear in itself, we must then understand the task of interpretation as limited to that of removing hindrances that prevent the verbal statement from functioning effectively as a vehicle of communication. The light of understanding is not something that is introduced from outside the statement but something that emerges from the statement itself once hindrances to understanding are removed.

A similar view of the task of interpretation emerges from the Reformers' view of the Bible as the supreme authority for theological understanding. Their view implies, of course, that the Biblical meaning is not something introduced from without. The Bible, say the Reformers, is clear in itself and interprets itself. Wittgenstein's view of the clarity of meaning-

---

[10]A. Nygren, *Meaning and Method: Prolegomena to a Scientific Philosophy of Religion and a Scientific Theology* (trans. P. S. Watson; Philadelphia: Fortress, 1972) 331.

[11]G. Ebeling, *Word and Faith* (trans. J. W. Leitch; Philadelphia: Fortress, 1963) 318-319; "The Word of God and Hermeneutic," in J. M. Robinson and J. B. Cobb, Jr., *The New Hermeneutic* (New York: Harper, 1964) 93 ff.

[12]Terry, *Hermeneutics*, 71.

ful utterance therefore has its counterpart in the Reformers' doctrine of the clarity of Scripture.

For Luther the question of the authority of the Bible was at the center not only of his controversy with the Roman Church but also of all his theological and exegetical work. "Scripture alone," he says, "is the true lord and master of all writings and doctrines on earth."[13] Calvin, who emphasizes the "internal persuasion of the Holy Spirit" in the formation of faith, agrees with Luther's view of the authority and indispensability of the Scriptures. The work of the Holy Spirit is not to make Scripture superfluous. On the contrary, says Calvin, it is only through the Scriptures that we can expect the Spirit of God to speak. "This, then, must be considered as a fixed principle, that no man can have the least knowledge of true and sound doctrine, without having been a disciple of Scripture."[14]

Perhaps the most straightforward formulations of the *sola scriptura* principle are found among the Baptists, for whom the principle sometimes constitutes the whole content of Christian confession. "The Holy Scripture," declares the Second Confession of the English Baptists (1677), "is the only sufficient, certain, and infallible rule of all saving knowledge, faith, and obedience."[15]

As Schaff points out, the creeds of Christendom have consistently been viewed within Protestantism as relative and limited, always subordinate to the Bible as ultimate authority. Hence the value of the creeds

> depends upon the measure of their agreement with the Scriptures. In the best case a human creed is only an approximate and relatively correct exposition of revealed truth and may be improved by the progressive knowledge of the church, while the Bible remains perfect and infallible.[16]

Accordingly the fundamental concern of Protestant theology has always been the correct exposition and interpretation of Scripture.

Two implications of the *sola scriptura* principle are of particular importance here. The first is the principle that Scripture is its own interpreter. Protestantism denies that the authority of the Bible depends in any way, as the Westminster Confession puts it, "on the testimony of any

---

[13] *Luther's Works* (Philadelphia: Muhlenberg, 1958), 32. 11. A full account of Luther's view of the Bible, of course, would require consideration of a number of qualifications—e.g. "Christ is King and Lord also of Scripture," "No man perceives one iota of what is in the Scriptures unless he has the Spirit of God," "The Scriptures are to be understood within the church" (by which he does not mean the Roman Church as institution, of course).

[14] J. Calvin, *Institutes of the Christian Religion*, 1.6.2.

[15] H. Bettenson, ed., *Documents of the Christian Church* (New York: Oxford University Press, 1947) 353.

[16] P. Schaff, *The Creeds of Christendom* (New York: Harper, 1919), 1. 7.

man or church, but wholly upon God, . . . the author thereof." Hence "the infallible rule of interpretation of Scripture is Scripture itself."[17]

The appeal to Scripture as its own interpreter presupposes the coherence of Scripture as a whole. If the interpetation of Scripture as a whole were to lead to inconsistency or self-contradiction within the Biblical message, then that message would be incomprehensible. A coherence test is implicit in the apparently tautological rule of interpretation as followed by the older Protestant theology: "The norm for interpreting Scripture and for judging the truth or falsity of interpretations of sacred Scripture is sacred Scripture itself, which is the voice of God."[18]

The Protestant polemic was addressed against the alleged insufficiency of Scripture and the supposed need for support from the teaching office of the Church in the understanding of the Bible. Against these allegations the *sola scriptura* principle declares the autonomy of Scripture in interpreting itself.[19] As the sole source of divine revelation the Bible speaks for itself, and this means that it interprets itself. "Faith depends upon the Bible for its language and so for its life. But the Bible shows faith how to use its own words."[20] As Barth puts it, "the door of the Bible texts can be opened only from within."[21]

The second implication of *sola scriptura* is the principle of the clarity of Scripture. Luther's most forceful and direct argument for the principle of *claritas scripturae* appears in *The Bondage of the Will* (1525), his polemic against Erasmus. In contrast to the irenicism of the great humanist, Luther responds with an explosion of "sheer disgust, anger, and contempt" to Erasmus' call for a balanced view of the authority of Scripture and of the Church.

The heart of the issue, as Luther views it, concerns the sufficiency of Scripture. Implicit in the appeal to the authority of the Bible, Luther contends, is the assumption that it is clear in itself. To Erasmus' contention that there are some passages in the Bible that are obscure or abstruse and thus in need of clarification by experts, Luther replies that every word of Scripture is perfectly clear. Parts of it may be obscure at any given time to a given reader because of his ignorance of the vocabulary or grammar of the text, his ignorance of the historical circumstance surrounding the text,

[17] Bettenson, *Documents*, 347.

[18] Polanus, *Synt. Theol. chr.* (1609) 683. Quoted by K. Barth, *Church Dogmatics* (Edinburgh: T. & T. Clark, 1956), 1/2, whose paraphrase takes certain liberties with the text.

[19] Cf. the recent statement by E. Schillebeeckx: "The church's teaching authority is not a criterion of orthodoxy since it is itself subject to the Word of God," *Understanding*, 74.

[20] Ebeling, *Introduction*, 189. Cf. G. Ebeling, *The Word of God and Tradition* (trans. S. H. Hooke; Philadelphia: Fortress, 1964) 127.

[21] Barth, *Dogmatics*, 1/2. 583.

his spiritual blindness, and so on. And there is much about God himself that we must admit is beyond human knowledge. But not a word of Scripture, says Luther, is obscure in itself. It cannot be obscure and remain the ultimate authority for faith.

> Those who deny that the Scriptures are quite clear and plain leave us nothing but darkness. . . . In opposition to you [Erasmus] I say with respect to the whole Scripture, I will not have any part of it called obscure.[22]

That the Bible is the Word of God implies that it speaks for itself and is clear and understandable in itself. "Clarity," as Barth says, "is intrinsic to the Word."[23] The Word of God as such requires no explanation, and human thought has no power to establish its authority. The objective clarity of the Word of God is not at all subject to the care or responsibility of any human interpreter. On the contrary, it is the presupposition of all human responsibility for interpretation.

> All the explanation of Scripture for which we are responsible can be undertaken only on the presupposition that Scripture is clear in itself as God's Word; otherwise it will at once disintegrate. And all Scriptural exegesis for which we are responsible can lead only to the threshold beyond which Scripture is clear in itself as God's Word.[24]

The Bible, as Terry says, is not an obscure Delphic oracle, calculated "to bewilder the heart by utterances of double meaning." It is no purpose of the Biblical writers to be misunderstood. "Nor is it reasonable to suppose that the Holy Scripture, given by inspiration of God, is of the nature of a puzzle designed to exercise the ingenuity of the reader."[25] The Word of God is clear, and that clarity is the basis of the understandability of the Church's proclamation of the Word of God.

III. UNDERSTANDING AND PROCLAMATION

Although the categories for analyzing the stages of Biblical interpretation have varied widely throughout the history of hermeneutics, it has been customary to distinguish between understanding and proclamation (*expli-*

---

[22] *Luther's Works*, 33. 94. Cf. F. Beisser's interpretation of Luther's view: "Gott, der ein Bestimmter ist und ganz Bestimmtes tut und ganz Bestimmtes will, offenbart sich uns, indem er in seinem Wort zu uns spricht. Unsere Haltung ist die des Hörens." (God, who is the determiner of things and does and wills things in an entirely determinate way, reveals himself to us in that he speaks to us in his Word. Our responsibility is to hear.) *Claritas scripturae bei Martin Luther* (Göttingen: Vandenhoeck and Ruprecht, 1966) 82.

[23] Barth, *Dogmatics*, 1/2. 719.

[24] Ibid., p. 712.

[25] Terry, *Hermeneutics*, 72, 143.

catio and *applicatio*) as logically independent phases of the process of interpretation. In the Protestant tradition it has been emphasized that the preservation of this distinction is essential to the doctrine of the authority of Scripture.

The distinction has been drawn by theologians of a variety of persuasions using quite different terminology. Doedes says in his *Manual of Hermeneutics* (1867): "In order to be able to explain anyone's words to others, one must understand them oneself, otherwise one cannot render them intelligible to others."[26] Hirsch says that the possibility of validity (invalidity) in the interpretaion of a text requires us to view understanding as prior to and logically different from interpretation.[27] Barth warns against the temptation of the Church to substitute for the authoritative word of Scripture something that it wishes to proclaim.[28] The entire work of Bultmann may be viewed as an attempt to show how the Church's proclamation of the gospel may be based on understanding the Bible: "The church's preaching, founded on the Scriptures, passes on the word of the Scriptures."[29] Moving within the same general framework as Bultmann, Hans-Georg Gadamer says, "Scripture is the Word of God, and that means that it has an absolute priority over the teaching of those who interpret it."[30] And Ebeling, who adds a perspective formed in part by his extensive Luther research, says, "The real rub in the hermeneutical problem, as it presents itself for theology, consists in the connection between exposition of the text as proclamation that has taken place and execution of the text in proclamation in the present."[31]

Interpretation of a message, as contrasted to original creation of a message or imaginative contemplation stimulated by receipt of a message, takes its point of departure from the meaning of the message itself. Hermeneutics, as Hirsch says, presupposes the distinction between validity and invalidity in interpretation.

> The crucial problem in the theory and practice of interpretation is to distinguish between possible implications which do belong to the meaning of a text and those that do not belong. I have argued that if such a principle of determinacy did not exist (a principle under which we accept or reject possible implications) communication and interpretation would be impossible.[32]

[26]Quoted by ibid., p. 465.

[27]E. D. Hirsch, Jr., *Validity in Interpretation* (New Haven: Yale University Press, 1967) 129.

[28]Barth, *Dogmatics*, 1/2. 691.

[29]R. Bultmann, *Existence and Faith* (ed. and trans. S. M. Ogden; New York: Meridian, 1960) 168.

[30]H. Gadamer, *Truth and Method* (London: Sheed and Ward, 1975) 295.

[31]Ebeling, *Word*, 109.

[32]Hirsch, *Validity*, 62.

With Barth we must recognize the essential importance of Polanus' definition of Biblical interpretation: "The interpretation of sacred Scripture is the exposition in truth of the sense and the use of that which is intended by the clear words to the glory of God and the edification of the church."[33] On this view the basic orientation of interpretation is to the true sense (*verus sensus*) and the true use (*verus usus*) of the Scriptures, which speak for themselves. The truth of Scripture may call for explanation (*explicatio*), but the point of reference for all such explanation is the clear language (*verba perspicua*) of the text. In approaching the scriptural message we must understand that it has a meaning that it carries in itself, as contrasted to any meaning that we may bring to it, and that it has a truth and importance that exceed those of "even the best and most necessary things that we ourselves have said or can say."[34]

Luther was particularly concerned to warn against the danger of misinterpretation in Biblical exegesis. "The Scripture has a wax nose," he said. Hence he attached central importance to hermeneutics. The interpreter of Scripture, said Luther, must bring to his task an extraordinary devotion to Scripture itself so that he may learn to understand its message on its own terms. Above all he must avoid doing violence to the text by appropriating it from an idiosyncratic point of view. He must not approach Scripture from a previously established position, looking for his own answers to his own questions, but must be open to an encounter with God's Word on its own terms.[35]

Or, as Terry puts it,

> The first and great thing is to lay hold of the real spirit and meaning of the sacred writer. There can be no true application, and no profitable taking to ourselves of any lessons of the Bible, unless we first clearly apprehend their original meaning and reference.[36]

IV. THE DIALECTICS OF INTERPRETATION

The process of interpretation, however, is extremely complex. And there is always the possibility that an appeal to the "clear meaning of Scripture" may be nothing but a rationalization for theological dogmatism or arbitrariness. Recognition of the complexities of Biblical interpretation might give a conscientious reader pause before dogmatically pronouncing his understanding of a text.

Understanding a text involves a number of elements, each of which presents its own difficulties. There is the grammatical and lexicographical

[33] Quoted in Barth, *Dogmatics*, 1/2. 714 (my translation).
[34] Ibid., p. 719.
[35] G. Ebeling, *Luther: An Introduction to His Thought* (trans. R. A. Wilson; Philadelphia: Fortress, 1970) 97.
[36] Terry, *Hermeneutics*, 470.

understanding, which often calls for a high degree of linguistic competence. There is the understanding of the historical circumstance surrounding the text, which is often highly problematic at a distance of several centuries. There is the complexity of developing an understanding of the text in its relevance to the present, which may present circumstances that the original application of the text could not possibly have contemplated. And there is the further complexity that strikes at the very possibility of objective determination of the meaning of the text on grounds of the philosophical doctrine that all human understanding is limited by each individual's "conceptual framework" and cultural conditioning. No theory of Biblical interpretation can be accepted in the twentieth century if it fails to come to terms with the complexities of the process of understanding in all these phases. Indeed the difficulties presented by the recent analysis of the process of interpretation have created an unprecedented crisis for the doctrine of the clarity of Scripture.

The so-called "problem of hermeneutics" is posed by recognition of the difficulties encountered by the reader of Scripture in seeking to apprehend its "original meaning and reference." The problem is well illustrated in the profound and erudite work of Hans-Georg Gadamer.

Gadamer finds in all forms of hermeneutics (e.g. legal, literary or Biblical) the common assumption that the point of departure for interpretation is the meaning of the text. "Neither jurist nor theologian regards the work of application as making free with the text."[37] Gadamer's analysis of hermeneutics is dominated, however, by the conviction that no interpreter can completely avoid his own historicity. Moving in the tradition of Husserl, Dilthey and Heidegger, he contends that anything presented as a particular existent in our experience "is given in terms of the world and hence brings the world horizon with it."[38] Every individual's experience is conditioned by the perspective or "horizon consciousness" out of which particulars are given to him. Accordingly every act of understanding is conditioned by the "horizon" of the individual who understands. Consequently the form of interpretation that seeks "the rehabilitation of a text's original conditions" is, according to Gadamer, a futile undertaking.[39] No method of interpretation can transcend the interpreter's own historicity. The most that can be expected is a fusion of the perspectives of author and reader (*Horizontverschelzung*) which will permit a rendering of the text's meaning in terms of the reader's context of understanding.

The process of interpretation as Gadamer conceives it is dialectical. The interpreter must make the text speak—not through a kind of ventriloquism but through a kind of dialogue. The dialogue is possible, however, only insofar as the interpreter is able to place himself within the "horizon"

[37]Gadamer, *Truth*, 297.
[38]Ibid., p. 217.
[39]Ibid., p. 159.

of the text while at the same time (and unavoidably, in any case) preserving the perspective of his own "horizon."

> The reader does not exist before whose eyes the great book of world history simply lies open. But nor does the reader exist who, when he has his text before him, simply reads what is there. Rather, all reading involves application, so that a person reading a text is himself part of the meaning he apprehends. He belongs to the text that he is reading.[40]

The motto that Gadamer has chosen for the crucial Second Part of his work on hermeneutics is the saying of Luther: "Whoever does not understand the matter (res) cannot extract the meaning out of the words." But Gadamer construes this "matter" of a text as the "question" to which the text is a reply. The reader's understanding of the "matter" of the text will be conditioned by his own sense of the question with which the text deals. The "hermeneutical horizon," in other words, is "the horizon of the question within which the sense of the text is determined."[41] Collingwood is right, says Gadamer, in saying that we understand a text only when we understand the question to which it is an answer. But "the reconstruction of the question from which the meaning of a text is to be understood as an answer, passes over into our own questioning. For the text must be understood as an answer to a real question."[42] Our understanding of a text is based on our reconstruction of its question. But a "reconstructed question" can never stand purely within its own original "horizon." It stands as "reconstructed" in the horizon of our own questioning.

From this point of view every interpreter may be said to be engaged in the attempt to understand an author better than he understood himself.[43]

---

[40]Ibid., p. 304.

[41]Ibid., p. 333.

[42]Ibid., p. 337.

[43]The recent literature of hermeneutics has been very much taken up with a remark by Kant in commenting on Plato's theory of ideas (Critique of Pure Reason [trans. N. K. Smith] 310; A 314, B 370): "It is by no means unusual, upon comparing the thoughts which an author has expressed in regard to his subject, whether in ordinary conversation or in writing, to find that we understand him better than he has understood himself. As he has not sufficiently determined his concept, he has sometimes spoken, or even thought, in opposition to his own intention." Schleiermacher, in turn, formulated the task of hermeneutics in the following way: "To understand the text at first as well and then even better than its author. . . . Since we have no direct knowledge of what was in the author's mind, we must try to become aware of many things of which he himself may have been unconscious" (F. Schleiermacher, Hermeneutics: The Handwritten Manuscript [ed. H. Kimmerle; trans. J. Duke and J. Forstman; Missoula: Scholars Press, 1977] 112). Similarly Dilthey: "The final goal of the hermeneutic procedure is to understand the author better that he understood himself; a statement which is the

"All textual interpretation," according to Gadamer, "must go beyond the author, must mean more than he or any individual interpreter could know or understand."[44] The task of interpretation begins, of course, with the text itself. But every interpreter not only can but must find in the text a meaning that goes beyond that intended by the author. Hermeneutics must always be prepared to go beyond the stage of mere reconstruction. "All understanding is always more than the recreation of someone else's meaning."[45]

V. INTERPRETATION AT A DISTANCE

Conservative interpreters of the Bible have traditionally understood the aim of interpretation primarily in terms of understanding the original meaning of the text. However, under the dominance of the view that all verbal communication is culturally conditioned and that the "horizons" of understanding are not fully sharable across centuries of history, contemporary interpreters of the Bible have come to accept it as self-evident that no one can understand the Bible simply as the authors intended it to be understood or as the original readers would have understood it. The crisis for Biblical scholarship posed by this development is the "battle for the Bible" in the deepest sense.

"The understanding of something written," Gadamer contends, "is not a reproduction of something that is past, but the sharing of a present meaning."[46] This view of interpretation separates a text from its author and from the contingent and historical factors that conditioned its origination. Ironically the historico-critical method of Biblical exposition, which was once thought to be opposed to the authority of the Bible, has now been supplanted by a new form of anti-Biblicism based on banishment of the authors of Scripture and leaving interpretation free to be occupied only with the text itself.

Paul Ricoeur says, for example, that the appropriation of a text by a reader is no longer to be understood in terms of his apprehending the intention of the author of the text. Rather such appropriation is to be conceived as "understanding through distance, at a distance." The reader comes to self-understanding through the text. One understands oneself before the text and lets oneself be exposed to the meaning of the text—

---

necessary conclusion of the doctrine of unconscious creation" ("The Development of Hermeneutics," in W. Dilthey, *Selected Writings* [ed. and trans. H. P. Rickman; London: Cambridge University, 1976] 259, 260).

[44]Gadamer, *Wahrheit und Methode* (quoted in his own translation by Hirsch, *Validity*, 123).

[45]Gadamer, *Truth*, 338.

[46]Ibid., p. 354.

perhaps in the way in which one might let oneself be exposed to the performance of a piece of music. As Ricoeur says:

> All writing provides the text with a certain autonomy in relation to the intention of the author. What the text means may no longer coincide with what the author meant. Verbal meaning (i.e. textual meaning) and mental meaning (i.e. psychological meaning) are henceforth disconnected.[47]

Biblical scholars have always hoped for a dynamic and progressive enlargement of the Church's understanding of the Scriptures. And they have hope too that every reader might come to better understanding of himself before the Word of God. But Ricoeur's hermeneutical proposals seem to go far beyond such hopes. Indeed his view of interpretation is incompatible with the very idea of communication by means of language. According to Ricoeur, if the text is viewed as autonomous as compared even with the intention of the author then, once created, it is free to speak for itself—irrespective of the author's intention. And the reader in turn is free to allow the text to speak to him as "the reader it seeks"—again irrespective of the author's intention. Thereby the principle of the autonomy of the text is transformed into the principle of the creative independence of the reader, and the text becomes nothing more than an occasion for the exercise of the reader's own inspiration. The text is no longer a vehicle for the communication of the speaker's meaning.

On such a view of interpretation the text becomes something like an aesthetic object that the reader is free to appreciate as his own subjectivity permits. Gadamer says, "When we understand a text, what is meaningful in it charms us just as the beautiful charms us."[48] The notion of being charmed by a text thus replaces the traditional notion of correctly understanding what is meant by a text.

That the autonomy of the text gives place to the autonomy of the reader seems to be acknowledged by Gadamer despite his eagerness to disassociate his view from subjectivism:

> What is stated in the text must be detached from all contingent factors and grasped in its full ideality, in which alone it has validity. Thus, precisely because it entirely detaches the sense of what is said from the person saying it, the written word makes the reader, in his understanding of it, the arbiter to its claim to truth.[49]

By this extraordinary formulation of the hermeneutic principle it becomes quite possible, as Schillebeeckx says, for an interpreter to say of

---

[47]P. Ricoeur, *Philosophical Hermeneutics and Theological Hermeneutics: Ideology, Utopia and Faith* (Berkeley: Center for Hermeneutical Studies, 1976) 5.

[48]Gadamer, *Truth*, 446.

[49]Ibid., p. 386.

an author that he did not really mean what he said or that he did not say what he really meant. "The comfortable consequence of this for the interpreter is that he can insert his own meanings into the text, and it seems fully justified because the text did not in fact say what it intended to say."[50]

For Bultmann, interpreting the NT in the twentieth century means construing the witness of the apostles in terms of the scientific world-view. Bultmann's approach to NT interpretation is really a kind of apologetics in reverse. The interpreter seeks to construe the NT in a manner that will enhance its understandableness (in the sense of credibility) to modern readers, whose thought pattern is vastly different from that of apostolic times.[51] The question of course is whether Bultmann's apologetics are purchased only at the price of doing violence to the Biblical text.

In an earlier time the rationalization of Christian faith might take the form of a translation of the language of the Bible into the language of philosophical theology, the aim being to make the Biblical doctrine more understandable (i.e., credible) to persons who accept the validity of the philosophical discourse. So, for example, the He Who Is of the OT might be identified with the First Cause of the philosophical argument. This reinterpretation of Scripture in terms of the categories of scholastic philosophy seemed to Luther to be a confusion of categories and a serious threat to the autonomy and authority of the Bible.

> It is an error to say that without Aristotle no one becomes a theologian. On the contrary, one only becomes a theologian when one does so without Aristotle. The assertion that a theologian who is not a logician is an abominable heretic, is itself abominable and heretical. . . . In short, the whole of Aristotle is related to theology as darkness to light.[52]

The same kind of rejoinder (less Luther's exuberance) must be made today to the new hermeneutics, which presumes to add to the clarity and authority of the Biblical text by the strategies of demythologization and existential interpretation. Such strategies are misplaced from the point of view of both critical philosophy and Christian theology.

[50]Schillebeeckx, *Understanding*, 57.

[51]At times, however, Bultmann seems to disavow such a view of the task of interpretation. For example, in *Kerygma and Myth II* (182, 183) he replies to Jaspers' charge that he wants "to salvage faith in so far as it can be salvaged in the face of scientific insights that cannot be ignored; that I want to give the unbeliever 'a means to persevere in his faith with a good conscience'. Now this is certainly not my intention. The purpose of demythologizing is not to make religion more acceptable to modern man by trimming the Biblical texts, but to make clearer to modern man what the Christian faith is."

[52]Quoted by Ebeling, *Luther*, 89 (from *Disputatio contra scholasticam theologiam*, 1517).

VI. Interpretation Without Pre-Understanding

The principle of *sola scriptura* is contradicted by a hermeneutical principle that proposes that Scripture should be read through the screen of the reader's "conceptual framework," whether that framework be scholastic, scientific or existentialist. This claim that all human understanding is conditioned by a "conceptual framework" is simply doctrinaire and gratuitous. There is no philosophical necessity for adopting any such assumption. Nor is it necessary to suppose that the change in world-views that has occurred over the centuries is the decisive factor affecting modern man's understanding of the Scriptures. Indeed the whole notion that the validity of Christian theology is dependent on the vicissitudes of philosophical thought is based on a mistaken view of both the nature of philosophy and the method of theology.

There is simply no way for hermeneutics to make a Biblical text more believable (in an objective sense) to modern man. Hermeneutics is no more capable than any other science of resolving an ultimately religious issue. Nor is there anything about the logic of religious discourse that confers on the interpreter of Scripture the right, as Gadamer puts it, to act as "the arbiter of its claim to truth." There is no human science that can presume to have as its task to determine whether or not some expression is the Word of God. On the contrary, when an interpreter supposes that his interpretation will somehow add to the meaning, importance, relevance or credibility of a text of Scripture, that presumption is a sure indication that he does not think of the text as the Word of God. For to say it is the Word of God would imply that it was clear in itself, that it was authoritative without the benefit of scholarly support.

The Biblical message must be assumed to speak for itself and to be independent of any contingent historical framework for understanding. The point of departure for a constructive approach to the task of Biblical interpretation is the principle of the clarity of Scripture.

The interpreter of a message—particularly an authoritative message— is not allowed to change it, to create it, or even to reconstruct it. It is certainly misleading to call the interpretation of a message the re-creation of the message. The task of an interpreter of the Biblical message can surely be no more than to establish and maintain conditions under which the message can speak for itself on its own terms.

The recent literature of hermeneutics has served to heighten awareness of the central importance of a proper approach to Biblical interpretation in the experience of the Church. The life of the Church as well as of its members must be dominated by interpretation of the Bible. In this connection it is incumbent on each individual who recognizes the authority of Scripture to accept responsibility for its interpretation and application.

The principles of Biblical interpretation can permit no substitute for the Word of God. All human interpretation of the Scriptures must be carried out under the authority of the Scriptures themselves. The interpreter must assume that the Scriptures are clear in themselves, that they interpret themselves, that they need no human scholarship to make them more understandable or credible (in the objective sense).

The principle of *sola scriptura* establishes limits for the interpretation of Scripture as well as for Christian theology in its doctrinal content. We must presuppose with Barth "that an interpretation and application of the Word actually comes to pass in human freedom under the Word."[53]

Herein is the completion of the divine condescension—the Word of God presents itself in the form of language for human interpretation. The issue to which the recent hermeneutical literature has directed attention in the Church is: How may humanity have the right to interpret the Scriptures? Or to put the issue in another light: How may humanity in its freedom be placed at the service of the Word of God? Says Barth, "No disqualification of our humanity (neither presumptuousness nor despair) can give us the occasion or the right to evade or resist the course of the Word of God."[54]

Hence the interpretation of the Bible must continue at the center of the Church's life. Two themes present themselves for the continuing edifying contemplation of the Church. One is the significance of the Church's recognition of the authority of Scripture as the Word of God. The other is the significance of the fact that the Word of God is to be shared, that it is present in the Church. The key to the life of the Church is ultimately the openness of the believing community to the Word of God.

[53] Barth, *Dogmatics*, 1/2. 710.
[54] Ibid., p. 701.

Italics in English Bible Translation

JACK LEWIS

DESPITE the numerous studies of the use of italics in English Bible translation,[1] erroneous ideas of the merits of the practice continue to be held by the common Bible reader. Some have given the use of italics credit for being a special mark of integrity on the part of a translating group. This attitude makes an evaluation of the purpose of and success of the use of italics essential, particularly in view of the completely different use of italics that is being made in current English translations.

I. HISTORY OF ITALICS IN BIBLE TRANSLATION

The practice in Bible translation of indicating words not specifically represented in the original language that have been supplied by the translators is credited to Sebastian Münster who bracketed such words without change of type in his Latin OT of 1534-35. Münster published his Latin text along with his edition of the Hebrew Bible.[2] His version gave an impetus to OT study similar to that which Erasmus, by his publication of the Greek NT, had given to the study of the NT.[3]

At the same time (1535) Pierre Robert (usually called Olivetan), a relative of John Calvin, in a French Bible printed by Pierre de Wingle at Neuchatel[4] used type of a smaller font for all words not represented in the Greek text, and from these sources the practice spread to the Geneva Bible.

[1]D. M. Beegle, *God's Word Into English* (New York: Harper, 1960) 111-116; J. Eadie, *The English Bible* (London: Macmillan, 1876), 2. 280-285; F. H. A. Scrivener, *The Authorized Edition of the English Bible (1611)* (Cambridge: University Press, 1910) 61-81; W. F. Specht, "The Use of Italics in English Versions of the New Testament," *Andrews University Studies* 6 (1968) 88-109; W. L. Wonderly, "What About Italics?", *BT* 6 (1956) 114-116.

[2]T. H. Darlow and H. F. Moule, *Historical Catalogue of Printed Editions of the Holy Scriptures in the Library of the British and Foreign Bible Society* (London: Bible House, 1903-11) 5087, 6115 (hereafter cited as D&M); H. W. Robinson, *The Bible in Its Ancient and English Versions* (Oxford: Clarendon, 1940) 135-136.

[3]B. Hall, "Biblical Scholarship: Editions and Commentaries," *The Cambridge History of the Bible* (ed. S. L. Greenslade; Cambridge: University Press, 1963), 3. 70.

[4]R. A. Sayce, "Continental Versions to 1600: French," *Cambridge History*, 3. 118; D&M 3710.

Meanwhile the Great Bible used small type to supply in the text phrases found in the Latin Vulgate Bible that are not in the Hebrew and Greek texts as they were then known, such as "*and the bryde*" (Matt 25:1).[5] These words, today called textual variants, were about 130 cases in number, most numerous in Matthew (15), Acts (17), Romans (16) and Revelation (12). Mark, Ephesians, Philippians, Colossians, 1 Timothy, Titus, Philemon and 2 John had one case each. The Thessalonian epistles and 3 John had none. There were minor variations on the practice in successive editions.

Theodore Beza in his Latin NT of 1556-57[6] reverted to the practice of Münster of indicating supplied words (as opposed to textual variants) by different type. Then William Whittingham in his NT of 1557,[7] which was printed in roman type, marked words not in Greek by italics. The Geneva exiles in their Bible of 1560 said in their preface:

> Moreouer whereas the necessitie of the sentence required any thing to be added (for suche is the grace and proprietie of the Ebrewe and Greke tongues, that it can not but ether by circumlocution, or by adding the verbe or some worde be vnderstand of them that are not wel practised therein) we haue put it in the text with another kynde of lettre, that it may easely be discerned from the common lettre.[8]

The Geneva Bible in this way became the first complete English Bible printed in roman type and the first to use italics for words not in the original.[9] It also used italics for marginal references and for contents before chapters.[10]

The Bishops' Bible in 1568 and 1572 followed the practice of indicating added words. This Bible, however, was printed in black type, and roman type was used for the added elements.[11]

The 1611 edition of the *KJV* was printed in black letter with some foreign words like "Talitha cumi" (Mark 5:41) and the cry from the cross (Matt 27:46) printed in smaller type. There was not consistency, however,

---

[5] J. F. Mozley, *Coverdale and His Bibles* (London: Lutterworth, 1953) 221.

[6] D&M 6140.

[7] T. H. Darlow and H. F. Moule, *Historical Catalogue of Printed Editions of the English Bible, 1525-1961* (ed. A. S. Herbert; London/New York: British and Foreign Bible Society/American Bible Society, 1968), No. 106 (hereafter cited as *Historical Catalogue*).

[8] *Historical Catalogue*, No. 107.

[9] P. M. Simms, *The Bible in America* (New York: Wilson-Erickson, 1936) 91; W. Newcome, *A Historical View of English Translations* (Dublin: John Exshaw, 1792) 72.

[10] *Historical Catalogue*, p. 62.

[11] C. C. Butterworth, *The Literary Lineage of the King James Bible, 1340-1611* (Philadelphia: University of Pennsylvania, 1941) 176.

for other phrases like "corban" (Mark 7:11), "Ephphathah" (7:34) and "Anathema Maranatha" (1 Cor 16:22) were in regular black type. The supplementary words were in smaller roman type. Though the rules of procedure outlined for the translators[12] said nothing of the treatment of supplemental words, the sixth item in the report to the Synod of Dort, 20th of November, 1618, said

> that words which it was anywhere necessary to insert into the text to complete the meaning were to be distinguished by another type, small roman.[13]

When it became customary to print the *KJV* in roman type the supplementary words were printed in italics as is the custom today. According to Scrivener,[14] as early as 1612 roman type was used for some printings of the *KJV*,[15] and the supplied words were then in italic type. However, other editions in black letter continued to be printed from the 1611 edition. Interesting deviations from the practice of using either smaller type or italic type include Bibles printed in 1795[16] and 1800,[17] which instead of italics placed a dot under the first vowel of the supplied word.

Catholic translators were not only slower than their Protestant contemporaries to produce translations but were also slower to adopt the practice of indicating supplied words by italics. Italics were used in the Rheims version (1582) to indicate quotations of Scripture, but it was not until 1730 that Robert Witham in a translation from the Vulgate used italics for the supplied words.[18] Witham said:

> If the reader find in this Edition sometimes a word or two in a different character [italics] it is meerly because, tho' they are not express'd in the very *letter* of the text, yet they seem'd necessary, to represent to the reader the true and literal sense.[19]

In the fifth edition of the Rheims version (1738)[20] italics were used. Richard Challoner whose editions began in 1749[21] at first used italics

---

[12]The text is in G. Burnet, *The History of the Reformation of the Church of England* (ed. E. Nares; London: Scott, Webster & Geary, 1837), 4. 391-393.

[13]Reprinted and translated in A. W. Pollard, ed., *Records of the English Bible* (London: Henry Frowde, 1911) 337, 339.

[14]Scrivener, *Authorized*, 62.

[15]*Historical Catalogue*, No. 313.

[16]Ibid., No. 1399.

[17]Ibid., No. 1442.

[18]Ibid., No. 1009.

[19]Quoted in H. Pope, *English Versions of the Bible* (rev. S. Bullough; St. Louis/London: B. Herder, 1952) 350.

[20]*Historical Catalogue*, No. 1041.

[21]Ibid., No. 1086.

sparingly, but they increased in later editions, especially in the third (1752).[22] A Rheims edition printed by John Murry Company in New York and Baltimore, carrying the approbation of James Cardinal Gibbons in 1899, italicized quotations from the OT, chapter summaries, some allusions to the OT that used phrases but were not direct quotations (e.g., Matt 24:15; Acts 2:30), and also the supplementary words.

Scrivener's detailed analysis of the use of italics in the 1611 Bible showed that italics were used for many more purposes than the common reader has been aware.[23] Scrivener classified the examples under six general headings: (1) "When words quite or nearly to complete the sense of the sacred writers have been introduced into the text from parallel places of Scripture." In these cases the text seems to have lost necessary words. (2) "When the compactness of the Hebrew language, intelligible enough to those well versed in it, yet [is] hardly capable of being transformed into a modern tongue." (3) When "an expression which strictly belongs to but one member of a sentence, with some violation of strict propriety, is made to do duty in another." (4) When "inserting . . . a word or two, in order to indicate that abrupt transition from the *oblique* to the *direct* form of speech, which is so familiar to most ancient languages, but so foreign to our own." (5) To "indicate that a word or clause is of doubtful authority as a matter of textual criticism." (6) The case where "the words supplied are essential to the English sense, although they may very well be dispensed with in Hebrew or Greek." Category number six covers more instances than the other five put together, and the practice of indicating them is of the most doubtful practical value.

The number of italicized words in printings of the *KJV*, not a fixed number unchanged from the 1611 edition, has been fluid, changing from edition to edition. It is known that the Cambridge edition of the *KJV* in 1629 made revisions: "Considerable care appears to have been exercised as to the words printed in italics, punctuation, etc."[24] In the Cambridge editon of 1638 "the revisers took special pains to render uniform the use of italics."[25] This Cambridge edition remained the standard text until 1762.[26] F. S. Paris in an edition of 1762[27] made a serious attempt to correct the text by "unifying and extending the use of italics."[28] Further modification came in 1769 with the editorial work of Benjamin Blayney.[29] Still other

---

[22] Ibid., No. 1099.

[23] Scrivener, *Authorized*, 61-81.

[24] L. Wilson, quoted in *Historical Catalogue*, p. 158.

[25] *Historical Catalogue*, No. 520.

[26] Ibid., p. 176.

[27] Ibid., No. 1142.

[28] Ibid., p. 274; cf. Scrivener, *Authorized*, 28-29.

[29] *Historical Catalogue*, No. 1194. A report published in *Gentleman's Magazine* 39 (October 25, 1769) 517 is reprinted in Scrivener, *Authorized*, 238-242.

modifications came with Scrivener's publication of the *Cambridge Paragraph Bible* in 1873.[30] The *Historical Catalogue* describes Scrivener's publication as an edition in which "the use of the italic type [is] made uniform." The effort to italicize supplied words had its widest use in this *Cambridge Paragraph Bible*. However, modification of italics has continued into the twentieth century as the following material makes clear.

In a passage like Exod 32:18, thirteen Hebrew words are translated with 36 English words. Five were italicized in 1611. These became eleven in the *Cambridge Paragraph Bible* (1873) but are then reduced to ten in the American Bible Society printings of the *KJV*. Psalm 84 (83) had nine words or phrases in roman type in twelve verses in 1611. These became fourteen italicized phrases (a total of eighteen words) by 1873 and are now thirteen in the American Bible Society printings. "Of" in the phrase "God of hosts" (v 8) is now in regular type.

In the gospel of Matthew, the 57 marked words of 1611 were expanded to 165 in 1623, to 244 in 1638, and the number had become 583 by 1873.[31] In the current American Bible Society edition the number is 363. In 1611 the *KJV* carried six marked words in Matthew ("are" [5:11], "thou" [5:22], "so" [13:2], "they" [23:4], "one" [23:8], "to" [24:1]), which are no longer italicized in *KJV* printings. Of these the 1611 edition was clearly in error on Matt 5:11, which has *este* in the Greek text. It was inconsistent at 10:27 where "that" rendering the same imperative structure is once italicized and once not. One may take a phrase like "her that had been the wife" (Matt 1:6). The 1611 edition marked "*that had been.*" The *Cambridge Paragraph Bible* (1873) italicized "*her that had been*" and "*wife*" but not "the," and the American Bible Society now italicizes "*that had been the wife*" but not "her." The Matthew phrases "*the*" (1:6), "*for*" (2:18), "*against*" (10:1) and "*which is done*" (21:21) had been italicized in 1611, were not in 1873, but now again are in the American Bible Society printings of the *KJV*.

The gospel of John, chap. 11, had no marked words in 1611, but the 1638 edition carried fifteen. These had become 34 by 1873, and the American Bible Society printings now have seventeen.

In 1611, 1 Corinthians 11 had seven italicized words: "*unto you*" (v 17), "*this is*" (v 20), "*other*" (v 21), and "*hee tooke*" (v 25). By 1873 these had become forty in the *Cambridge Paragraph Bible*. That number has now been reduced to 24 in the American Bible Society printings.

In spite of all the care that has been expended on italics, great inconsistency still exists in current printings of the *KJV* on the use of italics. One reads "Ye *are* to pass" (Deut 2:4) and "thou art to pass" (2:18), and "*even* unto Uzzah" (2:18) and "even unto this day" (2:20) for the same

[30] *Historical Catalogue*, No. 1995.

[31] J. R. Dore, *Old Bibles* (London: Eyre and Spottiswoode, 1888) 339-340.

sorts of structures. The same Greek phrase is "them all" (Luke 17:27) and "*them* all" (17:29); "this *man*" (Heb 3:3) and "this man" (8:3).

This continuous process of change justifies the conclusion stated by the 1885 revision committee which, after mentioning some of those who had introduced changes in italics prior to that date, said of the changes, "None of them however rest on any higher authority than that of the persons who from time to time superintended the publication."[32] When various printings using italics for supplied words use the same words (as is true in some of the above examples) and some italicize them and some do not, what dependence can an English reader put on italics as an indication of what the original text had and what is supplied?

Realizing the need to attempt to bring order into a very confused situation, the Revision Committee of Convocation in rule number seven of the General Principles for the revision of 1881-85 provided for a revision of italics in the Bible. The revisers of the NT say that

> we have acted on the general principle of printing in italics words which did not appear to be necessarily involved in the Greek. Our tendency has been to diminish rather than to increase the amount of italic printing; though, in the case of different readings, we have usually marked the absence of any words in the original which the sense might nevertheless require to be present in the Version; and again, in the case of inserted pronouns, where the reference did not appear to be perfectly certain, we have similarly had recourse to italics. Some of these cases, especially when there are slight differences of reading, are of singular intricacy, and make it impossible to maintain rigid uniformity.[33]

The revisers of the OT adopted the rule "that all such words now printed in italics, as are plainly implied in the Hebrew and necessary in English, be printed in common type."[34] The preface then proceeds to say:

> But where any doubt existed as to the exact rendering of the Hebrew, all words which have been added in order to give completeness to the English expression are printed in italic type, so that the reader by omitting them may be able to see how far their insertion is justified by the words of the original. This of course is especially true of those renderings for which an alternative is given in the margin, where the roman and italic type play exactly opposite parts.[35]

In keeping with that announced policy the revisers of the *ASV* made considerably less use of italics than did the *KJV* translation. In Psalm 84 none of the words overlapping the *KJV* are italicized, but the *ASV*'s own

[32]"Preface to the New Testament," Revised Version.
[33]"Preface to the Edition of A.D. 1881."
[34]"Preface to the Edition of A.D. 1885."
[35]Ibid.

addition "*to Zion*" (v 5) is. Whereas the current *KJV* printings of Joel have 39 italicized words, the *ASV* has only eight. In the gospel of Matthew it has only 97. In John 11 there are only three italicized words. Little objection is to be taken to many instances such as "*How is it* that we could not cast it out?*" (Mark 9:28) and "the more *the prophets* called them, the more they went from them" (Hos 11:2). However, the rules of italicization were inconsistently applied. The *ASV* (as the *KJV*) renders *arsen* as "manchild" (Rev 12:5) but also as "man *child*" (12:13). *Pneumatikos* is "spiritual gift" (Rom 1:11) but also "spiritual *gift*" (1 Cor 12:1).

Numerous cases can be found where words supplied to complete the meaning were not italicized—for example, "may" (Ruth 1:11), "aught" (1:17), "fast" (2:8). "Could" is inserted by both the *KJV* and *ASV* (Judg 1:19) without italics to supply what seems a defect in the Masoretic text. The *ASV* freely supplies possessive pronouns without italicizing them (e.g., "his child" [Matt 10:21], "his philosophy" [Col 2:8], "our redemption" [Eph 1:7; Col 1:14]). The paraphrase "God forbid" (cf. Luke 20:16; 1 Cor 6:15) occurs a total of fifteen times without italics.

The *ASV* also has its cases of italics continued from the *KJV* that unduly change the meaning of the passage. Both the *KJV* and *ASV* were reluctant to have Stephen pray to Jesus. The *KJV* had him "calling upon *God* and saying, Lord Jesus . . ."; the *ASV* had "calling upon *the Lord* and saying . . ."; but the *RSV* and *NIV* correctly drop the unjustified addition and read, "He prayed, 'Lord Jesus, receive my spirit'" (Acts 7:59). Another case is in the addition of *our* in the phrase "finisher of *our* faith" (Heb 12:2 *ASV*). The addition goes back to Tyndale. Without the addition it is Jesus' own faith that is perfected, while with the addition it is the believer's faith.[36]

II. ITALICS IN TWENTIETH-CENTURY BIBLE TRANSLATIONS

The *RSV* (1952) abandoned the effort to indicate supplied words by italics.[37] Supplied page headings for the text and alternate readings cited in the notes are italicized. With the exception of the *NASB* and the New Scofield Bible, the latter of which is only a modified *KJV*, translations made since the *RSV* have followed its pattern in not indicating supplied words. Italics are used, but for other purposes. The *RSV* does indicate in footnotes some cases where an addition has been made. The translators' guess that "instruction" is given to the wise man (Prov 9:9), which carried italics in the *KJV*, *ASV* and *NASB* but gets a footnote in the *RSV*. In numerous other instances attention is called to the fact that the Hebrew

---

[36]Principal Brown, "Some Minor Gains of the Revised Version of the New Testament and Some of the Reverse," *ExpTim* 3 (1891-92) 260.

[37]M. Burrows, *Diligently Compared* (London/New York/Toronto: Nelson, 1964), Nos. 6, 20-23.

lacks a word or phrase (e.g., Gen 4:8; 10:5; 21:9; 44:4; Num 9:16; 34:6; Deut 30:16; 33:8; Judg 16:14; etc.), that a phrase in Hebrew has been omitted (e.g., Gen 9:10; Lev 20:10; etc.), that a Hebrew phrase is obscure (e.g., Exod 17:16; 23:5; Lev 6:21; Deut 18:8; Judg 5:10; etc.), or that for some other reason there is a departure from the Hebrew text.

The *NEB* uses italics for page and section headings, which have been supplied for the guidance of the reader, and for introductory phrases (like "Or" or "That is," etc.) in the note material. Supplied speaker identifications in the Song of Songs are italicized. The transliterated phrases in Belshazzar's vision (Dan 5:25-27) and in the gospels (Matt 27:46; Mark 15:34; 5:41; 7:34) and "*Marana tha*" (1 Cor 16:22) are italicized. No effort is made to indicate supplementary words.

The New Scofield Bible carries the italicized words of the *KJV* comparable to those of the American Bible Society printings but then carries in brackets with accompanying center reference notes cases where it has modified the vocabulary of the *KJV*.

The only translation produced in the second half of the twentieth century to attempt to indicate supplied words in italics is the *NASB*, which inserts words in italics in at least 2029 instances in the NT alone. Some of these cases are words already supplied and italicized in the *ASV*—for example, "*shall come*" (Num 24:24). A preference for inserting the word "some" is observable: "*some* tax-gatherers" (Luke 3:12), "*some* soldiers" (3:14), "*some* Pharisees" (5:17), "*some* grainfields" (6:1), "*some* bread" (22:19).

The use of italics left the *NASB* translators free to encroach on the domain of the commentator in their supplements to the text. Frequently an idea is sharpened or restricted by an added word when no addition is actually necessary: "you *alone*" (Gen 7:1), "*single* cubit" (Matt 6:27; Luke 12:25), "that *very* hour" (Matt 8:13), "shall *more* be given" (13:12), "*firm* root" (13:21), "*right* at the door" (24:33; Mark 13:29), "*any* one prisoner" (Matt 27:15), "*only* temporary" (Mark 4:17), "*all* about" (5:16), "last *of all*" (12:6), "*merely* the beginning" (13:8), "the Father *alone*" (13:32), "*appointed* time" (13:33), "go *as a forerunner* before Him" (Luke 1:17), "How shall I know this *for certain?*" (1:18), "*properly* clothe yourself" (17:8), "*real* cause" (Acts 19:40), "accursed, *separated* from Christ" (Rom 9:3), "you stand *only* by your faith" (11:20), "*refreshing* rest" (15:32), "*mere* men" (1 Cor 3:4), "*first* went forth" (14:36), "*only* a man's covenant" (Gal 3:15), "God is *only* one" (3:20), "the need *of the moment*" (Eph 4:29), "do not *merely* look out" (Phil 2:4), "*true* circumcision" (3:3), "a *mere* shadow" (Col 2:17), "we *really* live" (1 Thess 3:8), "examine everything *carefully*" (5:21), "*only* fitting" (2 Thess 1:3), "*ever* greater" (1:3), "*only* just" (1:6), "*only* one wife" (1 Tim 3:12), "*too* hastily" (5:22), "goodness *actually* is a means of great gain" (6:6), "*still* called today" (Heb 3:13), "*only* of milk (5:13), "*only* when men are dead" (9:17), "a *mere* copy" (9:24), "*only* a shadow" (10:1), "*any* offering" (10:18), "sprinkled *clean*" (10:22), "*only* one Lawgiver" (Jas 4:12), "the *very* world of iniquity" (3:6), "*just* a vapor" (4:14), "external *only*" (1 Pet 3:3). The insertion of the word "including" (Acts 6:9) excludes the exegetical possibility that "Freedmen" (*Libertinōn*) could be a geographical term along with the other geographical terms of the verse.

In some instances the *NASB* translators have inserted side comments in italics. Representative passages are: "*He added*" (Mark 6:9), "*with the saliva*" (7:33), and "*the passage about the burning bush*" (12:26; Luke 20:37). The statement, "the old is good *enough*" (Luke 5:39) has a different implication from "the old is good." Other cases include "*Roman* cohort" (John 18:3), "you say *correctly* that I am king" (18:37), "Hellenistic *Jews* ... *native* Hebrews" (Acts 6:1), "*human* hands" (7:48), "translated *in Greek*" (9:36), "no *longer* consider" (10:15), "*divinely* directed" (10:22), "*just* a man" (10:26), "the days of *the Feast* of Unleavened Bread" (12:3), "led away *to execution*" (12:19), "*the meeting of* the synagogue" (13:43), "the dust of their feet *in protest*" (13:51), "speaking boldly *with reliance* upon the Lord" (14:3), "The God-fearing *Gentiles*" (17:17), "*that is coming*" (Col 4:16), "from one *Father*" (Heb 2:11), "tempted in all things *as we are, yet* without sin" (4:15), "spirits *now* in prison" (1 Pet 3:19), "*the will* of God" (4:6), "a *special* gift" (4:10), "*Christian* love" (2 Pet 1:7), "*earthly* dwelling" (1:14), "*really* of us" (1 John 2:19), "a *good* testimony" (3 John 12).

In many cases a possessive pronoun has been substituted in italics for the definite article or supplied where there is no article in the original. Examples occur in "*his* child" (Matt 10:21), "*their* journey" (Mark 6:8), "*His* name" (Acts 5:41), "*His* resurrection" (26:23), "*my* offering" (Rom 15:16), "*our* brother" (2 Cor 1:1), "*their* children" (12:14), "*our* faithful and beloved brother" (Col 4:9), "*my* true child" (1 Tim 1:2), "*our* doctrine" (6:1—but 6:3 has "the doctrine"), "*His* Son" (Heb 1:2), "*their* body" (Jas 2:16), "*our* life" (3:6), "*your* faith" (1 Pet 5:9), "*their* greed" (2 Pet 2:3), "*their* lawless deeds" (2:8), "*its* corrupt desires" (2:10), "*their* mocking" (3:3).

When two words are required in English where there was one in Greek or Hebrew, like "fiery *serpent*" (Num 21:8) or "corner *stone*" (Ps 118:22; Eph 2:20; 1 Pet 2:6), the second word is italicized. The italics are superfluous. "Stone" is as justified in the translation as "corner" is. The word was spelled "cornerstone" in Job 38:6 and Isa 28:16. The verb supplied in a sentence translating the Hebrew nominal sentence is at times italicized despite the fact that it is impossible to make an English sentence without the verb: "Now the Canaanite *was* then in the land" (Gen 12:6), but the verb "to be" is unitalicized at Amos 7:14: "I am not a prophet."

Though italics are abundantly used, they cannot be depended upon invariably to tell the reader whether a word in the text has been supplied or was in the original. If a literal rendering is given in the margin the translators felt no need to use italics in the text, but elsewhere also there are supplied words in no italics. "Own" in the phrase "his own sons" (Deut 33:9), "may" (Ruth 1:11), "influences" (Isa 2:6), "some" (Amos 2:11), "in the sight of" (Acts 7:20), "day" (Mark 16:2, 9; Acts 20:7; 1 Cor 16:2) and "actually" (Acts 22:28) are all supplied. "False" is not italicized in the phrase "false circumcision" (*katatomē*, Phil 3:2), though "true" in the next phrase, "*true* circumcision" (*peritomē*, 3:3), is. None of the words of "spiritual service of worship" for *logikēn latreian* (Rom 12:1) are italicized. "Long" in the phrase "all day long" (Matt 20:6) has no italics, but "hour" in "eleventh *hour*" does. "Prove" in the phrase "prove to be my disciples" (John 15:8), "still" in "still more excellent way" (1 Cor 12:31) and the words "just as" for *kathōs* (1 John 3:2, 3, 7, 23) are not italicized. "Seared in their own consciences as with a branding iron" (1 Tim 4:2) carries no italics.[38] The definite article is supplied without italics in many instances beginning with the first verse of Genesis: "In the beginning." The reader can never be certain whether the original had the definite article or not.

Italics may be used where a textual variant has been followed, though the reader is not so informed. The *ASV* used "Jesus" in Matt 4:23, calling attention to the variant "he" in the margin. The *NASB* italicizes "*Jesus*" with no marginal note. Other cases of italicizing a versional reading include the supplied numerals in 1 Sam 13:1. "Like" is inserted in Isa 21:8 ("*like* a lion" for the Hebrew "a lion") and "as" at Ps 11:1 ("*as* a bird" for a vocative) without a note that a version is being followed instead of the Masoretic text.

A distinctive feature of the use of italics in the *NASB* is its use for "began" where that word is used in rendering the Greek imperfect tense when it is considered to be inceptive. The italics distinguish this use of "begin" from the translation of the Greek word ordinarily meaning "begin." The practice leads to "overtranslation," and instances can be seen in Matt 20:17; Mark 9:25; Luke 15:32; Acts 3:5; Gal 2:12.

Italics in the Living Bible Paraphrased have little in common with the usage in the *KJV*, *ASV* and *NASB*. A paraphrase does not lend itself to indicating what has been supplied by the paraphraser. Kenneth Taylor has used square brackets to enclose the more obvious glosses he has made on the text, often with a footnote claiming that the content of the gloss is implied (e.g., John 12:32; 16:24; 20:8; Acts 2:34; 10:12; 11:6; 12:15; 16:3; Rom 3:2; 5:13; 9:6; 1 Cor 7:29; 2 Cor 4:10, 13; 5:13; 11:33; Heb 9:18; Jas 5:9; 1 Pet 2:5; 1 John 1:9; etc.). That the gloss is actually implied is debatable enough in some instances.

---

[38]W. L. Lane, "The New American Standard Bible—New Testament," *Gordon Review* 9 (1966) 156.

Taylor has used italics for speaker identifications (Gen 16:8; 25:30 ff.; 27:1 ff.; John 8:57-58; etc.), for headings (Gen 5:1 ff.; 46:22; Rev 1:4; 2:1, 8, 12, 18; 3:1, 7, 14), for book titles (Num 21:14; 2 Kgs 1:18; 15:6, 21, 26), for a ship title (Acts 28:11), for the words "From" and "To" at the beginning of letters (15:23; 23:26; Phil 1:1), and for instructions from the paraphraser to the reader (as "continued in the next chapter," Exod 7:25). There is no apparent reason for the italicization of 1 Kgs 8:10-11 and Matt 8:2-4.

In following current literary usage, Taylor italicizes words on which he wishes to place emphasis: "the *center* of the garden" (Gen 3:3), "to *give* you the land" (Lev 25:37), "*living* water" (John 4:10), "*I was blind and now I see*" (John 9:25), "*I am that disciple!*" (21:24), "*God's* garden . . . *God's* building" (1 Cor 3:9), "*eternal life*" (1 John 2:25), "and we really *are*" (3:1), "*born again*" (3:9). The cases are not of such frequency as to void the impact of the italics. Nevertheless, the rules by which such emphasis has been determined defies systematization, and the italics are perhaps only a guide to Taylor's religious orientation.

The instances include whole statements: "*Listen! the virgin shall conceive a child*" (Matt 1:23), "You can pray for *anything* and *if you believe, you have it*; it's yours" (Mark 11:24), "*Watch for my return*" (13:37), "*keep close to me*" (Luke 9:23), "*There is forgiveness of sins for all who turn to me*" (24:47), "*they are my glory*" (John 17:10), "*but you dishonor him by breaking them*" (Rom 2:23), "*if you are counting on circumcision and keeping the Jewish laws to make you right with God, then Christ cannot save you*" (Gal 5:2), "You ask him for *anything* . . . yes, ask for *anything*" (John 14:13-14), "*For God's secret plan, now at last made known, is Christ himself*" (Col 2:2), "*so you have everything when you have Christ*" (2:10), "*to love one another*" (1 John 2:8).

Perhaps Taylor's nearest approach to the older practice of italicizing supplementary words is encountered in his glosses: "*for he says we have sinned*" (1 John 1:10), in his repetitions for emphasis: "never, *never*" (Heb 13:5), in adverbs: "*really* love" (John 21:16; 1 John 3:18), "follow me *now*" (Matt 8:22), "*still waiting*" (Heb 4:9), and in adjectives: "*that* kind of faith" (Jas 2:14). The most serious snare in Taylor's practice is that the reader will be receiving emphasis from a gloss (whose content Taylor thinks is implied) rather than from that which was actually in the text. No notes are given to guide the reader in the meaning of the italics system.

Making no effort by italics within the text to indicate textual problems or words supplied by the translators, the Good News Bible (*GNB*) has sparsely used italics for printing subheadings supplied in the text. Such headings include the listing of the plagues (Exod 7:14 ff.) and other lists (Num 1:5 ff.; Ezra 10:18; Neh 10:2 ff.; Amos 1:3). Supplied speaker designations are also italicized (cf. Job 3:2; 4:1; Song 1:1 ff.; etc.), and those at Job 24:18; 26:5 are also bracketed. Book titles within the text are given in italics (Num 21:14; 1 Kgs 11:41; 15:7; 2 Chr 9:29; 24:37; 35:27; etc.). In

certain cases the measures *ephah, bath* and *homer* (Ezek 45:11 ff.) are
italicized, and the *number, weight* and *division* (Dan 5:26) of the explanation of the handwriting on the wall in Belshazzar's vision are.

Italics are not used in the OT of the *GNB* for a transliterated phrase
like "Jegar Sahadutha" (Gen 31:47), but in the NT transliterated phrases
"*Talitha, koum*" (Mark 5:41), "*Ephphatha*" (7:34), "*Eli, Eli, lema sabachthani*" (Matt 27:46; cf. Mark 15:34), and "*Marana tha*" (1 Cor 16:22) are
italicized. Italics are used for emphasis in the phrase "*Greetings from Paul*"
(1 Cor 16:21; Col 4:18; 2 Thess 3:17) and in the phrase "*I, Paul, will pay
you back*" (Phlm 19).

In the *NIV*, subject headings in italics (not a part of the original text
and not intended for oral reading) have been supplied for the guidance of
the reader. Suggested speakers in the Song of Songs and phrases from
Belshazzar's vision (Dan 5:26) are italicized. Psalm 136 is printed with the
responses in italics, suggesting responsive reading.

More obvious words or phrases not represented in the original text,
but supplied by the translators for clarification, usually are enclosed in half
brackets (e.g., Lev 11:26; Judg 2:3; 1 Sam 13:1; 2 Sam 1:21; 21:2, 16; 22:15;
23:9; 1 Kgs 10:16; 11:24; 20:34; Neh 6:9; 10:37; 12:36; Ps 45:13; 57:2; 58:9;
68:17; 78:61; 137:5; 141:7; 144:6; Isa 27:7; 37:9; 41:22; Eccl 5:6; 7:18, 28;
Ezek 20:24; 24:17; 48:28; Dan 8:12; 9:27; Nah 1:8, 11, 12, 14; 2:1, 7; John
1:14, 18; Gal 2:4; 4:17).[39] The brackets indicate that there may be uncertainty about the addition. Not to be identified with the earlier translation
effort to put all supplied words in italics, the brackets are not numerous.
But their presence should not lead to a false confidence, for cases of words
supplied without brackets can be found (e.g., "instruct" [Prov 9:9], "your"
[Matt 13:32], "for a while" [John 1:14], "truly" [21:15, 16], "spiritual"
[1 Cor 1:7], "setting our hearts" [10:6], "group" [Gal 2:12], "party" [3:20],
"to which he has called" [Eph 1:18], "kingdom" [Col 1:12], "shed" [1:20],
"produced," "prompted," "inspired" [1 Thess 1:3], "really" [3:8], "suffer"
[5:9], "evil" [Jas 1:14], "the truth" [1 John 2:20]).

The New King James Bible has abandoned the italics system of the
KJV but uses italics for topic headings that have been supplied throughout
and for OT Scripture quotations that are used in the NT (e.g., 1 Cor 15:27,
32, 45, 54-55). Foreign words whose translation is explained in the text,
like "*Talitha, cumi*" (Mark 5:41), "*Ephphatha*" (7:34), "*Eli, Eli, lama
sabachthani?*" (Matt 27:46; Mark 15:34), "*Abaddon*" (Rev 9:11) and
"*Armageddon*" (16:16) are italicized.

---

[39]P. Doebler, "New Bible Translation Computerized for Automatic Setting of
Editions," *Publisher's Weekly* 204 (October 1973) 56-62.

III. Cautions About Italics

Rather than being a guarantee of the "honesty of word translation," italics have proved to be a mixed blessing to the reader. Certain cautions are in order.

(1) Italics are not an infallible guide to what has or has not been supplied by the translators. They are not a basis for complacency so that the reader can assume that an unitalicized word must be represented in the original. No translating group has consistently italicized all words it supplied to complete the meaning. Furthermore, the use of italics has been fluid rather than constant in the various printings of the *KJV*.

(2) In certain cases the use of italics is actually superfluous. A nominal sentence in Hebrew has no expressed verb, but to translate it into English some form of the verb "to be" must be used. To italicize these verbs is superfluous, and the translations using italics have been inconsistent in doing so.[40] Examples of this sort of sentence are seen in the *KJV*: "And darkness *was* upon the face of the deep . . . and God saw the light, that it *was* good . . . the waters which *were* under the firmament from the waters which *were* above" (Gen 1:2, 4, 7). "A *good* name *is* better than precious ointment" (Eccl 7:1). Greek does not use a verb in the beatitude "Blessed *are* the poor in spirit" (Matt 5:3). In the supplying of "are" the translators have not supplied an unnecessary item. The sentence could not be translated into English without it. The last verse of the *KJV* (Rev 22:21) has the word "*be*" in a sentence of this sort. Examples of superfluous italics for other reasons are encountered in "Rachel weeping *for* her children" (Matt 2:18) and "Provoke not your children *to anger*" (Col 3:21).

In some instances the need to supply a phrase is created by the effort to maintain the word order of the original when it differs from normal English order. Recasting the sentence into normal English order would eliminate the need of the addition. Such a case is seen in "the *sword*" (*KJV*) or "*Even the sword*" (*ASV*) of Rev 19:21. The phrase could be "the sword coming out of the mouth of the one sitting on the horse" without any change of meaning.

In certain cases the added phrases are italicized in the *KJV* but are unnecessary additions: "*he shall be chief and captain*" (2 Sam 5:8), "*as though he heard them not*" (John 8:6), "*the image of*" (Rom 11:4), "*for us*" (Heb 9:12), "*they are commanded*" (1 Cor 14:34). "*He shall be free*" (Matt 15:6) would be unnecessary if an unitalicized "and" had not been supplied at the beginning of the verse.

---

[40]T. W. Chambers, "The Plan of the New Bible Revision," *The Presbyterian Review* 2 (July 1881) 465-466.

The opposite side of this problem is the case in which the *KJV* made unnecessary additions without italicizing the added words. Some examples are "Ho" (Ruth 4:1) or "thine" in the phrase "thine alms" (Matt 6:2—not italicized in 1611 but now italicized in American Bible Society printings). The word *philagathon* becomes "a lover of good men" (Tit 1:8, *KJV*), but the *ASV* correctly omits "men." In the phrase "The rest of the dead lived not again (*ezēsan*) until the thousand years were finished" (Rev 20:6) there is no reason to supply the word "again." The definite article is supplied in numerous cases without italics—e.g., "the eternal gospel" (Rev 14:6, *KJV*). Such an addition may intensify the idea as the word "very" does in the expression "that very hour" (Matt 15:28; 17:18).

(3) In certain cases, to have italics at all is clearly an error. "*For the Son of man is*" (Mark 13:34, *KJV*) is more accurately "It is as when a man." "Dry *land*" (Heb 11:29) for *cheros gēs* did not carry italics in 1611 but did in the *Cambridge Paragraph Bible* (1873) and does in the American Bible Society printings. "*Any man*" (Heb 10:38, *KJV*) is in error. "If he draws back" would be accurate.

(4) There are places where the insertion seems to be a wrong one. For example, "the pleasant *places* for their silver" (Hos 9:6, *KJV*) seems more accurately translated in the *ASV* and *RSV* as "things of silver." "It *shall be given to them*" (Matt 20:23, *KJV*) is better rendered "it is for those." "*Venomous* beast" (Acts 28:4, *KJV*) adds an unnecessary adjective. The Greek merely has "creature" as in v 5. "Took not on *him the nature of angels*" (Heb 2:16, *KJV*) is more correctly in the *ASV* "For verily not to angels doth he give help."

(5) The fact that in current use italics signifies emphasis may invite the reader to place an emphasis on that which is not in the original text at all. The following examples are in the *KJV*. In 1 Kgs 13:27 "saddled *him*" becomes an improper emphasis. In Ps 19:3, "*where* their voice is not heard," the addition changes the meaning of the statement. In John 3:34 "*unto him*" limits the sense. Perhaps the most striking case is "*unknown* tongue" (1 Cor 14:2, 4, 13, 14, 19, 27), which is surely partly responsible for the glossolalia movement. The rendering of the same Greek phrase in the plural but without the addition occurs in this same setting at vv 5, 6, 18, 22, 23, 26 (singular), 39. In the phrase "this *man*" (Heb 7:24) a proper emphasis should not be on "man," nor should it be on "did" in the phrase "a better hope *did*" (7:19).

(6) Italics have been used to turn the reader to an interpretation the translator or editor (as the case may be) wished him to accept as opposed to other alternatives. Job 19:25-26 (*KJV*) carries the words "that," "that," "day," "though," "worms," and "body" in italics, and these words made the passage clearly a resurrection passage. 1 Cor 7:36-37 (a difficult passage) carries "her" (vv 36, 38) in the *KJV*, but the *ASV*, removing these italics, supplied "daughter" (vv 36, 37, 38) in italics while leaving its supplied word

"own" unitalicized. Though "virgin," omitting "daughter," is given as the marginal alternate, the *ASV* clearly suggests an unmentioned "father" as the antecedent of the masculine pronoun in the passage. "Spiritual things with spiritual *words*" (margin: "spiritual things to spiritual men" [1 Cor 2:13, *ASV*]) gives preference to taking a dative case as instrumental rather than as an indirect object. "*The church that is* at Babylon" (1 Pet 5:13, *KJV*) excluded the possibility that the unnamed antecedent of the feminine pronoun is a lady. "*God's* heritage" (5:3, *KJV*) for *tōn klērōn* would be better as "those in your charge" (*RSV*). The italics unduly restrict the meaning in the statement "Hereby perceive we the love *of God*" (1 John 3:16).

(7) The use of italics has been relatively ineffective in safeguarding the reader from forming a theology on supplied (italicized) words. The reader has ignored the italics. The phrase "for God giveth the Spirit not by measure *unto him*" (John 3:34) has been used to develop the idea of measures of the Spirit in which Jesus had the Spirit without measure while other people have it "by measure."

(8) The use of italics has proved a snare where the interpreter has supposed that every unitalicized word is represented in the original and then proceeds to make a supplied word the chief point of the thought of the passage. Such cases are encountered in the *KJV* and *ASV* in the use of the term "office" for occupational activities: "office of a bishop" (1 Tim 3:1), "office of a deacon" (3:10, 13, *KJV*) and in "usurp authority" (2:12, *KJV*). This last case is commonly understood to mean that any sort of authority can be exercised as long as it has been duly given by leaders of the congregation. A false emphasis is placed on "usurp."

(9) How extremely pedantic the effort to italicize supplied words can become is seen when the American Bible Society printing of the *KJV* has *dikaioi* as "righteous *men*" (Matt 13:17) and renders *malaka* as "soft raiment" and as "soft *clothing*" in the same verse (11:8). *Houtos* is rendered "this *fellow*" (12:24) or as "this *man*" (13:54), but neither "fellow" nor "man" is an unnecessary addition in these verses.

(10) A large measure of subjective judgment enters into determining what words to italicize. In cases using completely the same wording the *KJV* has one set of italicized words while the *ASV* has others. An example may be seen in 1 Cor 15:41 where the *KJV* italicizes "*there is*," "*one*" and "*another*" but the *ASV* italicizes nothing.

IV. CONCLUSION

The use of italics to indicate supplied words developed late in the transmission of Scripture and as used in existing translations has not proved to be an effective safeguard against danger. The high percentage of the cases of italics that are superfluous and thereby worthless leaves the reader without direction to know when an important issue is at stake. When the use of italics has become an excuse for license, the danger is the greater, for later printers are almost certain to print the material without the italics, leaving the reader with the impression that the phrases are legitimate translation. That italics have now the more common significance of indicating emphasis makes them more dangerous than helpful to the uninitiated reader. Ordinarily the introductory material of an English version does not explain to the reader this specialized use of italics.

It might be wholesome to remind any who would exalt the tradition of using italics into a saving virtue that when the Greek Scriptures are cited in the NT they are considered as authoritative but are unencumbered by devices that call attention to their deviation in details from features of the Hebrew originals.

The Bible the Foundation for a World and Life View

Harold Lindsell

T RADITIONALLY theology has been called the queen of the sciences. In theory at least it meant that theology topped the list in man's never-ending quest for knowledge and particularly for ultimates. Hidden in theology's queenship was the notion that all of life and conduct including the political, economic, social, ethical and philosophical had its "ground of being," to use Tillich's phrase, in theology. Life was rooted in theology, informed by theology, and found to be false or true to the extent that it corresponded to theological realities.

Theology in turn was grounded in God's self-revelation, and this was commonly held to be the Word of God written. This Word not only revealed the incarnate Word; it also formed the framework that gave meaning to all of life. This idea that theology was queen and that all thought was related and subject to it was held by Jonathan Edwards, who, as much as any man, influenced eighteenth-century American religious life. His biographer says:

> Throughout his mature life as well there would be the recurring ambition to bring vast areas of knowledge within an orderly system, in which everything would have a place, part relating to part. He once dreamed of writing *A Rational Account of the Christian Religion*, in which all art and all science would find center and meaning in theology.[1]

I share Edwards' view, but I shudder at the failure of evangelicals to make regnant in life what most of them pay lip service to in principle. I am not speaking of nonevangelicals, for many of whom theology is irrelevant. I am not speaking of those who follow the current fads of intuitionism, humanism, subjectivism and nontheistic existentialism. Rather I have in mind those who profess to believe that life is of one piece, that objective absolutes underlie all reality, and that the theology derived from Scripture has something to say to men in the arts, the sciences and the social sciences.

Unhappily, even among evangelicals theology has been divorced from the other disciplines found in the curriculum of the average Christian

---

[1] *Jonathan Edwards: Basic Writings: XII* (New York: New American Library, 1966), Foreword.

institution. Most of the historians, political scientists, sociologists and economists, to name a few in the soft sciences, have been educated in secular graduate schools where Christian theology was never brought to bear on these disciplines. Once these social scientists graduated they gravitated to teaching posts in evangelical schools where they now pursue their studies, teach their classes, and indoctrinate their students as though theology had nothing to say to them. They read their Bibles, say their prayers, attend their churches, and confess their commitment to Christ— but they live in two worlds, separated one from the other without intersecting at any point. The theologians do no better. Steeped in their preoccupation with God's revelation, they do not often relate what they know to politics, economics, sociology and the like. The theologians know little about the social sciences; the social scientists know little about theology. Each without the other, without interdisciplinary study, without cross-fertilization, is bound to be truncated, bound to remain infantile, and certain to be ineffectual if not misinformed, arriving at conclusions that are sure to be misleading.

Let me illustrate why I believe that all of human life involves theological questions and how the teachers in the major disciplines of all liberal arts curricula are forced to render theological verdicts whether they do so knowingly or at the subconscious level. I refer first of all to economics.

I. ECONOMICS

American economic life until recently has been characterized by individualism and free enterprise. During the nineteenth century these were markedly influenced by social Darwinism, which had its roots in biological evolution and particularly in the principle of the survival of the fittest. The robber barons, some of whom were certainly Christians, accepted the biological concept of the survival of the fittest and applied it with a vengeance to industry. The weak were eliminated, and even as nature appears to be capricious and has no regard to morality per se, so the strong often had little regard for morality as they eliminated the competition by collusion, kickbacks, preferential freight rates, price wars and the like.

But the scene has changed dramatically in the twentieth century. Free enterprise and individualism as they were known in the nineteenth century are dead. So is social Darwinism, whose demise has not included a repudiation of biological evolution on which it rests. And this anachronism alone is worthy of somebody's special research and reflection. America is moving toward socialism and has already embraced the welfare state as an economic reality. One need not go beyond the halls of academia to realize how many university and college professors are admitted socialists. Kenneth Galbraith and Arthur Maier Schlesinger, Jr., are two who come to mind as well as the retired columnist Walter Lippmann, who influenced a generation of academic minds.

One of the consequences of the trend toward socialism has been increased government intervention in all phases of economic life. Richard Nixon, who at least in theory claimed to be a supporter of free enterprise and individualism, by his actions denied these principles. He was the one who opposed wage and price controls. But he was also the one who used them. Kenneth Galbraith predicted two years earlier that he would be forced to do so.

Moreover, America has by its economic policies in the international market built up a balance-of-payments deficit far greater than our ability to pay in gold. Technically the nation faces bankruptcy, and even devaluing the dollar will not finally stave off financial disaster. The crisis at home and abroad has been accelerated by increasing the supply of paper money through the use of the printing press. This has fed inflation with the result that the purchasing power of the dollar has declined, and this in turn has worsened the wage-price spiral that continues unabated.

What has happened economically is dynamically related to the state of mind of the American people. In an increasingly materialistic-oriented culture a dominant characteristic of the American mind is the desire for economic security. And this is true even for many of those who call themselves Christian. Moreover, belief that you can get something for nothing is widespread. This does not necessarily imply that people are stupid. They may be avaricious instead, so long as they are on the receiving end. This belief in something for nothing has been exacerbated by a corollary doctrine: the idea that the state owes every man a living. But the state has no wealth of its own. Therefore it can dispense no largess that it does not secure first from the taxpayer. Thus when I adhere to the view that the state owes me a living, this should really be translated that other people should support me.

If life is of one piece and if the Bible deals with the whole man, then any consistent theology neglects economics at its peril. The Bible does say something about private property, balanced budgets, free enterprise, the work ethic, capital formation, and employer-employee relations. When the principles revealed in Scripture are not practiced, disaster is sure to come. Even when Biblical principles are acknowledged, given the fallen nature of man it is exceedingly difficult to get men to operate in accord with these principles. Moreover unregenerate men, of whom there are many, deny Biblical principles at the outset. The Marxist-socialist states most clearly demonstrate this. They deny the Biblical principle of human freedom and keep men in bondage as they suppress their rights and control their destinies. It is time for evangelicals to speak to the economic realities the world faces and to do it from the Biblical perspective.

II. POLITICAL SCIENCE

Dean Acheson, one-time secretary of state, now deceased, made this statement: "We can see—if we will only open our eyes—that one of the ideas we have discussed must be a guiding principle. Power can be limited only by counterbalancing power. Without that, treaties, international organizations, and international law are of no use whatever. The possessor of unopposed or unopposable power can sweep them aside and make his will law."[2]

George W. Ball, who reviewed Acheson's book, said of this statement: "If that was an unpopular idea when Dean Acheson made his speech sixteen years ago, it is rank heresy today, but for him the truth was not to be found through Gallup Polls or in the fashion pages, but from logic and experience."[3] Whether we like it or not, the balance-of-power concept has governed the relationships of nations from time immemorial. In contemporary life NATO and SEATO were brought into being to offset the power of the Communist bloc just as the Warsaw Pact of the Soviet Union was designed to balance the power of the west.

International relations more frequently than not are amoral rather than moral or immoral. World War II provides a good illustration. It was waged by the democracies against fascist totalitarianism. But the Soviet Union, no less totalitarian than Germany and Italy, fought on the side of the democracies. The morality or immorality of Soviet totalitarianism did not enter the picture. The policies of the democracies and the Soviet Union coincided at this point, and it was in their common interest to fight side by side against the fascists. When the war was won, the common cause that bound the democracies and the Soviet Union together ceased to exist. And from that day to this the balance of power has been operative between the Soviet Union and its erstwhile partners of World War II.

More recently the involvement of the United States in Vietnam divided the nation and produced serious internal convulsions. Curiously enough, people like Jane Fonda, who have no Christian convictions, suddenly developed a particularistic interest in morality. They labeled the war as immoral and obscene even as its defendants argue that it was the fulfillment of treaty obligations and a deterrent to larger Communist aggression. Whoever goes the moralistic route enters the realm of theology immediately. And moralistic approaches have little to commend them unless there are absolute, objective standards by which it can be reasonably determined what is and is not moral. Indeed to say that something is immoral presupposes the moral, and that in turn makes an absolute necessary. If all things are relative then there is no basis for speaking of

[2]D. Acheson, *Fragments of My Fleece.*
[3]G. W. Ball, *Book World* (November 21, 1971) 5.

anything as either right or wrong, and each man's opinion is equally normative. And this leads to nihilism.

The Pakistan-India (1971) war illustrates perfectly the complexities of relating Biblical principles to international affairs. Here a democracy, India, warred against Pakistan, a nondemocratic state. Each of the protagonists was backed by a strong Communist power—the Soviet Union and the People's Republic of China. India, the overt attacker, sought to justify its actions on moral grounds. Pakistan, which had certainly acted less than justly in its relations with East Pakistan, sought the support of the world on the moral ground that India had committed aggression against it. What should the attitude of the Christian be to such a situation, and can he make a decision unless both theological and political science insights are brought to bear?

Developments with reference to the People's Republic of China further illustrate the point. For years American policy had been moralistic, based on the fiction that Taiwan represented all China. Yet it was plain that whatever our opinions about the rightness or wrongness, the goodness or badness of a Communist regime, mainland China was a viable political entity with hundreds of millions of people. And if we could have diplomatic relations with East Germany, which is also a divided situation, and with the Soviet Union, which is a Communist nation, why should we not recognize the People's Republic? Moreover, any expectation that Taiwan might invade the mainland and replace the Communist regime is wishful thinking. In this instance the American position flip-flopped. We recognized Red China and de-recognized Taiwan. If moral standards had anything to do with the decision it is difficult to perceive what they were and how they had any bearing on the action we took. The ambiguities are obvious.

Moreover, Scripture itself poses ambiguities concerning the relation of believers to pagan states and their rulers. Joseph served the Pharaoh in Egypt and did so in good conscience. Daniel served Nebuchadnezzar and his successors and did so also in good conscience. They had divine approval even though their monarchs were wicked men whose decisions were hardly in accord with Biblical principles.

Perhaps the dilemma can be highlighted by the response Lord Carradan gave in reply to questions when he addressed the World Council of Churches in Uppsala in 1968. He was asked why Britain had initiated economic sanctions against Rhodesia but had failed to do so in the case of South Africa. Since the issue of racisim was at stake in both cases, the questioner wanted to know why there was unequal treatment. Lord Carradan expressed himself explicitly. For Britain to initiate sanctions against South Africa, he said, would be to ruin Britain economically. Therefore expediency based wholly on pragmatic considerations caused Britain to forego economic sanctions against South Africa. Morality would have dictated sanctions, but when faced with the consequences Britain decided on what it felt to be the lesser of two evils: It would be more immoral to break Britain economically than it would be to initiate sanctions against South Africa. Thus it may be seen from these illustrations that decisions in international relations are not only political; they are moral as well. Thus there is a real need for political scientists and theologians to sit together to forge out a life and world view in this arena.

III. SOCIOLOGY

We shall now take a look at some matters that generally concern the sociologist and have to do with social relationships. Surely one of the most vexing and as yet still unresolved problems is racism. This of course is a theological as well as a social problem. It is manifested not only in the area having to do with the pigmentation of one's skin. Nor is it, in this form, limited to white racism. There is yellow and brown and black racism as well. There is also national racism, which exists between people of the same skin color but coming from diverse national origins. The Czechs versus the Slavs, the Irish versus the English, the Arabs verses the Israelis, the Poles versus the Germans and the Russians are just a few of them. Then there is a racism based on religion: Catholic versus Protestant, Jew versus Christian, Mohammedan versus Hindu, and even atheist versus theist. And who can deny the racism that exists because of sex distinctions: male versus female? These are certainly moral as well as sociological questions and as such require interaction of sociologists and theologians. Behind racism lies the question: Is racism wrong? And if so, why is it wrong? This is not a sociological question; it is a religious question. Therefore Christian theologians need to inform the sociologists what revealed truth has to say about the question.

Consider also the rapid development of urbanization around the world. Eveywhere man is faced with mammoth ghettos with all the economic maladjustments they bring. Vast hordes of people have been uprooted from the land and the security it brought with it. The urban dweller easily develops an anxiety syndrome because he has nothing to fall back on during times of extensive economic dislocation and mass unemployment. When such contingencies arise, and even when they do not exist, people want safeguards against them, and so they turn to the welfare state. More frequently than not, the promise of bread makes people (and that means us too) willing to suffer the curtailment or loss of their freedoms for this form of security.

May it not be that the social situation is responsible in a large measure for the cop-out syndrome that has affected numbers of our younger generation and older ones too? Faced with massive contemporary problems that seem overwhelming and for which there seem to be no adequate answers, withdrawal is an appealing alternative. In a materialistic culture that emphasizes gadgetry, those who do not have enough money to buy them or who do not want them use the cop-out technique.

Copping out is not a new response. It has existed from time immemorial, although current conditions make it especially attractive. David the warrior king of Israel has left us a record of his own desire to cop out. In Psalm 55 he records this experience. He said: "My heart is in anguish within me, the terrors of death have fallen upon me. Fear and trembling come upon me, and horror overwhelms me. And I say, 'O that I had wings like a dove! I would fly away and be at rest; yea, I would wander afar, I would lodge in the wilderness, I would haste to find me a shelter from the raging wind and tempest'" (vv 4-8). Disenchantment, or copping out, has theological implications.

Social justice is one of the torturing questions facing society today. To talk of justice is to assume the existence of some standard outside man that has invariable certitude. If this were not true then justice would be ephemeral, for when each man determines for himself what justice is then it would vary from one to another and have no binding effect on anyone except the individual who made the decision. It is here that situation ethics displays its barrenness. Since only the individual in the existential moment can make the decision and since nothing is prohibited, then nothing is ultimately forbidden. Whichever road a man takes, however, involves theological considerations. Thus the sociologist needs the services of the theologian even as the theologian needs the services of the sociologist in order to understand the range of the problems and to view the problems from a sociologist's as well as a theologian's perspective. Of one thing we can be sure: Life is of one piece, and sociology does not exist in a theological vacuum whether the sociologists sense it or not.

IV. Ethics

This brings us to the ethical dimensions of man's existence. Even those cultures that profess to be atheistic, such as the Soviet Union and the People's Republic of China, cannot escape involvement in this area of life. It was James Reston of the *New York Times* who, on his return from Red China, stated that its ethical precepts are far higher than those of the United States and indeed are close to America's former Puritanism. It was C. S. Lewis in his thoughtful and perceptive book *The Abolition of Man* who quoted Aristotle as saying that the purpose of education is to teach youth what they ought to do. But this is impossible unless there are ethical oughts. Lewis argues that nature itself, irrespective of one's specific religious attachment, proclaims ethical absolutes that have found common consent and expression in all religions and, it might be added in the case of Red China, in a country with no religion.

The acceptance of certain forms of conduct in no way validates these actions unless they are consonant with the ethical oughts to which men and history bear witness and which time has shown reinforces the fabric of society and furthers legitimate relationships among men. In America today there is a great struggle being waged to make forms of conduct socially acceptable that have heretofore been regarded as illicit. Thus fornication, adultery, pornography, homosexuality and abortion are advocated and practiced by at least a significant minority of the population, a minority determined to make these things licit in law and acceptable even to people who do not choose to practice them.

Two specific cases are presented here, not with the view to passing judgment in either instance but to illustrate the need for ethicists and theologians to work together to demonstrate that conscience in and of itself is no reliable guide. Indeed multitudes of people commit heinous acts in good conscience with no particular thought that what they have done is in any sense immoral.

The first case has to do with Desi Arnaz, Jr. He was described as the all-American boy, a tennis-playing athlete, open by nature, outgoing and pleasant. He wore a crucifix around his neck and spent much of his spare time reading. At eighteen his illegitimate son was born. He said, "I love him just as I love his mother. But the relationship between Patty and me has altered. Our passion is not as tempestuous as it once was. Because she is an honest and decent and forthright girl, Patty has told me only a few days ago that she has now fallen in love with some other lucky young man and plans to marry him. . . . Naturally my male vanity is a trifle shattered that she has fallen out of love with me and in love with someone else. But at the ripe old age of eighteen I feel sure I will be able to overcome it." His father wrote him a man-to-man letter in 1969 in which he said, "Persevere. Keep swinging. And don't forget that the Man upstairs is always there, and all of us need His help."[4] It is not necessary to mention all of the specific ethical issues raised by this illustration but this much is clear: Neither Desi nor his father have the foggiest notion of a holy, transcendent God of righteousness, justice, wrath or judgment. For them, he is the Man, not the God, upstairs—anthropomorphized and brought down to man's level. There is no awareness that he who performs the deed shall eat the fruit of it. Rather it illustrates a modern notion of God as a glorified Santa Claus who exists to be used by man for his pleasure.

The second illustration is a question-and-answer situation. The writer from Dayton, Ohio, asked the following question and received the answer:

> Q: I just read Norman Mailer's book, "The Prisoner of Sex" and I am dying to know who he is talking about when he says he "captured the mistress of a Potentate of 'Time' (magazine)." Who is he talking about?

[4] *Parade* magazine, October 17, 1971.

A: Henry Luce—who else? Mr. Luce brought the lady, then in her early twenties, to New York from a romantic idyll in Europe and put her to work in his magazine empire. At one point, a Luce associate asked the lady if she would please return to her native England because circulating rumors of the liaison were "threatening Henry's moral leadership of America." About this time Mailer stepped in and saved Henry from himself. Mailer married Lady Jean Campbell, granddaughter of the press tycoon, Lord Beaverbrook, and fathered one child by her. They are now divorced but still fond of one another.[5]

One need not elaborate on this illustration either, except to ask whether there is any vital connection between the profession a man makes and his conduct. Both illustrations open the door wide to an understanding of relativistic ethics in our day as well as to the question of whether what one says he does in good conscience is a reliable guide. It was John Knox who when Queen Mary objected to what he said by claiming that her conscience said it was not so replied that conscience needs to be educated, and that from the Word of God. The ethicist has need of the theologian even as the theologian needs to understand and grapple with the problems faced by the ethicist.

V. PHILOSOPHY

It would be imprudent not to mention the realm of philosophy, which plays a vital role in determining what the life and world view of men will be. Even those who have never studied philsophy have been influenced by it, and every painter, writer, musician and movie producer in one way or another makes use of philosophy's viewpoints whether he has studied it or not. The philosophers have made available to men a large variety of options across the years. Space makes it impossible to mention all of the options or even to discuss more than one or two of them. Each of us is familiar with logical positivism, empiricism, agnosticism, secularism and humanism. I would like to say a word about two options that have captured the minds and the allegiances of many people during the course of this century. I refer to dialectical materialism and atheistic existentialism.

Dialectical materialism is beset by two basic errors that disqualify it for serious consideration by theologians and also by philosophers. It presupposes that matter, not spirit, lies behind all reality—i.e., the material rather than the nonmaterial. If matter is basic then nothing precedes it, including God. Materialism is therefore atheistic. It is not and cannot be agnostic, for that would then leave open the possibility of a nonmaterial postulate. But once having settled on materialism it must be atheistic. Its second presupposition has to do with the dialectic, and here it supposes the unity of opposites. This is expressed in the concept of thesis, antithesis and

[5]"The Gossip Column," *Washington Post*, September 26, 1971.

synthesis. The antithesis is the opposite of the thesis, and from the interaction of opposites a new synthesis comes into being. This view destroys the traditional law of antithesis on which logic and philosophy have relied for centuries. But here it is that philosophy as it devises an apologetic needs the theologian who affirms the notion of God's self-revelation in Scripture. And the theologian needs the interaction of the philosopher to teach him logic, orderly processes of thinking and objective detachment.

Atheistic existentialism goes beyond dialectical materialism, for it declares that life is meaningless. Jean-Paul Sartre said that "there is no human nature, since there is no God to conceive it. Not only is man what he conceives himself to be, but he is also only what he wills himself to be after his thrust toward existence. . . . Man is nothing else but what he makes himself." So also Joseph Wood Krutch, former Columbia University professor, said, "We know that man is only an animal, and that there is no purpose for him in the universe."

In existential painting it makes no difference which way you turn the canvas. The message comes through clear and sharp. "Life has no meaning." In music John Cage put together a series of notes selected at random. He calls his method "purposeful purposelessness." Translated it says that "there is no meaning to life." In the theatre Bergman produces the film "The Ritual," of which *Time* magazine said, "Reality is distorted and logic becomes madness." Of the movie "Stolen Kisses" it was said that the hero "doesn't know where he's going and couldn't aim himself in the right direction if he did." For life has neither rhyme nor reason.

Historians know that the Renaissance and the Enlightenment changed the course of western culture. Before that era men acknowledged the supremacy of the Judeo-Christian faith as the foundation for all thought and learning. This presupposition was abandoned, and in its place the autonomy of man and his supremacy over nature and over God took shape. Across the years secular humanism has come to dominate the landscape to such a degree that the Christian Church has itself been secularized in large measure, and the notion that the Bible is the foundation for a world and life view has lost credence. In the process the social sciences have lost their moorings in Christian tradition and have come to rest on pragmatic and relativistic foundations. As a result the idea espoused by Jonathan Edwards that all art and all science would find their center and meaning in theology has been discarded even in practice by those who may still pay lip service to it.

A theological "dark age" has come upon us in the sense that the dominant consensus is anti-Biblical and pro-humanist. The great centers of learning neither care about nor use the Bible in their thinking and teaching. The world and life views they articulate, as a result of this failure, are sterile and offer no hope for man in the life to come. And if the revelation of God is regarded seriously it can be affirmed that any world and life view divorced from Scripture offers no enduring hope in this life either. Thus the destinies of men and nations in the here and now are inexorably bound to the presuppositions from which they operate. For the Christian to be a Christian requires that he seek to do two things: (1) He must call men back to Scripture as the only source from which a world and life view that has true meaning and cosmic usefulness can be developed; and (2) he must relate Scripture to life and apply its principles to the social sciences until they become a true image of God's revelation and are used by men in society for their well-being. Anything short of these two objectives spells decline and decay and must result in disaster in the long run.

Symbolism, Modeling and Theology

William A. Dyrness

A call to the re-evaluation of symbolism in theology from one point of view seems presumptuous. From the very beginning theology has made use of symbols. Originally a "symbol" (from the Greek *syn-ballein*) was two parts of a ring or staff brought together to identify a guest or messenger. From this it came to have the meaning of treaty and, in the Church, the common profession of faith (the "symbols"), and finally the objects and acts in which this faith was expressed.[1] Traditionally then symbolism involved two distinct things understood together, and thus the reference of a symbol was largely denotative. Two developments have recently initiated a rethinking of the nature and role of symbols in theology.

On the one hand it is becoming increasingly obvious that traditional symbols do not communicate with their former force. The Church is only one of the modern institutions finding old patterns of ritual and order losing their hold on people. As Gilbert Cope notes: "It is characteristic of many ancient symbols that their immediate impact is diminished today, and it also seems to be the case that long verbal explanation does not restore their psychic energy for a sophisticated people."[2] Not that the modern age is bereft of symbols; quite the reverse. But their purveyors are usually the technicians rather than the theologians.

On the other hand anthropologists have suggested that symbols are far more important to culture than we had imagined. Symbols are not isolated places and objects but sense-giving patterns that permeate our whole social life. Then too the relationship between symbol and reality is much more complex than traditional theories of symbolism suggested. Symbols and culture stand in a reciprocal relation to each other.

The theologian must obviously be intensely interested in both these developments. While we intend to say nothing further about the death of symbols, in this paper we will survey current discussion in the social sciences on the function of symbols and seek to assess this discussion from a theological point of view. It may well be that such a study will give a clue

[1]J. Splett, "Symbol," *Encyclopedia of Theology* (ed. K. Rahner; New York: Seabury, 1975) 1654-55. J. N. D. Kelly discusses the debate over the meaning of *synbolon* in *Early Christian Creeds* (London: Longmans, Green, 1950) 52-61.

[2]G. Cope, *Christianity and the Visual Arts* (London: Faith Press, 1964) 73.

as to why symbols die and offer suggestions to the theologian-communicator for regaining the symbolic vitality that is the birthright of theology. It should be clear from the beginning that we are working on the level of the understanding and communication of Christian truth. It is not a question of theology looking to social science as a source of dogmatic material or even for a confirmation of revelation. Rather we seek to gain an understanding of how knowledge is constructed and thus of what actually takes place in the doing of theology.

Behind the use of symbolism in theology, Hans-Georg Gadamer asserts, lies the assumption that "it is not possible to know the divine in any other way than by starting from the world of the sense."[3] As a mediating agent the symbol or icon was given a privileged position in the history of the Church. This position, it is true, did not always go unchallenged. During the eighth and ninth centuries the Eastern and Western churches were engaged in bitter debates over the place of images in worship. At the Reformation the Swiss reformers again challenged the importance of visible symbols by insisting that no finite being can communicate infinite reality. Zwingli for example banned images from the churches as turning man's mind from God. For him the prime symbol of unbelief was the visible image.[4] On the linguistic and philosophical level it was Immanuel Kant who in 1790 first challenged the unique status of symbols. Kant recognized that in an aesthetic experience we are not concerned with the object but with the representation of that object "by means of analogy." In what he called symbolic representation, a concept is not presented directly but only indirectly in "which the expression does not contain the proper schema for the concept but merely a symbol for reflection."[5] Thus in calling attention to the symbolic way in which language can function he opened the way to a more generalized understanding of symbol. What is particularly important to note is that for Kant symbols tied together conceptual levels and not, as previously, metaphysical levels. Significantly, he commented in this connection, these things need further investigation, which he was not able to give them.

One in Kant's own tradition to follow up this suggestion was Ernst Cassirer. For our purposes two areas of Cassirer's philosophy of symbolic forms call for comment. Within the framework of idealism Cassirer first of all suggested that man creates his world through the symbols he uses. Kant

---

[3]H. Gadamer, *Truth and Method* (New York: Seabury, 1975) 66.

[4]See C. Garside, *Zwingli and the Arts* (New Haven: Yale University, 1966).

[5]I. Kant, *Critique of Judgment* (trans. Bernard), par. 59, p. 250. Cf. Gadamer, *Truth*, 67: "This concept of symbolic representation is one of the most brilliant results of Kantian thought. He thus does justice to the theological truth that had found its scholastic form in the *analogi entis* and keeps human concepts separate from God."

had believed that our knowing presupposes certain forms and categories of the mind. Cassirer with his background in the study of myth and depth psychology felt it was rather a people's whole language and symbol system (which he took to be inseparable) that determines what the world will be.[6] Images and signs in the second place are not merely reflections of (another) reality. They are themselves what give shape to that reality. They are instruments of cognition. Knowledge is a result of the total process of understanding. Cassirer notes: "Only within these categories which are required to constitute its form can it [knowledge] be described at all." A sign or symbol is not the accidental cloak of a thing "but its necessary and essential organ."[7] Symbols are not only vehicles by which content is conveyed but the arena in which this content is elaborated.

Anthropologists about this time began to understand cultures similarly as symbolic systems. The so-called structuralist anthropologists, following earlier leads in de Saussure and Freud, observed that society provides people with a ready-made order in terms of which they must live. These ready-made orders or, as they are sometimes called, "models" of and for experience, we may call a society's culture. Claude Lévi-Strauss developed a highly articulated system of analyzing cultures on the principle of binary oppositions as a means of locating symbolic systems.[8]

Significantly, structuralism had first emerged as a theory of linguistics. Older linguists had approached language atomistically, wherein each word was taken to stand for something. This led early in this century to Bertrand Russell's famous attempt to create an ideal emotion-free language. Literary critics (such as I. A. Richards) soon pointed out that it was the use of words (not the words themselves) that was emotive and that such discourse —especially in poetry—could actually illumine reality in an indirect ("symbolic") way. On the one hand structuralists elaborated the view that the meaning of the word is a function of the relationships it sustains with other words in a particular "field" or lexical system and cannot be defined outside of these relationships.[9] On the other hand philosophers, influenced by the later Heidegger, began to discuss the ability of symbolic language to uncover underlying structures of human experience. Paul Ricoeur, for

[6]M. C. Beardsley, *Aesthetics: From Classical Greece to the Present* (New York: Macmillan, 1966) 348-349.

[7]E. Cassirer, *Philosophy of Symbolic Forms* (Eng. trans; New Haven: Yale University Press, 1953-), 1. 76, 86.

[8]C. Lévi-Strauss, *The Raw and the Cooked* (trans. J. Weightman; New York: Harper, 1969). For a concise summary of structuralism see H. W. Scheffler, "Structuralism in Anthropology," *Structuralism* (ed. J. Ehrmann; New York: Doubleday, 1970) 56-79.

[9]See J. Lyons, "The Meaning of Meaning," *Times Literary Supplement* (London; July 23, 1970) 796.

example, believes that metaphor stands in a privileged place in the structure of language and thus can uncover basic structures of human experience.[10]

Anthropologists working within a structuralist framework point out that the systematic interrelationship characteristic of language extends to the whole of culture. In a recent discussion of this in the context of communication Edmund Leach argues:

> *All* the various non-verbal dimensions of culture, such as styles in clothing, village lay-out, architecture, furniture, food, cooking, music, physical gestures, postural attitudes and so on are organized in patterned sets so as to incorporate coded information in a manner analogous to the sounds and words and sentences of a natural language.[11]

Clifford Geertz has been one of the most important anthropologists to study religion from this structural point of view. Religion, he insists, is really a cultural system—that is, religion is a set of symbols (acts, objects or events that are vehicles for a conception) that serves to build up and retain significant moods and motivations in a society. This system expresses and shapes the general order of existence in such a way that it appears of indubitable reality and helps make everyday life graspable.[12]

It is clear from this that structuralists analyze cultural facts in such a way as to discover the rules and codes of a society. While such analysis is often helpful, its dangers have not gone unnoticed. Critics point out that the implicit rationalism in structuralism sometimes forces the data to fit its schema. Does every motion or object stand in some symmetrical relation to some other? Recently an attempt has been made from within the structuralist framework to define a theory of symbolism that avoids this criticism. Dan Sperber argues that symbolic interpretation is not a matter of decoding but rather an improvisation based on implicit knowledge.[13] He believes that symbolism has for too long been hampered by semiological interpretation —i.e., one that seeks to explain symbolism as a language-like code. He calls symbolism a cognitive rather than a semiological system. The human symbolic mechanism, he believes, is a kind of "handyman" (*bricoleur*) of the mind that seeks to "establish by its own means the relevance of the defective representation" (p. 113). He discusses the symbolic function of certain smells as an illustration. Smells set up direct links between the individual's inward state and nature observed. While dependent on con-

[10]P. Ricoeur, *The Rule of Metaphor* (trans. R. Uzerny; Toronto: University Press, 1977) 41.

[11]E. Leach, *Culture and Communication: The Logic by Which Symbols are Connected* (Cambridge: University Press, 1976) 10 (italics his).

[12]See C. Geertz, "Religion as a Cultural System," *Reader in Comparative Religion* (ed. W. A. Lessa and E. Z. Vogt; New York: Harper, 1972) 167-178.

[13]D. Sperber, *Rethinking Symbolism* (Cambridge: University Press, 1975) xi.

ceptualization this link cannot be verbalized (p. 118). As a function of a person's shared conceptual (though not verbalizable) orientation to the world, symbolic response can in this way determine parallel "evocational fields" while allowing the individual freedom of response and determination on the rational level. Sperber summarizes: "Cultural symbolism creates a community of interest but not of opinion" (p. 137). So language and gesture, as well as more traditional art objects and icons, all have a symbolic function to play. But Sperber implies that symbolism may operate at yet another level, the more comprehensive level of basic orientation, what he calls "interest."

We will return to this further on, but first we pause briefly to take note additionally of parallel discussions in recent sociology, what is called the sociology of knowledge. Peter Berger and Thomas Luckmann in a programmatic essay broadened the idea of knowledge in a society.[14] Generally a person's relation to his environment is characterized by unspecific drives (compare Geertz' "mood" and Sperber's "interest") and world-openness. "The process of becoming man takes place in an interrelationship with an environment" (p. 48). There is thus a reciprocal relationship between man and his social setting. By a process Berger and Luckmann refer to as the externalization, habitualization and then internalization of this relationship man builds his world "symbolically." Institutions grow out of typified habitualization and rest on the internalized knowledge of all concerned. Most interesting for the theologian is the discussion of the process of legitimation of social worlds. They see this taking place on four (symbolic) levels (pp. 94-97). The first consists in linguistic objectification of experience (calling someone "cousin" legitimates immediately certain conduct). The second level contains rudimentary theories like those found in parables and maxims. The third level contains more explicit theories (such as an economic theory of cousinhood) explained by those commissioned to pass down traditions. Finally a society builds "symbolic universes" that "integrate different provinces of meaning and encompass the institutional order in a symbolic totality" (p. 95).[15] In this way a people creates a whole world that is a social product with a history. Moreover, the reality of this world must be maintained (as it has been developed) through time and internalized by each member who will find his or her identity in that society.

---

[14]P. Berger and T. Luckmann, *The Social Construction of Reality: A Treatise in the Sociology of Knowledge* (New York: Doubleday, 1967) 14.

[15]The idea of religion as a symbolic construct can be traced to Emile Durkheim: "When a certain number of sacred things sustain relations of co-ordination or subordination with each other in such a way as to form a system having a certain unity, but which is not comprised within any other system of the same sort, the totality of these beliefs and their corresponding rites constitute a religion." *The Elementary Forms of the Religious Life* (New York: Free Press, 1965) 56.

Even in our brief survey we have come upon significant insights into the way people "construct" their worlds. The relationship between the person and his world is not a fixed one. He seeks symbolically—that is, by objects that bring together elements in his world—to orient himself in his environment, and in turn he is shaped by the structure that he has made. Religions extend the range of meaning, giving signs to the whole of life, and provide a world in which the person is comfortable. Symbolism (better, symbolisms) function(s) on many levels, from pre-theoretical to complex rational formulations, all of which together makes it possible to understand the world.

Our account of these things has of necessity been sketchy, and we have passed over many of the problems involved. But before going further we must seek to face at least the most serious of these. We noted at the outset that we are working on the level of understanding and communication of reality. In the social sciences then we are interested in the descriptive characterization of human society. We assume that certain techniques and insights can be used while others are resisted. We accept, for example, that one can take a functional perspective toward religion without reducing religion to its function. But it is just here that we must admit a difficulty. Behind these developments lies a particular way of looking at reality. One does not have to read far to feel the hand of Immanuel Kant in these discussions. We have already noticed his part in the historical development, and so we are not surprised to find the following confession by Lévi-Strauss:

> What we are attempting to do is well described in Paul Ricoeur's qualification of our effort as "Kantianism without a transcendental subject." We see no indication of a lacuna in this restriction, instead we see the inevitable consequence, on the philosophical level, of the ethnographic perspective we have chosen.[16]

Specifically Kant's influence is to be seen in the implication of structuralism that symbols are ultimately self-referential. A symbolic system constructs a world. It does not refer to something outside itself. A religious system then—to use Frege's distinction—has sense but not reference. In Kantian language there is no way from the phenomena to the noumena. We obviously cannot assess Kant's contribution to modern thought here. But we may suggest that while the relationship between man and his world is a dynamic one, there is no reason to deny, and much reason to affirm, that

---

[16]C. Lévi-Strauss, "Ouverture le Cru et le cuit," *Structuralism* (ed. Ehrmann) 45. Ricoeur had called Lévi-Strauss' transcendental more "a Kantian unconscious than a Freudian; a categorical unifying consciousness." *Archivo di Filosofia* 1-2 (Roma, 1963) 9, 24.

the structures of our understanding may conform to reality as it is. Especially is this true if we consider our symbolic framework as a hypothetical perspective that can be confirmed and/or corrected by our further involvement with the world. As T. F. Torrance notes, one can agree that it is the a priori structures of our consciousness that make knowledge possible without claiming that "the conformity of the object to the mind of the knowing subject is attributed to our power of knowing or is predicated of our human nature."[17] As in current discussions of hermeneutics (which are not unrelated to the discussion we have been following), it is possible to learn from the debate without accepting the neo-Kantian metaphysics with which proponents are sometimes allied.

A second equally pressing problem is that of terminology. Words like "symbol" and "metaphor" are used in many senses in these discussions. There is often less unanimity than we might have implied. Where can one find a consensus? Is anything to be gained by reaching the final level, where the whole universe is a symbolic construction? If everything is symbol, then perhaps nothing is particularly symbolic. These are good questions, and they deserve to be answered. We have neglected definitions so far—and we will postpone the attempt even longer—because it is our view that definitions must come at the end of the survey rather than the beginning. We are in the midst of a fundamental shift in our conception of knowledge (what Thomas Kuhn has called our acute methodological crisis), a shift in which the discussions we have reviewed have played and will continue to play a fundamental role. The best we can hope for is to discern some basic directions and take our reading from these. It is our view that these directions can be charted and offer important help to theologians.

What then are the areas where the view of symbolism being developed today may be of interest for theology? We limit ourselves to three statements that will prove important to later discussion. Many social scientists today have come to view men and women as world-open symbolizing creatures. People are not biologically fixed but rather define themselves socially by explicit and implicit understandings about their world and those around them. Their unique capacity to make symbols of their "understandings" gives their world its shape. Moreover, their setting out and experiencing of symbols is the actualization of their freedom. A person forms his world as a conversation between himself and his environment. A person first internalizes his social world and then contributes as well to its structure and maintenance by his cooperation. Or he discovers for himself another "world" with another structure and new legitimations. Implicit to this line of thinking is assumed structural correspondence between a

[17]T. F. Torrance, *Theological Science* (Oxford: University Press, 1968) 89. Torrance goes on to say: "It is precisely because Kant did do this that the temptation to discount the thing-in-itself as a mythical projection was so strong."

person's mind and the objective world we referred to a moment ago.[18] But we do not mean to imply that this view is necessarily the anthropological statement of Hegel's idea of the concept exteriorizing itself or of Karl Rahner's idea of real symbol (though idealist theologians have been quick to see it as such). Human symbolism is not able to penetrate to another (divine) level of being. It is rather the way man orients himself within his creaturely level. Symbolism brings together areas of experience but has no special capacity to reveal divine dimensions of reality.[19]

Secondly, what we call our "world" or culture must be understood as a single unified whole. Each part, object or gesture has its part, however humble, to play in the functioning of the whole. As Sheldon Hodelman says, "the reality of the object consists in the full texture of all its relationships with its environment."[20] A symbolic object—for example, a ritual or a sacred text—must obviously be interpreted in its context. It must be seen in terms of the values that produced it and the meaning it holds for members of that society. But the reverse is true as well: A society can also be interpreted by its symbols. Both the whole and the part play a symbolic role.

Finally, this whole discussion points up the role of nontheoretical (not to say nonrational) factors in world construction, leading to the suggestion of Sperber that symbolism involves evocation in the knowing process. What is fundamental for the person is not his rational understanding alone but rather his whole world orientation in which ritual/gesture and "interest" play a formative role. Mary Douglas has admitted that

[18]Cf. P. Ricoeur: "In the sacred universe the capacity to speak is founded on the capacity of the cosmos to signify." *Symbolisme* (ed. J. E. Ménard; Strasbourg: University Press, 1975) 155. The idea of "analogy" has of course been important in the history of theology. Battista Mondin believes that the analogy of intrinsic attribution—that is, the likeness between the creature and God based on the similarity of cause and effect—is the most adequate tool for the interpretation of the God-creature relationship. *The Principle of Analogy in Protestant and Catholic Theology* (The Hague: Martinus Nijhoff, 1968) 100-102. Though these discussions overlap, our proper concern in this paper is not the analogy between God and the creature but between man and his world.

[19]It was the error of romanticism—seen most clearly in Schelling's idea that aesthetic intuition is metaphysically constitutive—to tie symbolism and revelation together. The danger is displayed clearly in J. R. Barth, *The Symbolic Imagination: Coleridge and the Romantic Tradition* (Princeton: University Press, 1977). For Coleridge (and Wordsworth) symbol becomes "the vehicle for the expression of . . . the sacred depths of the self" (p. 142). The most important modern exponent of this view is of course Paul Tillich, who ties his important discussion of symbolism explicitly to the revelation of divine being. *Systematic Theology* (Chicago: University Press, 1951), 1. 106 ff.

[20]S. Hodelman, "Structural Analysis in Art and Anthropology," *Structuralism* (ed. Ehrmann) 81.

implicitly I find myself returning to Robertson Smith's idea that rites are prior and myths are secondary in the study of religion. For it would seem that recent shifts in Christian doctrine which are taking place in the long theological debates since the Reformation are attempts to bring intellectual positions into line with deeply imprinted, personal attitudes to ritualism.[21]

Such an attitude fits well with the awakening understanding of the relationships between fact and theory (as in Thomas Kuhn) and between myth and reality. Philip Wheelwright has said:

Myth . . . is not in the first instance a fiction imposed on one's already given world, but it is a way of apprehending that world. Genuine myth is a matter of perspective first, invention second.[22]

Theologians also have spoken of fundamental pre-theoretical orientations, called variously faith commitments or presuppositions. Perhaps, we will argue, a dialogue at this point with the social sciences may enlarge our understanding of how such positions are formed and how they function in the doing of theology.

In turning to the role of symbolism in theology we must first face the question of definition. What is a symbol? We may call a symbol any meaning-giving act, object or event that brings together elements of experience. Any object may serve in a symbolic way provided that it is made to stand out in contrast to its setting or brought to focus by a design so that we may dwell on it.[23] Moreover, this "standing out" serves to illuminate the setting. In short, a symbol is a means to our conceptual orientation to the world. Then too symbols function on various levels. Language itself is of course a symbolic system, but the symbolism we speak of in theology involves the special use of language in connection with other (often nontheoretical) factors. The various levels of symbolic activity that we will describe are tied together by a certain family resemblance and by their ambition to give varying expression to a single theological and religious reality.

Models then are symbols that function on a higher level of generality. They suggest a correspondence between a set of parallels rather than between one thing and another.[24] Models have been classified in various ways. Frederick Ferré analyzes models by type (picturable or theoretical),

[21]M. Douglas, *Natural Symbols* (London, 1970) 11.

[22]P. Wheelwright, *The Burning Fountain: A Study in the Language of Symbolism* (Bloomington: Indiana University, 1954) 150.

[23]Compare Berger and Luckmann's similar definition: "Any significant theme that . . . spans spheres of reality" (*Social*, 40) and M. Beardsley, *Aesthetics* (New York: Harcourt, Brace & World, 1958) 292.

[24]Cf. P. Toon, "Models and the Development of Dogma," *Reformed Journal* (July-August 1974) 19.

by scope (whether they refer only to individuals or groups) and by status (how do they correspond to reality?). But all of them link divergent domains of understandings "to make sense of observations."[25] Similarly Max Black distinguishes scale models (where proportions correspond), analogue models (where structures correspond though the medium is changed) and theoretical models (hypothetical models that serve a heuristic function). In brief, models serve as a kind of metaphor. Black says of this way of thinking: "Metaphorical thought is a distinctive mode of achieving insight, not to be conceived as an ornamental substitute for plain thought."[26]

We will see presently that models function on various levels in theology. Some are essentially picturable, though picturability is not essential to a model so long as inferences can be drawn. In every case the more inclusive truth "shows through" the simpler or more immediately recognizable surface: In Scripture God is seen in the good shepherd or in the forgiving father of the parable. Our thesis is that because of the objective analogy between man and nature and the consistency of God's purposes in history it is possible to recast or re-enact Biblical materials both as a means of understanding and orientation and also as a way of allowing the reality of Scripture to show itself. Here there is a parallel with the way a scientist works. Max Black points out that scientists often "worked not *by* analogy, but *through* and by means of an underlying analogy."[27] The correspondence was not invented. It was actually there. In allowing the scientist to perceive it, the metaphor simply uncovered it.

In theology the fundamental model or basic orientation precedes (and informs) all theoretical formulation. Our basic model is the root of our religious life, wherein our commitment to Christ directs and informs our world-building. We may formulate this model variously in basic statements: The Lord is my Shepherd, or God is our Father. In his helpful article, F. Ferré distinguished between model and theory in theological and scientific procedure. The "model" is the formal understanding and the theory is the abstract formulation. He believes that in theology the model is primary and the theory is secondary but entailed (while in science it is the reverse). For it is in the models rather than the abstract theory, he insists, that all intelligible theological ideas are rooted.[28] We might illustrate this point by reference to OT theology. In a pioneering series of articles on law and covenant, G. E. Mendenhall pointed out the distinction in legal theory

---

[25]F. Ferré, "Mapping the Logic of Models in Science and Theology," *Religion and Philosophy* (ed. J. Gill; Minneapolis: Burgess, 1968) 270-276.

[26]M. Black, *Models and Metaphors* (Ithaca: Cornell University, 1962) 237.

[27]Ibid., p. 229 (italics his).

[28]Ferré, "Mapping," 284-285. He claims that in science models are changed more often than theory, while in theology, though theory can change, models do not.

between policy and procedures.[29] In our terms the policy is the model, the legal basis of the community: Israel's self-understanding as a covenant community. The procedures—legal theory—were outlined in the law and were occasionally emended or elaborated (as for example during the exile or the intertestamental period). But the policy remained the same.

Obviously theology cannot dispense with such models. As Ferré argues:

> Even the theologian's technical vocabulary is not so independent of his model as he might think. Is "God's transcendence" under discussion? An analyst need not look far before he finds the thinly disguised spatial metaphor that underlies the term. Everywhere the model peeps through, and it is more difficult than many realize to be rid of it and still to *say the same thing* that was intended before. "Transcendent? That means above the universe. Above? Well, not really above, but *beyond*. Beyond? No, not in space—but simply not exclusively in the universe. *In* . . . ?"[30]

The reason for this of course is that we are creatures of space and time, and God has dealt with us in historical terms. But unless one sees this fact as a handicap, one cannot fault theology for speaking in spatial and temporal metaphors.

Secondly, for the theologian the data of revelation provide a system of models that include God's activity and theoretical elaboration of that activity, both policy and procedure. In the most inclusive model this includes all of nature, man and God in what Ferré calls the key metaphysical model.[31] At the other end of the spectrum there are proverbs and parables that image the reality of God's presence and working. Ferré notes that parables are of the form: "Here is how you may think about it, if you like . . . ; but here is how it really is. . . ."[32] Recent studies on the parables in fact see them as not only illustrating the kingdom of God but as presenting *in nuce* Jesus' own self-understanding.

In between these levels are a series of images shaped jointly by the Holy Spirit and cultural/personal forces. These of course do not present one symbolic world but many. There is the Hebrew world of the kings and their self-confident and majestic cult where God is enthroned as King.

---

[29]G. E. Mendenhall, "Ancient Oriental and Biblical Law," *BA* (1954) 26 ff.

[30]Ferré, "Mapping," 284 (italics his). D. F. Wells makes a similar point in his fine book *The Search for Salvation* (Downers Grove: InterVarsity, 1978) 166-169. Discussions with Wells have proven of great value in the preparation of this paper.

[31]Ferré, "Mapping," 282. This model is of such a scope that it has been accused of being unfalsifiable. M. Black notes that its breadth may result in the model's becoming a "self-certifying myth" (*Models*, 242). But B. Mitchell has argued that a cumulative case may be made for such a model just as for any large paradigm. *The Justification of Religious Belief* (New York: Seabury, 1973), Part 2.

[32]Ferré, "Mapping," 283.

There is the picture of Jesus that Mark draws for poor and perhaps suffering Christians in Rome, a Savior who understood their temptations and who himself shared their humiliation and suffering. There is the Greek world of Hebrews, perhaps Alexandria, where the influence of Greek philosophy and its metaphysics is evident and Jesus is the Mediator who passed through the heavens. There is the Jesus of John who sets the Lord's ministry as a reflection of the liturgy of the early Church (perhaps in Ephesus) and its symbols, the wine (vine), the bread, the water.[33] These give us a richness of imagery that together shows the reality that permeates them. If we study these with patience and in dependence on the Holy Spirit they converge, and immersed in their power we have a multitude of counselors (models) in which Scripture tells us there is much wisdom. The uniqueness of these models lies in the fact that their unique historical truth conveys the redemptive reality of God's self-revelation. Our re-enacting and retelling then can become vehicles of God's presence, not by virtue of their symbolic character but through their congruence with the Biblical model(s) —i.e., only as it is based upon the redemption God brought about in Israel and Christ.

We can go even further: The central model can be expressed as the historical movement of God, which not only reflects his love but actually becomes itself what it shows in image. T. F. Torrance describes this central model:

> In Jesus Christ the discrepancy between theological statements and the reality to which they refer has been overcome, and in him that relation between human statements and the objective facts to which they refer, which cannot be put into words, nevertheless shows itself.[34]

Reference to this symbolic movement indicates how Biblical imagery reaches out to embrace the whole of man's history. As Pierre Prigent sums up:

> In this way the history of the world up until the end finds in the death and resurrection of Christ (symbolized by the exodus, passover and creation) its final meaning, its real contents.[35]

[33]P. Prigent says of John, "The history of Jesus has become a symbol." "Le symbole dans le Nouveau Testament," *Symbolisme* (ed. Ménard) 108.

[34]Torrance, *Theological*, 186. His tendency to identify this showing forth only with Christ, rather than to see it in an analogous way throughout Biblical (and even Church) history, leads Torrance to call theological formulations tools rather than pictures. These then can be dispensed with when they have gotten us to Christ (p. 19). Now there is no doubt that our personal experience with Christ goes beyond our conceptual images. But insofar as we speak at all of knowledge (even of personal knowledge) it is hard to see how we can avoid mental conceptions.

[35]Prigent, "Le symbole," 110. Though he is speaking of John his words apply to the whole of Scripture. The fact that these Biblical images present the reality they

Although the further ramifications for theological method lie beyond our scope, it is worth noting the promise offered by the model of "dramatic movement." Here dramatic activity and history would become guiding images in theology, replacing more static conceptual patterns. Significantly it has been Latin American theologians who have pointed this out to us. Church historian Enrique Dussell notes that Jesus and the prophets were working with a very different logical process from our own. They "found the meaning and import of the present movement in the past history of their people." Where the Hebrews found meaning in history, the Greeks found it in the idea and so were able to get beyond the anecdotal in history and ratiocination in theology.[36]

We have said that our part is to recast and re-enact the Biblical material in the idiom of our time and place. This takes place on various (symbolic) levels—liturgical, theoretical and social—which all feed on and grow out of the Biblical materials but form themselves dialectically in terms of culture and traditions.[37]

We begin on the liturgical level. Here we "proclaim" (1 Cor 11:26) Christ's death during this interval until he comes again. We remember his death while we await his coming in glory. The movement of the service of worship signifies our sharing in God's gestures toward the world. Indeed in our proclamation of the Word of God our liturgy becomes (by the Holy Spirit) that movement itself as God calls people to himself. We have a graphic picture of this in OT worship. An early confession is preserved for us in Deut 26:5-11. Each generation is to say: "My father was a wandering Aramean. . . . The Egyptians mistreated us. . . . Then we cried to the LORD. He heard us." In Exod 13:8 in the Passover ritual the father is to say to the son: "It is because of what the LORD did for me when I came out of Egypt." This actualizing interpretation (as Prigent calls it) is confirmed by the Passover ritual found in the Mishna, which Rabbah Gamaliel explains:

> In every generation a man must so regard himself as if he came forth himself out of Egypt. . . . He has brought us out from bondage to freedom, from sorrow to gladness, from mourning to a festival day, from darkness to great

---

refer to offers a fine analogy with the theory of symbolism developed by Susanne Langer (who was heavily influenced by Cassirer): "We never pass beyond the work of art, the vision, to something separately thinkable, the logical form, and from this to the meaning it conveys. . . . Symbolic form, symbolic function, and symbolized import are all telescoped into one experience, a perception of beauty and an intuition of significance." *Problems in Art* (New York: Scribners, 1957) 34.

[36] E. Dussell, *History and Liberation of Theology* (New York: Orbis, 1976) 19.

[37] P. Toon suggests a methodological model of the interaction between "structuring elements" and "structured elements," which he prefers to either the model of "logical implication" or that of "progressive understanding of nature (as in science)." "Models," 18-20.

light, from servitude to redemption. So let us say before him: Hallelujah
(*m. Pesaḥ.* 10:5; ed. Danby).

Since, as we have seen, in Israel and Christ the whole history of man is
included symbolically, when we celebrate that history we merge with it, we
"present" the movement of it, we actualize in our place its unique redemptive truth. As the words of the prayer book put it: "Allelujah. Christ our
Passover is sacrificed for us. Therefore let us keep the feast. Allelujah." The
language of confession and praise then is the primary theological language.
It constitutes the fundamental level of theological activity.

The next level is that of theoretical explication or, as Ferré calls it,
interpretive theory. Though this level moves on a higher level of abstraction
it can also be seen as a symbolization, in this case a verbalization and
systematization growing out of (and into) our fundamental orientation,
which we express in worship. In Wilbur Urban's distinction, if the first level
presented "symbolic truth" the second lays out the "truth of the symbol."
Though secondary to our basic models it is entailed and shaped by them.
As Torrance expresses this:

> The scientific structure of dogmatics, its compound analogues and disclosure-
> models, or doctrinal formulations, are not simply the theoretic instruments
> through which the objective reality is discerned with some exactness and
> precision, but the hermeneutic media through which it is heard in its own
> self-interpretation and articulated in our disciplined response to it.[38]

Here the dramatic action of God finds its suitable formulation in self-
consistent statements. But these too in their own way, when they are
successful, are "transparent." They have as their goal to allow the reality
they refer to to show itself in the language of a particular time and place
and in a particular manner of thinking. It grows out of what we called the
fundamental theological language that it seeks to present and interpret.
Jean Ladrière explains this interconnection:

> The primary language (of worship) calls for an interpretation. The task of
> theological discourse, insofar as it responds to this call, is to furnish the
> meaning announced with a conceptual space where it can unfold itself.[39]

It is perhaps for this reason that the best theology from each generation,
often written for the common believer, is characterized by clarity and
intuitive grasp.

Finally, God's dramatic procession expresses itself in the day-to-day
life of the Church. This reality is founded on the fact that creation itself

[38]Torrance, *Theological*, 346.

[39]J. Ladrière, "Le Symbole: Discours Theologique et Symbolique," *Symbolisme*
(ed. Ménard) 116.

reflects God (Rom 1:20) and can become the bearer of deeper meaning. Man himself as *imago Dei* carries unmistakably (if enigmatically) the image of his Maker. The social sciences agree here with theology that man realizes his freedom in his (symbolic) interaction with creation and his fellow man. In theology the fundamentally world-oriented and interpersonal character of human life is displayed in its rites and rituals as well as in its instructions for living. Christians find each other in common symbols: in their feasts and festivals, in their corporate caring, their foot-washing and burden-bearing. As we repeat in our worship: "Let us go forth into the world rejoicing in the power of the Spirit." In Biblical ethics the theme of the imitation of God and Christ points up the fact that Christian living can become an image through which God's love can be seen. Matt 24:34-46 indicates that when we place ourselves in the midst of God's action in the world we minister as God himself. Our gestures and his converge (cf. John 20:21).

We must avoid the temptation of seeing this level as the application of theology. It is rather what we might call concrete theology—a part of the way we appropriate and proclaim God's revelation. Again Latin American theologians have helped us see our theological task in more concrete terms. José Miguéz-Bonino reminds us of the "unavoidable historical mediation of Christian obedience" and urges us to form "concrete hypotheses" in which we work out our commitment.[40] The reality of the dramatic direction in which we share is vividly embodied in the Biblical symbol of the new earth (Rev 21:22). Here is the fulfilled reality toward which we move and which by our love and praise we foreshadow. Here too is pictured the impetus of theology, its intrinsic character of reaching forward to its promised future.

Before leaving this sketch we must underline the interconnection of these levels. Empirically they often overlap and coincide. Indeed we have said that the whole is to be seen as a single movement of symbolization in which under the guiding images of Scripture and the energy of the Holy Spirit each level interrelates and all levels mutually interpret one another. Our knowing of God is fulfilled on all levels together. Imagination and will are as fully engaged as the intellect. As Jerry Gill reminds us, "there is a sense in which one does not become aware of certain realities until he responds in certain ways."[41] Our fundamental faith orientation fulfills and explains itself at many points of our knowing and doing. All this together when self-consciously related is the doing of theology.

[40] J. Miguéz-Bonino, *Doing Theology in a Revolutionary Situation* (Philadelphia: Fortress, 1975) 98 ff.

[41] J. Gill, *The Possibility of Religious Knowledge* (Grand Rapids: Eerdmans, 1971) 188.

By way of conclusion we must try to ask honestly what gains there are in looking at theology in this way. We must avoid the temptation of seeing this way of looking at things as the only way. Theology has been done and will continue to be done by those who give no thought to symbols (except perhaps the sacraments). But at least we hope to have shown that, whatever name it goes under, "modeling"—the use of guiding images, in short, metaphoric language—is indispensable to doing theology. This is a necessary corollary to the meaning-bearing nature of reality and man's nature as symbol-maker, and it is a vital characteristic of Biblical revelation. We may put the matter in another way: Symbolizing is a necessary though not a sufficient condition of theology.

Especially in our use of Scripture we need to avoid seeing any single mode of discourse as sufficient to understand all that is there. While there are varying images of God's loving concern, there is also command, explication and direct address. These elements must all be understood together.[42]

Are there advantages to seeing the whole of theology as a symbolic process? Seeing Christianity as a symbolic system might help us see the interrelation of various aspects of our religious life that at present are all too fragmented. To see the mutual relationship might make it possible on the one hand to better understand certain concrete images (e.g., the Church as the body of Christ) and on the other hand to end the mutual hostility often noted between the so-called theoretical and practical disciplines in theology. Applying Ricoeur's idea of metaphor to the use of case studies in theology may allow us to find intelligent alternatives to traditional teaching techniques.[43]

Secondly, the insights of the sociology of knowledge may lead us to a more realistic (and imaginative) idea of the way in which theological perspectives are actually formed. Knowing how religious faiths are built up in dialogue with other symbolic universes and how they are legitimated may help us guard against illicit borrowings and a false sense of autonomy. Such insight, we believe, will only reinforce what the Bible insists is our fragile, temporary hold on life and our need to work our way through together to clarity, which will not come finally until Christ comes again.

As we begin to learn more from Third-World theologians we may see how limited is our western statistical and linear way of looking at reality.

---

[42]G. Fackre, *The Christian Story: A Narrative Interpretation of Basic Christian Doctrine* (Grand Rapids: Eerdmans, 1978), is a very helpful attempt to understand theology as story and underline some of the points we have made. At the same time it shows the difficulty of fitting everything into a single rubric.

[43]Cf. Ricoeur, *Rule*, 247: "Metaphor is that strategy of discourse by which language divests itself of its function of direct description in order to reach the mythic level where its function of discovering is set free."

We may begin to see the role that intuitive and aesthetic dimensions play in our knowing, and in the process we may come to see Scripture in a whole new light. Perhaps we will begin to have not only a rational idea of God's program but also a "feel" for what he is doing in the world.

Finally, all of this will certainly help us see the mistake of a whole direction in modern theology. Beginning with Schleiermacher and up to Bultmann and his disciples there has been advanced the strange notion that God must be limited (and thus distorted) by our attempts to picture him. It is not God but we who are limited to pictures. As Hilary of Poitiers put it: "Every analogy is to be considered as more useful to man than as appropriate to God, because it hints at the meaning rather than explains it fully" (*De Trinitate* 1.19). God for his part has made man and the world so that pictures can accurately reflect reality. He has in fact stooped to our imaginings (in Israel) and become the Image (in Christ).

The Bible in an Age of Revolution

Harold Kuhn

I⊤ has been for some time a commonplace to say that ours is a revolutionary age. For well over a decade, in our nation and abroad, not only existing institutions and structures but also long-accepted norms have been called into question. Principles long taken for granted have had to stand trial for their lives, and ideals that had come to be regarded as imperishable are now compelled to justify their continuance as guiding norms for human conduct. The forms of revolutionary (as opposed to evolutionary) social change observable in our land reflect the spectrum of issues that engage most of the nations of the western world and indeed most of the Third and Fourth Worlds as well.

The 60s showed forms of revolutionary activity that had been, of course, observable at other periods in history. But new dimensions were added, particularly as radical movements for revolutionary change began to demand not mere reforms within existing systems but the total replacement of existing forms by new and revolutionary ones. Such student slogans as "Smash the system!" or "Bring the present order to a halt!" became watchwords. True, such movements passed from the American scene with surprising rapidity when Vietnam was no longer an issue and when college and university youth faced a buyer's market as they sought for employment.

The demand, however, for a replacement of existing systems with radically new ones did not die with student protests, for in many quarters of the earth the writers who felt the pulse of their peoples no longer spoke of "a revolutionary age" but rather of "an age of revolution." And much of the agitation for the total replacement of existing systems occurred with little or no reference to the spiritual issues that were involved. It may be said that revolutionary movements rose and began to implement themselves outside the sphere of influence of the Scriptures.

Within conciliar Christianity the question of the theological bearings of contemporary revolution came to focus during the third session of the World Conference on Church and Society held in Geneva in 1966 under the auspices of the World Council of Churches. This third plenary session, held on July 14, heard three major speakers attempt to formulate a "theology of revolution" in terms of three separate conceptions of the task of the ecumenical Church in the world. Heinz-Dietrich Wendland of the

University of Münster in West Germany, Archpriest Vitaly Borovoy of Leningrad and Geneva, and Richard Shaull of Union Theological Seminary made the major presentations.

In the discussions at Geneva it was noted that the fundamental facts of our world today compel us to face the existence of "total revolution" in place of the more conventional forms of political and social revolution of the past, which were usually limited both in extent and in depth. Today there are massive upheavals in every area of modern life, which came in part as a result of technological and scientific discoveries, particularly in communications, and which have assumed global proportions. This posed for the Christian Church the problem of whether or not the Church ecumenical should assume a role of total involvement in such a global movement for accelerated social change and even upheaval and, further, whether this involvement was to be merely institutional, whether involvement should be indirect as her members became concerned and involved or whether the Church should involve herself theologically in the structures making for change.

In this connection one substantive question presented itself: Has the revolutionary element in the Christian gospel contributed to making the contemporary world to be revolutionary? If so, then "what is the connection between the revolutionary element in the Christian message and revolution in history?" The question is, in other words, whether one can distinguish between the so-called "revolutionary element" implicit in the Biblical revelation on the one hand and "secular-revolutionary absolutism or fanatical Utopianism" on the other.[1]

Wendland held that the Christian gospel is brought to bear upon revolution indirectly—that is, not by fomenting rebellion or by the use of political and military force but through what he called "quiet" personal influence of Christian persons through the structures of society, working as individuals, but as individuals conscious of being united in Christ. Archpriest Borovoy of the Russian Orthodox Church spoke out of the perspective of a Church that has not only lived for fifty years in a revolutionary situation but that has been the heir of a millenium of Byzantine ideology, which tended to react affirmatively to social and political systems and thus to contribute to the sanctification of the *status quo*.

The conclusion of the archpriest was that "Christianity is by its very nature revolutionary; and the new life required by Christian social ethics is more radical, more profoundly revolutionary, more novel than any other social system or doctrine which has grown up outside Christianity."[2] What was sought by these two men was a way in which Biblical Christianity

---

[1] J. M. Lochman, "Ecumenical Theology of Revolution," *SJT* 21/2 (June 1968) 171.

[2] Ibid., p. 174.

might exercise a positive influence upon the historical process. It was indicated that this must occur basically within the area of the penetration of the mentality of men and women in "the new revolutionary and socialist societies."

Neither of these two presentations seemed to satisfy the claims of the mentalities of the representatives of the Third World, particularly the younger delegates from the underdeveloped nations. More to their liking was the address of Richard Shaull, who pleads for a "revolutionary theology" that should formulate a new strategy of revolution. He sought to test all contemporary forms of theology—historic orthodoxy, neo-orthodoxy, and emerging forms of ecumenical theology—in terms of whether they have any longer any appeal to the younger revolutionary thinkers, particularly in the Third World. This would seem to place the burden of theological decision upon acceptance by revolutionaries, whether they be within the Christian movement or outside it.

Reference is made to the Geneva conference here because of the three different definitions of revolution that they heard and with which the conference had to grapple. The first two definitions, the one Lutheran and the other Eastern Orthodox, adhered in general to lines laid down by historic Christianity—although neither the typically Lutheran nor the more "incarnational" forms might prove completely adequate for us as evangelical Christians. It is the third view, expressed by Shaull, that attracts our attention, particularly since his view seemed to gain large acceptance with the Third World, in which revolutions of a violent nature seem to be taken somewhat for granted.

A bit of further attention is given to Shaull's position paper at Geneva in view of the fact that it was prepared and delivered under the rubric of "Theological Foundations" and since John C. Bennett gave it place as chap. 1 in his symposium entitled *Christian Social Ethics in a Changing World*. It is fair, we think, to note in this connection that this address stood at the cutting edge of ecumenical thinking in the sphere of "the theology of revolution."

Shaull's concern was for the placing of a revolutionary theology in what he called "theological perspective." He is not concerned with Wendland's analysis of the traditional Lutheran "theology of orders," feeling that it makes too much of the right of the state to maintain itself, if necessary, by the use of force. Nor does he seem to have been overly impressed by Archpriest Borovoy's emphasis upon the parallel between the concept of revolution on the one hand and the Biblical concepts of "conversion," "change of heart" and "new life in Christ."

One looks in vain in the pronouncements of Shaull for any clear dependence upon Biblical insights. He speaks rather of man's historical existence and of "human fulfillment" as the goal for God's action in history. At this point his writings share a certain fuzziness with respect to

what "makes human life more human" as the objective allegedly sought by
Jesus as the liberator and humanizer of society. (This same lack of precision
marks the work of Paul Lehmann.)

More precisely, Shaull regards such an historic term as "transcendence"
as applied to God as being not metaphysical and ontological but historical
and eschatological. Biblical statements that have been traditionally associated with God's reality are utilized by him as paradigms for the manner in
which God breaks the power of oppressors and establishes a new and
"messianic" world. In this new order man's humanity (i.e., true human
existence) must be found in the future, since the present order denies this
to him.

Perhaps enough has been said to indicate that at Geneva in 1966 there
was laid the theological foundation for an age of revolution, so that much
that has been done subsequently is founded upon that base. It is one of the
ironies of our time that in the final pronouncements of that conference
Biblical statements and references were kept at a minimum level. To be
sure, such references were there, but those utilizing them were not in the
long run the decisive voices in the gathering. It was the element of "re-
doing of theology" in terms that were only superficially theological and
basically ideological that was taken up as normatively Christian by the
world to which they were directed. Thus in the thinking of the Third
World, where restructuring of the socio-economic order was most needed,
there was projected a pattern of thought in which Biblical insights were
utilized only in an oblique manner.

If the third plenary session of the World Conference on Church and
Society in Geneva on July 14, 1966, was a landmark in the shaping of our
time as not merely a revolutionary age but an age of revolution, another
conference became determinative for giving form to a specialized type of
"doing theology" whose significance is widespread and influential in our
time. It was the Second General Conference of Latin American Bishops
held at Medellin, Colombia, in mid-August of 1968.

The central concern of this conference was allied to that of the Geneva
conference already noted—namely, the character of the revolutionary age
for the special needs of Latin America. At Medellin the overall quest of the
assembled bishops of Latin American Catholicism was to understand "the
salvific mission of Jesus Christ" with special reference to the imperative
need for the liberation of great masses of the population of the lands south
of the border. There hovered over the conference the conviction that the
Church in Latin America, to which the large majority of Latin American
peoples are adherents, was ready to articulate and implement a new set of
insights relating to its people. In contrast to the Geneva conference, whose
use of the Scriptures was oblique and lateral, the Medellin conference
sought frankly to relate its concerns and insights directly to the Bible.

The theme was, as is well known, liberation. The elaboration of the theme began with such Scriptures as Heb 1:1-2; Gal 4:4; and Rom 1:3-4. It was recognized also that the term "liberation" was burdened by ambiguities, and it seems clear that an honest attempt was made to define it in Biblical terms. This was done in recognition that the discussion faced the constant danger of becoming merely political in nature.

In defining the term "sin" the conference drew heavily upon such Scriptures as Matt 6:11-12; 7:11; John 3; Rom 3:9-12; John 1:29. From these and other references "sin" was defined in both its personal and its socio-cultural meanings. Emphasis was laid upon the "principalities and powers," in terms of which the conference sought to understand the sinfulness of human institutions.

It follows that the statements of Medellin concerning sin are basically in harmony with the Biblical insights at this point, if we understand that these insights are pushed farther in the direction of applying them to the unjust structures of society. Whether or not there was some eisegesis at this point by the writers, especially of the *conclusiones*, is open to question, since the Bible does not deal specifically with earthly institutions (unless we regard the Hebrew monarchy or the temple priesthood as institutions). But we see here a sincere attempt at elaboration of the question of human evil in terms of the Biblical undersanding of sin.

As for the term "liberation" itself, the Medellin Conference explored especially the account of the exodus (Exodus 14), finding there not only an instructive illustration of God's delivering power but also a paradigm for the expected deliverance of the oppressed of our time as God's special objects of his saving concern. In the discussion of liberation, the dimensions of both spiritual and material, of temporal and eternal, as well as the areas of personal, social and even cosmic deliverance were explored—with the ideal in mind of discovering the Biblical bases for the identification of these dimensions and areas.

It is in the area of the elaboration of the concept of liberation that we come to some problems of exegesis. The Medellin declarations contain many terms of the type of "integral liberation," "our true liberation," "liberation from every enslavement" and "full liberation." It is certainly true that the gospel envisions freedom for men and women in every dimension of their lives. Moreover, the exodus was "integral" in that it removed God's ancient people from their pitiable life-style as slaves. After all, our Lord's redemptive mission is not to pure spirits but to spirits organically related to bodies—and to institutions. In view of this, spiritual liberation is not complete without more social and "material" forms of freedom.

We can agree that the exodus was political and cannot be reduced to transcendent terms. What is to be questioned is whether the parallel between Israel's deliverance at the Reed (Red) Sea and the envisioned freeing of peoples of Latin America from the forms of unfreedom imposed by Latin America's creole minority, by the disproportionate relation of population (and its vast increase) to resources, by the multinational corporations, and by discriminatory forms of marketing, of import-export regulations, and of monopolistic control of markets—whether this parallel is adequate as a source of expectation of a divine intervention in behalf of the marginated peoples of Latin America.

What is questioned is not that Scripture is used as a source for a model of liberation but whether the model is correctly applied. This will remain a question for debate for a long time to come. Nor can we fail to appreciate the manner in which the miracles of our Lord are seen by Latin American theologians to be more than "signs" designed to confirm the truth that those performing them were proclaiming. Many of the miracles, notably the feeding of the hungry or the casting out of demons, have deep social significance.

In the light of this we applaud the work of Medellin in pointing out the wider cosmic significance of our Lord's liberating miracles (John 12:31; Col 2:15; etc.). The needs of the marginated poor of the earth are seen as part of the total package of ills under which the creation travails and from which the cosmos will finally be delivered from its torturing burden (Rom 8:22; Revelation 21-22). Here liberation through the Son is envisioned as embracing both mankind and the authentic universe "out there."

Medellin grappled also with the question of the manner in which our Lord related himself to the social situation of his day. The conference proceedings called attention to the complexity of our Lord's relation to society, noting that he did not live in a social and political vacuum. He was, it is said, accused of being a subverter of the nation (Luke 23:2), a troublemaker (John 7:11) and an opposer of the highest civil authority (Luke 23:2; John 19:12). Thus it appears that Scripture was taken very seriously as a key to understanding Jesus' socio-political attitude. Reporting this analysis by Medellin, James T. O'Connor notes that

> to admit that His person and message were unsettling, transforming, liberating —even revolutionary to the extent that He was executed purely for political motives, is not to propound the claim that the Lord was the Che Guevara, the Camilo Torres, the Mao of the first century. Such an understanding of His life and work is absurd.[3]

Thus in relation to liberation Medellin relied heavily on Biblical insights drawn directly from statements rather than by inference and indirectly.

---

[3]J. T. O'Connor, *Liberation: Toward a Theology for the Church in the World*, 38-39.

With regard to the motif of "conversion" Medellin insisted "on the conversion of man" as a prerequisite to structural change (*conclusiones*, p. 52). Thus the [Holy] Spirit is basically the Spirit of conversion, revealing to man his alienation from self and from society and showing him what he ought to be (1 John 2:20).

It is significant that today's Latin American theology of liberation moves far beyond Medellin in its appeal to Scripture. Nowhere is this more clear than in the attempts of "revolutionary theology" to deal with the problem of violence. Juan Luis Segundo notes that "all the remarks we find in the Bible about violence or non-violence are *ideologies*."[4] Thus such Scriptures as Matt 5:21-22, set against the statement (Mark 3:5) concerning the Lord's "looking around at them with anger," seem to him to contain something other than direct mandates.

The same author notes passages that suggest a relativity of application (Rom 14:1-2; 1 Cor 8:7-13; 10:23-33).[5] Again Segundo cites our Lord's seeming abandonment of John the Baptist to his fate as an indication that he condoned violence, in some cases at least. A similar pointing away from absolutes is indicated in his interpretation of Mark 7:16, 18-23, in which he sees what comes from within a man as making "him moral or immoral."[6] (p. 171).

From the foregoing we derive certain conclusions with respect to the use of the Bible at the cutting edge of the age of revolution. First, those who grapple with the question of revolution usually feel some need to relate to the Bible and its mandates. Second, representatives of conciliar Christianity tend to be less specific in their application of the Bible to their situations than their Roman Catholic counterparts. Third, the Catholic hierarchy tends to be more literal and specific in its understanding and use of Scripture than many of its parish priests and its laypersons. Fourth, and as a result, the leaders of the most prominent of today's revolutionary movements (i.e., the Latin American theology of liberation) are less inhibited in applying Scripture to the needs of their *praxis* than their clerical counterparts. This leads to a higher degree of politicizing of their exegesis of the Scriptures.

There stands out above these statements the evident need for most leaders of the activistic movements in the age of revolution to find some justification for their attitudes, whether these be conservative or radical, in the Christian Scriptures. Somehow the Bible "will not down" but maintains its historic vitality. Even in cases when exegesis becomes eisegesis and when Scripture is "adjusted" to fit or at least give plausibility to alien models it tends to reassert itself as powerful over the consciences and actions of men.

[4] J. L. Segundo, *The Liberation of Theology*, 166 (italics his).
[5] Ibid., p. 167.
[6] Ibid., p. 171.

The Use of the Bible in World Evangelization

ARTHUR P. JOHNSTON

MUCH attention is rightfully directed toward the questions of inspiration and hermeneutics, but additional consideration needs to be given to the use of the Bible in evangelism at home and abroad. By this it must be recognized that a sound doctrine of Biblical authority must undergird the use of the Bible in evangelism. This was the crucial and formal cause of the sixteenth-century Reformation, and its application gave rise to the modern and contemporary world evangelistic movement of this century and the last one.

I. ISSUES RELATING TO THE USE OF THE BIBLE

The effective use of the Bible in evangelism is subtly undermined by at least four sources beside the more academic issues of inspiration and hermeneutics. First, the behavioral sciences have focused our attention on methodology so that more attention is given to technique and organization than is given to the dynamics of the Scriptures and the power of the Holy Spirit. Whether in the local church or in parachurch movements, a well-organized and implemented plan of evangelization is not only desirable but necessary. Nevertheless, the secondary means of evangelization easily displaces the primary where shallow hearts or those with nonevangelical roots apply these methods, and the result is culturally-conditioned Christians who have never been "born of the Spirit" by faith in the Word written, the Holy Scriptures.

The second danger diminishing the importance of Scripture arises from what is often a well-intentioned effort to inspire both godliness of conduct and service in the Church and in the world. This is expressed in various ways. Some insist that the Christian must "incarnate" Christ so that the world will believe. Others speak of the "authentication" of the gospel by our good works. Both have a commendable motive but, first of all, there was only One who was truly incarnate, and no one can in any measure replace him. Seeking to so incarnate him who was without sin can only discourage the sincere and zealous yet sinful personal evangelist. As it could be said, "If every Christian is an incarnation, nothing is an incarnation." The believer is united with Christ and he dwells within, but this is

309

not the primary source of convicting the unbeliever of sin, righteousness and judgment. In like manner our good works will glorify our Father in heaven. But they will not "authenticate" the gospel but only attract attention to the gospel, for "faith comes by hearing" (Rom 10:17). Here again attention is directed away from the use of Scripture and the ministry of the Holy Spirit to the life and good works of the believer in his witness. It is upon this basis that many succumb to a euphoric concept of "holistic" evangelism: We must minister to the body and mind as well as the soul.

Third, it is true that the unity of the Church is related to evangelism (John 17:21-23), and it is unquestionable that many seem to have been turned away from the gospel, from Christ and from the local church because of strife and schism within a congregation. Others, of course, have insisted upon the world-wide organizational unity of Christendom as incumbent upon effective evangelization. Who will deny that evangelistic conquest may suffer because of an "Achan in the camp" (Joshua 7) or because of ecclesiastic genocide in the name of "truth"? Nevertheless, some remarkable examples of body life are not also noted for their evangelistic fervor, and some seem to degenerate into "fellowship worshipers" where the mutual "love" for others does not transcend their cultural or social boundaries. In like fashion, some united or uniting churches have been brought to organizational union by their common evangelistic sterility rather than by their spiritual virility. More thought needs to be given to that spiritual unity given unconditionally to all those "born from above" and, also, to the true meaning of unity akin to that of the Trinity. In some cases divided and dividing churches who rightly use the Scriptures are among those that seem to flourish the most. This does not justify division but points to the power of Scripture.

Fourth, the Reformation debate on the authority of Scripture has been revised in two ways that are destructive to evangelism. Some are unable to divorce evangelism from the authority of the Church. This is expressed by some nonevangelicals who have lost confidence in the inerrancy of Scripture: Because we cannot be sure of the words of the texts giving assurance of personal salvation we must look again at the centuries of Church tradition. It is the unique tradition of the Church and the Bible that validate faith and permit a hope beyond the grave. Some of this first group have placed tradition as a parallel source of revelation, and others place the Bible within the tradition of their Church. In these and other similar relationships the use of the Bible is contingent upon the validity of the tradition of the Church: The evangelist must proclaim the validity of a visible Church or denomination and its tradition along with the use of the Bible. Thus some depreciate the use of Scripture alone by an appeal to the Church as an institution, and others appeal to the tradition of the Church.

Lastly, another wing of evangelicalism is depending upon the authentication of Christianity based upon a personal experience with God. This designation of the use of Scripture is, perhaps, one of the most subtle of all because it is so closely related to the great Reformation reaffirmation of the inner witness of the Spirit of God as to the reliability of Scripture and to the assurance of the believer's relationship to God in Christ. In an extreme expression it says that it does not make any difference what you or your church believes about the essential doctrines of Scripture. The important thing is to have had an experience with God in Christ that Christians generously accept as the "new birth." An example might be that of one who does not hold to the deity or bodily resurrection of Christ (in consideration of Rom 10:9-10) and yet affirms the "new birth" based upon a personal religious experience. Yet this experience is negated by a cursory examination of Biblical teaching implicit in Biblical evangelism. Christian experience, the assurance of salvation, and the authenticity of Scripture are not luxuries of apostolic Christianity but necessities. Nevertheless, religious experience without a foundation in divine revelation is groundless and void of eternal value.

II. The Reformers' Return to the Authority of Scripture

The theological basis for the use of Scripture is grounded and predicated upon the authority of Scripture. Because Scripture alone mediates truth in all its purity to mankind, the Bible judges finite sinful man, his rational processes, his deeds, his traditions of the Church and even the Church itself.

Martin Chemnitz (1522-1587) cites 2 Tim 3:16 and 2 Pet 1:21 to show that the Scriptures came forth from God and that God chose certain definite persons to write them so that there would be no doubt that what they wrote was divinely inspired. The Scriptures possess

> canonical authority chiefly from the Holy Spirit by whose impulse and inspiration it was brought forth; thereafter from the writers to whom God gave more and special testimonies of the truth. After this it has authority from the primitive church as from a witness at whose time these writings were published and approved.[1]

He rightly insists that the Church has not bestowed authority upon the canonical Scriptures any more than the Church can bestow authority upon what the Church transmits and teaches without any testimony from Scripture. The Scriptures have authority, first, by their inspiration by the Holy Spirit; second, by the divinely-appointed apostolic writers; and lastly, by their recognition by the primitive Church, not by later Church councils.

How did this last acceptance of the canon by the primitive Church take place? Not by the councils, Chemnitz says:

[1]M. Chemnitz, *Examination of the Council of Trent* (trans. F. Kramer; St. Louis: Concordia, 1971) 176.

> It is foolishness when some babble that the Scripture is called canonical
> because that authority was bestowed on it by a canon of some council, for
> they cannot even name or invent any council in which such a canon of
> Scripture was first set up, as if the Scripture had not had such authority
> before.[2]

To the contrary, it is the Church that receives its authority from Scripture,
he insists. Some have gone so far as to say that the Scriptures are without
authority divorced from the authority given by the Church.

> It is, however, manifest blasphemy that, if the present church, namely, the
> Roman pontiff with his prelates, would desert the Scripture with their [sic]
> authority, it would of itself have no more authority than Aesop's fables.[3]

The prior authorities of the Holy Spirit and the apostolic authors are
understood even by the manner in which the Scriptures were received, he
explains.

> Finally those divinely inspired writings were at the time of their writing laid
> before, delivered, and commended to the church with public attestation in
> order that she might, by exercising the greatest care and foresight, preserve
> them uncorrupted, transmit them as from hand to hand, and commend them
> to posterity. And as the ancient church at the time of Moses, Joshua and the
> prophets, so also the primitive church at the time of the apostles was able to
> testify with certainty which writings were divinely inspired. For she knew the
> authors whom God had commended to the church by special testimonies; she
> knew also which were the writings which had been composed by them; and
> from the things which she had received by oral tradition from the apostles she
> could judge that the things which had been written were the same teaching
> which the apostles had delivered with the living voice.[4]

Thus the primitive Church discerned that which the Spirit inspired and
which was the source of her own authority.

While the Christian Church preceded the NT canon by its appearance
and manifestation at Pentecost, it is the witness of the apostolic authors
who preceded the Church and guided the Church in the content of her
truth (cf. Luke 24:48; Acts 1:21-23; 2:32; etc.). Gaussen affirms that the
certainty of the first canon was established by historians in the latter half of
the second century but that these NT books have a far earlier historical
testimony.

Thus the very nature of the Scriptures is spiritual: Their use by
believers in evangelism results in the calling out of the world of those who
are born again by the proclamation of the gospel. The Church is primarily

[2] Ibid., p. 169.
[3] Ibid., p. 176.
[4] Ibid.

spiritual and invisible as a result of the divine and inward work of regeneration by the Spirit through the Scriptures. It is the authority of Scripture alone that remains the solid foundation for world evangelization. For this reason the apostle Paul admonished Timothy to "preach the Word" (2 Tim 4:2). The author of the epistle to the Hebrews likewise saw the Word as "living" and "active" (Heb 4:12).

III. CONTEMPORARY REVIVAL OF THE AUTHORITY OF THE CHURCH AND TRADITION

James Burtchael of Notre Dame University believes that when the Reformers threw off the authority of the Church at Rome they were obliged to develop the authority of the Bible as a last resort. Divine inspiration of Scripture was stressed, and interest in the Bible was revived. Now, he says, after three centuries the discovery of "many inadequacies and inconsistencies" by the Protestant theologians has reversed the roles of the Roman Catholic Church. During the Reformation centuries she played down Scripture and highlighted the Church as the supreme interpreter of religious truth by correcting the understanding of the written text and supplementing the text with unwritten tradition. Now "New Criticism and Modernism reversed the roles of the Church and the Reformers and inerrancy became a Catholic 'cause.'"[5]

Confidence in the authority of Scripture has been eroded by those following in the footsteps of Emil Brunner. He destroys the confidence of a minister to preach the Word of God with authority. He says, for example, that

> there is "preaching" which, dogmatically speaking, may be in complete accordance with that which an Apostle, a Paul or a John, may say, yet it may not be, on that account, in the very least the preaching of the Word of God. Authoritative preaching is guaranteed neither by the legal ordination of a Church nor by a period of training in an orthodox theological college. . . . It is plain that the divinely present Word cannot be tied to a correct doctrine, any more than to an official position in the Church. Again and again we see that authoritative preaching, even in view of correct doctrine, is the free gift of God. We can learn orthodox theology, and anyone who has learned it can use it, but we can never "possess" the Word of God; we can only pray that it will be granted us when we have to preach.[6]

This divorce of Scripture from the Word of God by Brunner represents the direction that many in Protestantism have taken.

[5] J. T. Brutchael, *Catholic Theories of Biblical Inspiration Since 1810: A Review and Critique* (Cambridge: University Press, 1969) 285.

[6] E. Brunner, *Revelation and Reason* (trans. O. Wyon; London: SCM, 1947) 144-145.

Because of higher criticism of the Biblical text, because we do not possess the originally inerrant "Bible X" and because "the word of the Bible is only the means of the real Word of God, Jesus Christ . . . therefore, in spite of its priority as the original witness, fundamentally it stands upon the same level as the testimony of the Church."[7] Brunner has again raised the level of the authority of the Church to the same level as that of Scripture. An errant Bible became the source of a subjective and mystical Word of God not to be identified with doctrinal orthodoxy or the Bible itself.

Furthermore, and even more serious, the resultant use of the Bible is limited as an evangelistic instrument of "thus says the Lord." It can only be "thus says the Lord to Moses, John, or Paul." The Bible has lost its normative nature and direct application to the individual. "The individual reader of the Bible," Brunner writes, "thinks that he can be 'saved' by himself, so long as he has his Bible, and he ignores the fellowship of the Church."[8] He considers it an error that one can become a Christian "through the Bible alone." Here again there is the non-Reformation assumption that the nature of the Church is primarily visible and institutional. Parachurch evangelism has been eliminated.

Some opponents of the Reformation spoke of Scripture as a dead letter that "cannot speak or pass judgment on itself." "The Holy Spirit does not speak through Scripture" for the Spirit speaks through men. Men who have the Spirit of God pronounce right sentence and judgment with the help of Scripture. But this key to understanding the Bible was not granted to one man alone, for the help, advice and intercession of the other faithful in Christ was required. Nowhere can one be more assured of the assistance of the Spirit, it was said, than in a Council of the Church because it is there that men who have the Spirit make pronouncements and decisions with the help of Scripture that "does not by itself understand."[9]

Because of their failure to confine apostolic inspiration to the text of Scripture these opponents appeal to the Spirit's influence upon that which was preached by the apostle but never written down. Thus, it is said, these unwritten traditions are now "their living voices."[10] Tavard offers a solution of the dilemma between Holy Writ and Holy Church by suggesting a theology of ecumenism that opens the way to a more inclusive concept of Scripture and the Church. He proposes that

> Scripture cannot be the Word of God once it has been severed from the Church which is the Bride and Body of Christ. And the Church could not be the Bride and Body, had she not received the gift of understanding the Word.

[7]Ibid., p. 145.

[8]Ibid.

[9]G. H. Tavard, *Holy Writ or Holy Church* (Westport, CT: Greenwood, 1978) 128.

[10]Ibid., p. 166.

. . . They are ultimately one, though one in two. The Church implies the Scripture as the Scripture implies the Church.[11]

This position seems to be gaining ground as confidence in the authority of Scripture wanes in much of historical Protestantism. The Bible is seen more and more as part of the tradition of the Church and intimately linked to a visible organization institutionalized by God.

IV. THE AUTHORITY OF GOOD WORKS

Bernard Ramm rightly questions the expression that "the Church is the extension of the incarnation."[12] He notes, first of all, that the Church was founded by both redemption and special revelation. The Church did not originate them and has no existence apart from them. Rather the Church exists because of them:

Salvation and revelation are the absolute presuppositions both logically and temporally for the salvation of every single person and therefore for the entire Church. The Church by definition is the redeemed and enlightened people of God. Before there is a church there must be both revelation and redemption. No real headway can be made in the debate over tradition until it is clearly seen that revelation and redemption are absolutely prior to the Church.[13]

Second, Ramm rightfully insists on the priority of Scripture over the Church and tradition. Third, he warns that to apply the incarnation in the continuity of the Church is dangerous because it could make her "become a lord of revelation and a dispenser of salvation."[14] This same principle may be applied to those who speak of the individual "incarnating" Christ in the world today by our good works. This doctrine opens the door for the individual to "get in the act" of a once-for-all revelation and redemption. This oversteps the boundaries of Scripture and becomes a corrupting teaching in the life of the Church as well as the individual.

In addressing the question of incarnation or holistic evangelism it becomes more and more apparent that these terms represent a departure from sound Biblical proclamation evangelism. The authority and power for evangelism are the result of the Word proclaimed and the dynamic of the Holy Spirit. This in no way eliminates the necessity of good works in the life of the believer nor an essential growth in grace or sanctification. Christian citizens have a responsibility to grow in loving concern for other believers and even for the whole world. This sanctification is founded upon

[11] Ibid., p. 246.
[12] B. Ramm, *Special Revelation and the Word of God* (Grand Rapids: Eerdmans, 1961) 171 n.
[13] Ibid., pp. 170-171.
[14] Ibid., p. 171.

justification by faith alone. Social concern and social action are the fruits of the new life. Yet they, in themselves, do not validate or authenticate the believer's testimony. This is the divine work of the Scriptures and the Spirit. Contemporary evangelicalism must be careful not to politicize the ministry of the Church which God in his Word has Spirit-ized. This would be a return to another form of the pre-Reformation confusion of justification and sanctification.

V. The Internal Witness of the Spirit

Few doctrines need to be emphasized more than the great inward witness of the Holy Spirit, the *testimonium spiritus sancti*, for a fundamental understanding of Biblical evangelism. Bernard Ramm has isolated the Reformation struggle with Catholicism now revived in Protestantism where the Church becomes the custodian of Scripture and, consequently, the Lord of Scripture.[15]

Calvin, Ramm says, placed the Scriptures above the Church and insisted that the Church is governed by the Word and the Spirit. Therefore all traditions and ecclesiastical hierarchies must submit to the lordship of Scripture. Instead of the voice of the Church proclaiming that the Scriptures are God's Word, Calvin says the Bible teaches that this assurance comes by the internal witness of the Holy Spirit. This was the experience of the patriarchs:

> When God gives his revelation, he gives along with it a certainty that it *is* revelation. When speaking of the revelation given the patriarchs, Calvin asserts that God so inwardly persuaded and impressed them that they were convinced that the doctrine received by them was from God (*Institutes*, 1, vi, 2).[16]

This inward persuasion and firm conviction is the inward witness of the Holy Spirit. Certainty comes from the Spirit through the Word written, not from the Church, nor from an experience of revelation divorced from Scripture, nor by a demonstration of the truthfulness of Christianity by purely rational evidences.

Calvin opposed rationalistic Christian apologetics in evangelism because the Scriptures do not make their appeal by rational arguments but to the sacred name of God (*Institutes*, I, vii, 4). Rational arguments would result in human assurance but not in divine. Only probability of personal salvation can result, and the mind is left in suspense and uncertainty. The problem resides with the human mind whose darkness does not make it a fit instrument to prove Christianity.

[15] B. Ramm, *The Witness of the Spirit* (Grand Rapids: Eerdmans, 1959) 11.
[16] Ibid., pp. 11-12.

The authority of the Church was opposed by the Reformer because an inner voice is needed, and the Church of his day was composed of humans who treated the Spirit with contempt: She despised the Spirit-inspired quality of Scripture and its self-validating quality, the *autopistia*. Why? Because men were redeemed prior to the formation of the institutional Church, and it was Scripture that was the foundation of the Church. The sign of the Church is not the presence of the Spirit, said Calvin, but the sign is the Word of God, for "the Spirit governs *by* the Word."[17]

There is no revelation apart from the Scriptures, "for the Lord gives his children illumination of the Spirit *through the Word*" (*Institutes*, I, ix, 3). The ways, doings, and all actions of the Spirit conform to Scripture for the Spirit is consistent within himself. Consequently it is a union of the Word and the Spirit that provides the *testimonium*. Our *testimonium*, or inner witness, is an absolute persuasion given by God. This witness is one persuading us that the Scriptures are true and witnessing to our personal salvation. "The Scriptures become the Word of life to the believer when impressed on our hearts by the Holy Spirit, *when the Scriptures exhibit Christ* (I, ix, 3)."[18]

Likewise the Lutheran historical theologian, Robert Preus, speaks of the supernatural work of God whereby Scripture itself has the power to make us divinely certain of its authority. Scripture is self-authenticating: "The Spirit testifies through Scripture that Scripture is Divine."[19] When we read and hear God's Word, God moves and enlightens our hearts to faith in his Word and promises. The witness of the Spirit is never immediate—without Scripture—but always by Scripture, *per verbum*. It is a living witness in the believer's heart and not something external to or apart from man.

Because of the primary struggle with the authority of the Church, Preus expressed concern that the *testimonium spiritus sancti internum*, the inner witness of the Holy Spirit, was neglected by old Lutheran dogmaticians in its application to Christ as the object of saving faith or in reference to the believer's personal assurance of faith.[20] This is understandable although not excusable, and it may account for that post-Reformation spiritually dead orthodoxy of the seventeenth century. Lutheran Pietism, however, broke through the confessional doctrinal structure, recognized the ministry of the Holy Spirit and the Bible and focused attention upon world evangelization. The result was seen in the great century, the nineteenth, of world missions.

[17] Ibid., p. 15.
[18] Ibid., p. 19.
[19] R. Preus, *The Inspiration of Scripture* (London: Oliver and Boyd, 1955) 108.
[20] Ibid., p. 115.

VI. Scripture and Evangelism

The evangelical evangelism and missionary pioneers of the eighteenth century were nourished by the theology of Philipp Jacob Spener, the father of pietism. Germane to his theology was the Reformers' doctrine of Scripture: The authority and power of the Church and tradition was replaced by the power of the Holy Spirit and the authority of Scripture. Several of his *Theological Thoughts* apply directly to evangelistic methods revived from the apostolic and post-apostolic era of missionary endeavor.

First, Spener wrote, the Scriptures possess the inherent power of God to enlighten man's reason and to so act upon his will that man will be brought to conversion.[21] He spoke of the sufficiency of the Scriptures to bring individuals to personal conversion because they are neither a "dead letter" nor impotent. They have the ability to perform the function for which they were given. While this principle did not divorce Scripture from the Church it recognized that the evangelists' primary appeal and call to faith must be rooted in the verbal proclamation of the Word written. The right and discriminate use of the Bible regained its place as the first pillar of world evangelization. Neither good works nor personal piety in themselves can serve as a divine ground of faith. Only the living word from the living God can effectively bring life to those dead in sin (Heb 3:12; 4:12; Eph 2:1-3).

The second pillar of truth related to a full Biblical recognition of the person and work of the Holy Spirit. Spener said that "the Holy Spirit is at all times with, by and in the Word of God to bring men to illumination, conversion and the new birth."[22] Thus we note that while it is the Holy Spirit who gives these graces to men, subjective experience is always anchored to divine objective revelation. The Holy Spirit is always present working with the Scripture that is read and rightly proclaimed. It is the power and ministry of the Holy Spirit by the Word that is necessary to lead to saving faith in Jesus Christ. While signs, miracles and gifts of the Spirit may accompany the proclamation, they are no more essential to Biblical evangelism than a ministry to physical and social need is essential to saving faith (Rom 10:17). G. C. Berkouwer rightly comments that the relationship between the Word and the Spirit "is no theoretical or merely dogmatical question but a life-and-death issue in the preaching of the Church."[23] He quotes the Belgic Confession as declaring that true faith is worked in many

---

[21]P. J. Spener, *Theologische Bedenken* (Halle: Verlegung des Waysen-Hauses, 1700), 1. 159.

[22]Ibid., 1. 160. For the complete text in German and commentaries cf. A. P. Johnston, *World Evangelism and the Word of God* (Minneapolis: Bethany, 1974) 30-32, 259-262.

[23]G. C. Berkouwer, *Sin* (Grand Rapids: Eerdmans, 1971) 213.

"by the hearing of the Word of God and the operation of the Holy Spirit."[24]

Reformed and Lutheran theologies have historically been distinguished from a "spiritualist" position that speaks of the Spirit working without Scripture, *sine verbo*. The traditional Lutheran position is *per verbum*, by the Word: "*Per* suggests the meaningful function of the Word which is proclaimed, and agrees with those scriptural passages which point to the power of the Word."[25] They are Isa 55:11; Heb 4:12; 1 Thess 2:13; Acts 4:33; 2 Cor 10:4; 2 Tim 4:17. *Cum verbo*, with the Word, represents the Reformed position, which gives emphasis to the Spirit who opens the heart and causes the Word to be efficacious. This is to say that there is "a subjective efficacy which must always *accompany* the objective Word."[26] *Cum* suggests that the preaching in itself does not have an automatic effect but emphasizes that the Word is appropriated in faith only by the power of the Spirit.[27] "Though the acceptance of the Word would seem to be a matter of our own choice and activity, yet *in that choice* the power of the Spirit is at work."[28]

The Scriptures have their dynamic and living quality because of their origin in and inspiration by a living God and a living Redeemer (Heb 3:12; 7:25; 9:14; 10:31; 12:22). For this reason the living God supernaturally accompanies the living Word by the Holy Spirit as it is read, proclaimed and taught (4:12).

Thus the evangelist is to proclaim the Holy Scriptures (2 Tim 4:2). In so doing, God's purposes for the salvation of believers are accomplished (Isa 55:8-11). The Scriptures have never been proclaimed in vain, for they are able to break down the most resistant sinner's will (Acts 9), or they remain as a stern and ultimate judgment upon those who reject God's revelation of himself in creation (Romans 1) or in Christ (John 12:47-48).

This use of the Bible in world evangelization is described by Merle D'Aubigné, noted historian of the Reformation. What he spoke concerning Luther's translation may well apply to those who proclaim and translate the Scriptures into the multiple tongues of the world.

> The bond that unites to Christ will be everything to the believing soul. . . . Thus, as the doctrine of the Bible had impelled Luther's contemporaries toward Jesus Christ, their love for Jesus Christ, in its turn, impelled them toward the Bible. It was not, as some in our days have supposed, from a philosophical necessity, or from doubt, or a spirit of inquiry that they reverted to Scripture, it was because they found *there* the word of *Him they*

---

[24]Ibid., p. 214.
[25]Ibid., p. 217.
[26]Ibid., p. 215.
[27]Ibid., p. 217.
[28]Ibid., p. 218.

loved. "You have preached Christ," said they to the Reformer, "let us now
hear him himself." And they caught at the sheets given to the world, as a
letter coming to them from heaven.[29]

The man or woman of God may share with confidence the appropriate
message of the gospel, the good news, assured that "thus saith the Lord"
whose Spirit works in, with and by Scripture.

[29]J. H. M. D'Aubigné, *History of the Great Reformation* (3d ed.; London:
D. Walther, 1840), 3. 104.

GENERAL INDEX

Abba^cilum-Yarimlim treaty   35
Abraham   11, 14, 16, 32, 33, 35–46,
   132
   —(Abram)   164, 188
   —his faith   38–39, 43
Abraham, Isaac and Jacob   14, 41, 204
Achaia   169
Achan   310
Acts,
   —book of   113, 149, 150, 152, 154,
      169, 172, 172 n. 6, 179, 180, 181
Adam   10, 11, 12, 14
Adam and Eve   12, 60
Adriatic Sea   168
Aesop's Fables   312
Age of Reason   207, 208
Ahab   17, 21
Ahaz   79, 80, 81, 82, 83
Akkadian,
   —language   34, 35
Alexander the Great   26
Alexandria   157, 294
Alexandrian/Byzantine
   —(textual traditions)   171, 172, 176,
      181, 182
Amaziah   64
American Bible Society   259, 262, 268,
   269
Ammon   93
Amos   62, 63, 63 n. 7, 64, 65, 66, 67, 68
   n. 15, 69, 70
"Amsterdam" position   201
"Amsterdam School"   198
Anabaptist   86, 87, 99, 107
Ananias and Sapphira   233
animals
   —laws concerning   19
   —sacrifice   44
Antioch
   —on the Orontes   158, 177, 177 n.
      19
   —Syrian   158
Antiochus Epiphanes   26
anthropologists   283, 285, 286

apocalyptic literature   26
   —Jewish   88 n. 6
Apocrypha   202, 213
apostles   137, 149, 153, 170, 210, 213,
   215, 312, 313
"apostolic decree"   171–183, 171, 172,
   172 n. 6, 176, 180, 181
Aquinas, Thomas   193
Aramaic
   —language   90 n. 11, 93 n. 16, 94,
      217
Aramean   295
archaeology, archaeological   47
   —importance for OT study   11
Arminians (Remonstrants)   208, 219
Aristotle   220, 251, 277
Aristotelian (philosophical principles)
   208
   —Aristotelianism   193
Arnaz, Desi Jr.   278
Arndt, John   208
Arpad-KTK treaty   32 n. 4
Asia   167
Assyria, Assyrian(s)   80, 81, 83
ASU   260, 261, 262, 264, 267, 268, 269
Athens   123, 169
Augustine   193, 235 n. 31
Baal (Hadad)   17, 68, 70, 71, 149
Babylon, Babylonian   191
   —invasion of Judah   18
   —exile   20, 23
   —language   34
Baptists   242
Barga^cayah-Mati^cil treaty   35
Barnabas   158
Barth, Karl   211, 212
Basnage, Jacques   221
"beast," the   191
beatitudes   87
Beaverbrook, Lord   279
Belgic Confession   318
Bellarmine, Cardinal   213, 217
Belshazzar   266
Blayrey, Benjamin   258

Beza, Theodore   221, 256
Bezalel, son of Uri   120
Bible, Biblical
—arrangement   64
—as Word of God 14, 197, 198, 237, 244
—authority   200, 251, 309, 311–313
—believing interpreters   75, 84
—Christian religion   167
—clarity of   237–253, 242, 252
—content, teaching of   9, 13, 128, 135, 137, 146, 230, 230 n. 20, 230 n. 21, 243, 304, 307, 315, 318
—concepts   303
—courses 9
—criticism   207, 220
—division of (OT/NT)   125
—English   255–270
—errors in   226, 229, 230, 314
—God's self–revelation   194
—hermeneutics, interpretation 209, 240, 241, 242, 244, 245–248, 248 n. 43, 252
—historians   137ff.
—history, times   59, 129, 131, 133, 139, 144, 145
—imagery 294
—in evangelism   309–320
—inspiration   200, 201, 207–223, 225, 244
—institutes, colleges (etc.)   10
—Jewish background, roots of   126, 128, 132
—languages   209
—materials   292, 294 n. 35, 295
—nature of   59, 60, 62, 64, 126, 199, 236
—principles   273, 275
—purpose of   226 n. 7, 227 n. 10, 227 n. 11, 228 n. 15, 235, 241, 243, 271–281
—self-authenticating   317
—scholars   147, 249, 250
—study of   199, 202
—symbols   292-299
—terms   305
—text(s)   13, 86, 123, 232, 251 n. 51, 252

—translation   255–270
—truth of   223, 225–236, 227 n. 9, 227, n. 11, 228 n. 15
—use of   307, 310, 319
—view of life   123
—writers/authors   225, 226, 229, 244, 249
—world   123
Biblias (Rhone Valley martyr)   177
Bishops Bible   256
Bonfrere, Jacques   221
Book of Jubilees   21
Britain   275, 276
Brunner, Emil   193
Bullinger, Heinrich   211
Bultmann, R. 237, 251, 299
Caesarea   118, 121, 122, 169
Cage, John   280
Cain   14
Calov   210, 214, 215
Calvin, John   209, 210, 212, 214, 219, 255, 316, 317
Cambridge Paragraph Bible   259, 268
Campbell, Lady Jean   279
Canaan, Canaanite   12, 16, 17, 44, 48, 231 n. 24, 263
—burial practice   48ff.
Cappel, Louis, Younger   222
Carradan, Lord   275
Cartesian (philosophical principles)   208–210, 217
Cenchrea   159
Challorer, Richard   257
Charybdis   45
"Christ event"   140, 141, 144
Christian(s)   45, 72, 85, 89, 102–105, 108, 112, 123, 126, 129, 131, 134, 135, 150, 171, 173, 175 n. 13, 175 n. 14, 183, 185, 271, 273, 274, 280, 303, 304, 309, 315
—American   65
—Biblical   236
—doctrines, teaching, theology   126, 129, 139, 185, 186, 237, 238, 239, 251, 252, 253, 272, 284ff., 291
—early   150, 176, 181, 182
—ethics   85, 86, 95, 107, 175, 181
—era   11

—evangelical 126, 303
—faith 125, 126, 132, 138, 140 n. 17, 142, 150, 155, 237, 251 n. 51
—Gentile 174, 174 n. 11, 176, 177
—Jewish 90 n. 11, 173, 174, 177
—legalism 179
—missionaries 158
—obedience 297
—salvation 172, 173
—suffering 294
—theologians 194
—truth 235
Christian colleges 124, 131
Christianity 123, 124, 125, 128, 129, 132, 205, 307, 310, 316
—Jewish source of 124, 125, 175
—and historical interp. 140
—universality 160
—liberalism in 195
—conciliar 301
Christ's missionary to the Gentiles 157
Chronicles, book(s) of 199, 225 n. 1
Chrysostom, John 125
Church 10, 45, 59, 66, 72, 87, 109, 111, 113, 116, 123–135, 149, 170, 173, 181, 187, 188, 195, 208, 209, 212, 218, 243, 245, 252, 253, 283, 296, 304, 309, 311–318
—age 116 n. 17
—authority 310
—Christian 28, 194, 280, 314
—councils 311, 314
—early 137, 172, 174 n. 11, 176, 181, 182, 294
—ecumenical 30
—evangelism 159
—growth, expansion 67, 153, 171 n. 4
—history 129, 221, 284
—Jewish orientation of 175
—leaders 132
—local 310
—missionary calling of 188
—primitive 311, 312
—proclamation of 244, 245
—tradition 310
—unity of 310
Cicero 220

circumcision 39, 43, 164, 264
City of God 191
Clement of Alexandria 211
Cocceius, Johannes 212, 214, 222
Communication
—clarity and meaning in 238–241
Copernicus, Nicolaus 208
Corinth, Corinthian 157, 159, 163, 181
—Church 103, 153
—1st Epistle to 174 n. 11
Council of Jerusalem (Jerusalem Council) 171, 172, 172 n. 6, 174, 179, 180, 182, 183
covenant(s) 11, 12, 17, 33–46, 62, 65, 164, 165, 188
—Mosaic Siniatic 18, 32, 40, 42–44
—Abrahamic 31–46, 36 n. 23, 165
—Davidic 31, 40, 42, 43
—etymology 33–35
—people 91, 92
—Noahic 42
—of promise 120
—of grace 45
—New 12, 62 n. 6, 109, 109 n. 2, 113, 120, 122, 181
—ancient 165
Covenant theology 161
creation
—the goal of 28–29
cultural symbolism 287
Cypriote
—pottery at Dothan 51
Cyrus 103 n. 38
Dalmatia 168
Damascus 79, 80, 82
Daniel
—man, prophet 120, 275
—book of 120
David 12, 24, 31, 32, 122, 204, 220, 229, 234, 277
—dynasty of 22, 26, 27, 80
—son of 22, 23, 27
—house of 24, 26, 27, 80, 83
—throne of 27
—covenant (see covenants)
—descendants 204
David and Solomon 22, 42
day of the Lord 110, 111, 112, 113,

114, 115, 115 n. 14, 115 n. 16, 120, 122

D-(codex Bezae)   171, 176, 179
  —(text)   180, 182
D document   12
Dead Sea   24, 27
Dead Sea Scrolls
  —1QS 1:9–11   93
Decalogue   107
demons   188
demythologizing   251
Descartes, Rene   208
Des Marets, Samuel   222
Deuteronomic Code   18, 19
Deuteronomy, book of   12, 13, 20, 120, 161, 165
Dialectical materialism   279
"dictation theory"   214
Didascalia   171
Dilthey   237, 247
dispensational, dispensation(s)   161
  —and OT studies   10
  —writers   109 n. 2
documentary hypothesis (see also Graf-Wellhausen theory)   11
Dominus et Deus   185
Domitian   185
Dothan   47, 50–58
  —Tomb One at   50, 50 n. 10
  —excavation of   50
  —burial deposits   51
  —theological and sociological inferences of mortuary practice   52–56
dualism
  —in Platonism   127
DuMoulin   219
Dutch theologians   220
East Germany   275
Eastern Orthodox   303
ecumenical theology   303
Eden   16
Edom   111
Egypt, Egyptian   14, 16, 17, 18, 25, 34, 43, 44, 65, 121, 134, 149, 157, 192, 275, 295
  —cultural background   123
El Greco   169

Elijah   17
Elisha   19
English deists   208
Enlightenment   280
Enoch
  —apocryphal work of   118
Epaenetus   167
Ephesus   294
Ephraim   79, 80, 81, 82, 111
Epistle of Barnabus   171
Erasmus   243, 255
Esarhaddon   80
Essene(s), Dead Sea Sect   98
Euphrates   22, 41
Europe   159
Eusebius   170
evangelists   215
Eve   233
Evolution   195
Existentialism   280
existential theology   139
Exodus, the   18, 123, 294, 305
  —and conquest   31
Ezekiel, man   25, 111, 111 n. 4, 118, 122
Ezra and Nehemiah   26
"false prophet", the   191
Feast of Tabernacles   25
Feast of Weeks   117
Fonda, Jane   274
form criticism,   11
Francke, August Hermann   208
free enterprise   272, 273
Free University of Amsterdam   198
Fuller Theological Seminary   198, 225, 225 n. 1, 225 n. 4, 236
fundamentalists   198
Gadamer, Hans-Georg   237, 247
Galatia(n)
  —letter   163, 172 n. 6
Galbraith, John Kenneth   272, 273
Galileo   208
Genesis, book of   10, 40, 62, 97, 264
Geneva   217, 222, 223
Geneva Bible   255, 256
Gentile(s)   27, 45, 119, 120, 122, 124, 125, 154, 157, 158, 162, 163, 164, 165,

166, 167, 168, 169, 171, 173, 174, 176, 179, 183, 188
—uncircumcised 172, 173
—Jew-versus (contrast) 162–163
Gerhard 212, 214
German pietism 208, 318
Germany 217, 274
Gnostic(s), Gnosticism 127, 128
God
—activity, intervention into history of 111, 140, 141, 143–146, 190, 191, 194, 196, 201, 203, 293, 294, 296, 303
—anger, wrath of 61, 62, 65, 69, 174 n. 10, 191, 204
—as king 293
—author, source of Revelation 13, 153, 194–205, 211–218, 221, 228, 311
—character of 189, 229, 279
—commands 159
—counsel of 158
—covenants 11, 12, 14, 31–46
—creator (creation of) 15, 37, 62, 127, 129, 130, 186, 187, 191, 192, 196, 197, 204, 243, 299
—deliverer of His own, the 188
—doctrine of 185, 194–205
—eternity of 186
—existence of 141, 209, 237
—Father 62, 104, 117, 133, 212, 292, 310
—fellowship with 122, 127
—fidelity of 165
—fullness of 149, 151
—future work of 116, 190, 191
—grace of 31, 37, 62, 187, 189
—glory of 216, 246
—immanence of 194, 195, 201, 204
—independence of 191
—intention of (in Scripture) 229, 231, 232
—jealousy of 72, 114
—Judge, the 116, 192
—judgment 66, 115 n. 14, 188, 189, 190
—justice of 187–189

—living 318, 319
—love for 12, 71
—love of 14, 61, 127, 155, 204, 267, 297, 298
—of blessing 129
—of heaven 129
—of Israel 25, 98, 142, 167, 234
—of NT 86, 181
—of OT 86, 181
—omniscience (knowledge) 61, 195
—plan, purposes of 110, 122, 155, 163, 164, 187, 188, 190, 191, 292, 299
—power of 189, 192, 195, 305, 318
—reality of 304
—relation to men 191–192, 290 n. 18
—righteousness of 192
—ruler 187
—saving activity 127, 165
—servants of 152
—sovereignty of 155, 186–188, 221
—transcendence 194, 197, 203, 205, 293, 304
—Triune, the 212
—voice of 13
—"wholly other," the 197
—will of 97, 106, 155, 162, 187
God's Revelation 110, 111
"golden rule"
—negative form 171, 176, 180, 180 n. 21
Gomar, Francis 222
Good News Bible (GNB) 265, 266
gospel(s) 45, 159, 163, 164, 179, 228 n. 12, 245, 310, 320
—of God 167
Graf-Wellhausen theory 10–11
—(see documentary hypothesis)
great commission 117, 159
Greece 169
Greek
—cultural background 123
—language 90, 91, 91 n. 12, 92 n. 12, 93 n. 16, 100, 103 n. 38, 124, 217, 256, 258, 260, 263, 267, 268, 283

—literature 130
—people 295
—philosophers 127
—text (of Bible) 256, 259, 270
—world 130
Grotius, Hugo 221
Guevara, Che 306
Gulf of Aqaba 25
Halakah 92, 94, 94 n. 20
—oral 92
—written 92
—rabbinic 92, 94, 96
—Pharisaic 92, 94
Hasmonean(s) 26, 27
Hebraic (culture) 123ff
Hebraic (view of faith) 132
Hebrew
—language 24, 34, 35, 36, 36 n. 25, 78, 82, 114, 114 n. 12, 13, 118 n. 22, 131, 134, 217, 232 n. 26, 258, 259, 260, 263, 264, 267
—nation (see Israel) 41, 154, 295
—text (of Bible) 111, 255, 256, 270
—burial practice 48ff.
Hebrews
—epistle to 14, 113, 204, 313
Hebrew Scriptures (Bible) 123, 125, 134
Hegel 290
Heidegger, Johann Heinrich 210, 213, 215, 223, 237, 247, 285
Heilsgeschichte 142, 146
Hellenism
—pagan 125
Herbert of Cherbury, Lord 208, 221
higher criticism 200, 221, 314
Hillel 20, 96 n. 24
historical criticism 137, 138
historical-critical method 138 n. 5, 139, 139–140 n. 16, 142, 144, 146
history
—philosophy and Bible interpretation 137–148
—as revelation 138ff., 144
—Biblical 144, 145
—proleptic view towards 145, 146
Hobbes, Thomas 208, 221
Hodge, C. A. 193
Holy Spirit, Spirit 28, 81, 107, 112,

112 n. 5, 113, 114, 116–122, 117 n. 18, 118 n. 24, 149–155, 157, 158, 161, 165–168, 179–181, 202, 208–217, 219, 228 n. 12, 242, 269, 293–297, 307–319
—and Scripture 209, 210, 213, 311
—baptism of 118
—fruit of 152
—gifts of 153
—indwelling 28
—love of 170
—manifestation of 149–155
—new 119
—power of 166
—regeneration of 151
—relation to Christ 152
Hoornbeek, Johannes 222
Horeb 12
Horizontuerschelzung 247
Hosea 17, 63, 63 n. 7, 65, 70
Hoshea 82
Husserl 247
Hyrcanus, John 26
idolatry 70, 72
Ignatius 125
Illyricum 157, 166, 168
Immanuel 79, 80, 81, 81 n. 24, 83
"inerrancy" 199, 205, 207, 219, 225, 226, 228, 229, 236, 313
"infallibility" 207, 219–221, 231 n. 24, 242
International Council on Biblical Inerrancy (council) 200, 201, 205
Irenaeus 171, 177 n. 18, 180, 181, 182, 185
Isaac 39, 40, 41
Isaiah 62–73, 63 n. 7, 75–84, 118, 118 n. 24, 122, 162, 165, 186, 188, 198
Israel
—covenant community 293
—house of 113, 116, 118
—Jacob 44, 111
—land of 15, 23, 109, 119, 173
—nation, people 11, 12, 17, 42. 63–66, 68, 69, 81 n. 24, 109, 112–116, 119 n. 25, 120, 124, 134, 135, 149, 163, 164, 186, 188, 195, 202, 294, 296, 299, 305, 306
—promises to 164

—society 69
—worship of God 69
Israelites 13, 17, 39, 93, 165
Italy 274
Jacob 44, 111
James 154, 173
Jeremiah 31, 35, 40, 63, 63 n. 7, 64, 66, 69, 70, 113, 120
Jerome 128, 171 n. 4
Jerusalem 18, 24, 25, 27, 32, 99, 111, 123, 124, 155, 157, 166, 168, 169, 170, 177 n. 19
—church 153, 175 n. 13
—congregation 153
—officials 172
Jesus Christ 10, 12, 14, 18, 21, 23, 25, 27–29, 37, 45, 46, 62, 70, 72, 78, 81, 84, 85, 87, 88 n. 7, 89, 90 n. 11, 91–103, 103 n. 38, 105–107, 106 n. 40, 111, 116, 117, 120–122, 139, 141, 143, 147, 149, 151, 153, 157, 159, 160, 164–167, 170, 180, 185, 203, 230, 231, 235 n. 30, 238, 261, 262, 265, 269, 293–297, 294 n. 34, 303, 304, 307, 309–311, 314, 317–320
—Alpha and Omega 186
—atonement of 194
—authority of 190
—blessing of 170
—body of (church) 135, 153, 175, 230 n. 21, 298, 314
—bride of 314
—call of 152
—cause of 150
—death of 117, 118, 153, 204, 295
—deity of 181, 194
—disciples, followers of 96, 101, 104, 105, 152
—end of the law, the 160
—entombment of 147
—ethic of 87, 101, 105, 177
—faith in 144
—gospel of 151, 166
—humanity of 194, 203
—incarnate Word, the 271
—incarnation of 140, 309, 315
—Jew, the 124
—Lamb (of God), the 185, 188
—life and ministry 149, 153
—Lord and Savior 122, 152, 161, 176, 192, 294
—mediator 294
—name of 153
—Redeemer 191, 305, 319
—resurrection of 139, 140 n. 17, 142, 144, 145, 147, 161, 189, 230 n. 21
—sacrifice of 189, 204
—second advent, coming 111, 298
—service of 154
—speeches of, sayings, words of 159, 164, 225 n. 3, 234
—teaching of 85–108, 159
—on divorce 96–98
—on oaths 98–100
—on retaliation 100–106
Jewish theology 124
Jewish Scriptures 185
Jezebel 21
Joel
—book of (prophecy of) 109, 111, 111 n. 4, 112, 112 n. 5, 113, 114, 115, 116, 116 n. 17, 118, 119, 119 n. 25, 120, 121, 122
John 213
—gospel of 96
—apostle 313, 314
John Murry Company of New York and Baltimore 258
John the Baptist 27, 307
Jonah 231
Jordan
—river 23, 24, 25
Joseph 71, 234, 274
Joshua 12, 312
—days of 41
Josiah
—reform of 31
Jubilee, year of 21
Judah
—Nation of and land of 20, 79, 81, 116
—tribe 111
—house of 113, 116
Judaism 88, 124, 125, 129 n. 11
—orthodox 87
—proselytes to 158

Jude 213
Judea 153
Judean kingdom 186
Judeo-Christian faith 280
Judges, book of 192
Jurieu, Pierre 223
justification by faith 62
Justin Martyr 124, 125
Kadesh Barnea 17
Kant, Immanuel 288
Kerygma 153
Kidron Valley 24
Kierkegaard, Soren 193
Kepler, Johann 208
Kingdom 28
—of God 26, 27, 28, 43, 83, 97, 98,
    99, 106, 106 n. 40, 188, 293
—millennial 112
—of Christ 10, 46, 96, 99, 191
—ethics 100
Kings, book(s) of 199, 225 n. 1
KJV 100, 104, 114, 115 n. 16, 163, 256,
    257, 258, 259, 260, 261, 262, 264,
    266, 267, 268, 269
—Cambridge Edition 258
—New KJV 266
Knox, John 279
lake of fire 191
Latin America 304, 306
law 12, 14, 87, 88, 88 n. 7, 89, 90 n. 11,
    92, 94, 96, 98, 99, 102, 106 n. 40, 134,
    165, 179, 186
—Jewish 101, 177
—of works 161
—of righteousness 161
—of God 234
—concerning slaves 19
law-grace 10
law of retaliation (lex talionis) 100, 101
"Laws of the sons of Noah" 173, 173
    n. 9
Lebanon 22
Levi,
—tribe of 26
Leydekker, Melchior 209
Leyden Synopsis 214
Leibnitz, Gottfried 208
Lippmann, Walter 273
linguistics 285

Locke, John 208, 221
Lord of hosts 111
Lord's Supper 175
Louis XIV of France 208
Luce, Henry 279
Luke 157, 168, 169, 198, 213
—gospel 102 n. 36, 104, 149, 153,
    164
Lutheran
—church 207, 217, 303, 319
—theologians 213, 317
—Pietism 317
Luther, Martin 210, 211, 212, 219, 245,
    251, 319
—views on the Bible 242 n. 13
Maccabaeus, Judas 26
Macedonia 168, 169
Maher-Shalal-Hash-Baz 78, 79, 80
Malachi, book of 10, 98, 164
Marcionite heresy 62
Marcion 124, 125
Marcus Aurelius 150
Mari 34, 35, 48
Mark 91, 213, 294
Marriage
—in Christian thought 128, 128 n.
    9
—in Hebrew thought 128
Mary 80
—immaculate conception of 128
Masius, Andreas 221
Masoretic Text 261
Mastricht, Peter Van 209, 212
Matthew
—gospel 86 n. 3, 91, 97, 100, 102,
    102 n. 36, 107, 164, 261
Mediterranrean (sea) 23, 24, 25, 168
—regions, churches of 159
Mekilta 100
Messiah 14, 80, 81 n. 24, 82, 83, 111,
    112, 118 n. 22, 121, 124, 125, 164
—Jesus as 153
Messianic 81, 82, 112
—-King 115 n. 16
Messianic community, people 149, 151,
    152
Meyer, Ludwig 209
Micah 64, 81
Micaiah 234

Middle Ages
—concept of salvation 129
Midrash 174 n. 10
miracles 138, 147, 149, 150, 194, 195, 197, 202, 205, 306, 318
Mishna 95, 100 n. 28, 101, 101 n. 33, 295
missions, missionary 158, 162, 163, 167, 168
—Christian 158, 159, 160, 168, 169
—apostolic 166–168
Moab 93
Moesia 168
Moffatt (translation) 115 n. 16
monotheism 175
Montanism, Revived 208
Moriah 39
Morin, Jean 221
Mosaic tradition 87, 106
Moses 10, 12, 13, 14, 42, 87, 90 n. 11, 91, 96, 97, 98, 106, 107, 118 n. 23, 120, 128, 135, 154, 160, 161, 163, 215, 218, 220, 234, 312, 314
—law of 26, 86, 87 n. 4, 88, 90, 90 n. 11, 91, 107
Mount of Olives 25
Mount Sinai 12, 14, 134
Mt. Zion 23, 31, 32
Münster, Sebastian 255, 256
Mycenaean
—pottery at Dothan 51
Naboth 21
NASB 114, 117, 261, 262, 263, 264
nativity narrative
—Luke's 27
NATO 274
NEB 63, 100, 115 n. 16, 262
Nebuchadnezzar 275
Neo-orthodoxy 197
Nero 185
"new birth" 311
New Testament (NT) 10
—canon 312
—scholarship 137
Nicodemus 116
Nile 17, 25
—river of Egypt 41
NIV 114, 115 n. 16, 117, 235 n. 30, 261, 266

Nixon, Richard 273
Noah 11, 14, 16, 119, 231
North Africa
—church of 159
Notre Dame University 313
Obadiah 111, 111 n. 4
Old Testament (OT) 9
—approaches to teaching (methods of studying) 10–14
—historical development 42
—inductive theological-historical-cultural approach 12–14
—theology 292–293
Origen 171, 177, 177 n. 19, 182
Orr, James 199
P45 (Chester Beatty papyrus) 171, 176, 182
P document, source 39
Pakistan 275
—East Pakistan 275
Pakistan-India War (1971) 275
Palestinian 82
Palestine 169
Pannonia 168
Parachurch evangelism 314
Paris, F. S. 258
passover 117, 294, 295
—Christ our 296
patriarchs, patriarchal 122, 215, 316
Paul 19, 29, 44, 45, 70, 89, 99, 100, 103, 105, 106, 117 n. 18, 120, 121 n. 33, 124, 129, 130, 134, 154, 157–170, 172, 177, 202, 225, 230 n. 22, 231, 234, 266, 313, 314
—missionary travel 169
—Christ's Ambassador 158
—Christ's Servant 158
—(Saul) 158
—Pharisee 130
Peace of Westphalia; 1648 207–208
Pekah and Rezin 82
Pentateuch 11, 12, 14, 18, 44, 91, 92, 97, 100, 101, 162, 173, 221
Pentecost
—day of 28, 109, 112, 112 n. 5, 113, 114, 116, 116 n. 17, 118, 120, 121, 121 n. 29, 122, 312
People's Republic of China 275, 277
Pereira, Bento 221

Pergamum 181
Persia, Persian(s)
—empire 26, 186
—language 103 n. 38
Peter 46, 109, 112, 112 n. 5, 113, 114,
115 n. 14, 116, 121, 151, 154, 177,
220
Peyre, Isaac de la 221
pharaoh 192, 275
Pharisee(s) 87, 89, 94, 95, 97, 98, 204,
262
Philippi
—Greek jailer at 130
Phoebe 159
Plato 127, 220, 248 n. 43
Platonic thought 125
Platonism 127, 128 n. 9
Polansdorf, Polanus von (Amandus)
221
Polanus 215
Pompeii 47
post–exilic period 26–27
Princeton Seminary 200
—"old" 193
Princeton theologians 193
"promise," promises 12, 31, 32, 38–41,
45, 46, 125, 164, 165
prophetic foreshortening 110ff.
prophets, Prophets 12, 14, 17, 19, 23,
31, 41, 63, 65, 71, 88, 89, 90, 90 n. 11,
92, 96, 98, 106, 106 n. 40, 107, 109,
110, 120, 149, 153, 161, 162, 165,
186, 210, 213, 215, 229, 234, 312
proselytes 24
Protestant 85, 125, 133, 237, 238, 242,
245, 276, 313, 315
—Reformers 89, 208, 210, 211, 213,
214, 216, 219, 241, 242, 284, 311,
317, 318, 320
—Reformation 167, 207, 211, 218,
284, 310, 311, 313, 314, 316, 317
—"newer Protestantism" 210
—theologians 221
—theology 242, 243
—translators 257
Psalms
—book of 123, 165
Psalms of Solomon 27

pseudo-Clementine Recognitions 90 n.
11, 177 n. 17
Queen Mary 279
Quenstedt 214
Qumran 171 n. 4
—community of 27
Rabbi Gamaliel 165, 295
Rabbi Ibn Ezra 119
rabbinic, rabbinism 88 n. 7, 94, 94 n.
21, 101, 102 n. 34, 202
—literature 87, 88 n. 6, 93, 95
—law 101 n. 33
Rachel 267
racism 276
Rahner, Karl 290
Rechabites 17
Reed (Red) Sea 306
Reformed (position, interpretation) 86,
89, 199, 207–223, 227 n. 10, 319
—theologians 207, 211
—church 207, 208
Religions-geschichtliche Schule 138, 143
Renaissance 280
Revelation/Apocalypse 181, 185–192
revelation of God 139, 142, 148
—in the Bible 193–205, 207–223,
238, 272, 281, 292, 297, 298
—in the history of Israel 139, 143
—in Christ 139, 141–143, 143 n.
29, 176
—self, the 140, 140 n. 18, 141, 195,
238, 280, 294
—Jewish context 142, 195
—in all things 196–197
Revision committee of convocation 260
Rheims version 257
Rhodesia 275
Richards, I. A. 285
Rijssen, Leonard van 218, 219, 223
Robert, Pierre (Olivetan) 255
Roman Catholic Church 85, 86 n. 3,
133, 207, 208, 217, 218, 219, 276,
307, 313, 316
—translators 257
Roman pontiff 312
Rome, Roman(s) 27, 83, 158, 159, 166,
168, 169, 170, 294
—law 101

—cultural background 123
—empire 155, 157, 177
—epistle 157, 165, 167, 168, 170
—church(es)
    —congregation 158, 163, 164, 167, 170, 313
    —believers 159, 163, 164, 169
    —senate 185
"root of Jesse" 165
RSV 75, 78, 88, 117, 175, 235 n. 30, 261, 268, 269
RV 115 n. 16
Sabbath
    —day, laws of 18, 88 n. 7, 94, 20
    —year, laws of 19, 20, 21
Samaria 118, 121, 122, 153
Samuel 198
    —book(s) of 199
Satan 218, 233
Saul
    —messengers of 120
scarabs 52
Schleiermacher 299
Schlesinger, Arthur Maier Jr. 272
Schwenkfelders 208, 219
Scofield Bible, the (New) 10, 261, 262
Scotland 217
Scottish common-sense realism 193
Scripture, doctrine of 193–205
Scylke 45
SEATO 274
Second-Commonwealth Judaism 173, 174
Second Confession of the English Baptists (1677) 242
Second General Conference of Latin America Bishops (Medellin) 304, 305, 306, 307
seminaries
    —conservative 125
Sennacherib 24
Septuagint, LXX 119 n. 26, 162, 165, 186
Sermon on the Mount (SM) 85, 86, 86 n. 3, 87, 87 n. 4, 89, 91, 92, 103, 105
"servanthood" 105–106
Servant of the Lord 118
Seven churches of Asia 181

Shammai 96
Shear-Jashub 78, 80
Shechem 37
Silas 130
Simon
    —from Cyrene 103
Simon, Richard 208, 220, 221
Sisera 192
Social Darwinism 272
Socinians 208, 219
Sodom
    —king of 37
Sodom and Gomorrah 66
Solomon 22, 41, 234
    —day of 26
    —reign of 41
Son of Man 27, 28
Song of Songs 262, 266
South Africa 275, 276
Soviet Union 274, 275, 277
Spain 158, 160, 162, 163, 166, 167, 168, 169, 170
Spanheim, Friedrich Younger 219, 222
Spencer, Philip Jacob 208
Spinoza, Baruch 208, 221
Spirit of truth 117
Stephen 261
Stoic(s) 150
Suffering Servant 117
symbolism in theology 283–299
Synod of Dort, 1618 257
Syria 25, 168
Syrian Language 217
Syro-Palestine 182
Taiwan 275
Talmud 134, 173, 173 n. 9, 176 n. 16
Targums 92 n. 13
Taylor, Kenneth 264, 265
Temple,
    —Second 25
Ten Commandments 188
Tertullian 171, 176, 179, 180, 181, 182
textual criticism (lower) 199, 200, 258
theology of liberation 307
"Theology of the Word" 139
Thessalonian(s) 181
Third World 301, 303
Thirty Years' War 207

Thyatira   181
Timothy   157, 313
Titus   157
tombs   47–58
Tolstoian   99
Torah   64, 68, 90 n. 11, 92, 94, 96, 98,
    100, 102, 106, 107, 107 n. 41, 134,
    161, 173, 175
    —"new Torah"   107 n. 41
Torres, Camilo   306
tree(s)
    —of knowledge of good and evil   16
    —of life   16
    —laws concerning   19
trinity   310
Trinity Evangelical Divinity School
    200
Tronchin, Louis   219, 223
truth, theories of   226–228
Turretini, Francois   213, 216, 217, 218,
    220, 223
Tyndale, William   261
typology
    —as a study method   10
Ugarit   48
Ugaritic   78 n. 16
Ugaritic Texts   48, 49, 57, 58
    —Aqht A [vi]   48 n. 4
    —Aqht C [iii]   48 n. 5, 49 n. 8
    —Baal, g I*AB [ii]   48 n. 6
    —Keret   48
    —Baal, h I*AB   49 n. 7, 57 n. 19
    —Aqht A [i]   57 n. 18
    —Krt A[i]   57 n. 19
    —Krt B[u]   57 n. 19
    —Baal, g I*AB [vi]   57 n. 20
    —Aqht C [iv]   58 n. 22
United Nations   40
University of Basel   221
University of Halle   208
University of Leiden   209, 217, 222, 223
University of Tübingen   221
University of Utrecht   209, 217, 222,
    223
Uriah   220
Vespasian   185

Vietnam   274, 301
Voetius, Gijsbert   209, 210, 213, 217,
    222
Voss, Isaac   221
Vulgate   257
Warfield, Benjamin B.   193, 214
Wheaton College   2ff., 9, 50
Weigelians   208, 219
Weltanschauung   67
Wendelin, Marcus of Speyer   213
Western text   171, 176, 177 n. 18, 180,
    180 n. 21, 181
Westminster Confession of Faith
    —(1646)   125
    —(1647)   220, 242
Whittingham, William   256
William B. Eerdmans Pub. Co.   198
Wingle, Pierre de   255
Wittich, Christoph   209
Wolleb, Johannes   221
Wolzogen, Ludwig   209
Word of God (God's Word)   9, 14, 59,
    60, 61, 63, 64, 66, 163, 197, 198, 203,
    207, 211, 212, 215, 216, 217, 218,
    219, 228, 237, 238, 240, 243 n. 19,
    244, 245, 246, 250, 252, 253, 271,
    279, 295, 313, 314, 316, 317, 319
World Council of Churches   275, 301
World Conference on Church and So-
    ciety (Geneva)   301, 304
World War II   274
"Writings"   165
Yahweh   16, 17, 18, 20, 21, 22, 23, 24,
    25, 68, 71, 80, 81, 174, 186
    —worship of   26
    —covenant of   31
    —day of   110, 111
Yugoslavia   168
Zadokite, high priest   26, 27
Zedekiah   82
Zelophehad   21
Zephaniah   111, 111 n. 4
Zion   66, 71
Zondervan Publishing Company   200
Zurich   217
Zwingli   209, 210, 284

SCRIPTURE INDEX

Genesis

1	154, 231
1-11	14
1-9	174
1:1-2:4a	15
1:2	267
1:4	267
1:7	267
1:28	15
1:31	128
2	231
2:2-3	18
2:4b-3:24	16
2:8-17	16
2:16	44
2:17	233
3:3	265
3:4	233
3:11	44
3:15	12
3:17-19	16
3:17-18	29
4:8	262
5:1ff.	265
5:29	16
6:3	234
6:11	174
6:13	119
7:1	262
9:4	175
9:10	262
9:20	16
10:5	262
12-50	14
12-22	32
12	36
12:1-3	36, 37, 39, 40
12:1	36, 43
12:2	36
12:3	164, 188
12:4-5	39
12:4	36
12:6	263

12:7	37
14:22-23	37
15	32, 33, 35, 36, 44
15:1-6	32
15:6	45, 77
15:7-18	32
15:9-10	37
15:9	35, 36
15:18	35, 36, 41
16:8	265
17	43
17:1-2	37
17:1	36, 37
17:2	36
17:3	38
17:4	38
17:7	36
17:9-14	36, 38, 39
17:9	38, 40
17:10	38
17:13	36
17:23-27	39
18:19	39
21:9	262
22	77
22:2	36, 39
22:3-10	39
22:16-18	39
22:16	36
22:18	40, 43
25:8	49
25:30ff.	265
26:4-5	40
26:5	36, 40, 43
27:1ff.	265
31:47	266
35:29	49
37:17	50
37:35	48
42:16	234
44:4	262
46:22	265
46:27	219
47:29	232

Exodus

2:24	43
3:6	43, 204
3:14	186
6:4-5	44
6:8	43
7:14ff.	265
7:25	265
13:8	295
14	305
17	213
17:16	262
19:1	10
19:3-6	43
19:5	40
20:1-17	18
20:2	43
20:8-11	18
20:13	92
20:14	92
21-23	18
21:1-6	19
21:12	92
21:24	92, 100
22:26-27	102
23:4-5	19
23:4	93
23:5	262
23:10-11	20
23:14-17	18
23:31	41
24	44
24:3-8	18
31:2-3	120
32:13	44
34:21	18
34:22	117
34:24	18
35:3	18

Leviticus

3:17	175
4:2	234
4:22	234
4:27	234
5:15	234
5:18	234
6:21	262
7:27	175
11:26	266
17-26	18
17-18	173
17:10-14	175
18:5	161
18:6ff.	161, 175
19:12	92, 98
19:18	92, 93
19:26	175
19:27-28	48
19:33	93
20:10	262
22:14	234
23:15-21	118
24:20	100
25:1-6	20
25:8-17	20
25:8ff.	21
25:20-22	20
25:22	20
25:23-24	21
25:37	265
26:40-45	36
26:42	44

Numbers

1:5ff.	265
8:15-19	120
9:16	262
11:5	17
11:29	120
12:6	120
15:24-29	234
15:28	234
15:32ff.	18
20:28-29	58
21:8	263
21:14	265
24:24	262
28	68
34:6	262
35:11	234
35:16-33	92
36:1-12	21

Deuteronomy

1:7	41
1:8	41, 44
2:4	259
2:18	259
2:20	259
4	13
4:24	63
5:6-21	18
5:12-15	18
5:26	119
7:7-8	44
11:10ff.	17
11:22-25	41
11:24	41
12-26	18
13	163
13:14	232
15:1-6	20
15:9-10	20
15:12-18	19
17:4	232
18:8	262
18:15	90
18:18	90
18:22	234
19:21	100
20:19-20	19
22:1-4	19
22:6-7	19
22:8	19
22:10	19
22:20	232
23:3-6	93
23:12ff.	19
23:21-23	98
23:21	92
24:1-4	92, 96
24:1	97
25:4	19
26:1-11	17
26:5-11	295
26:14	48
28:15-68	40
28:45	81
30:11-14	161
30:12	161
30:14	161
30:16	262
31:9	13
31:17-18	115
31:19	213
32:21	163
32:43	165
32:50	49
33:8	262
33:9	264
34:8	58

Joshua

1:4	41
7	310
20:3	234
20:9	234
21:43-45	41
24:14	41

Judges

1:19	261
2:3	266
3:8	42
4-5	120
5:10	262
5:20	192
8:32	49
9:16	232
16:14	262
16:31	49

Ruth

1:11	261, 264
1:17	261
2:8	261
4:1	268

1 Samuel

2:1-10	128
13:1	264, 266
13:2	266
19:20-23	120
28:14	56

2 Samuel

1:2 57
1:21 266
2:6 232
3:31 57
5:8 267
7:18 24
7:28 232
14:2 58
21:2 266
21:12-14 49
21:16 266
22:15 266
23:9 266

1 Kings

2:10 49
4:20-21 41
4:20 22
4:25 26
4:26 225
8:10-11 265
8:26 234
9:4-9 41
10:16 266
11:24 266
11:41 265
11:43 49
13:27 268
15:7 265
15:8 49
17-18 17
17:24 232
20:34 266
21:3 21
22:16-22 234
22:16 232

2 Kings

1:18 265
3:18-25 19
6:13 50
10:15-16 18
15:6 265
15:21
15:26 265
15:29 80

16:5 79
16:7-8 80
17:1-23 42
17:28 115
17:35 35
22:14 120

1 Chronicles

16:15-18 44

2 Chronicles

9:25 225
9:29 265
15:3 . . . . 115, 232
16:14 56
18:15 232
20:7 33
24:37 265
35:25 57
35:27 265
36:21 20

Ezra

4:2 80
10:18 265

Nehemiah

6:9 266
9:13 232
10:2ff. 265
10:37 266
12:36 266
13:13ff. 18

Esther

4:1 57

Job

3:2 265
4:1 265
10:21-22 48
12:16 234
17:16 48
19:25-26 268
24:18 265
26:5 265

36:22 115
38:6 263

Psalms

6:1-5 58
11:1 264
18:49 164
19 160
19:3 268
19:4 163
22 229
30:9 232
36:10 216
45:13 266
46:4-5 24
51:11 122
55:4-8 277
57:2 266
58:9 266
65:2 119
65:5 119
68:17 266
72:6 115
72:7-8 22
72:8 41
72:16 22
78:61 266
80:11 41
84 . . . . 259, 260
84:5 261
84:8 259
88:1-14 58
89 41
94:17 48
94:20 71
104:27 119
105:8-11 44
110 204
116:10 117
118:22 263
119:67 234
119:105 216
119:151 232
119:160 232
119:163 234
132:11-12 41
136 266
136:25 119

137:5 266
139:21-22 93
141:7 266
144:6 266
145:9 119

Proverbs

5:13 115
9:9 . . . . 261, 266
14:25 . . . . 232, 234
25:21-22 106
30:19 78

Ecclesiastes

Book of 28
3:1ff. 94
3:4 150
5:6 . . . . 234, 266
7:1 267
7:18 266
7:28 266
10:5 234

Song of Solomon

1:1ff. 265

Isaiah

1:2-4 65-66
1:5-9 66-67
1:10-15 68-69
1:15-23 69-72
1:24-31 73
2:6 264
3:14-26 71
5:2-3 76
5:8-12 . . . . 71, 72
5:8 18
6 186
7-12 76
7 81
7:1 79
7:3 78
7:5 79
7:6 . . . . 79, 82
7:8 80
7:9 80
7:11 80

7:13 . . . . 80, 81
7:14-16 . . . . 79, 81
7:14 . . . . 75, 76, 77,
78, 79, 80,
81, 82, 84
7:15-17 81
7:15 . . . . 81, 83
7:16 . . . . .81, 82, 83
7:17 . . . . 81, 83
7:22-23 81
7:22 81
8 78
8:1 213
8:3-4 79
8:3 . . . . .78, 79, 81
8:4 . . . . 79, 82
8:7 82
8:8 . . . . 75, 79
8:10 81
8:18 80
9-11 75
9:6-7 75
9:6 75
9:7 75
9:13 66
10:19 232
11:1 75
11:6-9 22
11:10 . . . . .75, 165
13:5 111
13:6 110
15:2-3 57
16:9 80
19:20 81
20:3 81
21:8 264
24:5 41
27:7 266
28:9-10 63
28:16 . . . . .161, 263
29:13 68
30:9-11 63
30:27 63
32:15 118
33:21-22 24
35:1 23
35:5-6 23
35:10 23

37:9 266
37:30 81
38 58
38:7 80
38:22 80
:0:1-45:25 186
40:5-6 119
41:4 186
41:8 33
41:22 266
42:1 118
42:6-7 188
44:3 118
49:6 188
49:26 119
52:7 162
52:15 . . . . .166, 168
53:1 163
55:8-11 319
55:11 . . . . .232, 319
55:13 81
57:19 120
58 70
58:1-12 68
59:2-15 68
59:21 118
61:1 118
65:1-2 163
65:17 29
66:16 119
66:20 119
66:22 29
66:23 119

Jeremiah

Book of 42
1:6 120
1:18-19 64
2:6ff. 65
2:30 66
2:32ff. 65
3:1-8 97
4:1-2 40
5 68
5:3 66
5:23 69
6:8 66
6:10 64

7 68
7:6 70
7:11 69
7:28 66
8:8-9 64
9:5 232
9:17-19 57
10:10 232
11 68
11:21 64
14 68
17:21ff. 18
22:13-19 71
22:29 64
23:5-6 23
23:29 63
26:7-11 64
31:15 77
31:31-34 113
31:31 113
31:34 120
33:14-16 23
34:5 56
34:8 35
34:18-20 35
34:18 35
35:1-11 18
36:2 213
44:16 64
48:37 57
51:35 174

Lamentations

2:10 57

Ezekiel

8:17 174
11:18-19 119
18:8 232
20:24 266
24:17 266
26:16 57
27:31 57
30:3 110
33:23-26 42
36:26-28 119
37 59

37:12-14 119
39:28-29 118
40-48 23
44:3 24
45:11ff. 266
47:1-12 24
47:17-20 41
47:22-23 24
48:1 41
48:28 . . . . .41, 266

Daniel

2:9 234
5:25-27 262
5:26 266
8:12 266
9:27 266
10:21 232
12:4 229

Hosea

1:2ff. 65
1:11 77
2 68
2:5 70
2:8 . . . . 17, 70
4:1 63
5 68
6 68
7 68
8 68
8:14 . . . . 71, 72
9:6 268
11:2 261
12:13-14 65

Joel

1:13-14 114
1:15 . . . . .110, 111, 114
2:1 . . . . .110, 111, 114
2:2-11 114
2:12-17 114
2:18 114
2:19-27 . . . . 114, 115
2:23 115

2:26-28 113
2:28-32 . . . . 109, 112, 114,
                        115, 116, 121
2:28-29 114
2:28 . . . . 114, 115
2:29 . . . . .114, 115, 116
2:30-31 . . . . .113, 114, 121
2:30 114
2:31 . . . . 115, 116
2:32 . . . . .111, 114, 162
3:1-8 116
3:14 111
3:18 25
4:19 174

Amos

1:2 63
1:3 265
2 68
2:6-8 70
2:10ff. 65
2:11 264
2:12 64
3:1-2 65
3:8 63
3:10-15 71
4 68
4:1-5 70
4:6-11 66
4:13 62
5 68
5:5-9 62
5:10-15 71
5:18 22
6:1-8 71
7:10-17 64
7:14 263
8:5 18
8:10 57
9:5-6 62
9:9-15 113
9:11-12 173

Obadiah

15 110

Micah

2:6 64
7:11-12 41

Nahum

1:8 266
1:11 266
1:12 266
1:14 266
2:1 266
2:7 266

Habakkuk

2:2 213

Zephaniah

1:7 110
1:14 110
4:25 234

Zechariah

2:13 119
4:10 25
9:9 77
9:10 41
14:1 111
14:4-5 25
14:8-9 111
14:8 25
14:10 25

Malachi

2:13-16 98
4:5 115

Matthew

1:6 259
1:18 . . . . 76, 80
1:20-23 81
1:20 76
1:22 . . . . .76, 77, 94

1:23 . . . . 76, 77, 265	6:24 70
1:25 76	6:27 262
2:15 . . . . 77, 91	7:11 305
2:17 77	7:28-29 107
2:18 . . . . 259, 267	8:2-4 265
3:3 91	8:13 262
3:11 118	8:22 265
4:14 91	10:21 . . . . 261, 263
4:23 264	10:27 259
5-7 85	11:5 103
5 . . . . 86, 94, 95, 96	11:8 269
5:3 . . . . 27, 103, 267	11:13 106
5:10 27	12:24 269
5:11 259	13:2 259
5:17-48 88	13:12 262
5:17-20 88	13:17 269
5:17-18 88	13:21 262
5:17 . . . . 87, 88, 89,	13:32 . . . . 225, 266
90, 96	13:33 100
5:18 88	13:54 269
5:19-20 95	15 256
5:19 88	15:6 267
5:20 96	15:11 177
5:21-48 . . . . 88, 90, 91	15:17-19 177
5:21-22 307	15:28 268
5:21 . . . . 91, 92	17:18 268
5:22 . . . . 89, 259	18:16 235
5:23 92	19:7-9 97
5:27 91	19:8 97
5:28-29 89	20:6 264
5:31-32 96	20:17 264
5:31 91	20:21 297
5:33-37 98	20:23 268
5:33 91	21:4 77
5:34 99	21:21 . . . . 106, 259
5:37 98	22:31 94
5:38-42 . . . . 100, 104	22:32 204
5:38 . . . . 91, 100	22:34-40 . . . . 12, 133
5:39-42 100	22:45 204
5:39 . . . . 85, 95, 100,	23 124
101, 105	23:4 259
5:40 102	23:8 259
5:41 103	23:16-22 99
5:42 . . . . 85, 104	23:21-22 99
5:43 . . . . 91, 92, 93	24:1 259
5:48 37	24:15 258
6:11-12 305	24:33 262

24:34-46 297	16:9 264
25:1 256	16:15 159
26:63-64 99	
27:15 262	*Luke*
27:32 103	
27:46 . . . . .256, 262, 266	1:17 262
28:18-20 117	1:18 262
28:19-20 159	2:24 94
28:20 117	2:38 27
	3:12 262
Mark	3:14 262
	3:16-17 118
Book of 256	4:19 . . . . 21, 23
1:8 118	4:21 23
2:27 18	5:17 262
3:1-5 94	5:39 263
3:5 307	6:1 262
4:17 262	6:27f. 93
5:16 262	6:29 102
5:41 . . . . .256, 262, 266	6:30-34 104
6:8 263	6:35-36 104
6:9 263	7:22 23
7:1-16 94	9:23 265
7:11 . . , ... 257	10:25-28 12
7:16 307	12:25 262
7:18-23 307	15:32 264
7:19 106	17:8 262
7:33 263	17:27 260
7:34 . . . . .257, 262, 266	17:29 260
8:31-9:1 27	20:16 261
9:25 264	20:37 263
9:28 261	22:19 262
10:1-12 90	22:28-30 28
10:42-45 28	23:2 306
11:24 265	24:27 165
12:6 262	24:47 265
12:26 263	24:48 312
12:28-32 12	
13:8 262	*John*
13:29 262	
13:32 262	1:14 . . . . .232, 266
13:33 262	1:17 232
13:34 268	1:18 266
13:37 265	1:29 305
15:21 104	3 305
15:34 . . . . .262, 266	3:10 116
16:2 264	3:11 96

3:14 10
3:34 . . . . .163, 268, 269
4:10 265
4:22 126
5:31 235
5:33 234
7:11 306
7:37-39 117
7:37-38 25
7:38-39 118
7:38 25
8:1-11 106
8:6 267
8:17 235
8:14 235
8:44-45 232
8:44 . . . . .232, 233
8:56 45
8:57-58 265
9:25 265
11 . . . . .259, 261
12:31 306
12:32 264
12:47-48 319
13:17 122
13:34 . . . . .89, 107
13:35 89
14:6 . . . . .231, 232
14:13-14 265
14:16 117
14:17 117
14:23 117
14:25-26 117
15:8 264
15:26-27 117
15:26 152
16:7-11 117
16:12-15 117
16:24 264
17:8 163
17:10 265
17:15 100
17:21-23 310
18:3 263
18:22-23 95
18:37 263
19:11 106

19:12 306
20:8 264
21:15 266
21:16 . . . . .265, 266
21:24 265

Acts

1:4-8 117
1:5 118
1:21-23 312
1:26 10
2 112
2:1ff. 28
2:15 150
2:16-21 109
2:19-20 121
2:30 258
2:32 312
2:34 264
2:38 120
2:39 120
2:40 121
2:41-47 151
3:5 264
3:25 188
4:33 319
5:1-4 233
5:29 153
5:41 263
5:42 153
6:1 263
6:9 263
7:14 219
7:20 264
7:43 219
7:48 263
7:59 261
8:1 153
8:4 153
8:15-17 118
9 . . . . .172, 319
9:6 157
9:36 263
10:12 264
10:15 263
10:22 263

10:26 263
10:45 120
11 172
11:6 264
11:15-17 117
11:16 118
11:28-30 20
12:3 263
12:15 264
12:19 263
13:1-4 158
13:4 158
13:40 94
13:43 263
13:51 263
14:3 263
15 . . . . 124, 154, 172,
174, 179, 181
15:1 172
15:5 172
15:8 117
15:9 . . . . 173, 179
15:11 . . . . 173, 179
15:13-18 113
15:15-18 173
15:20 . . . . .171, 172, 183
15:23 265
15:28 179
15:29 . . . . . 171, 172, 175, 179, 180
16:3 264
17 256
17:17 263
18:3-4 158
19:21 168
19:40 262
20 169
20:7 264
20:35 159
21-28 169
21:25 . . . . 171, 172
22:10-21 157
22:28 264
23:26 265
24:8 . . . . 232, 234
24:11 232
26:23 263
27:1 169
28:1 169

28:4 268
28:11 265
28:30 169

Romans

1-8 158
1 . . . . .65, 319
1:3-4 305
1:5 44
1:11 261
1:20 297
1:26ff. 181
2 65
2:20 233
2:23 265
2:29 134
3:2 264
3:9-12 305
4:11 134
4:16 134
4:18 94
5:13 264
5:15 10
6:1-2 45
8:3 232
8:19-24 28
8:22 306
9-11 159
9:1-3 164
9:1 99
9:3 262
9:6 264
9:12 94
10 . . . . 159, 160
10:4 160
10:5-9 . . . . 160, 161
10:5-6 161
10:5 161
10:9-10 311
10:10-11 . . . . 160, 161
10:12-13 . . . . .121, 160, 162
10:14-15 . . . . 160, 162
10:15 . . . . 169, 170
10:16-21 . . . . 160, 163
10:16 163
10:17 . . . . .163, 310, 318
10:18 160

11-14 163
11:4 267
11:6 167
11:17-24 126
11:20 262
11:25 167
11:27 113
12:1 264
12:14-21 105
12:17 100
12:20 106
12:21 264
13:1ff. 106
13:10 89
14 . . . . 164, 167
14:1-2 307
15 . . . . .160, 163, 166
15:1-8 164
15:8-33 159
15:8-31 163
15:8 . . . . 163, 164
15:9-13 164
15:9 165
15:12 75
15:13-16 158
15:14-33 168
15:14-21 . . . . 164, 166
15:14-15a 167
15:14 167
15:15b-17 167
15:16 263
15:18-21 168
15:19-20 157
15:22-23 . . . . 164, 168
15:22 168
15:23 170
15:24 . . . . 168, 170
15:26 169
15:27 169
15:28 . . . . 168, 170
15:29 170
15:30 170
15:31 169
15:32 262
16 256
16:5 167
16:13 104
16:26 44

1 Corinthians

1:7 266
2:13 269
2:14 216
3:4 262
3:9 265
4:4-13 103
6:1-8 103
6:15 261
7 159
7:29 264
7:36-38 268
8:1ff. 181
8:7-13 307
8:8 177
9 170
9:7 170
9:9 19
10:1-11 10
10:4 202
10:6 266
10:19ff. 181
10:33 307
10:31 129
11:17 259
11:20 259
11:21 259
11:25 259
11:26 295
12:1 261
12:13 . . . . 118, 134
12:31 264
14:2 268
14:4 268
14:5 268
14:6 268
14:13 268
14:14 268
14:18 268
14:19 268
14:22 268
14:23 268
14:26 268
14:27 268
14:34 267
14:36 262
14:39 268

15:10 167
15:12 230
15:23 167
15:24-28 29
15:27 266
15:31 99
15:32 266
15:41 269
15:45 266
15:54-55 266
16:2 264
16:21 266
16:22 . . . . .257, 262, 266

2 Corinthians

1:1 263
1:23 99
4:10 264
4:13 . . . . 117, 264
5:13 264
8:9 103
10:4 319
11:33 264
12:14 263

Galatians

1 172
1:20 99
2 172
2:4 266
2:11ff. 177
2:12 . . . . .220, 264, 266
2:16 45
3:6 45
3:8 45
3:15 262
3:20 . . . . 262, 266
3:26-29 134
4:4 305
4:17 266
5:2 265
5:6 38
5:19-21 174
5:19 181

Ephesians

Book of 256
1:7 261

1:9-10 28
1:13 233
1:18 266
2:1-3 318
2:8 117
2:13 120
2:14 124
2:17 120
2:20 263
3:10 218
4:25 234
4:29 262
5:5 70
5:8 216

Philippians

Book of 256
1:1 265
2:4 262
3:2 264
3:3 . . . . 262, 264
3:8 103

Colossians

Book of 127, 256
1:12 266
1:14 261
1:20 266
2:2 265
2:8 261
2:10 265
2:15 306
2:17 262
3:5-9 174
3:5 70
3:21 267
4:9 263
4:16 263
4:18 266

1 Thessalonians

Book of 256
1:3 266
2:13 319
2:14-16 124
3:8 . . . . 262, 266
4:15 230
5:2-6 83

5:9 266
5:21 262

2 Thessalonians

Book of 256
1:3 262
1:6 262
2:12 233
3:17 266

1 Timothy

Book of 256
1:2 263
2:12 269
3:1 269
3:10 269
3:12 262
3:13 269
4:2 264
4:3-4 128
4:4 128
5:22 262
6:1 263
6:3 263
6:6 262

2 Timothy

Book of 170
3:15 . . . . 228, 232
3:16 . . . . 213, 311
4:2 . . . . 313, 319
4:4 233
4:17 319
6:5 233

Titus

Book of 170, 256
1:8 268
1:15 129

Philemon

Book of 256
19 266

Hebrews

1:1-2 . . . . 153, 305

1:2 . . . . 116, 263
2:11 263
2:13 81
2:16 268
3:2-6 118
3:3 260
3:12 . . . . 318, 319
3:13 262
4 62
4:3 94
4:9 265
4:12-13 60
4:12 . . . . 313, 318, 319
4:14 10
4:15 263
5:13 . . . . 216, 262
5:14 216
7:19 268
7:24 268
7:25 319
8:3 260
8:8 113
9:12 . . . . 10, 267
9:14 319
9:17 262
9:18 264
9:24 262
9:28 10
10:1 263
10:18 263
10:22 263
10:31 319
10:32-34 103
10:38 268
11:8 41
11:13-16 42
11:17-19 40
11:29 268
12 62
12:2 . . . . 153, 261
12:6 61
12:22 319
13:5 265

James

1:14 266
2:14 265
2:16 263

2:20-23 45
2:23 . . . . 33, 77
2:24 . . . . 265... 45
3:6 263
4:7 100
4:12 263
4:14 263
5:9 264
5:12 99

1 Peter

1:10-12 112
1:10-11 229
1:19 10
1:23 216
2:1 213
2:5 264
2:6 263
2:21-23 106
3:3 263
3:9 106
3:16 106
3:19 263
4:3 174
4:6 263
4:10 263
5:3 269
5:9 263
5:13 269

2 Peter

1:3-11 46
1:7 263
1:14 263
1:21 311
2:3 263
2:8 263
2:10 263
3:3 263
3:10 29

1 John

Book of 127
1:6 131
1:9 264
1:10 265
2:4 232

2:8 265
2:19 263
2:20 . . . . 266, 307
2:25 265
3:1 265
3:2 264
3:3 264
3:7 264
3:9 265
3:16 269
3:18 265
3:23 264

2 John

Book of 256
4 233
6 233
8 233

3 John

Book of 256
12 263

Revelation

Book of 191
1:1 . . . . 187, 191
1:4 186
1:5 189
1:7 191
1:8 186
1:18 189
2 192
2:1 265
2:8 265
2:9 103
2:12 265
2:13 187
2:14 181
2:18 265
2:20 181
3 192
3:1 265
3:7 265
3:14 . . . . 233, 265
4 . . . . 186, 190
4:1 . . . . 187, 190
4:2 187

4:8-11	187	13:2		187
4:9	187	14:3		187
4:10	187	14:6		268
5	190	15:1		191
5:1-14	187	16:10	187,	188
5:1	187	16:11		188
5:6-7	188	16:16		266
5:6	189	18:2		191
5:7	187	19:2		189
5:9-10	189	19:4		187
5:13	187	19:20		191
6:16	187	19:21		267
7:9	187, 189	20:6		268
7:10	187	20:11-12		187
7:11-12	187	21-22		306
7:14-17	187	21:5	189, 191,	233
7:15	187	21:6	186,	187
9:11	266	21:22	42,	297
9:20-21	188	22:1		187
11:15	191	22:3		187
12	256	22:5		192
12:5	261	22:13		186
12:13	261	22:21		267

AUTHOR INDEX

Acheson, D. 274
Ahlström, G. W. 115
Alexander, J. A. 77, 80
Allen, L. C. 114, 115
Allen, R. 157
Allis, O. T. 43, 44
Althaus, P. 139
Amiran, R. 47
Anderson, B. W. 11, 13, 135
Archer, G. L., Jr. 41, 76, 78, 204
Aristotle 226
Arnold, T. K. 121
Augustine 87, 97, 235
Bacon, F. 7
Ball, G. W. 274
Banks, R. 86, 87, 88, 90, 93, 99, 102, 107, 108
Barnet 72
Barth, J. R. 290
Barth, K. 126, 139, 140, 145, 197, 198, 210, 211, 212, 214, 217, 243, 244, 245, 246, 253
Basnage, J. 221
Bavinck, H. 226
Beardsley, M. C. 285, 291
Beckford, G. 72
Beebe, H. K. 11
Beecher, W. J. 110
Beegle, D. 76, 79, 83, 201, 225, 255
Beet, J. A. 161
Beisser, F. 244
Bennett, J. C. 303
Berger, P. 287, 291
Berkhof, H. 109
Berkouwer, G. C. 198, 202, 203, 228, 318
Bernard 284
Bettenson, H. 242, 243
Beveridge, J. 210
Beza, T. de 221
Bizer, E. 208, 209, 210
Black, M. 292, 293
Bodenstein, W. 138
Boice, J. M. 200, 201, 204

Boman, T. 134
Bonfrere, J. 221
Bonhoeffer, D. 151, 152, 155
Borovoy 303
Bourke, J. 111
Bower, A. 59
Bowne, B. P. 195, 196
Breuer, I. 134
Brichto, H. C. 54
Briggs, C. A. 209
Bright, J. 11, 31, 32, 40, 41, 43, 45, 68, 126
Brinsmead, R. D. 38, 44, 45
Bromiley, G. W. 208, 215
Brown, C. 227
Brown, P. 261
Bruce, F. F. 118, 153, 172
Brueggemann, W. 109
Brunner, E. 228, 313, 314
Brutchael, J. T. 313
Buber, M. 133, 135
Bucan, W. 214, 215
Büchler, A. 173
Bullough, S. 257
Bultmann, R. 138, 139, 145, 245, 251
Burnet, G. 257
Burrows, M. 171, 261
Butterworth, C. C. 256
Calov 214, 215
Calvin, J. 37, 42, 62, 82, 87, 97, 98, 106, 115, 210, 212, 214, 219, 242, 255, 316
Campenhausen, H. von 145
Camus, A. 59
Cappel, L. Y. 218, 222
Cassirer, E. 284, 285, 295
Chambers, T. W. 267
Chemnitz, M. 311
Childs, B. 232
Cobb, J. B., Jr. 141, 241
Cocceius, J. 212, 214, 222
Cochrane, C. 67
Coleridge 290
Collingwood 248

Collins 72
Cope, G. 283
Craigie, P. C. 13
Cullman, O. 150
Culver, R. D. 157, 159
Dahood, M. 115
Dajani, R. W. 47
Danby, H. 296
Darlow, T. H. 255, 256
Daube, D. 94, 95, 100, 101, 102, 106
D'Aubigné, J. H. M. 319, 320
Davies, W. D. 85, 87, 90, 98, 107
Davis, S. T. 231
Des Marets, S. 215, 218, 220, 222
Dewette 12
DeWolf, L. H. 197
Dibelius, M. 87
Dilthey, W. 238, 248, 249
Dodd, C. H. 137
Doebler, P. 266
Doedes 245
Dore, J. R. 259
Douglas, J. D. 39
Douglas, M. 290, 291
Duke, J. 248
Durkheim, E. 287
Dussell, E. 295
Eadie, J. 255
Ebeling, G. 237, 239, 241, 243, 245, 246, 251
Edwards, J. 271, 280
Ehrmann, J. 285, 290
Eichrodt, W. 33
Ellul, J. 60
Emerson, R. W. 7
Epp, E. 180
Erasmus 243, 244
Eusebius 170, 177, 185
Fackre, G. 298
Feinberg, C. L. 112
Ferré, F. 291, 292, 293, 296
Finnerty, A. D. 67
Fitzmyer, J. A. 134
Fleming, T. V. 97
Foakes-Jackson, F. J. 172
Forster, W. 174
Forstman, J. 248

Free, J. P. 50
Freedman, D. N. 39, 41, 43
Freud, S. 285
Frymer-Kensky, T. S. 174
Fuller, D. P. 37, 225, 227, 228
Gadamer, H.-G. 245, 247, 248, 249, 250, 252, 284
Gardiner, F. 121
Gardiner, P. 146
Garside, C. 284
Garstang, J. 47
Gaster, T. 51
Gaussen 312
Geertz, C. 286, 287
Geisler, N. L. 229
Gelin, A. 134
Gennep, A. van 56
Gerhard 214, 215
Gerstner, J. 200
Ghormley, K. 120
Gibbons, J. C. 258
Gill, J. 292, 297
Gogarten 139
Goldsmith, O. 21
Goldsworthy, G. 42
Gomar, F. 216, 222
Goodwin, T. 118
Gordis, R. 133
Gordon, C. 78
Gottwald 13
Granskow, D. 140
Grant, E. 47
Gray, G. B. 111
Greenslade, S. L. 208, 221, 255
Greenstone, J. H. 173
Grogan, G. W. 117, 118
Grotius, H. 221
Guelich, R. A. 87, 90
Gustafson, J. 85
Guy, P. L. O. 47
Haenchen, E. 172, 175
Hall, B. 255
Hamilton, R. W. 47
Harder, G. 100
Harnack, A. 179
Harris, G. E. 174
Harris, R. L. 171, 214

Harvey, V. A. 137, 138, 140, 146, 147, 148
Hastings, J. 139
Heidegger, J. H. 213, 215, 223, 238, 247, 285
Heizer, R. 47, 48
Held, M. 34, 35
Hengstenberg, E. W. 81, 121
Henry, C. F. H. 76, 86, 87, 89, 92
Heppe, H. 211, 212, 213, 214, 215, 217
Herbert, L. 221
Herder 13, 143
Herrmann, W. 138
Hertz, J. H. 129
Hertzberg, A. 129
Heschel, A. J. 125
Hilary 299
Hirsch, E. D. 229, 230, 245, 249
Hobbes, T. 221
Hodelman, S. 290
Hodge, A. A. 200
Hodge, C. 162, 200
Holmes, M. W. 121
Hooke, S. H. 243
Hoornbeek, J. 220, 222
Howe, E. M. 183
Hubbard, D. A. 128, 199, 226, 227, 236
Hulst, A. R. 119
Hunter, A. M. 88, 93, 98
Hurd, J. C. 172
Irenaeus 171, 180, 181, 182, 185
Isbell, C. D. 76
James, W. 231
Jaspers 251
Jeremias, J. 87, 89, 93, 94, 99, 101, 103, 105
Jewett, P. K. 225
Johnston, A. P. 318
Josephus 103, 173
Jurieu, P. 219, 220, 223
Juster, D. C. 124
Kaiser, W. C., Jr. 12, 36, 42, 113, 115, 121, 229
Kant, I. 248, 284, 288, 289
Kantzer, K. 117, 205, 214
Kaplan, J. 47
Kehm, G. H. 140
Keil, C. F. 40, 41

Kelly, J. N. D. 283
Kenyon, K. M. 47, 54
Killen, R. A. 38
Kimmerle, H. 248
Kissinger, W. S. 86
Klein, R. W. 111
Kline, M. 12, 33, 35, 43
Knight, H. 210, 211
Koch, K. 142
Kramer, F. 311
Krutch, J. W. 280
Kuhn, T. 289, 291
Kuitert, H. M. 199, 202
Külling, S. R. 38
Kuntz, J. K. 11, 13
Kuyper, A. 228
Ladd, G. E. 96, 115
Ladrière, J. 296
Lake, K. 172, 175
Lane, W. L. 183, 264
Lange, J. P. 161
Langer, S. 295
Lapp, P. W. 47
Lappé 72
Larue, G. A. 11, 13
LaSor, W. S. 93, 125, 225
Leach, E. 286
Lehmann, P. 304
Leitch, J. W. 241
Lessa, W. A. 286
Lessing, E. 138, 143
Leupold, H. C. 75
Levi, R. 174
Lévi-Strauss, C. 285, 288
Lewis, C. S. 61, 149, 154, 155, 277
Lindsell, H. 219, 236
Locke, J. 221
Luckmann, T. 287, 291
Luther, M. 62, 87, 97, 106, 210, 212, 242, 243, 244, 245, 246, 248, 251, 319
Lyons, J. 285
Mailer, N. 278
Manson, T. W. 88
Marcel, G. 61, 66
Marks, J. H. 32
Masius, A. 221
Mastricht 212

Matheson, D. 138
McArthur, H. K. 86, 87, 88, 89, 94, 98
McCarthy, D. J. 45
McGonigal, T. P. 32, 33
McKenzie, J. 134
McNamara, M. 92
McNeile, A. H. 100
Meinardus, O. F. A. 169
Melito 185
Ménard, J. E. 290, 294
Mendenhall, G. E. 13, 35, 292, 293
Menoud, P. H. 171, 180
Merton, T. 126
Metzger, B. M. 172
Meyer, H. A. W. 103
Miguéz-Bonino, J. 297
Mitchell, B. 293
Mitchell, J. J. 33, 34, 35, 36, 37, 42
Mondin, B. 290
Moore, G. E. 239
Morin, J. 221
Motyer, J. A. 68
Moule, C. F. D. 107
Moule, H. F. 255, 256
Mozley, J. F. 256
Müller 72
Murray, J. 38, 39, 44, 87
Nares, E. 257
Neufeld, D. F. 33
Neve, J. L. 211
Newcome, W. 256
Newman, J. H. 6
Nygren, A. 241
O'Connor, J. T. 306
Ogden, S. M. 245
Origen 171, 177
Ory, J. 47
Packer, J. I. 194, 200, 201, 203
Pannenberg, W. 139, 140, 141, 142,
    143, 144, 145, 146, 147, 148
Payne, J. B. 39, 77, 78, 82, 83, 229
Pereira, B. 221
Peyre, I. de la 221
Pfeiffer, R. H. 12, 38
Pink, A. W. 32, 38, 39, 45
Pinnock, C. G. 140
Polansdorf, P. von 221
Polanus 243, 246

Pollard, A. W. 257
Pool, D. deS. 133
Pope, H. 257
Preisker, H. 120
Preus, R. 207, 212, 214, 233, 317
Preuschen, E. 171
Price, R. 75
Price, W. K. 112, 116
Priebe, D. 143
Prigent, P. 294, 295
Pritchard, J. B. 47
Quenstedt 214
Quinn, E. 140
Rackham, R. B. 153
Rad, G. von 32, 37, 38
Rahmer, K. 283
Ramm, B. 199, 315, 316
Rendtorff, R. 142
Reston, J. 277
Ribar, J. W. 54
Rice 81, 82
Richardson, P. 124
Rickman, H. P. 249
Ricoeur, P. 249, 250, 285, 286, 288,
    290, 298
Riddle, M. B. 161, 162
Rijssen, L. van 212, 218, 223
Rilliet, J. 211
Ringgren, H. 75, 115
Roberts, T. A. 137, 138, 146, 148
Robertson, O. P. 36
Robinson, H. W. 133, 255
Robinson, J. F. 215, 216, 218, 219, 220
Robinson, J. M. 141, 145, 241
Rogers, C. L., Jr. 32, 36
Rogers, J. 193, 198, 226, 227, 228, 235
Ropes, J. H. 172
Roth, C. 115
Rudin, A. J. 124
Russell, B. 285
Ryrie, C. C. 112, 113, 121
Saller, S. J. 47
Sartre, J.-P. 280
Sasse 214
Saucy, R. L. 109
Saussure, de 285
Sayce, R. A. 255
Schaeffer, C. F. A. 50

Schaeffer, E. 124
Schaeffer, F. 154, 200
Schaff, P. 242
Scheffler, H. W. 285
Schillebeeckx, E. 240, 243, 250, 251
Schlatter, A. 87
Schleiermacher, F. 238, 248
Schultz, S. J. 1, 112
Schumacher, G. 51
Scrivener, F. H. A. 255, 257, 258, 259
Segundo, J. L. 307
Shama, G. 40
Shaull, R. 303, 304
Sider, R. 72
Simms, P. M. 256
Simon, A. 72
Simon, M. 172, 175
Skinner, J. 81, 83, 84
Smeaton, G. 118
Smith, N. D. 240
Smith, N. K. 248
Smith, R. 291
Smith, W. 230
Soden, W. von 34
Spanheim, F. Y. 218, 222
Specht, W. F. 255
Spener, P. J. 318
Sperber, D. 286, 287, 290
Spinoza, B. 13, 221
Splett, J. 283
Spong, J. 130, 131, 132
Sproul, R. C. 200
Stanyon, J. S. 138
Stendahl, K. 150
Steuernagel, C. 51
Stewart, R. W. 138
Strack, H. L. 176
Suetonius 185
Taine 146
Tannebaum, M. H. 124
Tavard, G. H. 314
Taylor, K. 76, 264, 265
Temple, W. 196
Tenney, M. C. 39
Terry, M. S. 10, 240, 241, 244, 246
Tertullian 171, 172, 179, 180, 181, 182
Thomson, G. T. 210, 211

Tillich, P. 271, 290
Toon, P. 291, 295
Torrance, T. F. 289, 294, 296
Troeltsch, E. 138, 139, 140, 142, 143, 144, 145, 146, 147
Tronchin, L. 219, 223
Tufnell, O. 47
Tupper, E. F. 141
Turner, C. H. 182
Turretini, F. 213, 216, 217, 218, 220, 223, 227
Umen, S. 134
Unger, M. 112, 113
Urban, W. 296
Ursini, D. 215
Uzerny, R. 286
Vawter, B. 201
Veenker, R. A. 183
Voetius, G. 217, 219, 220, 222
Vogt, E. Z. 286
Voss, I. 221
Walvoord, J. F. 113, 214
Warfield, B. B. 199, 200
Watson, P. S. 241
Weightman, J. 285
Weinfeld, M. 13, 35, 42
Weingreen, J. 115
Wellhausen, J. 11
Wells, D. F. 140, 293
Wendland, H.-D. 301, 303
Wenger, J. 87
Wenham, D. 90
Wesley, J. 37, 38
Westermann, C. 38
Wheelwright, P. 291
Wilkins, L. 143
Williams, C. S. C. 172, 180
Williams, J. 11
Wilson, L. 258
Wilson, M. R. 124
Wilson, R. A. 246
Wilson, R. D. 78
Windisch, H. 87
Witham, R. 257
Wittgenstein, L. 238, 239, 240, 241
Wolf, H. 76, 77
Wolleb, J. R. 215, 221

Wonderly, W. L.   255
Wordsworth   290
Wright, G. E.   11, 47
Yadin, Y.   47
Yamauchi, E. M.   124

Yoder, J.   85, 87
Young, E. J.   75, 78, 79, 81, 83
Zahn, T.   87
Zwingli, U.   87, 89